COLLECTED WORKS OF MAURICE DOBB

RUSSIAN ECONOMIC DEVELOPMENT SINCE THE REVOLUTION

RUSSIAN ECONOMIC DEVELOPMENT SINCE THE REVOLUTION

MAURICE DOBB
ASSISTED BY H. C. STEVENS

Volume 5

Routledge
Taylor & Francis Group
LONDON AND NEW YORK

First published in 1928
Second edition 1929

This edition first published in 2012
by Routledge
2 Park Square, Milton Park, Abingdon, Oxon, OX14 4RN

Simultaneously published in the USA and Canada
by Routledge
711 Third Avenue, New York, NY 10017

Routledge is an imprint of the Taylor & Francis Group, an informa business

British Library Cataloguing in Publication Data
A catalogue record for this book is available from the British Library

ISBN: 978-0-415-52309-7 (Set)
eISBN: 978-0-203-11950-1 (Set)
ISBN: 978-0-415-52364-6 (Volume 5)
eISBN: 978-0-203-12083-5 (Volume 5)

Publisher's Note
The publisher has gone to great lengths to ensure the quality of this reprint but points out that some imperfections in the original copies may be apparent.

Disclaimer
The publisher has made every effort to trace copyright holders and would welcome correspondence from those they have been unable to trace.

MIX
Paper from responsible sources
FSC www.fsc.org FSC® C013604

Printed and bound by CPI Group (UK) Ltd, Croydon, CR0 4YY

RUSSIAN ECONOMIC DEVELOPMENT SINCE THE REVOLUTION

By MAURICE DOBB, M.A.

Assisted by
H. C. STEVENS

SECOND EDITION
WITH A NEW APPENDIX

LONDON
GEORGE ROUTLEDGE & SONS, LTD.
BROADWAY HOUSE: 68–74 CARTER LANE, E.C.
1929

Printed in Great Britain by
William Brendon & Son, Ltd.

CONTENTS

CHAPTER		PAGE
	PREFACE	ix
I.	THE POLITICAL BACKGROUND	1
II.	THE ECONOMIC POLICY OF THE FIRST EIGHT MONTHS	25
III.	THE PROCESS OF ECONOMIC DECLINE	66
IV.	THE PERIOD OF "WAR COMMUNISM"	98
V.	THE TRANSITION TO THE NEW ECONOMIC POLICY	129
	EXCURSUS TO CHAPTER FIVE: ON MONEY AND ECONOMIC ACCOUNTING	166
VI.	THE BEGINNING OF RECONSTRUCTION	182
VII.	THE NEW FORM OF INDUSTRIAL ORGANISATION	196
VIII.	THE "SCISSORS" CRISIS OF 1923	221
IX.	THE CLOSING OF THE "SCISSORS"	246
	EXCURSUS TO CHAPTERS EIGHT AND NINE: ON TRADE BETWEEN INDUSTRY AND PEASANT AGRICULTURE VIEWED AS A SPECIAL CASE OF EXCHANGE BETWEEN "NON-COMPETING GROUPS"	273
X.	THE PROBLEM OF FIXED CAPITAL	290
XI.	TOWN AND VILLAGE	333
XII.	ECONOMIC PROSPECTS	373
	A GLOSSARY OF TERMS	401
	A LIST OF SOURCES	403
	APPENDIX TO SECOND EDITION	409
	INDEX	431

PREFACE

TEN years have now been completed of a social experiment which has aroused more enthusiasm from some and more vituperation from others than any event since the storming of the Bastille. The importance which the events of 1789 had for the political theorist is now paralleled for the economist by the events of November 1917, and the 20th-century may be as profoundly influenced by the one as 19th-century Europe was shaken by the other. Yet the real facts of this experiment remain little known to the economist or the social theorist, and still less to the general public; while even among those with access to information bewilderment generally holds the place of understanding.

History, perhaps like genius, is rarely appreciated by its generation. The complex of events is too near the eye for the mind to group into patterns. Journalistic distortion and *ex parte* records, still unsifted, obscure the vision and give an edge to the temper. To pass judgment on contemporary history becomes as rash a task as to herald a prophet in his own village. Yet such rashness is necessary. If in the future we are to do more than dance as marionettes of the forces of history, contemporary history and the making of it must be known and understood. In the past mankind has stepped its macabre dance, unforeseeing and unwilling, either failing to learn the lesson of events or learning too late; and for this, perhaps, the cloistered timidity of the historian and social analyst must have no little share of blame.

This must serve as apology for what is attempted in this book. In writing of events which are still unfinished, one's work can hardly be perfect or complete. In telling of things which are hot in the memory one can hardly fail to touch the passions and rouse displeasure from some quarter, whatever one may say. Moreover, I have attempted to combine an objective description of facts with an analysis and interpretation of them, since a sense of perspective and of significance is as important to understanding as acquaintance with the chronological order of events. Possibly this combination of description and analysis is incompletely achieved, the inter-weaving of the two imperfectly done. Probably it will satisfy entirely neither those who look for a chronicle, nor those who desire ready-made generalisation. Inevitably the author's own assumptions have obtruded themselves into the framework of interpretation in which the record of events has been set.

In the search among sources of information I have not thought it necessary to disbelieve Russian records, whether "White" or "Red," unless there was definite reason in the particular case to do so. Otherwise the writing of this book would have been impossible. But considerable care has throughout been observed in the acceptance of evidence, particularly in regard to figures, a given statement being checked from several sources before any considerable reliance was placed upon it. Russian statistics have always been and still remain singularly imperfect. Figures relating to the village, owing to the difficulty of collecting exact data, have to be accepted with as much caution as before the war: a caution which does not, however, need to be observed to the same extent in relation to industry, where the collection of statistics has been greatly facilitated by the fact of nationalisation. Similarly, comparisons with pre-war production are no more than approximate, since figures of pre-war production are only estimates, just as are calculations of British production in the post-war years. Figures of pre-war Russian production were to hand from an industrial census of 1908, and annual figures for subsequent years were available for certain commodities, such as coal, oil, copper and iron, paper and cellulose, wood, cement, leather, chemicals and machine manufacture; and contemporary estimates exist of aggregate manufactures in 1912. These incomplete data have subsequently been supplemented from the records of nationalised factories and commercial houses. But so long as due allowance is made for the margin of error that is necessarily involved, one seems to be justified in using such estimates as an approximate guide. With regard to present-day Russian statistics, there does not appear to be valid reason for any suspicion of falsification or serious bias, as has sometimes been suggested. Departmental bias one may find in certain cases, which may act sometimes in one direction, sometimes in another. Discrepancies occasionally occur in the calculations presented by different authorities. But there seems no more reason to suspect a general bias in Russian figures as a whole in any particular direction than to suspect it in the statistics of Western countries. Indeed, economic affairs are generally characterised by a thoroughness of discussion and a frankness of self-criticism that is somewhat surprising to those who live in a country where business secrecy is a sacred rule.

In studying the economic organisation of present-day Russia I have had the opportunity of meeting, both in this country and during a visit to Russia in 1925, several persons actively engaged in the conduct of economic affairs, including Mr. Smilga and Mr. Bukhartsev of Gosplan, Prof. Hensel of Narcomfin, Prof. Kaffenhaus of Vesenha, Mr. Melnitchansky of the trade unions, Mr. Boiev formerly of Narcomprod, Mr. Khinchuk of Centrosoyus, and Mr. Emdin of the Textile Syndicate. Mr. Stevens, who spent three years in Russia in 1922–4 on relief work for the Society of Friends and has recently paid a second visit to Russia in 1926, is responsible for the translation of all the Russian material that has been used in the preparation of this work, and has given invaluable aid in correcting and supplementing my record of events from his own experience and his knowledge of Russian history. But for such opinions as are expressed in this book and for the general form and treatment he is not to be blamed. For suggestions as to sources and for the loan of books and documents I am under obligation to Mr. Maisky and Mr. I. Zvavitch, to Dr. Segal and Mr. Andrew Rothstein. Particularly am I indebted to Mr. J. M. Keynes and Mr. Dennis Robertson for reading parts of my manuscript and providing valuable criticism and suggestions both on practical and theoretical points.

As I write, time is making the end of my story incomplete. Already the passage of events may be revising such tentative generalisations as I have made. This I do not mind. Finality is never possible for those who write of history in the making. My endeavour has been to set down facts objectively without moral judgments, explicit or implied, to analyse their significance and to elucidate the motives and intentions of those who are guiding the course of events. That what is written to-day may to-morrow require rewriting does not seem sufficient reason for failing to assemble the large amount of material that is to hand and to begin to learn such lessons as it may hold. And to those whose chief desire it is, in the phenomena of the present as well as of the past, *rerum cognoscere causas* I dedicate this book.

M. H. D.

CAMBRIDGE,
November, 1927.

CHAPTER ONE

THE POLITICAL BACKGROUND

THE understanding of the situation in present-day Russia which one meets in Western Europe is in nearly all cases of an extremely cramped and limited kind. Nor is this confined to those whose mental food consists of the scenario caption or of the Fleet Street aphorism: it is found among persons usually intelligent and well-informed upon social and economic affairs. Indeed, it is precisely this customarily well-informed person who appears most ready to apply uncritically categories which have done service for classification in other spheres to this strange new social experiment: a thing which he seems to do in defiance of every Baconian principle, so as to render the result generally useless even as a working hypothesis. When the facts are little known, this method becomes specially dangerous: the temptation to fit facts to *a priori* notions and to invest mere hypotheses with dogmatic finality meets less resistance. The fact that Moscow and Leningrad are on the surface so surprisingly similar to other capital cities might seem to give some sanction to this facile uncritical approach. Actually, under the skin they contain so many entirely new elements, that one cannot arrive at much that is satisfactory in the way of interpretation on the basis of a little journalistic chatter in reviews and a smattering of club-room gossip.

The most common view that one hears expressed in competent circles is that Russian history of the last ten years marks the death of another utopia, the bursting of a giant social bubble in contact with economic reality. The Bolsheviks held a vision of a Communist utopia, which they tried to make actual by coercion and force. But this *a priori* utopia, being inconsistent with economic necessities, would not " work "; and only because of the surprising realism of Lenin was this fact realised in time—in time to beat a retreat in face of complete and devastating economic collapse. The new attention to facts, once started, involved the gradual reintroduction, one after another, of the methods of capitalism which had formerly been so bitterly denounced; while the ideal, which had been shown so futile in action, was retained by them in words to cover their withered spiritual nakedness, and as a weapon in foreign diplomacy to undermine by propaganda the position of their enemies. " Communism," says Mr. Norman Angell, " has been all but completely abandoned (in Russia); . . . every day gets farther away from it." But " Moscow has been careful to retain all the old battle cries."[1] A cruder view which had much currency in the early days of the Russian Revolution regards the new rulers of Russia as a group of ordinary tyrants, who ambitiously seized power by a *coup d'état* like military conspirators in Latin America. But being cunning as well as avaricious, they knew well how to tune their ears to the murmuring of the crowd and to temper terror with concession; and finding their position threatened by economic collapse and famine, they performed a *volte-face* to appease the peasantry. Since when, while remaining tyrants, they have become in policy unprincipled opportunists. " This strong ruling caste," state two recent writers, " is determined not to let the power it has gained slip from its hands. . . . Rather than lose its grip on power it will even sacrifice some of its Communist principles."[2]

[1] *Must Britain Travel the Moscow Road?* 119–120.

[2] Makeev and O'Hara, *Russia*, 276. Cf. also " The present leaders of the Russian Communist Party, intent on retaining their position at all costs, are sacrificing one Communist ideal after another to the returning tide of capitalism " (*The Outlook*, Dec. 11th, 1926).

Some, again, argue plausibly that Bolshevism is merely the creed of Socialists in overmuch of a hurry. Every movement, according to this view, has its left wing and its right, its extremists and its moderates, the former born of an impetuous and impatient temperament,[1] the latter of a native cautiousness which is sceptical of a step without experiment. In a pioneer movement the extremist malady will be wont to appear in specially violent form, since its members, absorbed in propaganda, are divorced from the practical difficulties of administration. In Western Europe Socialism has been sobered by the contact of its leaders with the facts of political office. In Russia, debarred from such contact by the absence of democracy, the Labour movement nourished extremism with special force. But the very success of Bolshevism was of necessity its death-blow as a distinctive creed, since the responsibilities of power were bound to cool its ardour and calm its haste, until Leon Trotsky should differ in little save his terminology from Mr. Norman Angell or Mr. Sidney Webb. A slightly different view found among Socialists, is that Lenin sought to light the flame of world revolution to enable him to introduce Communism into Russia, and then, when other countries failed to respond to his call, he had virtually to admit his failure and to beat a disastrous retreat, in course of which Socialist ideals were ruthlessly sacrificed on the altar of American efficiency methods.[2]

To the plain man who reads his *Times* every morning and takes his *Weltanschauung* from its leader-writers such explana-

[1] Mr. H. G. Wells, for instance, defines Bolshevism as " the sabotage of civilisation by the disappointed " (*The World of William Clissold*, I, 194). M. Kollnai regards Bolshevism as a product of the Œdipus Complex—an obvious " paranoic regression " (*Psychoanalysis and Sociology*) ; while a certain medical writer has gone so far as to declare that all Bolsheviks and " Radicals " are persons with decayed teeth. Mr. R. W. Postgate defines Bolshevism as " Socialism at once " (*Bolshevik Theory*, 15, etc.), and Mr. Norman Angell describes it as " the policy of establishing Socialism at one stroke, as opposed to its gradual introduction " (op. cit., 115).

[2] e.g. Dr. Otto Bauer : " The new (economic) policy restored capitalism in Russia " (*The Austrian Revolution*, 185–6).

tions as these seem plausible and satisfactory enough. They appear sufficiently consistent with his circumscribed experience of social life and with his admittedly imperfect knowledge of the facts of the case. And in these days of tube trains and gyratory traffic and a Rothermere Press, with their love of terse and glibly turned formulæ in explanation of every phenomenon, such explanations may appear uncommonly liberal. But for those who wish not merely to find after-dinner epigrams or to " place " Russia in some existing mental pigeon-hole, but are bent on serious study of the Russia of the last ten years these explanations will prove so inadequate as to be scarcely more than so much useless baggage. They are useless simply because, when one takes any survey of the facts at all wider than that open to the reader of popular journals, they completely fail to explain the facts. Though perhaps—to parody the Lincolnian phrase—they may at their best explain some of the facts all of the time, or all of the facts some of the time, they cannot even by the ingenuity of a Mrs. Nesta Webster be made to explain all of the facts all of the time.

Clearly the fulcrum of the affair consists in a correct interpretation of that change of policy in 1921 which has been called the New Economic Policy, or shortly N E P. It is in the significance assigned to this, its place in the Bolshevik strategy as a whole, the tendencies inherent in it, that explanations differ. One may almost say that to interpret N E P aright is to understand that system of social ideas which has come to be called Leninism, and to have a key to the future trend of development of the new Russia. But N E P itself can only be appreciated aright against its background of the " war communism " of the civil war period, and this in turn is only rendered intelligible in relation to the previous declarations, actions and policy of the Bolshevik Party.

In England an accurate appreciation of the distinctive characteristics of Bolshevism is particularly rare, largely because English Socialism has been almost entirely non-

Marxian.[1] In theory as a whole English Socialism was always particularly poor as compared with the movement on the continent: its most conspicuous intellectual leaders, the Fabians, priding themselves on their concentration on concrete situations in which generalisations assumed a secondary place. And that part of it which was based on Marxian principles was quite negligible. Though Marx made the British Museum Reading Room his workshop, lived several years of his life in Hampstead and donned the vestments of constable of the vestry of St. Pancras, while Engels pursued the calling of a Lancashire cotton manufacturer, there succeeded to them in England no counterparts of Labriola and Ferri in Italy, of Kautsky, Bebel, Cunow or Luxemburg in Germany, of Hilferding and Bauer in Vienna, of Struve and Plekhanov in Russia. Nor did Marxism stir the waters of academic discussion in Oxford, Cambridge or London, as it did in Berlin, Vienna, Rome and Petersburg. It called forth no grand refutations, placed no appreciable imprint on intellectual thought, for the most part was noticed scarcely enough to be understood. Economists, sociologists and historians generally ignored it, having usually no more knowledge of it than was afforded by a cursory glance at Volume I of *Capital*. Students knew of Marx as a man who had misunderstood Ricardo, taught that value was determined by labour and ignored demand, absurdly exaggerated the importance of economic self-interest in shaping the course of history, and held a place in social memory as a propagandist and agitator rather than as a contributor to thought.

English Socialism took shape in the 'eighties of last century primarily as a reaction against *laissez-faire*, with the six different milkmen in six separate milk-carts going daily down the same street as the favourite illustration of its street-corner evangelists. *Laissez-faire* was assailed because it was inefficient and wasteful, and because it left the weak at the mercy

[1] Cf. " The British Socialist movement, which derives from Robert Owen, and (without its knowledge) from Bentham, has . . . at no time been predominantly or even appreciably ' Marxian ' " (Sidney Webb in *Econ. Journal*, Sept. 1926, p. 438).

of the strong to be driven to the sweat-shop and the poor law. Latterly there has been added to the indictment the count that *laissez-faire* gives free rein to monopolistic restriction of output on the part of combines, trusts and cartels. State intervention, particularly in the labour market, and in certain essential cases actual State operation of industry is, accordingly, marked out as the desirable line of advance. The devout Socialist climbs his " golden road to Samarkand " to the extent that he spends his working hours as a civil servant, travels home by a rate-subsidised tramcar, and in his leisure hours smokes State-made tobacco lit by State-made matches, and takes recreation on a municipal tennis-court or bowling-green. Whether this belief in the merits of conscious control of economic forces by the democratic State was the sum total of English Socialism, or whether it was merely the garment in which a more comprehensive emotional revolt against individual enrichment from property-rights in land and capital saw fit to clothe itself, may be an open matter. But at any rate it was as a doctrine of " State-ism " that Socialism was generally discussed, and " State-ism " which characterised it in general estimation.

It was natural, therefore, that Communism, as a thing distinct from Fabian Socialism, should be evaluated by English social thinkers in these same terms; and a certain confusion of anarchist communism with Marxian communism helped to the particular interpretation which arose. Socialism or Collectivism sought to replace the private captain of industry by the State nominee. Communism presumably wanted to go further and abolish all inequality of reward, all individual incentive, by substituting for the market a moneyless system of rationing, combined with certain rather vague ideas about extensive administrative decentralisation. When, accordingly, in 1917 the Russian Bolsheviks, or Communists, declaring themselves more extreme than the Socialists, appeared and prepared to seize power, they were quickly fitted into this category of apostles of a utopian scheme to abolish moneyed exchange and to revert to a " natural economy " of moneyless rationing. The fact that they were in such indecent haste to overturn society in this manner, and that they relied on force of arms to do it, was presumably to be explained by an " Asiatic temperament," or by the extreme disorganisation wrought by the war in Russia together with lack of acquaintance with democratic methods. In the West, particularly in England, such a movement was inconceivable. Since Marxian categories had not been used in the discussion of English Socialism, and were little known at all, they did not occur to English thinkers as means to interpret the actions of the apostles of this strange new thing. Lenin and Trotsky must be either overweening knaves or gigantic utopians. The " war communism " of 1918–20 was the formal embodiment of the communist dream; its abandonment in 1921 marked the acknowledged defeat of their crude ideal and a return to the ways of capitalism, or at least of ordinary, normal, comprehensible State Socialism.

What distinguishes Marxism is its conception of class, and of capitalism as a class system, from which arises the fact of class struggle. Of the many differences which divide society, differences occupational and intellectual, geographical, racial and national differences, the most important, tending ultimately to transcend them all, is the difference of *class*. This arises from the fact that ownership of economic property, and with it access to the commanding positions, the most lucrative professions and the choicest opportunities, is in the main confined to, or monopolised by, a minority of the population; and as a result of this the majority, shut out from such opportunities and from the instruments of production (save in a few quite special cases), have no choice but to work for the favoured class for a wage which leaves a surplus to accrue to the favoured monopolists as rent of their position of differential advantage. Hence, the compulsion of the " free " labourer under such circumstances to work for a master—the economic compulsion of absence of other opportunities of livelihood—only differs in form and degree from the compulsion of the serf or slave to work for his lord; and the master class owes its superior fortune as much to exploitation of the labourers' dependent position as did the feudal nobility or slave-owning aristocracy to the surplus labour of serf or slave.[1] Marx, therefore, used exploitation in a broad sense as the defining characteristic of the capitalist wage-system. Orthodox economic theory, on the other hand, characteristically confines the use of the term to a much narrower and less significant sphere. It confines the term to the extent to which wages through inferior bargaining power fall below the " economic wage " which would exist in a " perfect " labour market where " economic friction " was eliminated; and for this evil collective bargaining is usually deemed sufficient cure. Mr. J. A. Hobson has gone a little further by emphasising the cases of " economic friction "—imperfect mobility and information, unequal bargaining strength, sluggish competition—and the " surpluses " and the corresponding exploitation of the weaker party which these involve; and it is on this economic conception to a large extent that English Socialism in the writings of Mr. and Mrs. Webb apparently leans.

But since the assumption lying at the base of orthodox economic theory is that of a classless society[2]—or a society in which the influence of class is left out of account—this usual conception of exploitation is far too narrow for those who accept the Marxian definition of capitalism as true. For it leaves out of account all inequalities of reward—unduly high rewards in one case and unduly low in the other—caused by the monopoly enjoyed by one section, and the exclusion from opportunities which is suffered by the other section—inequalities due, not to " friction " in the labour market itself, but due, as Mr. Hawtrey has explained it, to

[1] Prof. Achille Loria treats slavery, serfdom, and the wage-system as three phases of what he calls the " coercive association of labour." In each case the coercion is more indirect than in the preceding one; but remains nevertheless, even though in less evident form. This coercion hampers productive development after a point, and must give place, therefore, to the " free association of labour " (*Econ. Foundations of Society*, etc.).

[2] Cf. the writer's *Capitalist Enterprise*, p. 143 *seq.*

the fact that the species of income called Profit is mainly excluded from those competitive influences in the labour market which tend to adjust earnings to effort.[1] To give an illustration: if a group of employers combined to exclude newcomers in their business and to exclude competition among themselves in the employment of labour, the resulting surplus profit acquired at the expense of wages would be treated by economists as a case of " exploitation "; but the case where the institutions of a class society limit the number of persons able to set up as capitalist employers, while making proletarians seeking wage-employment plentiful, thereby raising the income of the former and depressing that of the latter, is not included as a species of exploitation, and generally in economic theory does not figure at all.

Given, then, the Marxian assumption that exploitation in this more significant sense exists and is a dominant feature of capitalism, it follows that continual friction is likely to arise between the class which gains and the class which suffers from exploitation; and this friction growing in intensity, particularly when times are bad and wages are on the downward trend, comes to constitute a chronic class struggle. This is the more likely in that the economic fact causes cultural differences and social and psychological differences to arise upon its soil. The fact of ownership carries with it the power to command; and there develops the relation of superior and inferior, ruler and subject, between those who own, control and draw " surplus-value " in various forms and those who are ownerless, work for a wage and obey. The economic friction is reinforced by struggles which show themselves on a purely ideal plane.

It is from this interpretation of capitalism that the Bolshevik theory starts, and in the light of it that Bolshevik policy must be understood. The basis of this whole policy is the belief that the only solution of thc unstable equilibrium of the class struggle, the only way of saving civilisation from

[1] *The Economic Problem,* p. 34 *seq.* Cf. also *Capitalist Enterprise,* p. 75 *seq.*

decline, is the transference of power in society to the working class, the abolition by them of class monopoly and the introduction of a classless society; just as in a slave society torn by slave revolts on an increasingly wide scale the only solution would be the emergence of a new system in which the slave-relation was destroyed.[1] The aim—the new social equilibrium—is, accordingly, the classless society, where class monopoly has been abolished and is precluded from rebirth. Socialisation of the means of production is desired as the necessary form which the assumption of power by the workers and their liquidation of class monopoly must take. Whether industry operated by the State nominee promises to be more efficient than industry run by the private *entrepreneur*, whether the " planned economics " of State control will be superior to the " anarchy " of *laissez-faire*—questions such as these which hold the fore-stage in Fabian Socialism, though important additional considerations, become of secondary importance in the Marxian theory. The question of the form which administration shall take, at any rate, becomes, not a matter of first principles as the Guild Socialists would have it, but a matter, as Mr. Keynes has phrased it, of purely " experimental technique."[2]

So far, however, no more has been said than would secure the assent of many continental social-democrats, graduated in the school of Marx. We only reach the parting of the ways between the ordinary social-democrat and the school of Lenin

[1] Unless, of course, the ruling class were able to " buy off " the discontented rebels by affording them a continually ascending standard of life and abundance of " panis et circenses " (as may be said to have happened in Britain between 1850–1900, and in U.S.A. at the present time.) This possibility is, however, provided against by the second part of the Marxian theory. This asserts that capitalism as it develops will continually come up against periodic crises of partial and general over-production and falling profits (cf. below, in Excursus to Chapters Eight and Nine). This, occurring in periodic waves, will accentuate the instability of the workers' position in the shape of unemployment, and will in turn impel search for new markets in non-capitalist countries and the extension of capitalism to them, leading to Imperialist stuggles and wars, and so to ultimate economic decline.

[2] *A Short View of Russia*, p. 18.

when we come to political strategy and the position of the State. What was responsible for the " militancy " of Lenin, his alleged " sectarianism " and " undue haste," was the conviction that exploitation would only be abolished *after* power had been transferred to the workers, that this transfer of power would be resisted and would involve an open struggle, and that the strategy of this struggle for power must be the preoccupation of any genuine socialist party. At some stage in the " step by step " advance of the workers would come the situation, familiar to military strategists, where, to hold one position, several others would have to be taken at the same time, and where a general manœuvre all along the front would have to be conducted in order to make possible the main attack. The case would be the same whether or not the State was clothed in democratic forms, since in a class society democracy could never be more than a form—a convenient veil for the rule of the dominant class. True, the worker had the vote; but the capitalists had the Press and the funds and control of popular education. True, the workers' representatives might sit in Parliament and pass laws; but the financiers held the purse-strings of the Ministry, the lieutenants of the ruling class, trained in public school and university to be masters, staffed the executive departments, had command of the military forces and steered the judicial machine.[1] And should any of these bulwarks be too weak to withstand the proletarian onslaught, there remained in the background the " buying-off " of the workers' leaders and the methods of employers' " Pinkertons," " Black Hundreds " and Fascist squads. The workers' struggle, therefore, could not take a constitutional, and only in most exceptional circumstances a peaceful form. The State from its nature would be a hostile force ranged at every point to break up any general manœuvre, to hamper and to resist to the death the workers' expropriatory aims; and the workers

[1] Said Lenin : " The actual work of the State is done behind the scenes and is carried out by the departments, the chancelleries, the staffs. Parliament itself is given up to talk for the special purpose of fooling the common people " (*State and Revolution*, 1925 ed., p. 60).

in their struggle would need to fashion their own organs—workers' councils and trade unions—to overcome the bourgeois State and finally supplant it, first merely as organs of struggle and later as embodiments of legislative and executive power.

This struggle for power could not in a modern community bear the character of a conspiratorial *coup d'état*, such as military generals conduct overnight in undeveloped countries, as Baboeuf attempted in 1796 and Blanqui in 1848. And against such " Blanquist " delusions Lenin conducted relentless war.[1] Equally stern was he in condemning the opposite opinion, that on the appointed day of the final struggle the " spontaneity " of crowds of determined proletarians would suffice to win the power and keep it and set to building brick by brick the future socialist State. Such faith in " spontaneity " was mere childish dreaming, the romanticism of intellectuals who idealised the proletariat. To carry through the revolutionary struggle, a disciplined, organised revolutionary party, with singleness of purpose and of will, was required. But this must be neither a band of long-haired doctrinaires nor of soft-footed conspirators. It must be a party of the masses, composed predominantly of persons who were part of the mass in trade union branch, barrack-room and factory, intimately linked with the masses by years of contact in bread-and-butter struggles and holding their confidence, quick by long experience to sense their every change of mood and quick to harness it to an objective. In the struggle the directing brain would be the party executive,

[1] When charged with Blanquism in 1917 he wrote : " A military plot is pure Blanquism, *if* it is not organised by a Party of a determined class ; *if* the organisers of it do not justly estimate the correct moment ; *if* they have not on their side the sympathy (proved by deeds) of the majority of the people . . . *if* the slogans of insurrection have not acquired the widest diffusion and the greatest popularity ; *if* the advanced workers are not convinced of the desperate situation of the masses and assured of the support of the country workers ; finally, *if* the economic situation seriously allows hope in a favourable solution of the crisis by peaceful methods and the parliamentary way." (" Letter to the Comrades," Oct. 16–17, published in English in *On the Road to Insurrection*, pp. 129–30.)

the nerves the party apparatus, and the muscles and limbs the masses themselves. The party would represent the politically conscious elements of the class, and in a sense dominate it. But the party would lead, not as a sheepdog marshals a herd of sheep, but rather as a wolf or coyote comes to be the leader of his pack. And since history does not stand still, and there is such a thing as a " psychological moment "—perhaps a few weeks or a few days—when the workers are most strongly placed and most ready for action, and the ruling class most divided, hesitant and weak, it was necessary for a revolutionary party to be able to sense the presence of such a moment, to wait not upon democratic procedure, but to have the courage to strike then and to strike hard.

In the spring of 1917, when the Provisional Government had first been installed, the policy of the Bolshevik party, which for the first time led a legal existence, certainly was not leading towards the events of October. The democratic revolution was regarded as having transferred power from the Court and the aristocracy, not to the workers, but to the middle class—the bankers and industrialists; although through the influence of the Soviets of Workers' and Soldiers' and Peasants' Deputies, which had spontaneously arisen during the March days to focus mass feeling, the workers exercised a certain "pressure." The official Bolshevik policy at this time was to support the Democratic Government, and merely to strengthen this working class " pressure " through the Soviets, and later in the Constituent Assembly when it was called, with the object of securing Peace and furthering proletarian interests. To speak of a further, Socialist, revolution at this stage was considered absurd: for this backward Russia must wait upon the more developed West.

Lenin, however, on his arrival from Switzerland quickly called another tune, and for some months remained in a minority in his Party and was denounced as a Blanquist. Throughout the war he had preached a doctrine known as " revolutionary defeatism," that during a war the class interests of the workers must have precedence over national loyalty, to the point of seizing the hour of mass discontent and the divisions of their class enemies to make an offensive move to carry the coveted key positions. Now in 1917 he saw the time as growing ripe for such a movement in Russia, the " psychological moment " when the quickly changing objective situation was ripest for such a move as drawing near. For him it was necessary, not to support the Democratic Government, but to denounce it as a convenient mask for bankers' and industrialists' rule, and to prepare the masses for a movement against it to seize power. For him the Soviets were the self-created organs of working-class opinion, which must become the instruments of their struggle and ultimately the nucleus of the new Workers' State; and to wait, as his colleagues desired, for the Constituent Assembly was to acquiesce in the retirement of the Soviets, since with the coming of the Assembly the Soviets would certainly have to transfer much of their authority to other bodies and to take a subordinate back-seat. " We will not become partisans of national defence," he wrote, " *until after* the seizure of power by the proletariat, until after the offer of peace, until after the secret treaties have been cancelled and relations with the banks broken."[1] Agitation against the counter-revolutionary tendencies of Gen. Kornilov must be conducted while at the same time attacking Kerensky for weakness and vacillation. Early in September he was urging " the formation of a Government of Mensheviks and Social Revolutionaries (Kerensky's party) responsible before the Soviet," urging this compromise " only by way of exception, only in virtue of a special situation which will apparently last a very short time," " for the sake of a peaceful development of the revolution, in order to profit from this precious possibility such as is extremely rare in history."[2] But by the end of September the quickly changing scene had moved again.

[1] Letter to the Central Committee of the Bolshevik Party, *ibid.*, p. 9 ; cf. also a letter from Zurich, dated 23–24th March 1917.
[2] *Ibid.*, pp. 13–14.

The Kerensky Government had apparently shifted further "to the Right." There were many counsels inside and outside the Government to clip the wings of the Soviets and to take repressive measures against the Bolsheviks.[1] The feeling was growing that a "strong man" was needed who could restore discipline in workshop and army. At the same time the Bolsheviks had secured the majority in the Petrograd and Moscow Soviets, and were gaining increasing support among the troops of the Petrograd garrison. The peasants of the countryside were growing increasingly restive and the soldiers increasingly war-weary. Kerensky was reported to be sending the existing garrison regiments to the front and drawing more loyal troops to the capital. Lenin insisted that the hour had come to be uncompromising and to make the slogan *All Power to the Soviets* a reality; and he finally carried his Party with him in the demand that it should appoint a Military Revolutionary Committee, and "without loss of a minute organise a general staff of the insurrectionary *cadres*, concentrate the trustworthy regiments on the most important points, invest the Alexandra Theatre, occupy the Peter and Paul Fortress, . . . mobilise the armed workers, occupy simultaneously the central telegraph office and telephone exchange, instal *our* staff at the central telephone exchange, and get telephone connections with all the factories, all the regiments, etc."[2]

Even while the plans for this transfer of power to the workers' organs were being prepared in the former dormitories of the Smolny Academy for Young Ladies, there were strong elements in the Bolshevik Party who strenuously opposed the policy that was being pursued. Zinoviev and Kamenev in a letter of October 11th, published a week later in Maxim Gorki's paper, *Novaia Jizn*, declared it "inadmissible and a fatal step to take the initiative now for the armed insurrection." Time, they argued, was on their side; Bolshevik prospects in the coming elections for the Assembly

[1] Cf. Sir George Buchanan, *My Mission to Russia*, Vol. 2, 164–6, 189, 196, 203.

[2] Lenin, *op. cit.*, 61.

were " excellent "; hostile forces were too strong for an insurrectionary struggle to achieve success. Not "All Power to the Soviets," but " the Constituent Assembly and the Soviets—that is the combined type of State institution that we are approaching." Even after " the October days," when the seizure of power by the Soviets had been realised in Moscow and Petrograd and certain other cities, these same persons opposed the measures of suppression of the hostile Press which Lenin had undertaken, urged the abandonment of further military measures, the formation of a coalition government with the other socialist parties and the holding of elections to the Constituent Assembly as the future organ of governing power; and as a result there were several resignations of the dissenting leaders.[1] Among the " big names " of the " old Bolsheviks " Lenin stood almost alone in support of the policy that was taken: Trotsky, who was the moving spirit of the Military Revolutionary Committee, had only joined the Party in the course of the year and was still regarded as a tyro.

Clearly, these differences which arose were not merely differences in estimating the " ripeness " of the political situation for the proposed move—in estimating the extent of Bolshevik support among the masses, the attitude of the soldiers, the strength of the forces at the disposal of their opponents, the possibilities of support from the peasantry and from the workers of other countries, the tendency of the future to produce a balance of forces less or more favourable to the Bolsheviks than the present. They also represented an important cleavage of ideas as to the general character of the policy that it was desirable to pursue. It was a difference, not merely in the use of that strange intuitive perception of events in the political sphere which the business man is supposed to exercise in the sphere of the market, but a different conception of the line of advance and the rôle of a Bolshevik

[1] Namely, Rykov, Nogin, Miliutin, Teodorovitch, Shliapnikov, Kamenev and Zinoviev; while Riazanov and Larin supported the minority without resigning their positions.

Party. Lenin's ideas on this subject appeared, even in the ranks of the Bolsheviks themselves, as a quite new contribution, and, as most of those who opposed him within the Party in 1917 subsequently admitted, were imperfectly grasped and understood. The view held by many of the dissident section was that the revolutionary initiative could hardly be taken in Russia without definite promise of a similar movement in Western countries, by reason of Russia's " economic backwardness." All that could be done at present was to work within the bourgeois democracy, securing for working-class organisation and propaganda the maximum possibilities of development; and, by securing for the Soviets a constitutional place alongside the Constituent Assembly and for the factory committees a function in controlling production, to guarantee the maximum " pressure " on the trend of events and to exercise an encroaching partial control which could later be made absolute. Such a conception was not unknown to English Guild Socialist discussion, and appears to have resembled that held two years later by the German Independent Socialists and by the Viennese Social-Democrat, Dr. Otto Bauer.[1]

Lenin's view stood sharply separated from this. To him the economic backwardness of Russia was largely irrelevant to the political question of the seizure of power. The former certainly affected the problem of subsequent economic policy and economic reorganisation; but the latter was a political question with which the balance of class forces was primarily concerned. A victorious move in Russia would be just the event most likely to arouse a similar response among the workers of the West. When Lenin in August 1917 underlined Marx's statement that "the working class cannot simply lay hold of the ready-made State machinery and wield it for its own purposes,"[2] he was using a hitherto little-noticed passage as text of a new principle of political strategy. This

[1] Cf. his *Austrian Revolution*, 243 *seq.*

[2] Quoted from *The Civil War in France* (Eng. Ed. 1921), p. 28, in *The State and Revolution*, p. 48. The above wording is that of the former, which is a reprint of the original London edition of 1871.

principle declared that in the ripening of the class struggle the State machinery would be drawn in on the side of the existing ruling class, whether or not the workers held a formal Parliamentary majority; and the struggle must accordingly be developed by the workers' own organs aligning themselves against the State organs, challenging them and finally supplanting them. This rival State-in-embryo he saw in the Soviets, and he valued their advance, not in terms of ordinary political theory and study of comparative institutions, but solely because they focussed working-class power, whereas the machinery of the existing State was bound by a hundred threads to the ruling class. The "encroaching control" of the Soviets would take place, not as a game of chess played leisurely according to accepted rules, but as a manœuvre of opposing armies for position. In such a manœuvre great importance attached to possession of the initiative, and the time-factor was supreme. The situation in October was a transitory one of unstable equilibrium, in which the Soviets must either advance or retire—advance to the conquest of power, or retire before the growing influence of the Government, which, if given time to rally, would suppress the Soviets, or at any rate draw their claws, as was to happen later in Germany. There was no third way of standing still or preparing a checkmate by a series of leisurely moves.

This pre-eminence of the political issue of class power in Lenin's doctrine is of prime importance to a correct appraisement of subsequent events; and its reiteration is apparently necessary at least for an English audience, since Socialism in England has always been predominantly thought of in purely economic terms. Important also is it to appreciate that, given this primary assumption about the goal of strategy, the details of policy were not something deduced *a priori* a long period ahead, but were formulated from a given concrete situation as it arose. Flexibility in face of changing situations was almost Lenin's catchword. He was particularly insistent on not sketching plans too far ahead, but taking first things first and viewing only a few steps at a time; and he counselled this, not as a rudderless opportunist, but as a strategist sure of his goal while conscious that his own actions must adapt themselves to the partly unknown movements of a moving world. To plan in detail for the future when the future could only be dimly discerned was not only waste of time, but took one's eyes away from the present, and gave wing to utopian illusions which would gather later to cloud one's vision. The general lines of advance might be known well enough ahead; but detailed tactics must wait for the concrete situation to which they were meant to apply. In economic matters this was even more the case than in the realm of politics, for, given the transfer of power to the workers, the aim of the new ruling Party and the new Workers' State was to lay the basis of a classless society, and to guide society towards this classless goal. The economic forms to be adopted would be primarily governed by this consideration; but their precise character could only be decided on in relation to the actual situation which presented itself after the Revolution.

But even after the Bolshevik Commissaries had gone from the Soviet and installed themselves in the principal government offices, and the dissenting Commissars had reconsidered their objections and resignations and crept back to the fold, there remained for Lenin a further political problem to be settled, before it was possible to turn thought to more specialised economic affairs. The Bolshevik Party in the name of the workers had gained supreme power in the towns. How would they be likely to keep it in a peasant country where the town workers, many of them still half-peasants, constituted less than a sixteenth of the population? It was precisely his appreciation of the overwhelming significance of this peasant factor that made Lenin, who had scorned the caution of more timid colleagues on the eve of seizing power, now quick to adapt himself to this factor and to compromise, in order to hold the power that in the towns had been won. One would have expected the slave of an economic Utopia to have started on the discussion of "fancy schemes" for Socialism in the village, much as the German Liberals at Frankfurt in 1848 had involved themselves in dissertation on fundamental rights. Socialist doctrine had for years maintained the economic superiority of the large farm over the small. Yet, one of the first acts of the new Government was the Land Decree, which, while nominally declaring the land nationalised, directed the village Land Committees to take over the landlords' estates and to organise their systematic distribution among the peasants. "Fancy schemes" of rural collectivism were relegated to a purely experimental rôle, in the case of "plots of land scientifically cultivated—gardens, plantations, nurseries, seed-plots, greenhouses and others—" which according to the decree "shall not be divided, but transformed into model farms and pass into the hands of the State or of the community." This became the basis for the system of communal peasant farms and State model farms, which, though distinctly important from an experimental point of view, never covered more than a relatively insignificant area and certainly disappointed many of the exaggerated expectations placed upon them by enthusiastic advocates in the Commissariat of Agriculture.[1]

From an economic point of view this distribution of the land was without much doubt a retrograde step. The preponderating economic element in the village now became the "poor peasant" with a holding of less than 4 dessiatines[2] and often no cattle; while the proportion of farms owned by "rich peasants," owning several head of cattle and farming

[1] By the end of 1921 there were 4316 Soviet farms in R.S.F.S.R. and 15,121 "collective farms." In 1922 these covered 3·2 per cent of the cultivated area in 32 provinces of R.S.F.S.R. and 4 per cent in the Ukraine, making a total of 3·5 million dessiatines, and employing 1·5 per cent of the farming population. The average size of a Soviet farm in R.S.F.S.R. was 389 dessiatines (about 1100 acres). Many of these, however, were at this time in a bad way for want of capital and technical personnel. [A. Orloff in *Russian Economist* (London), Vol. III, No. 9, pp. 3115–17.] Cf. also: "The attempt at socialism in the sphere of agricultural economy has remained up to now unsuccessful" (Bronsky in *Yejegodnik Cominterna*, 1923, 323).

[2] 1 dessiatine = 1·09 hectares = 2·7 acres.

more than 8 dessiatines, declined between 1916 and 1919 from 8 per cent to 3 per cent of the total number, and the number of farms of less than 4 dessiatines increased from 58 per cent of the total number in 1917 to 82 per cent in 1922;[1] while the loss of productivity involved in the break-up of landlords' estates was little, if at all, repaired by the achievements of the vaunted Soviet farms. Certainly this economic revolution in the village carried an individualist rather than a socialist flavour. But politically for the Bolsheviks it had an opposite and more than counter-balancing significance. It was an act which won support for the new Soviet power, or at least passive acquiescence, among wide masses of the peasantry who would otherwise have viewed it with hostility as another alien tyranny imposed on them by the towns.

The second step taken by Lenin to the same end was more purely political: political alliance with the largest and most influential peasant party. His dissident colleagues were anxious, and were actually negotiating, for an alliance of all *bona-fide* Socialist parties, pending the result of the coming Constituent Assembly. At one stage a proposal was apparently being discussed with the Left Social Revolutionaries for the admission of the latter into the Government, from which Lenin and Trotsky and the Revolutionary Military Tribunal should be excluded. But on one point Lenin was adamant. He would admit of no coalition with other parties who did not accept the pre-eminence of the Soviets in the new State structure and the necessity of maintaining the sternest

[1] Farbman, *Bolshevism in Retreat*, 207; and *Industrial and Lab. Information* (Russ. Suppl.), Nov. 2, 1923; Bronsky in *Yejegodnik Cominterna*, 1923, p. 321. It is to be noticed, however, that the 3 year average output of 1923–5 compares quite favourably with the annual average for 1905–14, the average yield of cereals in quintals per hectare being 6·8 in the earlier and 6·6 in the later period for R.S.F.S.R., and 7·1 at both periods for U.S.S.R. as a whole, excluding Transcaucasia and Turkestan (*Abrégée des Statistiques*, L'Admin. Central de Statistique U.R.S.S., 1925). On the other hand, one would expect a smaller cultivated area to yield a higher average return on the principle of diminishing returns. However, part of the effects of the reduced size of holdings has, no doubt, been offset by improved agricultural methods—improved rotation of crops, deeper ploughing, extended use of tractors.

military measures against the counter-revolutionary forces which were already rallying at Mogilev for a counter-blow. In alliance with odd groups of Socialist intellectuals and leaders who had lost most of their flocks he was not particularly interested. To his mind, they would only serve to reinforce the counsels of weakness and timidity within his fold. But the case of a party which had a large peasant following and a membership playing a leading rôle in the villages was a different matter. Co-operation was worth the sacrifice of some principles, provided the fundamental requisite—unflinching maintenance of Soviet hegemony in the towns—was retained.

On November 18th, on the initiative of the new government, a Peasants' Congress met in the Alexander Hall of the Duma Building in Petrograd. This Congress had formerly been dominated by the great peasant party, the Social Revolutionaries; but by November this party had split into a "Right" section, led by the old Executive Committee which followed Kerensky, and a "Left" section which now constituted a clear majority of the Congress. The Bolsheviks, on the other hand, had no more than a fifth of the delegates; but so important did he regard it that Lenin himself participated as a rank and file delegate. For some time the issue of the Congress remained quite indecisive. Marie Spiridonova of the Left was elected to the chair; and Chernov, a man of the Centre, who was believed to have been intriguing with the counter-revolution at Mogilev, was shouted down. But on the other hand, Lenin himself could not secure a hearing for full ten minutes; while Zinoviev had to leave the rostrum amid jeers and shouts of "See how a Soviet Commissary sits in a mud-puddle!"[1] In the course of the Congress, however, the Right minority, led by the old committee, seceded to form a separate convention of their own, between which and the official Congress, Chernov went to and fro; and behind the scenes at Smolny negotiations were in progress between the Bolsheviks and the leaders of the Left S.R.'s.

[1] John Reed, *Ten Days that Shook the World*, p. 266.

Finally, after many hours of intricate negotiations, a compromise was effected between them. The Central Committee at Smolny, which had formerly represented only the soldiers and workers' Soviets, was now to be broadened to include an equal number elected from the Peasants' Congress; while members of the Left S.R. Party—the party of Marie Spiridonova and Kamkov and the revered and aged Nathanson—were to join the Council of Peoples' Commissaries and to be given certain ministerial posts. The leading influences in the villages and smaller townships were now supporters of the Soviet régime and pledged to carry into operation the new government's decrees.

By this timely compromise Lenin had secured the second principle of his policy, which always remained for him the *sine qua non* of any progress on the road to socialism in Russia. He had secured in the towns the hegemony of his own Party, basing itself on the interests of the factory workers. Now he had cemented, primarily by his land decree and secondarily by the outcome of the Peasants' Congress, that alliance with the poorer and " middle " peasants, who, in return for concessions of land and the right to control their own affairs in the village, were willing to leave to the Bolsheviks the rôle of leading partners in the enterprise with a free hand to take the road to socialism in the towns. Before the transfer of power in the towns Lenin had condemned compromise,[1] doubtless because he regarded the pre-October situation as a situation of unstable equilibrium in which one must needs either retreat some distance or else advance. But the October days had introduced for him a new equilibrium on a new level and on the basis of a new grouping of forces, to maintain which was possible, and only possible, if the passive support of the peasant masses was secured. Compromise before had been condemned as the start of a retreat in front of the enemies' forts which might become a rout.

[1] Except for the particular compromise early in September suggested to " meet a special situation " and " to secure a peaceful development of the revolution."

Compromise now was advocated after the forts had been taken to protect the flanks and to give a breathing space for consolidation and "digging in." And only when this political site had been obtained for a building was attention turned to what the details of the economic structure were to be.

CHAPTER TWO

THE ECONOMIC POLICY OF THE FIRST EIGHT MONTHS

WHEN one has said that for Lenin the economic problem was mainly a matter, not of applying principles, but of experiment, one has at once to modify it by admitting that all was not opportunism and that certain lines of the picture were, of course, drawn *a priori*. What is important is that these were the lines of general direction rather than a static, detailed diagram of formal structure. Moreover, the economic problem could not be dealt with in isolation from the basic political issue of Bolshevik policy—the issue of class power.

In the first place, it is clear that the question how much should be nationalised and how quickly it should be done was essentially bound up with the political prospect of the morrow of October. English theory has always tended to answer such a question from a strictly economic point of view, often answering it quite separately for each industry in strange contempt for the principle of composition. But for the Bolsheviks no such water-tight compartment could be maintained. If they viewed the question of the Press, of committees in the army and the workshop from the standpoint of the struggle for power, it was natural that they should view the question of nationalisation from this standpoint too; and the same reason that made control of the Kremlin, the telegraph office, the arsenal and *Isvestia* important counted in the matter of control of the banks and transport and big industry as well. Indeed, this would apply to almost any socialist government pursuing a vigorous and uncompromising socialist policy. For, whereas a Finance Minister of an ordinary government, following a policy in the line of accepted tradition, has little fear of finding in the Governor of the central Bank anything but a ready and sympathetic collaborator, a Finance Minister bent on expropriating property would certainly find the same Governor an unwilling helper and in all probability an implacable foe; and in such circumstances the replacement of the latter by a sympathetic nominee of the Government would be almost a *sine qua non* of successful execution of the Government policy. The nationalisation problem becomes part of the problem of "key positions."[1]

In the second place, in so far as the aim of Bolshevik strategy was the creation of a classless community, nationalisation was judged as an essential step to this end. Nationalisation was an act in liquidation of class monopoly, and this was the *leitmotif* of the whole. If the existence of a ruling capitalist class was rooted in ownership and the differential advantage which that ownership gave over the ownerless—if, in a word, the largest factor in inequality was income from unequally distributed property—it followed that the continued existence of capital in private hands represented a continuance of the capitalist class and its influence, and a persistence of differential advantage with its usual cumulative tendency. This would seem to suggest the criterion of size, quite apart from all technical considerations, in determining the order of expropriation; but the size of personal holdings of capital rather than the size of enterprises themselves. However, in Russia, where the complicating factor of the diffusion of bonds and preference shares among numerous small rentier investors (like Standard Oil with its 60,000 names on the share register) was comparatively undeveloped, the problem was simplified; and the nationalisation of large enterprises was approximately synonymous with the expropriation of large capitalists.

The more strictly economic factors, to which in England one is inclined to assign the leading place, undoubtedly

[1] Rykov said at the 1st Congress of Councils of National Economy that very largely "nationalisation was effected in view of the direct struggle with the bourgeoisie" (*cit.* S. Zagorsky, *La République des Soviets*, 36).

played some part in the Bolshevik attitude towards nationalisation, but apparently only a subordinate part. The feeling doubtless existed that a system of socialised industry was economically superior to a system of private enterprise, on very much the same anti-*laissez-faire* grounds as form the platform of Mr. Sidney Webb. Certainly these arguments were used; though used, one frequently suspects, as a kind of scientific seasoning to other arguments to impress the sceptic, as a don adorns a page with classical quotations to impress the reader with his learning. In September 1917, under the title of " The Approaching Catastrophe and How to Avert it,"[1] Lenin wrote to urge nationalisation as the only way of combatting the economic disorganisation by introducing centralisation and control; and he asserted that at present such measures were either precluded or *sabotaged* when introduced " for fear of encroaching on the capitalists," and could only be successfully introduced after the workers had attained power. There has always been much talk of the superiority over the " anarchy of production " of " planned economics "—planned by a sort of economic general staff formed " to do those things which at present are not done at all."[2] And Trotsky, in particular, seems to have been influenced by such economic considerations, even to the point at times of making centralisation and planning into a blinding obsession. Prof. Eugen Varga, writing on the basis of a brief experience as Soviet Commissar in Hungary, urges several reasons for the economic superiority of socialist over private industry: the breaking down of the barriers of vested interests, attention to welfare rather than money indices, the abolition of many unproductive occupations, the substitution of conscious planned control for economic anarchy, and so forth. At the same time he is careful to indicate that these advantages would hardly be obtained in the first days of the new proletarian régime—in fact, an initial decline in pro-

[1] Published in *On the Road to Insurrection*, p. 162 *seq.*: "To control, to inspect, to register—these are the ways to fight disaster and famine."
[2] J. M. Keynes, *End of Laissez-faire*, p. 47.

ductivity would almost certainly have to be faced.[1] But the fact that, while stressing this, he argued in favour of the most rapid possible nationalisation even of quite small businesses, shows that in his mind the political considerations which we have mentioned were the dominant ones, and that in regulating the speed and extent of the socialising process the purely technical issues counted scarcely at all. His summing up of the matter is definite enough: " Expropriation is an incident of the class struggle: (it) should be sufficiently sweeping to break the economic power of the bourgeois class —and that as speedily as possible."[2] Indeed, the chief rôle played by technical considerations, at any rate in Lenin's thought, was probably the exact opposite of what is commonly supposed. Instead of providing the reason for nationalisation, its main defence, they set its limits. The political considerations which were paramount would have dictated an expropriation of indefinite extent and speed. Economic considerations, administrative difficulties, called for caution and delay.

Principle, therefore, decreed that the character of the new economic system should be predominantly socialist, but left mainly to experiment and expediency the precise forms of administration which socialist industry might adopt. Yet, there remained a further matter of principle which had some influence, if not on the choice of forms themselves, at least on the substance in which the forms were clothed—on the actual relations established between groups and persons; and in certain cases it certainly acted as the balancing weight in the scales in favour of one type of organisation as against another. This further matter arose out of Lenin's theory of

[1] *La Dictature du Prolétariat : problèmes économiques*, 36 *seq.* G. Krshishanovsky, writing in 1921, discusses similar advantages as being among " the positive results of the (Bolshevik) revolution " (*Khosiaistvennie Problemi R.S.F.S.R.*, pp. 1–4).

[2] *Op. cit.*, 60. Cf. also S. Zagorsky, *op cit.* : " La problème d'une politique économique determinée n'était envisagé que comme un moyen de lutter pour la suppression de la bourgeoisie et pour l'établissement du régime soviétiste " (p. 6). They had no determined economic program (p. 7).

the State, to which reference has already been made. According to this, the State, as a strongly centralised organ imposing by coercion from above certain decrees and regulations upon the governed, was the product of a class system, and was in fact the instrument of the class which at the particular time was the ruling class. The State was an object of coercion imposed from above, reproducing in the political field the relation of master and servant, overseer and employee, in a sense in which an elected parish council and a voluntary association were not. In a society where conflict was only a conflict of individual wills on specific issues, a permanent apparatus of coercion was unnecessary: every such conflict could be dealt with *ad hoc* by the voluntary association of the majority; and the condition of affairs imagined in Rousseau's theory of the General Will would tend to prevail. But where conditions were such as to create potential conflict of a more far-reaching and persistent kind between rival herds, as a society based on some form of class privilege would naturally do, then some regular apparatus would be required to repress conflict and preserve the equilibrium of society on its existing basis by preventing the insurgent group from overstepping its appointed bounds. To preserve such an equilibrium, and by coercion to repress all efforts dangerous to class privilege, was the rôle of the class State.

In the transition period between capitalism and communism fundamental differences of classes would still remain. even though hegemony now rested with the working class. Society would still be an eddy of different elements and warring tendencies; and with such differences there would be potential conflict, dangerous to the equilibrium of the new society. Hence a State with a centralised apparatus and its usual coercive functions must still persist, though as an instrument of a working-class party, not of capitalist interests; and it must use its power against the remnants of the old ideology remaining among the workers and the intellectuals and stemming the new current of events, as well as against the old ruling class who actively or passively try to resist socialism or even to restore the *ancien régime*. But precisely in the degree that this State is successful in laying the basis of a classless society, the need for its coercive functions will disappear, and its former character will tend to " wither away."[1] Indeed, Lenin regarded as a necessary part of progress towards a classless society the progressive democratisation of the State, the decentralisation of administration and the breaking down of the barriers between officials and workers, so that governors and governed, administrators and administered, progressively mingled and merged. For, without such a development, there would tend to crystallise a bureaucratic " white-collar " caste, greedy of privilege, tinged with superiority and tending to reproduce in its dealings with the mass of the workers the old relation between master and servant—the relation of subjection of an inferior class to a superior. Accordingly, when Lenin spoke of " bureaucracy " and the need to fight against it, he meant not merely the derived journalistic sense of the term, inefficiency and " red-tape," but the existence of an official caste separate from the mass of the workers and imposing orders on them from above; and for him it was part of the essential rôle of the Party in this transition period to fight against bureaucracy in this sense by continually bridging the gulf between State administrators and the masses, forging a really organic unity between the two.

This conception of the " withering away " of the bureaucratic class State clearly had a voice in administrative methods and arrangements. It certainly influenced, as will be seen

[1] Lenin distinguished the " repressive " and the purely administrative functions of the State machine. He wrote in 1917 as follows: " Besides the preponderatingly ' repressive ' part of the apparatus, the standing army, police, officialdom; there is in the contemporary State machine another part, closely interconnected with banks and syndicates, fulfilling a great mass of work of account-keeping and registration, if one may so express it. This part of the apparatus cannot and must not be broken up. It must only be torn from subjection to the capitalists. From it must be cut off, broken, chopped away the capitalists, with their wire-pulling influence. It must be subjected to the proletarian Soviets. It must be made wider, more all-embracing, more popular " (*Will the Bolsheviks Maintain Power?*, 47–8).

later, the rôle assigned to the trade unions and the factory committees; and the concern shown prior to October 1917 to ensure contact between the Party and the masses was now partly transferred to the task of linking continually closer the State apparatus and the industrial workers. But in one respect it merely reinforced the experimental character of economic reorganisation. It suggested a continual, progressive modification of administrative forms as the general situation developed, the problem being one, not of realising a ready-made plan, but of creating and adapting instruments to fulfil a function in a continually changing set of circumstances. For the Bolsheviks the hegemony of their Party and the desire to guide society towards a classless goal remained constant factors in their problem. But the general economic situation was subject to variation and change. Their task in the economic sphere was regarded as an adaptation of economic forms to this objective situation, to the complex changing mosaic of material and ideal facts at a given time, as a schooner sets its sails and its course to the wind. But it was to be an adaptation designed to exert a reciprocal influence on the social environment, in order that the desired tendency towards a classless society might be achieved.

Nationalisation by the central government was not undertaken in the sudden and sweeping manner the day after the revolution that the popular imagination in Western Europe seems to picture. In the first eight months the new State acted towards industry in what may be described as quite a cautious manner—too cautious, as we shall see, for an important section of the Bolshevik Party. The State Bank, of course, passed into the hands of the new government without any formal break in its constitution, a Bolshevik, Piatakov, merely replacing the former President; while the step of declaring the other banks nationalised on December 13th was taken mainly as a move to stop the financing of the counter-revolution and the strike of civil servants which, it was alleged, was being conducted by these institutions.[1] This

[1] Cf. M. Philips Price, *My Reminiscences of the Russian Revolution* 209–11.

first stage in the nationalising process was, therefore, primarily a political move; and for the time being little more sweeping than this was done. In December the Supreme Council of National Economy (*Vesenha*) was formed in Moscow from representatives of the trade unions, factory committees and the government, together with technical experts and specialists, with the object of serving as a kind of economic general staff to control the economic system, to co-ordinate the somewhat chaotic activities of the factory committees, and to work out systematic plans for nationalisation as occasion arose. The merchant fleet and corn depôts were nationalised in the course of February 1918; but " it is not till May 1918 that we find a whole industry nationalised,"[1] when the sugar industry was placed under the administration of a Supreme Sugar Committee subordinate to Vesenha. The oil industry followed suit a month later. At the same time in the course of the spring certain trades were declared State monopolies, such as matches, coffee, spices, yarn and foreign trade.[2] But it was not until June 28th, 1918, that a general nationalisation decree was passed, declaring firms of over 1 million roubles capital to be national property,[3] their managers and personnel to carry on the enterprise pending detailed arrangements. And this decree also was primarily motivated by a political consideration.

Prior to June 28th, therefore, there was no general and indiscriminate nationalisation by the central government, as took place in Hungary in the case of both large and small enterprises within the space of one month.[4] Save in the cases

[1] *Labour Conditions in Sov. Russia* (Int. Lab. Office), 195.

[2] Zagorsky, *op. cit.*, 9; Piatakov in *Yejegodnik Cominterna, 1923*, 340.

[3] This was the figure given in most, but not in all, cases. Some elasticity was allowed for the different conditions of different industries. In mining a list of enterprises was given, in textiles all over 500,000 roubles capital were nationalised, in hemp over 200,000, tobacco over 500,000 and 300,000, glass and porcelain 500,000, cement 500,000. In the interim, while existing proprietors continued in control, the State assumed financial responsibility. At this time the rouble had fallen to about one-hundreth of the value of the pre-war rouble.

[4] Cf. Varga, *op. cit.*, 61.

of sugar and oil, there was no general decree applying even to a single branch of industry; and these two cases did not occur before May. The interference of the State in economic affairs was mainly confined to finance, to certain branches of trade and to general regulation and control, such as happened in most belligerent countries during the war, and had already under the Tsar acquired the name of "war socialism." When prior to June 28th specific enterprises were nationalised, this was usually due to some special circumstances applying to that particular business, or to the unauthorised action of local bodies, which tended in the early days to do most things on their own initiative and frequently to be somewhat scornful of centralised authority, particularly in areas where Left S.R. influence was strong.[1] The case of a group of factories in the Urals, which the central authorities had decided to leave in private hands, is fairly typical of the general situation. The local factory committees, declaring that the attitude of the owners was provocative, announced their intention of taking over the factories into their own hands. The Central Council of Trade Unions sent a delegation from Moscow to dissuade them, but without avail; and then followed it by telegraphed instructions forbidding the factory committees to take any action. To this telegram the only reply was a brief report stating the date on which the factories had been taken over by the local Soviet. Indeed, one of the chief reasons for the institution of Vesenha was

[1] At times during this early period local Soviets actually defied the orders of the central government. Says Baerlein: "Each local Soviet acted like an independent republic," and he refers to "the disregard of Moscow's authority by the self-willed Siberian Soviets" (*The March of the Seventy Thousand*, 126 and 138). In the case of the Tsar, when the Central Government sent its Commissary, V. Yakovlev, at the end of April to Tobolsk to bring the Tsar and his family to Moscow, Yakovlev met with severe opposition from the local Soviet, and was actually placed under arrest at Ekaterinburg and prevented from moving the Tsar further. (N. Sokolov, *Enquête Judiciaire sur l'Assassinat de la Famille Impériale Russe*, p. 66 *seq.*). The Anarchists at this time issued manifestoes such as the following with the aim of encouraging the maximum local autonomy: "Village! Ignore the orders of the city, disobey the Centre! Organise the Commune!" "Ye gulls of religion, destroy the Churches. Blow up the Universities!" (*cit.* E. A. Ross, *The Russian Sov. Republic*, 75).

to prevent unauthorised " nationalisation " and to co-ordinate the economic functions of the State according to some reasonable plan; and of the individual businesses expropriated prior to July 1918 only 100 were nationalised by decree of the centre and over 400 by local organisations.[1] The grounds for this nationalisation, in so far as they were legal, were governed by a decree of December 18th, 1917, which laid down the reasons for which factories might be " confiscated "—a decree which, it has been said, " read like penal enactments" rather than an economic measure.[2] The chief reasons were to be : the special importance of the enterprise to the State, refusal on the part of the owner to observe the rules laid down by order for certain measures of workers' control, and the closing down or abandonment of the works by the owner.

Thus, in February the large electrical company in Moscow, Electro-Peredacha, passed into State ownership " in view of its general importance to the State ";[3] and in December the Putilov works at Petrograd had been taken over for a similar reason. The Chaudoir Company was nationalised by decree of February 27th by reason of " governmental considerations of great importance "; and the Novorossisk mining and metallurgical works at Yuzovka were declared State property on March 3rd, both " in view of the impossibility of the company continuing its operations, and in view of the importance of the works to the State." In 50 per cent of the cases, however, where the reason was explicitly stated, the official reason given for nationalisation was the alleged " sabotage " of the owner,[4] and not infrequently the fact that he had actually closed his business and emigrated until fortune and the armies of the counter-revolution should

[1] I.L.O., *op. cit.*, 196; Prof. Benediktov in *Tyajolaia Industria S.S.S.R.*, 81. Quite half of these apparently belonged to the end of this period, namely between May 15th and June 28th.

[2] I.L.O., *op. cit.*, 194. Rykov in *Isvestia,* May 30, 1918, spoke of the early nationalisation as being often " of a purely penal character."

[3] Decree of 17 Feb. 1918, signed Lomov and Antipov for the President of Vesenha, *cit.* Labry, *Une Legislation Communiste*, 105–6.

[4] Pasvolsky, *Economics of Communism*, 36.

bring a happier turn of events. We find the Société Internationale des Wagons-lits and the Sergiev-Ufalenski mines nationalised because of " the refusal of the management to continue work in the workshops," and because of " the refusal of the management to submit to the decree on workers' control."[1] We find the business of M. Helferich-Sade nationalised in January because the management " had closed its factory and abandoned its principal office at Kharkov."[2] Similarly, the aeroplane works of Andréev, Lanski and Co. were taken over because of the declared intention of the company to dismiss its workers, the Sestronetsk metallurgical works for refusing to continue production, the Roentgen tube factory because its owner had abandoned the enterprise, and the Rostkino dye-works for " the categorical refusal of its owner to continue production, in spite of the reserves of materials and fuel in stock."[3]

But more important in these first eight months than nationalisation was the question of workers' control; and to a very considerable extent this latter issue dominated the former. Already under Kerensky factory committees had been given certain powers, and in some cases had assumed, or tried to assume, more powers than they were actually given, so that the industrialists were loudly clamouring for the suppression of the committees within reasonable bounds and the restoration of workshop discipline. Cases of actual seizure of factories by the committees were not unknown, though at that time were still exceptional.[4] But quite considerable " interference " with the management was more general; and seems to have been prompted in most cases by the desire of the workers to prevent the closing down of works and the dismissal of workmen.[5] As early as June 1917 the

[1] Decree of Dec. 29th, 1917, *cit.* Labry, *op. cit.*, 96–7.
[2] Decree of Jan. 13th, 1918, signed by Lenin and Shliapnikov.
[3] Decrees of Jan. 16th, Feb. 19th, and Jan. 13th, 1918, signed by Lenin and Shliapnikov.
[4] Piatakov, *op. cit.*, 327.
[5] Prokopovitch, *The Economic Condition of Soviet Russia*, 5; Khalatov in *Yejegodnik Cominterna*, 449.

factory and dock committees at Kronstadt were claiming and exercising " the right to inspect the accounts and the books of the management," and to see " that no materials left the premises without good reason "; while in the cable works the owner had actually been deposed by the local Soviet on the charge of trying to close down his works and to sell his plant to a foreign bank, and the concern was being administered by its factory committee which had sent its agents to Petrograd to purchase stocks of raw metal.[1] By October similar encroachments of power were being attempted in Petrograd, as in the case of a metal works on the Vassily Ostrov, where, in answer to wholesale dismissals by the management on the ground of insufficient raw materials, the factory committee decided to demand powers of controlling the raw material, examining the books and countersigning orders by the management.[2] Even outside " Red Petrograd " these events were happening; as at Rostov, where the workers' committees " presented demands for shorter hours, more pay and the right to name their own foremen," and then, when the employers rejected the demand concerning the foremen, " the malcontents in the biggest factory seized the general director, and wheeling him out in a barrow dumped him in the street."[3]

The industrialists on their side " were not slow to retaliate, some by ' sabotage,' some by closing their establishments, some by raising prices." They complained of the breakdown of discipline and the loss of authority by managers, the effects of the 8-hour day and the interruption of work occasioned by meetings and demonstrations, and declared that in some cases wages and salaries exceeded the gross value of output. This, added to the disorganisation of transport and shortage of materials, led to a wholesale closing down of cotton mills in Moscow, Vladimir and Ivanovo-Voznesensk and of the flour-milling industry, and a reduction of staffs in the metal

[1] M. P. Price, *op. cit.*, 39–40.
[2] *Ibid.*, 132–3.
[3] Baerlein, *op. cit.*, 63.

industry, while a general decline in production up to 30 or 40 per cent set in.[1]

Meanwhile, the moderate socialists of Kerensky's party and the Mensheviks groped uncertainly for a middle course. They could hardly fail to give sympathy to the workers' aims " in principle." But they were as disinclined to allow independent revolutionary action as they were to play into the hands of the Bolsheviks by appearing to the masses too reactionary; and in practice they also joined in the cry for " discipline " and for the curbing of independent action by State regulation of economic affairs. In face of the insistent demands of the industrialists, the Government was forced to take action to restrain the movement; and Skobolev, the Menshevik Minister of Labour, issued instructions to the factory committees not to interfere in the management, nor to obstruct in any way the owners' conduct of the undertaking.

Such action brought the Government and the Mensheviks into sharp opposition to the factory committees and to the Bolsheviks, who had issued a slogan of " workers' control," had urged on the factory committee movement to more militant claims and had organised the committees into a federation. This the Bolsheviks had done, not on fixed principles of political and social theory, but as part of the strategy of the class struggle. The matter was not viewed by them statically in the light of certain democratic " rights," but dynamically as part of a manœuvre, meaningless unless viewed in relation to the objective of the manœuvre as a whole. The factory committees brought to the fore keen and active workers of the younger generation, and focussed the riper and more militant temper of the present more quickly than did the trade union officialdom, elected some time previous, less responsive to and less in touch with mass opinion. They were regarded by the Bolsheviks as highly valuable instruments of the struggle for seizing power from the capitalists, doing inside industry what the municipal Soviets

[1] K. Leites, *Recent Economic Developments in Russia*, 38–9.

were doing in the wider political field. Moreover, their militant activity was regarded as forming an important educative force, a rallying point for class-conscious sentiment and opinion.

After the taking of the political " key positions " in October, the question of the factory committees and workers' control was still regarded from a tactical standpoint. Even at the outset the Bolsheviks—or at least an important section of them—were averse to allowing too great independence to the factory committees, now that the State was in their hands, lest this should introduce an anarchic element; and the central authorities were continually trying to restrain these committees and to keep them in line with the general State policy. But at the moment they were regarded, as a General may regard guerilla fighters, as useful instruments for encroaching upon and enveloping the positions which still remained in the enemies' hands. Industry still remained predominantly under the command of the capitalist; and an extensive system of workers' control, backed by the political influence of the new Bolshevik State, was regarded as the best way of ensuring that the continued rule of the capitalist in the industrial sphere should be no more than that of a limited monarch. In this second, post-October, phase of the struggle the factory committees were guerilla skirmishers thrown out in advance, until such time as the more ponderous main body could come up and occupy the remaining positions; and as such they were undoubtedly very important from the Bolshevik point of view in preventing the enemy from rallying and striking a counter-blow. They played a rôle in what has been termed the policy of " encircling the capitalist."[1] When nationalisation was finally effected, the circumstances of the case would be entirely altered, and the functions of factory committees would be reconsidered and revised.

What the new government principally feared was that owners of factories would try to bring pressure to bear by

[1] P. Miliukov, *Russia To-day and To-morrow*, 55.

closing down production and locking-out their workers, while commercial concerns might operate a partial blockade of "Red" Moscow and Petrograd, just as in November the League for the Regeneration of Russia had organised a strike of civil servants and officials of the State Bank, financing them, it was alleged, by credits from the private banks. They were concerned lest owners of enterprises, fearing nationalisation, might even sell out to a foreign syndicate, as had occurred in several cases already under Kerensky, or emigrate to the camp of the counter-revolution, with the accounts and keys and bank balances of their firms.[1] These fears strongly influenced the Decree on Workers' Control of November 14th, 1917. By Articles 1 and 6 the workers' committee was given the right to be consulted on matters of sale and purchase, of fixing the output program and even of determining selling price. If the committee, after full consultation, came to a decision contrary to the wish of the owner, this decision was nevertheless to become binding, subject to appeal to some superior economic organ (Sections 8 and 9). The committee, further, had the right of inspection of accounts and all relevant documents, and to demand explanations concerning them without regard to commercial secrecy (Section 7); and it was charged at the same time with the maintenance of workers' discipline (Section 10). On the other hand, Article 7 of the explanatory General Instructions, later appended to the Decree, reserved to the proprietor the sole executive right of giving orders as to the running of the concern, and expressly forbad the Factory Committee to interfere in this or to countermand such orders. In other words, the factory committee was given certain wide legislative powers in the conduct of the enterprise, and power of interpolating and securing information from the executive authority; but it was not allowed to interfere directly in the executive work concerned with the day-to-day running of the enterprise. Article 9 further emphasised this distinction by

[1] Cf. Leites, *op. cit.*, 70; Pasvolsky, *op. cit.*, 32; Prokopovitch, *op. cit.*, 5.

forbidding the committee " to take possession of the enterprise or to direct it," except by the sanction of higher authorities. The technical and clerical staffs were to join with the manual workers in the election of the factory committee (Article 2).[1]

This decree carried the powers of the factory committee considerably ahead of their position under Kerensky, and confirmed most of the hitherto illegal functions which these committees had often seized on their own initiative. Such an extension of powers had always been resisted by opponents of the Bolsheviks, first on the ground that it would hamper production, and second on the plea that it would merely " provoke " the enemy to violent and extreme action. To this argument the Bolsheviks had replied that productivity was not their concern until they had overthrown capitalism. Like Adam Smith, they insisted that at times " Defence is better than Opulence ": a General cannot concern himself unduly with the fact that the deploying of his troops may trample down the corn, and he may even at times have to shell a Rheims Cathedral. As for the " provocation," they declared that the capitalists would anyhow be provoked by any move aimed against the existence of capitalism; and to fear this " provocation " was to fear to gain the advantage of the initiative. Now that the Bolsheviks were the governing power, responsible for organising the economic life of the country, these arguments lost some of their force. The effect on productivity now reacted on the position of the Bolsheviks themselves; and " provocation " took on a somewhat new light when it was a question of a partially " encircled " enemy, not an unchallenged one—of the morrow, not the eve, of a Sadowa. That one result of this extension of direct workers' control was a considerable disorganisation of production, and that in many cases it provoked sabotage and emigration of owners and managers, just as it had in a smaller number of cases under Kerensky, can hardly be questioned. But that it created disorganisation and sabotage more than the in-

[1] Labry, *op. cit.*, 127–9, 131 *seq.*

fluences which would have operated in its absence seems a much more doubtful claim. Indeed, in the absence of some such pressure and regulation operated through the factory committees, rough and chaotic though it was, it is scarcely conceivable that more than a small percentage of owners, with the threat of nationalisation hanging over them and complete uncertainty of markets, would have continued their enterprise in anything approaching a normal way.

How far these measures were regarded as purely temporary measures is difficult precisely to determine. The question partly depended on how quickly or how gradually it was intended to accomplish general nationalisation; for, in a nationalised enterprise the immediate political requirements of workers' control would have disappeared with the passing of the private owner. Some Bolsheviks seem to have regarded it as a convenient transitional stage to complete nationalisation—as part of the policy of " encircling capital " —providing a sufficiently stable situation for a halt to be called before the complex tasks of economic reorganisation were taken up. Others, no doubt, regarded " direct democracy " in the workshop as having a certain permanent value for its own sake, as an educative force for the " creative spirit " of the masses, as a step towards the " withering away " of the State; and these claimed certain words of Lenin in support of this view. But Lenin himself, it seems, thought of the matter in terms of an immediate set of circumstances only, and was perfectly ready, as he later showed, to adapt his views on workers' control, as changed circumstances and the needs of production demanded. In those days of " touch and go " for the Soviet power few of the Bolsheviks looked further into the future than a week or two at a time.

But whatever intentions may have been, the actual outcome seems to indicate fairly strongly that the situation created by the Decree of November 14th could be no more than temporary. The state of affairs which the Decree created was a system of diarchy within industry;[1] and the whole available experience of Russia at this time and of other countries subsequently seems to indicate fairly forcibly that such a diarchy of two hostile forces is a position of unstable equilibrium which can be no more than short-lived. This seems true equally in the wider political sphere and inside industry, equally in the case of militant working-class organisations exerting political influence on the State through Soviets, as in the case of a workers' committee attempting to share powers of decision on industrial matters with the employer. In the latter case, in particular, instability disorganises economic life and so forces a conclusion of the matter; and it will generally happen that each party will be on the alert to take the first opportunity of establishing itself as at least the senior partner, if for no other reason than to forestall the anticipated action of the rival party; and when once the seniority is established, every care will be taken to preclude any questioning of that seniority in the future. This was the state of affairs in the political sphere prior to October. This is what occurred subsequently in Germany, where it was the Soviets that were ousted from the positions of influence which they had exerted in November 1918 and were relegated to a harmless rôle. In Austria there was a similar outcome after a somewhat longer transitional period, even though it was apparently the intention and hope of the workers' leaders to maintain this position of class diarchy for a considerable length of time.[2] In Italy a similar attempt by the agricultural labourers' unions to impose stringent conditions on the landowners led to the growth of Fascism in the rural districts and the restoration of equilibrium by the crushing of the unions. Of course, circumstances are conceivable where such a balancing of forces might by a convenient compromise be preserved for a considerable length of time; just as in a case of bilateral monopoly, where there

[1] Cf. Prokopovitch, *op. cit.*, 5–6.

[2] Cf. Otto Bauer, *op. cit.*, Part IV. Dr. Bauer speaks of it as the "Balance of Class Power."

are two monopolist traders in a chain of wholesale operations, the contestants may in certain circumstances cease their mutual efforts to subordinate or displace the other and effect a compromise. But such circumstances seem special and exceptional rather than the rule, and presuppose that the probability of gain to each party is small as compared with the loss to be incurred by it through any disturbance of the equilibrium. This may be the case where a test of strength has already taken place, and one party has already gained a partial victory, while the vanquished party has little hope of retrieving its fortunes by a counter-blow; or after a long period of costly struggle resulting in an exhausting stalemate. Such a situation will not be found on the eve of a decisive struggle for power. Indeed, at such a time the very formation of this diarchy would be regarded as a challenge by the party that had hitherto ruled. But on the morrow of such a decisive issue there might be some small chance of these circumstances being present.

It was not impossible, therefore, though it was improbable, that in 1918 a régime of diarchy in industry might have provided for a time a state of equilibrium with an "encircled capitalism." But, as it happened, few people thought that the new régime could survive for more than a week or two; and consequently employers were disinclined to submit quietly to the new decree. In a few cases matters went well, and production continued under the general supervision of the factory committee. Sometimes an owner who might otherwise have closed down his works submitted grudgingly to the order of the committee and kept it running; as, for instance, the English manager of an engineering firm at Odessa, who submitted to the demand that workers' representatives should be present at Board meetings, and found it "not entirely disagreeable."[1] But in what seems to have been the larger number of cases one of two extremes was quickly reached. On the one hand, it was not unknown for the employer by personal influence or by bribery to win over

[1] Article by "A British Manager" in *The Times*, Sept. 4, 1918.

the factory committee to acquiesce in his desires;[1] and in " several cases the vote of the factory committee was purely passive, and the former directors or proprietors continued for a long time to enjoy the powers they possessed under the old régime."[2] On the other hand, many owners defied the committees or emigrated, and the workers accordingly took over complete control of the enterprise; while in some cases the workers took over the enterprises without any serious attempt at joint running with the owner.

This gave rise to an entirely new problem—that of syndicalist and centrifugal tendencies among the factory committees. It was only to be expected when a group of workers took over an enterprise that they would tend to neglect wider social interests and even to develop a kind of proprietorial feeling of their own. Workshop discipline and production declined still further. Sometimes machinery and stocks were pillaged by the workers or sold collectively.[3] " Another proprietor came," wrote one of the leaders of the Metal Workers' Union, " who was equally as individualist and anti-social as the former one, and the name of the new proprietor is the control committee. In the Donetz area the metal works and mines refused to supply each other with coal and iron on credit, selling the iron to the peasants without regard for the needs of the State."[4] Piatakov speaks of " the elemental process of workers taking over enterprises through the organs of workers' control," which, carried to an extreme, " began to mean in many cases the transfer of the administration of enterprises into the hands of groups of workers instead of into the hands of the Workers' State."[5] In the case of the starch and molasses factory, " Jivilov," the concern was nationalised by the Government, but the

[1] As often happened in the Army in the case of officers; e.g. the case of the ex-Tsarist General who secured the appointment of a " shaky " political commissar to control him, and finally made the latter into a strong anti-Bolshevik (Sir Paul Dukes, *Red Dusk*, 211).

[2] I.L.O., *op. cit.*, 241; cf. also Zagorsky, *op. cit.*, 19.

[3] Cf. *Isvestia*, March 17th, 27th, etc., 1918.

[4] *Ibid.*, April 27th, 1918.

[5] *Op. cit.*, 328.

factory committee refused to hand over to the administrator whom Vesenha sent down to take charge.[1] When the District Economic Council of the Northern Region instituted a system of government inspectors to bring the metal works of Petrograd under its control, severe conflicts ensued between the inspectors and the factory committees.[2] In the railway shops there actually appeared an organisation terming itself the "Alliance of Workers' Representatives," agitating against centralised control and in defence of the "autonomy of the workers' committees."[3]

Thus, in place of nationalisation, there was a wholesale and chaotic "expropriation" of enterprises on local initiative, in some cases because the owners had refused to work them, in other cases in strict violation of Article 9 of the General Instructions on Workers' Control. The technical staffs were naturally more inclined to loyalty to the owners than to the manual workers, while the latter as a rule did little to conciliate them and secure their co-operation and often were actively hostile to them. The enterprises in the hands of their new directors were frequently cut off from their former markets and sources of supply, and work could only be carried on so far as existing stocks allowed, while to secure funds and food all manner of irregular trading in a purely local market had to be resorted to. Sometimes they lacked the information necessary to trade their goods and procure supplies; sometimes they lacked liquid resources; sometimes they lacked even the elementary expert knowledge of technical processes and regular accounting; not infrequently all three deficiencies existed at one and the same time. The ordinary links between economic units were largely broken down, and as a result the markets in the central towns and still more the villages were starved of essential manufactured articles; while in the immediate vicinity of factories anything that the workers could lay their hands

[1] I.L.O., *op. cit.*, 240.
[2] *Brit. Lab. Delegation Report*, 1920, 96.
[3] M. P. Price, *op. cit.*, 279–80.

upon, including parts of machinery, were being sold at "knock-down" prices, in order to secure funds for paying wages, and in country districts were being bartered with the peasants for food.

The chaos and disorganisation resulting from this situation was an important cause which forced the State to step in and take control where otherwise it would have been more tardy in doing so. It prompted the rapid creation of the machinery of State operation of industry, for the lack of which reliance had been placed on the organs of direct workers' control. The Supreme Economic Council (Vesenha) was set up, primarily with the object of regulating and giving some cohesion to the "elemental forces" which were shaping the economic situation; and among the leading figures on its Presidium were Rykov, Larin, Miliutin and later Krassin and Piatakov. In the first days of the revolution it was natural that much should be done on purely local initiative, and that the Government, obsessed with pressing political issues and poor in expert personnel, should be slow in bringing economic affairs under its control. The Bolsheviks in the winter of 1917 were doing no more than ride the whirlwind forces of revolution; not till later did they feel the reins; not, perhaps, till after 1920 or even later could they be said to have curbed the steed under their control. Accordingly, in these days many things useful to the new régime were done by local initiative, when without it they would not have been done at all; but at the same time many things were done that were senseless and disorganising. Gradually, therefore, the sheer pressure of events, rather than its own preconceived intentions, forced the Government to take a hand in controlling industry. In April the important step was taken of forbidding any local body to nationalise an enterprise without the sanction of Vesenha—an instruction which apparently was often disobeyed;[1] and in cases of essential industries Vesenha elaborated plans of organisation and itself sent officials from the centre to cajole or override the factory

[1] Piatakov, *op. cit.*, 340.

committee, conciliate the technical staffs, and start production again on some more satisfactory basis. At the same time the anarchism of the factory committees themselves was curbed by merging them with the trade unions. This was achieved after fairly prolonged negotiations; and the factory committees were made the units of trade-union organisation. The trade unions, though they had their points of difference on specific issues with the Government, were manned in their leading positions in the main by Communists, and had their representatives on Vesenha, and so were more alive to the needs of the general economic situation and considerably less separatist in tendency. Trade union influence could now be exercised to secure a uniform policy and observance of Government orders and decrees on the part of the factory committees.

The economic policy of this period, however, so far from being formulated in advance and imposed mechanically in *doctrinaire* fashion, was not introduced without considerable discussion and controversy inside the Bolshevik Party itself. Indeed, throughout this winter and spring of 1917–18 the Bolsheviks were so beset with political issues of first importance as to have little room for thought, still less for careful discussion of the principles of economic organisation. The spring was occupied with the protracted negotiations of Brest-Litovsk and eager hopes of the insurgent flame, fanned by Russian propaganda, spreading to the workers of Central Europe. The disappointment of this hope, and then the German advance into Russia, forced the immediate issue of a dictated peace or the proclamation of a new revolutionary war—an issue which nearly split the Party. The occupation of the Ukraine by the Germans, the formation of the Red Army under the driving force of Trotsky's organising genius,[1] the murder of Count Mirbach, the German Ambassador, by

[1] Sir Paul Dukes tells an interesting story of Trotsky's success in winning the co-operation of ex-tsarist officers, and describes the impression made by Trotsky on the officers of the Old Army, quoting the remark of one of them: "If Trotsky were not a Jew, the officers would follow him to a man" (*Red Dusk*, 221–2).

Left S.R.'s in the first week of July, and the armed revolt of the Left S.R.'s and Anarchists in the streets of Moscow against the Bolsheviks as " betrayers of the Revolution "—these events followed in quick succession. And after the first week of July came the advance of the counter-revolutionary forces of General Alexeiev from Samara and the North Caucasus, the revolt of the Czecho-Slovaks on the Volga, the commencement of Allied intervention in the North, the attempted assassination and wounding of Lenin, and the beginning of the Red Terror.

Economic controversy, accordingly, was always secondary to political discussion at this time. Nevertheless the grouping of opinions on political issues was to a large extent paralleled in the grouping on matters of industrial policy. The two sets of problems were not in practice distinct; no attempt was ever made to keep them in strict water-tight compartments; and so it was natural that certain differences of viewpoint should be reflected in both spheres at the same time. The political issue which shook the Party as much as or even more than the difference on the eve of October was the question of the signing of the Brest-Litovsk Peace, imposed under the bayonets of the advancing German army corps. The Left S.R.'s, and with them a powerful section of the Bolsheviks, were for refusing to sign and for continuing a revolutionary war of defence against German Imperialism. Lenin, on the other hand, counselled caution, pleaded the need to sign in order to secure a " breathing space," pointed out that the peasant soldier was war-weary and would not take up arms again, that the chances of the social revolution spreading in Germany were at the moment slight, while the technical organisation and supplies necessary for carrying on a war against well-equipped German troops were not available. Lenin's counsel won by a narrow margin; and Peace was signed by Chicherin on March 2nd. In relation to the economic problem, it was again Lenin who had his eye most intently fixed on reality; and that intuitive faculty which he possessed for grasping the essentials of a situation now made him the priest of caution, whereas it had made him on the eve of October scornful of all caution as cowardice. Lenin realised the immense difficulties involved in the economic organisation of a country like Russia, which could scarcely be said to have passed completely through the Industrial Revolution prior to 1914, and where much of the industrialisation which had taken place had been a kind of hot-house growth, achieved by foreign capital and foreign organising ability;[1] and he remarked about this time that although in the somewhat unique situation in Russia in 1917 it was comparatively easy to achieve the conquest of power, to hold the power and proceed to the work of achieving socialism would be considerably harder in Russia than in the more developed countries of Western Europe.[2] He realised the backward character of much of the semi-peasant factory proletariat, the insignificance of their numbers compared with the vast rural population with its strong individualist tradition. He realised Russia's poverty in the technical and organising ability necessary for large-scale economic administration—a poverty severe enough without any " sabotage " of experts or their estrangement by over-zealous factory committees. Hence his reiteration of the paradox: " We must learn from the capitalists how to organise the Socialist State." Hence his blunt declaration that " our efforts to organise the proletarian accounting and control of industry is obviously behind our expropriation of the expropriators."[3] Hence his plea in the economic as in the political sphere for a " breathing space."

Certainly Lenin did not intend nationalisation to be a sudden and devouring process, and envisaged nothing so sweeping as the policy which was in full swing by 1919.[4]

[1] Cf. Margaret Miller, *Econ. Development of Russia, 1905–14*, 219–20, 223, 298, etc.

[2] Lenin's Works, Russian Edition, Vol. XV, 233.

[3] *Cit.* Farbman, *Bolshevism in Retreat*, 169.

[4] Cf. Farbman, *op. cit.*, 118; Zagorsky, *op. cit.*, 7; Miliukov, *op. cit.*, 55–8. There seems no ground for the statement of Mr. Leites (*op. cit.*, 81) that Lenin was an advocate of immediate wholesale nationalisation. Lenin in his Theses of April 4th, 1917, had said: " Not the introduction

He was continually insisting to more impetuous colleagues that State Capitalism itself was a considerable step forward in so " mediæval " a country as Russia. What he had in mind was the socialisation of big industry, which would be relatively easy to organise on a national scale, and of enterprises important from a social and political point of view; while alongside socialist big industry would continue to exist smaller private enterprises, operating subject to State regulation and to a certain degree of direct workers' control. The fact that the State was transformed into a Workers' State, based on Soviets, and that it held the chief economic " key positions," would suffice to ensure that the " encircled capitalist " ruled merely as a limited monarch, and that the lines of progress were shaped in the direction of a classless community. It was this composite system that he referred to by the term State Capitalism—a composition " in which there is large-scale Socialist economy, private capitalist economy, and State enterprises temporarily leased to private capital "; superficially similar in form to what may sometimes be found in capitalist countries, but possessing the fundamental difference that power had been transferred to the organs of the working class.[1]

For certain enterprises, accordingly, particularly where foreign capital was required, Lenin considered seriously the participation of fairly large capitalists. One form of this was to be the " mixed company," in which the State and private capitalists should jointly own shares, but in the control of which the State presumably was to have the predominant voice. In industries where private concerns continued to

of socialism as our immediate task, but the transfer at once only to control on the part of the Soviets over the production and distribution of goods."

[1] Smushkov, *Economicheskaia Politika S.S.S.R.*, 23, 30; cf. also Bronsky, *op. cit.*, 308–9; Krumin, *v Borbye za Sozialism*, 74–7. Some Communists, however, were opposed to this use of the term " State Capitalism," declaring that the term " presupposes the capitalist State " (Bukharin, *op. cit.* (Chap. 7); also L. Kritsmann, *Geroicheskoe Period Vielikoi Russkoi Revolutsii*, 40). This objection seems to arise from an exclusive concentration on the position of industry, to the neglect of the village.

exist alongside State enterprises, an attempt was at first made to give representation to the private capitalists on the organising bodies set up in various industries to exercise general regulative functions, as the case of *Centro-textile*, which met on April 1st, 1918, and was composed of 15 representatives of the owners, 30 of the textile trade unions, and 11 of the central government organs, together with 6 technicians, 3 co-operators and 8 from other workers' organisations.[1] In the early summer a commission was appointed to frame conditions on which concessions might be given to foreign capital, and certain proposals of foreign firms were actually under consideration, as, for instance, a Norwegian firm and a Russo-Dutch syndicate for railway extensions in Siberia and the Donetz region.[2] In the course of March negotiations were in progress in Moscow between the Soviet Government and a group of large capitalists, headed by the wealthy Moscow merchant, Meschersky, for the formation of a mixed company, in which foreign capital should participate. The proposal, which originated from the side of Meschersky, was for the grouping of certain important enterprises in the metal industry into a vertical trust—the group of concerns which were later amalgamated to form the State trust, *Gomza*. At first Meschersky proposed to the Government a third of the shares and places on the Board; but later modified his proposal so far as to give 80 per cent, and finally 100 per cent, of Government participation, with the Meschersky group holding non-voting bonds, secured against 20 per cent of the share capital, and the Board being constituted jointly according to a five-year agreement. A similar proposal for a metallurgical trust in the Urals came from the Stakhaev company. Lenin apparently viewed the idea fairly favourably. But among the Communists there was important opposition to the scheme, Larin, who was in charge of the negotiations, himself declaring against it at a meeting of Vesenha on April 27th, on the ground that the State wanted "engineers not shareholders." In reply to the Stakhaev project, Vesenha

[1] Piatakov, *op. cit.*, 329.

[2] Labry, *op. cit.*, 168 *seq.*

proposed the personal participation of the authors in the construction of a State trust in the Urals, but apparently did not favour the participation of the capitalists as joint controllers of the concern on a footing of equality with the State. No agreement was reached; and the Meschersky negotiations finally also broke down. The official reason given was that many of the enterprises concerned belonged to foreign capitalists, and this involved the difficulty of arranging foreign participation in the concern. How, for instance, could any joint arrangement be made with both German and Entente capitalists, and how after the signing of Brest-Litovsk could an arrangement be made with either the one or the other alone?[1]

Against this conception of the immediate economic tasks of the new régime a very important alternative conception ranged itself among the Communists; and those who were in opposition on this issue were very largely the same elements who had opposed the signing of Brest-Litovsk, and had urged the heroic measure of withdrawing the capital of the new republic to the Urals and fighting a guerilla war against the German Eagle. The Left S.R.'s and Anarchists were, of course, opposed to any centralisation, regarding it as merely the substitution of a new irksome tyranny for an old one; and for them the independent syndicalist activity of factory committees was quite as it should be. The Left-wing Communists, however, were not averse to centralisation, at any rate, in theory, although they shared many points in common with the Left S.R.'s, and were evidently influenced by the ideology of the latter. What they chiefly seem to have desired was a much more rapid and sweeping confiscation of private enterprises, partly to "break the resistance of the bourgeoisie," partly for the psychological and symbolic value of a clean break with the forms of the past. Some of them, too, seem to have viewed workers' control as a matter of principle, and believed in a form of

[1] Cf. Leites, *op. cit.*, 84 *seq.*; Zagorsky, *op. cit.*, 37 *seq.*; Prof. Benediktov in *Tyajolaia Industria*, 81–3.

nationalisation which should embody a considerable measure of " direct democracy " and " committee management," in order thereby to express and develop the "creative impulses" of the masses. Communism in their eyes seems to have consisted largely of certain formal structures of economic organisation—formal structures which were mainly conceived *a priori* in utopian and *doctrinaire* fashion.

This Left-wing opposition among the Communists numbered among its leaders prominent intellectuals like Bukharin, Radek, Krestinsky, Ossinsky, Pokrovsky, Preobrajensky, Piatakov, Yakovlev. It constituted a separate fractional organisation within the Party, voiced its views through a newspaper of its own, *The Communist*, and held conferences with the Left S.R.'s.[1] The opposition of this group was chiefly levelled at the Brest-Litovsk Treaty and the " surrender to German Imperialism " which it was supposed to involve; but they also attacked the slowness of nationalisation, denouncing particularly the negotiations with Mescher-sky concerning a mixed company, and their propaganda was no doubt responsible for much of the hasty expropriation of enterprises which was effected on local initiative. How far they were explicitly hostile to the employment of former technicians and experts in industry is not very clear; but at any rate they looked askance rather than with favour at Lenin's insistence on generous treatment of " specialists,"[2] and their propaganda certainly did nothing to help the central authorities to curb the excesses of factory committees in this respect. Partly this point of view, which represented considerably more than a difference of emphasis on specific details, was the product of a *doctrinaire* utopianism common among intellectuals—similar instances are familiar among English Socialists—which in this case had provided a soil for certain strains of the ideology current among the Anarchists and Left S.R.'s. It was, however, something more than the theorising of a few individuals; and in so far as it

[1] Cf. L. Trotsky, *Cours Nouveau*, 37; M. P. Price, *op. cit.*, 271.
[2] e.g. in his pamphlet, *The Soviets at Work*.

touched a certain chord of response among the masses, one can probably say that it reflected the cultural backwardness of the Russian masses, the semi-peasant character of the factory worker in many areas and the somewhat limited horizon of his outlook. The view was characterised by what was, doubtless, a too narrow appraisement of the material limitations which stood in the way of economic reorganisation, and a too sanguine trust in the power of an imagined *élan* of the mass soul, if appropriately aroused, to turn back the waves and to change stones into bread.

Lenin lashed these persons ruthlessly in debate as " slaves of phrases," romanticists who wished always to live in the high-lights of melodrama, and he published against them his caustic pamphlet, *Left-wing Communism: an Infantile Disorder*. His answer to them consisted in a continual demand for realism: their proposals arose because their romantic vision was blind to the difficulties of the economic situation and exaggerated the possibilities of revolutionary help from the West. The opposition denounced his policy as State Capitalism. Did they not realise that in a backward country State Capitalism was an immense step forward, provided the State remained a Workers' State to steer society along the right lines? " When workers' delegations came to me with complaints against the factory owners," said Lenin, " I always said to them: ' You want your factory nationalised. Well and good! We have the decree ready and can sign it in a moment. But tell me: Can you take the organisation into your own hands? Do you know how and what you produce? And do you know the relations between your production and the Russian and the international market? ' And inevitably it transpired that they knew nothing. There was nothing written about such matters in the Bolshevik textbooks, or even in those of the Mensheviks."[1]

The breakdown of the diarchy in industry envisaged in the Workers' Control Decree to some extent played into the hands of the impatient " Left " by forcing the pace of

[1] *Cit.* Farbman, *After Lenin*, 43; cf. also L. Trotsky, *Lenin.*

nationalisation. In most cases where it had broken down, nationalisation was the sole alternative. Perhaps a strengthened interference by higher authorities might have reconstructed an equilibrium for a time on some such basis, at any rate in the smaller enterprises. But while the machinery of such regulation was being created, the machinery might as well be used for complete State operation; and the possibility of such a reconstructed equilibrium largely depended on the hopes which industrialists placed in the counter-revolution, since such hopes conditioned their willingness to compromise and to co-operate with the despised factory committees. With the occupation of the Ukraine by the Germans and the rallying of General Alexeiev's armies in the South, the hopes placed on an early overthrow of the new régime hardened the hearts of factory owners and moved them to spurn compromise. And after April, under the pressure of events and the need to bring some small order out of the economic chaos, the pace of nationalisation by sanction and plan of central economic organs very noticeably quickened.

On other points the opposition policy was worsted. On February 18th a joint meeting of the factory committees and the trade unions had achieved a merging of the two movements by a subordination of the former to the latter. At the Third Congress of Trade Unions on April 20th the further issue was raised of the subordination of trade union to State control in industrial management. On the ground that it would merely reproduce the old authoritarian relationship of master and servant, the Government proposal to introduce the principle of individual management and individual responsibility in industry was strenuously opposed. It was argued that such a measure would tend to destroy the independence of the trade unions as instruments for expressing the initiative of the workers, and would result either in their mechanical subordination to centralised State administration or else in their estrangement. Similar arguments were used in opposition to the proposal to introduce piece-rates, premium bonuses and scientific management in order to raise productivity—a proposal which was particularly denounced as "relics of capitalist exploitation" by a Bolshevik, Riazanov, who had recently resigned from his Party on this very point, and by the "Alliance of Workers' Representatives" and by Gorki's *Novaia Jizn* group. Instead, they proposed a system of "collective responsibility" of the factory committee and trade union jointly for a certain minimum program of production, the latter to be fixed by Vesenha in consultation with the union representatives. The declaration of a Bolshevik delegate at a meeting of the railway commission that there was need for "Americanising" the railway administration also called forth strong opposition. The spokesmen of the Government, on the other hand, argued that there was a wide gulf fixed between piece-rates and scientific management as used in the old days and when used under the new régime. There was now no question of using such methods to extort larger profits for shareholders and no fear of such methods being used to the detriment of the workers' class interests, seeing that it was a Workers' State which was in control, and the trade unions themselves had strong representation on Vesenha. Such methods, by leading to increased production, would raise the standard of life of the workers and would be strengthening the construction of socialist industry. Such methods were no more capitalist methods when used in a non-capitalist way than a stick is a murderous weapon when used as a staff and not as a cudgel.

The majority policy of the Bolshevik Central Committee finally carried the day. Individual management of factories by managers responsible to the higher economic body which appointed them was allowed in principle in cases where circumstances demanded it, although it was not generally introduced in industry until 1920, after the discussions at the 9th Party Congress. Payment by results and certain features of Taylor factory methods were also introduced in important cases and later gradually extended. In the case of the railways, administration was placed in the hands of a permanent Railway Department, whose decisions on purely administrative matters were to be binding on local trade unions and shop committees. In the realm of finance the power of local Soviets to impose indiscriminate levies on the *bourgeoisie* and to arrest persons as a means to distrain their property, as had been done in somewhat wholesale fashion in the provinces, was abolished; and authority to levy taxes was centralised in responsible regional finance departments which should carry out their work in conformity with the general principles and regulations laid down by the Central Government.[1]

Then suddenly came what seemed to be a *volte-face* of policy—an abandonment of State Capitalism as the transition stage and of gradual nationalisation. The decree of general nationalisation of June 28th seemed on this point a sudden complete surrender to the "Left." Nationalisation was now rapidly applied, not only to whole spheres of industry by a stroke of the pen, but also to quite small enterprises below the size mentioned in the general decree. The number of enterprises administered by the State rapidly rose in the second half of the year, until it reached the neighbourhood of 1000 at the beginning of 1919, and passed 3000 by January 1920.[2] A large and unwieldy centralised bureaucracy was quickly created under Vesenha, which endeavoured to eliminate market dealings as much as possible by organising a giant system of State barter in which the State financed the enterprises direct, often in kind, while the enterprises delivered their products direct to the State for the latter to distribute in the proportions which it thought fit to other

[1] Cf. M. P. Price, *op. cit.*, 280–5; Pasvolsky, *op. cit.*, 32–5; I.L.O. *op. cit.*, 244 *seq.*, 254–7.

[2] Figures on this point differ considerably. Prof. Prokopovitch quotes 830 and 3324 respectively for Jan. 1919 and 1920 (*op. cit.*, 13). Prof. Zagorsky mentions 1125 as the figure for Jan. 1919 (*op. cit.*, 35). Piatakov (*op. cit.*, 340) gives the following figures: Out of 6775 enterprises in the finishing industries, employing 1,185,000 workers, there were nationalised by Oct. 1919, 2522 employing 750,000 workers, by April 1920, 4141 employing 983,000 workers.

enterprises, to the countryside and to the army. The extreme point of this nationalising process was reached on November 29th, 1920, when Vesenha declared nationalised all enterprises with mechanical power employing over five workers and enterprises without mechanical power which employed ten.

But if concession seems to have been made to the desire of the " Left " to see all industry transformed at once into one glorious State department, their care for " direct democracy " and autonomy of trade unions and factory committees was, on the contrary, completely overridden. The policy of strictly centralised control and rigid discipline under single commanders, which had proved so successful in the lightning creation of the Red Army, was gradually to be applied to industry, finally in 1920, mainly under the influence of Trotsky, taking the form of the " militarisation of labour "; while, as " war communism " developed under the pressure of civil war, the trade unions and co-operatives lost most of their independence and became merely subordinate departments in the bureaucratic machine. Moreover, Lenin's attitude towards the problem of the bourgeois technical personnel found expression in Article 5 of the nationalisation decree, which included a recognition for the first time of the definite status of technicians and " specialists " as servants of the republic, and a guarantee of the continuance of their former salaries. At the same time the representation of " specialists " on Vesenha and on the advisory economic councils in each enterprise was increased, while the technical chief of an enterprise was given sole right of appointing technical employees and sole authority in all managerial matters.

Why did this sudden change of policy occur? One might, of course, speculate about a possible change in Lenin's conception of the transition period in face of the breakdown of the industrial diarchy and the growing strength of the counter-revolution, or on the possibility that he sought to strike a bargain with the " Left " tendencies among the masses by yielding to them swifter nationalisation in order the more readily to obtain greater centralisation and improved methods and workshop discipline. Whether influences of this kind played any part in the decision would be hard to establish definitely. Certainly, the unsatisfactory state of affairs connected with workers' control in the non-nationalised enterprises must have prepared the soil for the decree of June 28th. Where chaos had resulted from the sabotage of the owner or the syndicalist activities of the factory committee, it was evidently more satisfactory in most cases to declare the concern nationalised, and to send down a representative from the centre to restore a degree of order. For a recalcitrant factory committee would submit to the orders of an administrator appointed by the State—and even this they did not always do—where they would not have obeyed the order to submit to the former owner; and the latter policy might well have brought a severe estrangement between the Bolsheviks and their rank-and-file supporters. As the situation in June 1918, therefore, demanded action of some kind—either a step back or a step forward—it seems obvious that Lenin would be most inclined to take the step forward.

All this probably had something to do with the change. But the most important influence, and at any rate the immediate occasion of the Decree of June 28th, was a purely political issue. The Germans after Brest-Litovsk had advanced into the Ukraine and into the important industrial region of the Don. There were continued fears among the Russians that the Germans might proceed to occupy other industrial regions as well, and instal the former owners in their enterprises, and save them from danger of nationalisation by giving them the cloak, perhaps, of nominal German companies. Meanwhile in Berlin in the course of June there had been a buying of Russian industrial shares and a mild speculative boom. Larin, who was at this time in Berlin on a commercial mission, on the 25th telegraphed to Lenin that there was a likelihood of the German Ambassador in Moscow lodging a claim with the Soviet Government that certain important Russian enterprises were now owned by German citizens and were accordingly to be exempt from any nationalisation decree. Faced with this danger of an important part of Russian industry passing into German hands, the Council of People's Commissaries (*Sovnarcom*) hastily within the space of forty-eight hours prepared and passed the new decree; while Vesenha at an all night sitting drew up a list of the enterprises to which the decree should apply. The result was that the decree appeared in *Isvestia* on the very morning on which, in all probability, Count Mirbach was preparing to deliver his diplomatic note.[1]

But there seems no reason to think that even after the general nationalisation decree nationalisation would have been extended quite so far as it actually was by the end of 1920, or that the other features of industrial organisation which came to be called " war communism " would have appeared, had it not been for the recrudescence of Civil War and of armed intervention by Foreign Powers. Already on May 29th there had come news of the revolt of the Czecho-Slovaks in the Urals, and on May 30th martial law had been declared in Moscow and other principal cities, and in the first week of June General Krassnov and his Cossacks had attacked Tsaritsin; and the knowledge that the political " breathing space " was at an end must have influenced considerably the People's Commissaries in their attitude to the Decree of June 28th. On July 6th came the armed revolt of the Left S.R.'s on the northern outskirts of Moscow. On July 29th the Allied forces began to advance south from Murmansk; and on the day following the Czecho-Slovak forces occupied Kazan. On September 5th the attempted assassination of Lenin took place. Military necessities immediately took precedence over niceties of economic theory. As usually happens in a modern war, improvisation was governed by the need to bring some immediate return, to the exclusion of long period considerations; and as a result improvisation was consequently hasty and often intended to be no more

[1] Zagorsky, *op. cit.*, 40–1; M. P. Price, *op. cit.*, 285–6.

than a war-time temporary structure. The needs of the army and pressing necessities of life for the civilian population became the ruling obsessions; and under such conditions it was almost inevitable that there should be excessive centralisation, and that semi-military methods should be generally applied, particularly in the absence of an adequate administrative apparatus and personnel. " War communism " was, therefore, the product, not of theories, but of war-time improvisation.

Doubtless, there were many who regarded the forms which this " war communism " assumed as conforming to the ideal system which would any way have been reached eventually, even if more slowly, after a series of preliminary stages. At any rate, it seems probable that this was what many of the Communists of the " Left " had envisaged[1] and had sought to introduce more quickly and directly in the spring of 1918. Whether it was what Lenin had in mind as the ultimate form to be aimed at is more difficult to determine. But there seems no reason to think that it was. For the crux of the difference between himself and those whom he called Utopians was that the latter defined Communism as consisting in certain *forms*, which could be deduced *a priori* from first principles, based on postulates of what was subjectively desirable; whereas he defined Communism as a society erected on a certain base. This base was communal ownership and classlessness; and the forms of the superstructure would be those which experience should prove to be most adapted to and consistent with that base. Lenin, accordingly, logically refused to sketch the details of a situation until the basic elements of that situation

[1] e.g. Bukharin and Preobrajensky (*A.B.C. of Communism*, 333 *seq.*) state that " Communist society will know nothing of money," and that " as the work of building Communism is effected, the need for money will disappear." This is to be achieved (*a*) by payment of wages in kind, (*b*) by a " budget book " system, under which a worker shall have entered in his book the amount of work he has done, and this will entitle him to receive an equivalent amount of products from the co-operative store. How this equivalence is to be measured is not stated; but " a moneyless system of accounting " is referred to without being explained. The whole passage is a little reminiscent of Owen's Utopia-spinning.

had appeared. Broad, free-hand outlines he would draw, and frequently did draw, in advance; but they were regarded as no more than rough preliminaries, which played at very most the part of the working hypothesis to the scientific investigator. Even if he had envisaged some system like "war communism" as the goal of the future, it was characteristic of his whole philosophy that such a picture should not be regarded dogmatically, and should be quickly discarded for another if experience proved it wrong.

The fundamental feature of "war communism" was the displacement of the money system and the attempt to create a socially organised *Naturalwirtschaft*—a system, not of market exchange, but of State-organised barter. It was on this that the extreme centralisation of "war communism" largely depended, since, to organise the barter, all industry had to be concentrated into one large concern. On this also depended the replacement of appeal to the ordinary money-motives of industry by the sole available alternative, social coercion. There was a good deal of talk in the course of 1918 concerning the "replacement of the money system"; and a Congress of Vesenha actually adopted a resolution mentioning this as one of its economic aims. But the discussion seldom distinguished very clearly whether it dealt with the function of money as a means of exchange or as a measure. Presumably, to the extent that economic control is concentrated in large units, whether under the State or private trusts, the need for money as a means of settling debts will be reduced with the lessening of market transactions. This, together with the results of monopoly in place of competition, is presumably what Trotsky means when he refers to the gradual "elimination" of the importance of the market as Socialism develops. But this would not dispense with the need for some unit of measurement and calculation as a basis for accounting; and whatever unit one might take for this purpose would be performing this second function of money. Moreover, it might be practicable for the State to abandon the pricing of certain commodities if their supply had been so cheapened as to be exceedingly plentiful. But in all cases where the cost involved in production made it impracticable to supply every possible desire for the thing, either pricing or rationing would have to be resorted to in order to adjust consumption to the practicable supply. If the commodity in question is of a very standardised character and has a very inelastic demand, rationing by means of a direct payment in kind might be quite practicable.[1] But in other cases, at least in the case of more varied secondary wants, rationing would almost certainly be the more clumsy and inefficient method of the two. Though it is probable that the use of money as a means of exchange might well be narrowed in a socialist community in the case of standard necessaries, the extent of the narrowing would be a matter depending on the possibilities of cheapened production and plenty, not a matter that was the *sine qua non* of a classless community.

The question of money in general was, of course, always dominated by the particular monetary problems of the moment. As in all belligerent countries, the Government could not meet its expenditure at this time without resort to inflation. The view that the Communist aim was ultimately to destroy money promised, therefore, a halo for harsh necessity, and not unnaturally met a cordial reception among those whose consciences might otherwise have been uneasy. Moreover, a further balm to troubled conscience was the consideration that inflation was a means of expropriating those who held their wealth in money form; and the view came to be quite seriously accepted in the Finance Commissariat that progressive depreciation and eventual demonetisation was a process to be encouraged rather than restrained. It seems fairly clear that at this time Lenin had not formulated any defined views on the monetary problem; and in the only important pronouncement that he made on the question he was predominantly concerned with the immediate future of the existing paper issue; declaring, after an allusion to the

[1] e.g. to-day, supply of milk to infants, feeding of school children, etc.

desirability in the future of replacing money by a universal cheque system working through a central State clearing-house[1]—a future which he was careful to indicate lay a long way ahead—that the limitation of the currency of existing paper money to a certain date, by which all old issues must be exchanged for new " Soviet tokens," would be a convenient way of forcing hoarders to reveal the size of their hoardings, and so of facilitating a capital levy.

" War communism," accordingly, sprang into life in the " forcing-house " of a mortal struggle of the new régime—a struggle in which all things were subordinated to military necessity, and the problems of industry were simply regarded as predominantly the problem of military supplies. Those who held a rigidly formal conception of communism tended to see in certain features of " war communism " the realisation of their formal ideal; and in their eyes the system was not a hasty improvisation, but a creation of permanent value. The running of industry as a single unwieldy department of military supplies and the loss of a unit of accounting and measurement in a system of social barter and payment in kind were for them achievements to be prized and retained. Those who had their face so close to immediate issues as to have little chance to visualise the future marched with those whose thoughts were more frequently in the clouds; and when they required words to defend what they were doing, the former often spoke with the voice of the latter. These latter, when the ending of civil war brought the abandonment of " war communism," regarded the new course which circumstances demanded, not as a logical return to take up again the line of advance that had been broken so sharply in June 1918, and from which " war communism " was a deviation forced by pressure of military events, but as an abandonment of forms essential to communism and as a

[1] The disadvantage of any universal cheque system to replace money is, of course, that when cheques are used for small amounts the administrative costs of the system become prohibitive, this cost being a " function " not of the total value of cheque clearings, but of the *number* of cheques cleared.

regrettable defeat. It was natural that starting from this premise they should regard each subsequent adaptation of economic forms to objective circumstance as an abandonment of "the gains of the revolution," as steps towards the resumption of capitalist forms, and that they should grow increasingly fearful of "degeneration" of the State apparatus and increasingly sceptical of the possibility of building Socialism in Russia alone. Even those who took the class basis, rather than the forms of society, as their criterion of social development required a little distance to lend perspective to their view, had need of the "breathing space" which had been abruptly denied them by the events of June 1918 to raise their eyes to the horizon and to take their bearings.

CHAPTER THREE

THE PROCESS OF ECONOMIC DECLINE

THE economic development of pre-war Russia was always marked by certain traits which were not found in Western Europe. From one aspect her economic system seemed more akin to the undeveloped countries of Asia than to her industrial neighbours on the West. From another aspect her industrial development surprised one by its very maturity, and her manufacturing centres had a spiritual unity with the Ruhr valley, with Manchester or the Clyde. While less than 15 per cent of the population lived in towns, and less than 10 per cent were engaged in industry, the urban industry which existed was mostly equipped and organised on quite modern lines. While domestic industry still employed some 4 million persons (or nearly double the number employed in factories) and covered about 30 per cent of the total production,[1] and while, moreover, it continued to flourish and to grow, the number of workers employed in factories with more than 1000 hands was almost as great as in U.S.A., there being over 450 of such enterprises, covering 47 per cent of all factory workers.[2]

The somewhat unique character of this development appears largely to be explained by the very late survival of

[1] Cf. Rosenfeld, *Promishlennaia Politika S.S.S.R.*, 39 *seq.*, 140. To take a 1920 figure as a rough guide to the position before the war: of some 248,000 productive units of all kinds (including domestic workshops), only some 23,000 used mechanical power, with an estimated total horse-power of 2·4 million or ⅛ of that in U.S.A.; the average horse-power per worker in the 20,000 largest enterprises was ·92 prewar; while of the factories using mechanical power, the average number of workers per enterprise in 1913 was 98. (Piatakov, *op cit.*, 348–9; Raffalovitch, *Russia: its Trade and Commerce*, 107 *seq.*).

[2] A. Rashin in *Economicheskaia Obozrenie*, July 1926, 91; *Statistical Abstract of U.S. 1916*, 177. The number of workers in factories with over 1000 employees was respectively just over a million and 1·2 million. The number of such enterprises in U.S.A. was 648. In U.S.A. only 17·8 per cent of all wage earners were in such establishments.

feudalism in Russia. Strange though it may seem, this very fact was a reason for the appearance of a factory system as early as in any European country; and 18th- and 19th-century Russia affords us plentiful instances of those feudal industrial establishments, worked by serfs, which we meet with in mediæval Europe. Already at the very beginning of the 18th century Peter the Great, with his policy of industrial development and "Westernisation," was making grants both of the right to establish factories, and also of the services of State serfs, to numerous proprietors who were willing to undertake factory production (in a few cases to merchants, but more often to feudal nobility; in some instances to foreigners); and the second half of the century witnessed frequent strikes of these bonded workmen, particularly in the Ural iron works, culminating in the rebellion of the famous Pugachev, behind whose banner the peasants and workmen exultantly rallied.[1] Legislation between 1750 and 1770, limiting the purchase of serfs by purchase of land, had the effect of throwing "the ownership of the factories into the hands of those who possessed bondage right, i.e. into the hands of the nobility. This process went on at an accelerating rate in the last half of the 18th century, the social result being the practical elimination of the bourgeoisie from Russian society."[2] But, in spite of this, there existed by 1780 at least 75,000 of these "possessional peasants" who had been assigned to work in factories and workshops, in addition to the "*votchinal* peasants" who were set to work in factories owned by their own lord; while at the beginning of the 19th century there was already a factory, at Yaroslavl, employing 2½ thousand hands, and in 1825 as many as 210,000 workers were employed in industrial enterprises.[3]

As soon as the commutation of feudal services by the

[1] Cf. J. Mavor, *Econ. History of Russia*, Vol. I, 434 *seq.*; Max Gordon, *Ochork Economicheskoi Borbi Rabochikh v Rosii*, 30 *seq.*; Gessen, *Istoria Gornorabochikh S.S.S.R.*, Vol. I, 14–18.

[2] Mavor, *op. cit.*, 490. Foreign capitalists, however, were exempted from these limitations.

[3] *Ibid.*, 493; Gordon, *op. cit.*, 22–3, 37. In 1816 the Tula Treasury iron works employed 3½ thousand.

peasants for an *obrok* money payment became fairly general, an impetus was given to the growth of non-feudal factories, established by merchants of capital, and employing wage-labour; for the *obrok* payment left the peasant free to move into the towns and hire himself for wages. Then for the first time could the bourgeois *entrepreneur* compete on equal terms with the feudal proprietor who had plentiful supplies of serf labour. Indeed, the former came to have the advantage in competition, since the freely-hired labour proved everywhere more efficient than the bondmen; while a severe decline of agricultural prices in the twenties drove peasants off the land and filled the towns with cheap labour.[1] But it is here that we meet another of those paradoxes of Russian development: precisely this change caused a decline in the factory system to set in, since it now actually became cheaper for the capitalist, at any rate in textiles, to assume the rôle of *Verleger*, or " merchant manufacturer," and to give out work to be done on the domestic system. With the passing of bonded labour the factory, as an establishment where work was organised under the whip of an overseer, lost its *raison d'être*, until this was restored to it with the introduction of power-machinery after 1846. The result was a large development of the *kustar* peasant industry, particularly in textiles, in the first half of the 19th century, as a severe competitor of the older " possessional factories."[2] The initial effect of the Emancipation of the Serfs in 1861 was to cause a set-back to industry, particularly to the iron industry which had continued to rely very largely on serf labour.[3] But with the opening up of the Donetz area in the course of the next decade, and the introduction of the power-loom, the industrial revolution may be said to have definitely begun. The period between 1886 and 1890 showed the same speculative stock exchange activity as characterised England in the

1 Mavor, *op. cit.*, 528. About this time free-hired labourers formed about half of those employed in factories.

2 *Ibid.*, 546–7, 553.

3 *Ibid.*, Vol. 2, 369; M. Pokrovski, *Russkaia Istoria s. drevnyeyshikh Vremen*, Vol. 4, 111.

'thirties and 'forties; and 1870 saw in Petrograd the first modern strike.[1]

The economic development of Russia along modern capitalist lines came, therefore, somewhat late; and not until the 'nineties did Count Witte's vigorous transport development do for the economic unification of Russia on a more attenuated scale what Bismarck had done for the unification of Germany. Even so, many of the pre-conditions which in Western Europe favoured the rapid growth of capitalist industry were imperfectly matured. A certain class of considerable merchants existed in the towns; but they had little political influence, and hardly represented in 1900 as important a class as existed in the German towns in 1830. A significant class-differentiation was appearing in the villages. A class of peasant capitalists was in its beginnings, and was graduating from village usurers and middlemen, through organising *kustar* industry and small workshops, to be fully-fledged proprietors, like Morossov, of up-to-date factories in the towns, often buying up the "Cherry Orchard" of impoverished nobility on the way. At the bottom of the scale a landless class was forming, providing the cheap labour for the *kustar* industry, and eventually drifting into the towns as seasonal workers or as more or less regular factory hands. But both these tendencies were beginning rather than matured. Russia's *intelligentsia* was not a class steeped in a commercial *milieu*, with one eye close fastened on the problems of a cash register as were the scribes and prophets of English Manchester liberalism. Born of the poorer nobility and the peasantry, it had its roots in the village rather than the counting-house, and often had few surviving social roots at all, and its social creed as a result was woven of abstractions much in the manner of the German liberalism of 1848. Though the existence of large factories laid the basis for a developed proletariat which was highly class-

[1] Gordon, *op. cit.*, 59, 74–5. The number of factories with more than 100 workers rose from 644 in 1866 to 951 in 1890, and the number of workers employed in them from 231,000 to 464,000 (Balabanov, *Ochorki po Istorii Rabochevo Klassa v Rossii*, Vol. 3, 10).

conscious and had its strikes, both economic and political, and its unions so far as these were allowed, a large section of the workers was seldom separated by more than a few years from the village, returned there on the first favourable opportunity, and remained half-peasant in character and affections. The number of hewers in the Donetz mines or of workers in the textile mills, for instance, always declined considerably in the harvest months and revived again in late autumn.

As a result, considerable reliance had to be placed on foreign capital and on foreign technical personnel. One writer even goes so far as to say that industrialism " had been more or less grafted onto the natural structure of the country " by foreign capital.[1] By 1890 the industrial revolution had definitely begun, but was still only proceeding slowly. After that date there commenced the flow of foreign capital which was accompanied by the rapid industrial development between 1895 and 1914.[2] This foreign capital played a very considerable rôle. It has been estimated that of the capital invested by 1914 in the Donetz coal area 46 per cent was from abroad; in iron-mining 85 per cent, and metallurgy 90 per cent; while of the capital entering the oil industry in the four years before the war some 87 per cent was foreign and only 13 per cent Russian-owned.[3] In the two decades before the war Russia was able to finance a continually increasing volume of imports by borrowing from abroad each year to an average amount of 210 million roubles. The total foreign capital invested in Russian industry before the war has been estimated at 2200 million gold roubles, of which 32 per cent was French and 22 per cent British; and

[1] Margaret Miller, *op. cit.*, 223.

[2] Prof. Mavor attributes the rapid industrialisation of this period to the influx of foreign capital, to the growth of the railway system, and also to circumstances which accelerated the flow of peasants into the towns. Foreign capital had also been influential in the 'forties, e.g. Knoop of Manchester (*op. cit.*, 376 *seq.*).

[3] Miller, *op. cit.*, 255, 259, 266; cf. also *Ind. and Labour Information* (Russ. Supplement), 1.9.22, where the figure of 70 per cent is given for Donetz coal, over 70 per cent for oil, and 100 per cent for iron in Kertch district.

to this figure has to be added a further 5400 million of foreign capital invested in State and in municipal and guaranteed loans, making a grand total of some 7600 million roubles.[1] A considerable proportion of the cotton mills were staffed with English managers and foremen; and English and German technicians were equally common in the engineering works of the south. Russia, accordingly, on the eve of the world war was a country half-industrialised, living on foreign capital and managerial personnel, lacking the discipline of modern industrial methods, a part of her proletariat skilled and politically developed while few in numbers, and the rest of her workers half-peasant in character and of low efficiency: a country rich in materials, poor in equipment, technique and personnel. A high birth-rate was only prevented from producing a rapid natural increase of population by a death-rate that was the highest in Europe[2]; and Russia's national income per head was less than a quarter that of Britain.[3]

Such a country had, clearly, a very much smaller chance of surviving the economic strain of a modern war than had the economically tougher nations of the West; while anything that affected the inflow of foreign capital or the activities of the foreign managerial personnel was calculated

[1] L. Pasvolsky and H. G. Moulton, *Russian Debts and Russian Reconstruction*, 175–84. *The Economist* (Nov. 18, 1922) gave a lower figure for industrial investment, namely, 559 million roubles invested in foreign companies with undertakings in Russia, plus 784 million invested in Russian companies. On the other hand, the Memorandum presented to the Genoa Conference placed the foreign holdings in State, municipal, and guaranteed loans at a higher figure than that given in the text, namely, 6000 million.

[2] The death-rate in European Russia before the war was 27·3 per thousand and the birth rate 43·8; while in the area excluding the western border districts (not included in R.S.F.S.R.) and including Siberia the death-rate was 28·3. In 1923 the death-rate in the latter area was 21 per thousand. In 51 gubernias of R.S.F.S.R. it was 23·1, and in the Ukraine 17·1, the birth-rate being 42·6 and 35·4 respectively. The infant mortality rate was 25·6 and 19·4 per cent at the two dates respectively (cf. *Abrégé des Données Statistiques de l'U.R.S.S.*, 19–21).

[3] The Russian annual national income per head in 1913 was approximately 101 roubles (cf. Prokopovitch, *op. cit.*, 127 *seq.*). This at the current rate of exchange was equivalent to just over £10. An approximately comparable figure for the United Kingdom in 1911 is £45 ± 2 (Bowley and Stamp, *The National Income, 1924*, 49).

to remove an important prop of her industrial system. Before war had become the costly science which the 20th century holds as one of its prides, the economic effects of war were considerably less exhausting. Material devastation and loss of man-power were considerable; but warfare to-day is easily a match for the past even in these. As part of the cost of a modern war, however, such material destruction is a relatively minor item—the devastated areas of France and Belgium, for instance, were salvaged sooner than the German mark or the franc. The real burden of a war consists in the need to divert economic resources into the " unproductive " channels of military expenditure. Labour - power and machinery, formerly employed on making food and clothing, in building houses or railways or new factories to expand the productive powers of the future, have to be mobilised behind the firing-line for the making of munitions of war and army equipment, of tanks and bombing-planes and cruisers and submarines. Where the burden of this is not very considerable, the transfer of labour and materials can be achieved merely at the expense of superfluous luxury consumption indulged in during normal times mainly by the well-to-do, or by dint of improved organisation which facilitates more complete or more economical use of existing resources. How much of this surplus it will be possible to draw upon will be, of course, a complex question of public finance, depending on such factors as the available methods of taxation, the willingness of the well-to-do class to subscribe their money and the possibility of their resisting or evading levies when these have reached a large amount. Nevertheless, the existence of such a surplus over necessary consumption will create a *potential* fund of real resources for war purposes; and this fund will diminish in *greater proportion* than any fall in the national income per head, for the reason that a falling national income may very soon reach the point where such a surplus over necessary consumption has dwindled to zero. It will follow, therefore, that a country whose national income per head is only one-fourth that of a second country will almost certainly possess considerably *less* than one-fourth of the potential fund of real resources for war purposes possessed by the second country; while any factor which reduces the national income will progressively increase the difficulty of finding the means to support the conduct of the war.

Where exactly one is to draw the line of the minimum of necessary consumption, and how far it differs in different countries, is a hard question to decide. But two considerations are particularly relevant to the problem in Russia. First, this minimum limit of necessary consumption is not so much a single and definitive danger signal as a series of warning signals. There will be no one point, as the worker's ration is reduced, where he will drop from his lathe and cease to be productive; but below a certain point his efficiency will decline, and will decline progressively faster as the content of his ration falls. Second, there may be, in addition to such a physiological limit, what may be called an *incentive limit*—a limit below which, through lack of incentive and discontent, the producer will cease to exert himself so keenly, and in the extreme case will " ca' canny," down tools or lead a revolt. Such a limit, again, will not be a single line, but a series of them; and the upper edge of the series will probably be found in most countries not very far below the accustomed standard of life of wage-earners, varying from a high point in countries or in grades of labour accustomed to high wages and plenty to a level in poor countries or poorer grades considerably below the limit for full physiological efficiency. Moreover, it will be a limit that is variable and elastic according to circumstances, being relatively low where loyalty to the ruling class is strong and Government propaganda efficient, and relatively high where the working class is highly class-conscious and where profiteering and misgovernment give a sharper edge to discontent. It was here especially that the Achilles' heel of Tsarist Russia was found.

So far we have spoken only of the possibility of transferring resources to war purposes from the production of non-essential consumable goods. There remains also the possibility of transferring them from the production of capital goods which would have gone to replace or expand the capital equipment of the country. An individual who possesses a house and furniture and a few trinkets can in a crisis sell them to a neighbour and buy food, where the un-hoarding savage would have starved. A modern nation can sell its capital stock to foreigners—shares in its industries, its railways, liens on the taxpayer in form of Government bonds; and, most important of all, it can use the labour and resources which usually go to repair and add to railways, roads, buildings and plant for the production of the food or war material that it needs or of immediately exportable goods which can be used to procure those requisites from abroad. Similarly, the standard of life of the producers may be reduced: a form of reduced consumption which, though it may not react immediately on producing-power, may be undermining the efficiency of producers and that of their children for the future, or may persuade them, since their incomes are lower, to economise on education and technical training, thereby having an effect on productivity not in the present but in the years to come.[1] Moreover, capital equipment is of small use unless it is appropriately organised and is " in the right place." Railway wagons two mile deep in a siding, or locomotives kicking their heels in Vladivostok, corn sacks bulging in a warehouse without any means of transporting them thence, are all as useless and " unproductive " for the immediate present as a traction engine in a ditch or a lorry with a broken axle. Capital equipment which is producing to satisfy less intense wants when more intense wants are still unsatisfied is no less failing in the performance of its social function than plant which is old and deteriorated. In the one case a repair of material, in the other a repair of organisation is necessary—that is the only difference. In other words, there is a certain adjustment and

[1] This statement is equivalent to saying that the taxable capacity of a country is different for the short period from that for the long period.

balance of the various parts and agents in the economic system that in the existing state of wants produces the maximum results—a certain allocation of things and persons in their best proportions between places and uses; and this proper balance and adjustment it is the object of good organisation to achieve.[1] If it is not achieved, then the system is not working at its maximum efficiency: some persons and some things are producing less utilities where they are than they would do if they were in the place and use in which they ought to be. One of the ways of getting quick results in a crisis is to get those results at the expense of proper adjustment and balance in the economic system; and this, as much as letting plant and buildings fall into disrepair, is to supply the present at the expense of lowered producing-power in the future.

This power of a modern community to meet the requirements of a crisis by " living on its capital," while it affords a staying power and a respite, is at the same time an insidious means of hiding from men's eyes the real facts of the case and of piling up burdens for the future in profligate fashion —an abuse which is made more easy because the real nature of what is being done remains generally unperceived. The process is particularly dangerous because it is a cumulative one which will gather momentum and continue in motion on its own until some new force is applied to arrest and reverse it. If, of course, the financing of the war is done merely at the cost of new accumulations—of an extension of capital equipment—no retrograde step will necessarily have been made. The community will merely have " marked time " from the economic standpoint and sacrificed the economic progress that it would otherwise have enjoyed. Nevertheless, it is not always the case that there is no retrograde tendency even when no actual disaccumulation has taken

[1] Cf. *Capitalist Enterprise*, p. 26 *seq*. Prof. Pigou has enunciated the principle that this *optimum* arrangement is where resources are so distributed between various uses that their marginal net yield is everywhere equal.

place; for a community only really " marks time " when the expansion of material equipment—for instance, its housing facilities, its factories, its agricultural implements—proceeds proportionately with the increase in population. If that expansion lag behind the increase of population, then the national income per head will fall, *ceteris paribus*, and the tendency to decline will have set in. For the cumulative character of this tendency consists simply in this: that a smaller producing power and a smaller national income per head leaves a smaller surplus over necessary consumption available to provide for war purposes or to repair or add to existing capital equipment; and, with a shrunken available surplus, further inroads have to be made on existing capital resources, leading to a further decline of producing power and the beginning of the same causal cycle over again. Once the surplus resources that it is practicable to turn to war purposes are exhausted, therefore, either the necessary consumption of the masses has to be reduced, which brings a speedy reckoning, or future producing power in the form of capital equipment or organisation has to be mortgaged, which brings a reckoning a little later on. But whether the reckoning be faced to-day or left till to-morrow, it cannot under the crushing load of modern warfare be postponed for very long.

By the end of the third winter of the war the economic disorganisation in Russia had reached its breaking-point. Relatively poor to start with, Russia's difficulties were enhanced by the poorness of administrative personnel and organising ability, by stupidity and even corruption in high places, by the partial cessation of imports of manufactured goods and machinery from the West. Her transport facilities were inadequate to supply the needs of an army on a wide front and at the same time to bring increased quantities of food supplies from beyond the Urals across to the West. The rise in military demands from the pre-war figure of 1 per cent to a demand for 18 per cent of the total railway facilities represented a serious strain on the transport system. 16 per cent of the railway locomotives were out of action at the end of 1916, a figure which rose to 36 per cent in the course of the next year; while at the same time skilled workers were mobilised for the army, and a considerable number of railway shops were closed to their usual function and adapted to the manufacture of munitions.[1] " As early as 1916 the railway system was in a grievous condition. Car-loads of fresh roses came from the Riviera for the Petrograd aristocracy, but in the Viatka Government of North Russia there was no means of transporting the wheat."[2] Mr. Baerlein adds a story of the desperate attempt of the railway administration to effect the transport of wheat from Siberia by sending a special official in a special train across the Urals, armed with 130,000 roubles for bribes to ease the passage of the wheat trains.[3] Financial disorganisation was also taking its toll. While sums amounting to 7000 or 8000 million roubles had been borrowed from abroad, and while gold reserves had been shipped to France and England to the amount of some 460 million roubles in payment for war equipment, the deficit on the State Budget in 1916 amounted to 76 per cent of the whole expenditure, and inflation had swollen the currency issue by nearly four times to 9 milliard roubles at the end of 1916.[4] In industry the stoppage of the import of dyes and chemicals was especially felt, and also of imported cotton supplies on which she relied for half of her requirements in normal times. A general shortage of lathes, machines and fittings was beginning to develop—a shortage " that could not be made good because Russia was wholly unprepared to turn out such articles herself."[5] The winter of 1916–17 witnessed an acute food crisis in the towns, in part owing to the transport breakdown. M. Paléologue, the French Ambassador, notes in his diary for March 6th:

[1] Shatunovski in *Yejegodnik Cominterna*, 360 *seq.*, 368

[2] Baerlein, *op. cit.*, 45. [3] *Ibid.*, 46.

[4] Katzenellenbaum, *Russian Currency and Banking, 1914–24*, pp. 56 *seq.*; E. Epstein, *Les Banques de Commerce Russes*, 56 *seq.* Prices meanwhile had risen rather more slowly, having increased less than three times in the same period, mainly on account of peasant hoarding of money. [5] Leites, *op. cit.*, 27, 33.

" At the present moment 57,000 railway wagons cannot be moved." " Extreme cold has put more than 1200 engines out of action owing to boiler tubes bursting, and there is a shortage of spare tubes as a result of strikes." " Petrograd," he wrote, " is short of bread and wood. . . . At the bakery on the Liteiny this morning I was struck by the sinister expression on the faces of the poor folk who were lined up in a queue, most of whom had spent the whole night there." A few days later the patience of these " poor folk " had become exhausted : bakeries were being looted in the Viborg quarter and Vassili Ostrov.[1]

The critical events of 1917, however, came and followed one another in bewildering rapidity of succession, not so much because the economic system had come to the end of its tether as because it had come up against what we have termed the " incentive limit " ; and the existing relation of class forces, influencing the nature of war finance and war administration and the temper of the poorer classes, was probably as important a reason for this breaking-point being reached so soon, as was the greater weakness of Russia's economic system as compared with the countries of the West and the more developed process of her economic decline. Russia, with her semi-feudal remnants coexisting alongside 20th-century enterprise, was built on a dangerous instability of class forces, which her ruling class were less expert in controlling than its wiser Western neighbours ; and it did not require very much of war privation to set the edifice rocking, to provoke open class revolts against the *status quo* in town and country.

It is often said that Russia possessed one considerable advantage over other countries, at any rate over Britain, which acted as an element of stability. This advantage is said to have consisted in her self-sufficiency in primary foodstuffs owing to her predominantly agricultural character. But this element of stability can easily be exaggerated, and probably has very much less importance than many writers think.

[1] *An Ambassador's Memoirs*, Vol III, 213–15.

Her character as an agricultural country meant, of course, that the 80 per cent odd of her population that lived on the land was unlikely actually to starve—although 1921 showed this even fail to hold true. But for the towns there was as much a problem of importing food from the countryside as there was for England the problem of importing food from abroad, and the stability of her State and her existing social system was dependent upon the position of the towns. England's shipping problem was for Russia a railway problem, with distances nearly as great and more expensive, but without the equivalent of a submarine blockade. The towns could compel the villages to send them corn where Britain could hardly exercise the same compulsion on Canada or U.S.A.[1] But that was almost the whole extent of the difference. Russia was probably more hit by the partial cessation of imports of manufactured goods from the West than Britain by the submarine blockade. A country which has to look abroad for its foodstuffs, but has its industry sound, is usually in a stronger position than one that, while self-sufficient in foodstuffs, cannot get materials and spare parts to keep its industry and transport at work. From the standpoint of the towns the existence of her vast agricultural area placed Russia in a more favourable position than other countries only to the extent that the peasants were " squeezable," in the sense that they were willing to be taxed or to accept a lowered income, in the form of paper money, with a low purchasing power in terms of manufactured goods.[2]

[1] The facilities which Britain had to import from these countries on credit would be roughly analogous to the Russian Government's ability to purchase corn from the peasants by inflated paper issues. Both had their limit.

[2] This possibility depends on the peasants' desire for manufactured goods in terms of effort having *an Elasticity equal to, or less than 1.* Now, the Elasticity of Demand for real income (manufactures and foodstuffs combined) on the part of the wage-earner in terms of effort is probably not very large, although greater than 1. Near the subsistence level it may actually have an Elasticity less than 1 until the limit of increased effort has been reached ; and it is sometimes suggested that this Elasticity may be less just below the level of the accustomed standard of life than it is immediately above. The Elasticity of Demand of the peasant, however, for real income procurable through marketing

But events were to show that the " squeezing " process could not be pressed very far before the " incentive limit " was reached, and the peasant avoided the process by hoarding his corn and contracting his sown area to what was necessary for his own needs. Whether this " incentive limit " was reached sooner or later than that of the town worker, it was

his produce is likely to be rather greater than that of the wage-earner on the whole (at any rate at the lower ranges of income), since the peasant has *primary* necessities more or less assured, and only requires to market his produce to secure *secondary* necessities. This suggests that, *ceteris paribus*, the peasant is *less* " squeezable " than the town proletarian. This suggestion is modified, however, in so far as the peasant is possessed of a *money-hoarding instinct*. If he merely hoards any incidental surplus he may have after satisfying his most important needs for industrial goods, then his demand for command over real resources will not be rendered any less elastic. But if he has a fairly fixed amount in mind which he desires to hoard, this will make his demand *less elastic*, since the amount desired will be the constant thing to which he will adapt his actions. Which of these is most characteristic of peasant hoarding it is difficult to determine ; but it seems probable that on balance the peasants' demand for income in terms of effort will have an elasticity greater than 1 : how much greater it is not possible to say.

In the early stages of Inflation this fact of hoarding may have considerable importance in making it possible for the towns to obtain the results of peasant effort more cheaply by means of paper issues, without reducing appreciably the willingness of the peasant to put forth further effort. But as soon as monetary depreciation has gone a certain distance, the peasantry, realising that they are hoarding a depreciating asset, are likely to abandon the desire to hoard, and even to dishoard. This will probably cause their demand for income in terms of effort to become *more elastic* than before, and will set an immediate limit to the power of the towns to obtain peasant produce on easy terms without reducing the amount of effort which the peasants are willing to exert (and so reducing the quantity of produce coming onto the market). M. Kusovkov considers that this limit of " squeezability " was reached in the autumn of 1916 (*Sozialisticheskoe Khosiaistvo*, 1925, No. 3, 49). This view is supported by the fact that up to the end of 1916 prices rose more slowly than currency was inflated, while after 1916 the converse began to take place. M. Epstein states that at the beginning of the war the rise of prices of industrial goods had the effect of causing the peasants to increase their hoarding (not to reduce their effort and their sales of produce on the market) ; and he estimates this hoarding to have amounted in 1917 to 8·5 milliard roubles, or over half of the total currency circulation (*Les Banques de Commerce Russes*, 57–8). He further suggests that the time when they would be likely to dishoard would be when industrial goods again became cheaper. Actually, however, it would seem that dishoarding started long before this fortunate turn of the tide : it occurred as soon as there was serious fear of *further* depreciation. Anticipation of permanent recovery of the currency would probably cause hoarding of money to increase again rather than to diminish.

of the same nature; and the existence of a peasantry did not make the essentials of Russia's economic problem different, or considerably easier than the problem of more industrialised countries of the West.

The economic decline was hardly arrested by the events of March 1917, as the middle-class politicians who supported the overthrow of Tsardom had doubtless hoped. Fighting on the front continued, rising to the summer offensive, which ended in a disastrous and disorganising defeat. The workers and peasants, far from being appeased by the overthrow of Tsardom, seemed merely to be inspired by it to press forward revolutionary demands for which formerly they had not dared to hope, and, above all, to swell the clamour for "Peace"; and so to the effects of the war on the Western front were added the disorganising results of the growing class struggle. Between March and November the currency in circulation nearly doubled, while prices rose as much as 224 per cent—a significant change in the relation between currency increase and prices, which suggested that the peasant was no longer hoarding money, but rather dishoarding, and that the limit of "squeezability" in this direction was being reached.[1] This rapid rise in prices, at a considerably greater rate than the previous year, greatly increased the militancy of the town workers.[2] Factory committees pressed forward demands and sought a share in control, and employers complained of loss of discipline and decline of labour productivity. Desertion from the army, particularly of peasants to the village to aid their families with the harvest, which had

[1] Prof. L. N. Yurovsky, *Currency Problems and Policy of the Soviet Union*, 17–19.

[2] Food prices up to August 1917 did not rise as rapidly as prices of manufactured goods. Bread, which was carefully regulated, was little more than 3 times the 1914 figure, milk and butter and eggs about 5 times, and meat 7 times. Textile goods, clothing, boots, fuel, etc., had risen on the average about 10–11 times. Wages had increased by August 1917 on the average just over 5 times. One estimate makes real wages at the end of 1917 two points above pre-war; but during most of 1917 the rise of money wages probably lagged behind prices, thereby making real wages lower than this (cf. John Reed, *op. cit.*, 283–5; I.L.O. *Industrial Life in Soviet R.*, 169).

begun in 1916, increased to surprising proportions; and these returned soldiers, constituting a nucleus of active, discontented younger men in the countryside, were a powerful factor in swelling a rural agitation against the landed gentry for the distribution of the land of the great estates. Already in May we hear of aristocratic ladies in Moscow afraid to return to their estates because of the changed temper of the peasantry;[1] and in September this temper flamed into open peasant revolt in many districts, forcible seizure of estates, and sometimes violent treatment of the landowner.

One of the first acts of the Provisional Government was to declare a State monopoly of the corn trade, in an attempt to tackle the food problem and to prevent the rising price of corn. With the elimination of competition on the purchase side of the grain market it was hoped to prevent inflation from having its effect in raising agricultural prices. But this worsening of the rate of interchange between town and village from the peasants' point of view was now showing itself in a growing peasant refusal to offer his grain on the market: instead of hoarding depreciating paper money he now preferred to hoard grain; and against this more fundamental tendency the new policy had little chance of success. The food problem of the towns, accordingly, continued to be the crucial symptom of Russia's economic decline. Illegal speculation in foodstuffs, in evasion of the grain monopoly, grew apace; and the special "bagman" trade—illicit smuggling of foodstuffs in sacks from the villages for sale in the town—together with the crowd of returning soldiers, increased not inconsiderably the volume of travelling and added to the transport difficulties. No abatement, but rather a worsening of the transport chaos took place. By October 1917 the number of locomotives awaiting repair had increased to 5500, or nearly 30 per cent of the whole—an increase of some 2200 as compared with the previous autumn; while the average daily car-loadings stood at 16,000 as compared with 25,000 in 1915, showing a cumulative fall throughout the

[1] Paléologue, *op. cit.*, 339.

year. " This was the beginning of the complete breakdown of the railway system, which the Bolsheviks, in spite of extreme efforts, could not check or even retard."[1]

Together with an aggravation of the food crisis, and thereby of labour discontent, the transport disorganisation produced an acute fuel crisis, and this reacted in turn on the position of industry, and thereby once again affected transport itself in a vicious circle. Coal production in the Donetz was some 220 million poods less than the previous year. Blast-furnaces began to be drawn. In the Moscow district pig-iron output in 1917 fell even below 20 per cent of the previous year. Flour mills commenced to close in the course of October, and cotton mills, affected among other things by the shortage of raw cotton supplies from Turkestan, began in some districts to cease work entirely.[2] General Denikin states that the production of munitions fell some 60 per cent, and of aircraft as much as 80 per cent, while " only 16 per cent of the actual needs of the army were satisfied." Industry, he says, was " steadily falling into ruin."[3] Professor Prokopovitch estimates that industrial production on the average in 1916–17 was only 71 per cent of pre-war;[4] and by the autumn of 1917 it had probably reached a considerably lower level. Already in May M. Paléologue was writing: "Anarchy is spreading all over Russia " ; adding that the army was incapable of " any intense and continuous action . . . owing to the anarchy in its rear." " How on earth," he wrote in his diary on May 17th, " is he (Kerensky) to cope with the administrative disorganisation, the agrarian movement, the financial crisis, the economic *débâcle*, the universal spread of strikes and the progress of separatism? . . . I tell you, even a Peter the Great would not suffice."[5]

Civilisations built on a class system—a system where control is mainly vested in the hands of a privileged class—are

[1] Leites, *op. cit.*, 52. Cf. also Shatunovski, *op. cit.*, 360–1.
[2] Leites, *op. cit.*, 39–40.
[3] *The Russian Turmoil*, 117–19.
[4] *Op. cit.*, 20.
[5] *Op. cit.*, 334–5. Cf. also Nordman, *Peace Problems*, 98 *seq.*

likely to be unstable to this extent, that if a severe strain is placed upon the system, the discontent of the subject class against what it deems injustice and tyranny may break into open revolt. Russia was the weakest link in the chain of the pre-1914 European civilisation; and on it the unprecedented strain of the war had its first catastrophic effect. Russian workers and peasants rose and took into their own hands power which had formerly rested with bankers and industrialists and merchants and landowners. It was natural that they should do this at a time when the old system was weakest and the seizure of power could most easily be made; but in doing so they acted in defiance of the many Socialist theorists in Russia and outside who declared that it would be folly for Socialists to take over anything but a perfect machine at the peak of its efficiency—a counsel of perfection, indeed, which might well have banished the Socialist *Der Tag* to the millennium. It was the natural result of their audacity that the Bolsheviks should receive as a legacy an economic system which had already travelled a good distance along the road of economic decline and disorganisation.

Even given peace and a favourable combination of circumstance, it is doubtful whether the economic decline could have been arrested without a considerable organising effort, and then only after an interval of time. For the decline had entered on the cumulative course of " living on capital," which depreciates future producing power and so forces resort to further inroads on capital resources to make up the deficit; and disorganisation had reached the stage where it bred fresh disorder in reckless fashion.[1] Some bold positive action to stem disorganisation, to check the headlong process of capital depreciation and lowered producing power would have been necessary. To break the vicious circle

[1] It is this fact which renders the problem less simple than Prof. Prokopovitch assumes it to be when he allots responsibility for the decline by comparing the fall of production up to October 1917 with the fall subsequent to that date, and attributes responsibility for the latter entirely to the Bolsheviks (*op. cit.*, 19 *seq.*). The fact that a process of decline, once set in, is *cumulative* makes any such simple arithmetic computation completely misleading.

veritably needed, as M. Paléologue said, a greater than Peter the Great. Actually, the changes brought by October 1917 introduced certain new factors in the situation which might have favoured such a recovery, had not other counter-influences intervened. The distribution of the land among the peasants might have been expected to assuage their discontent and increase their willingness to supply food to the towns. Town workers—as subsequent events tended to show—might have been expected to tighten their belts and bend their backs rather more readily when the control was vested in themselves and the feeling that their labour was being exploited to swell the incomes of another class was removed. There was now a greater likelihood of a vigorous policy to co-ordinate and restore the creaking economic machine being enforced from the centre. Possibilities were opened of bringing fresh resources to the aid of the State exchequer and so filling the budget deficit by heavy progressive taxation and levies on the well-to-do, which had formerly been considered impracticable.[1] And it was to give these factors time to come into play that Lenin was so desirous of achieving a " breathing space."

As it happened, however, October 1917 brought in its train a number of other tendencies which actually hastened the process of economic decline. First, was the difficulty of personnel, shown in the hostility of the technical and managerial staffs to the new régime and their unwillingness or actual refusal to work with it, extending even to *sabotage* in some cases. Second, was the chaos and disorganisation resulting from the system of workers' control and the friction and inefficiency arising from the degree of committee-

[1] This influence showed itself quite clearly. In the first year of the Bolshevik revolution the Government trebled its taxation revenue (in paper roubles) while its expenditure increased by little more than 70 per cent, thereby reducing the Budget deficit to 66·6 per cent of total expenditure as compared with 81·7 per cent in 1917 and 74 per cent in 1915. As a result, until the renewal of the civil war in June 1918 the Government had less need of resort to paper issues than its predecessor and the pace of inflation appreciably slackened (cf. Katzenellenbaum, *op. cit.*, 69).

management that it involved. Third, the speed with which industry passed into the hands of the State, for reasons which have been discussed in Chapter Two, caused the demands on the new administrative apparatus to increase considerably faster than the apparatus itself could be erected and shaped to its required functions; and this resulted in a very serious amount of administrative chaos. Fourth, the various anarchic influences loosed by the revolution were some time in being bridled and curbed to central control, and in the meanwhile tended to have a centripetal and disorganising effect. Fifth, the Peace with Germany was only bought at the price of considerable loss of territory and of the occupation of the Ukraine and the valuable Donetz coal and industrial area by German troops. Sixth (and most fundamental), war on the Western front only ended to give place to a new civil war, which was in many ways more destructive than the previous war had been, since it involved fighting on several fronts —North, North-west, East and South-east—at the same time, and the occupation by invading armies of some of the most important agricultural and industrial areas of Russia. Moreover, the effect of these various influences in combination was greater than the sum of their separate effects, since the results of one tended to have a reaction in accentuating the other influences.

Most of the Bolshevik leaders seem to have been fully alive to the probability that the seizure of power in October would bring no immediate arrest of the economic decline, but might even aggravate it. Bukharin, at any rate, had no illusions on the matter. "Anarchy in production," he wrote, "or, as Prof. Grinevetsky defines it, 'the revolutionary disintegration of industry,' is an historically inevitable stage which no amount of lamentation will prevent. . . . The 'losses caused by revolution' (the decline of labour productivity, and the direct expenditure of social energy in the process of the civil war) is the price which human society must pay for the possibility of further development. The Communist revolution, like every other revolution, is accompanied by a diminution of productive forces."[1] Such measures as committee control in factories and decentralisation to encourage local initiative he declared to be necessary tactics in the class struggle, designed " to entrench the workers as the dominant class in all departments of economic life "; but at the same time he pointed out that " in a technical sense " such measures were " far from perfect," and would have to be stringently revised at a later stage of the revolution when " the basis of proletarian control had been more firmly established."[2] The main difference between Lenin and those, like Bukharin, who stood more to " the Left " at this time was that Lenin saw the extreme dangers, particularly to the relations between town and village and so to the food supply, of allowing the decline of industry to proceed any further. Accordingly he was willing to pay much to secure a " breathing space "; whereas they were more reckless, less alert to pressing economic facts, and less apprehensive of imminent economic collapse. But when the two-month " breathing space " afforded by Brest-Litovsk came to an end, and civil war blazed forth on every front, and complete blockade of Soviet Russia from all contact with the outside world was enforced for two years, it is not surprising that the cumulative process of decline proceeded at an accelerated speed. Once again there was need to divert resources to supply special military needs and to sacrifice the normal requirements of the economic system to the voracious demands of war. Russia continued to " live on her capital " and on her organisation—a capital and organisation that was already well depreciated; and the extreme centralisation of control which the circumstances demanded placed upon the immature administrative apparatus a burden which was far beyond its capacity to bear,

[1] *Economica Perihodnovo Perioda*, Chap. 3. He grouped the " real economic cost " of revolution under the following heads : (1) Physical destruction of the means of production ; (2) Human deterioration ; (3) Collapse of ties and relations between different branches of production ; (4) Redistribution of productive resources in the direction of " unproductive consumption " for the needs of the civil war (*Ibid.*, Chap. 7).

[2] *Ibid.*, Chap. 8.

and led in all but a few departments of work to administrative chaos.

The shortage of the goods for which Russia had formerly relied on imports from abroad was now rendered more acute than before. Such things as electric lamps, tubing for boilers, belting, etc., had formerly been imported almost entirely from abroad; and now factories had often to close for lack of them.[1] The occupation of the Donetz region, which in 1913 contained 71 per cent of Russian coal production, produced an acute fuel crisis and necessitated an almost entire transition to wood fuel for the railways; while oil supplies from Grozny and Baku were also cut off. By 1919 the total amount of fuel available for consumption (other than domestic) was little over a half that of 1917 and only 40 per cent of 1916.[2] Moreover, the Donetz in 1913 accounted for 75 per cent of the iron ore and 60 per cent of the pig-iron output of Russia. The Urals, where fighting was taking place in 1918–19, accounted for another 19 per cent of the pig-iron; while of the remaining 21 per cent Poland was responsible for nearly a half.[3] In the central area, which still remained in the Soviet sphere, the number of blast furnaces in operation fell from 13 in 1918 to 9 in 1919 and to 5 at the beginning of 1920; the number of rolling-mills from 14 in 1918 to 7 in 1920; and the production of cast-iron from 3·7 million poods in 1918 to 1·3 million in 1919 and to ·3 million in 1920.[4] The result was an all but complete stoppage of metal supplies for the engineering and munitions industry. The fuel shortage and difficulty of repairs added grievously to the disorganisation of transport, as did the added strain on the railway system from the military needs of several fronts, together with the direct destruction and disorganisation involved in the continual ebb and flow

[1] A. Heller, *The Industrial Revival in Russia*, 138.

[2] Larin and Kritsmann, *Ochork Khosiaistvennoi Jizni i Organisatzia Narodnovo Khosiaistva Sov. Russ.*, 28–9. The pre-war consumption of various fuels was in the following proportions: coal 65 per cent, oil 20 per cent, wood 13½ per cent, peat 1½ per cent.

[3] Cf. Miller, *op. cit.*, 288 *seq.*

[4] Leites, *op. cit.*, 142.

of the fighting front; and even before the effects of the civil war had been felt, Prof. Lomonossov, the Government's chief railway expert, reported that an early complete collapse of the railway system was inevitable. In many ways the civil war was a " railway war," since it took place along the main lines, and the railway was the only available means of moving troops, munitions and supplies any distance; and in 1919 50 per cent of the locomotives in action were being used for military purposes.[1] The proportion of disabled locomotives awaiting repair, which had stood at about 30 per cent at the time of the October revolution, steadily mounted to 47 per cent in December 1918, to 55 per cent in December 1919, and to 69 per cent in 1920; while the number of locomotives in the hands of the Government and in running order, which stood at about 14,500 at the end of 1917, quickly declined to under 5000 by the end of the following year and to 3900 in January 1920. Similarly, the proportion of wagons awaiting repair had in 1920 reached over 20 per cent.[2] The full extent of the disorganisation of economic life involved in the advance of the invading armies can be imagined from the fact that in 1918–19 about 60 per cent of the railway mileage of Russia was in the hands of the White armies, and consequently out of the control of the Soviet Government, and in 1920 80 per cent of the railroad was within the sphere of military operations. The direct destruction suffered by the transport system is estimated by the Soviet Government to have amounted to 3600 railway bridges, 1700 versts of permanent way, 380 engine depots and railway shops, in addition to the destruction of 3600 ordinary bridges and 86,500 versts of telegraph and telephone lines[3]

With the fresh strain on Budget expenditure there was little chance of the Government ceasing inflation and arresting the depreciation of the currency. On the contrary, in

[1] Larin and Kritsmann, *op. cit.*, 35.

[2] Pasvolsky, *op. cit.*, 362; Shatunovski, *op. cit.*, 366.

[3] Shatunovski, *op. cit.*, 362; League of Nations, *Report on Econ. Conditions in R.*, 14–15; Rudzutak in *Manch. Guard. Commercial*, Russian Supplement, June 26, 1924, p. 919.

spite of the possibility of new (though limited) sources of revenue by levies on the bourgeoisie, increased resort had to be placed on raising funds by printing paper currency. In the first eight months of the revolution—that is, up to the commencement of civil war and intervention in June 1918—the rate of increase of paper money was slower than it had been in the period of the Provisional Government. The currency circulation, which stood at 22·4 milliard roubles on November 1st, 1917, did not pass the 30 milliard figure until March 1918. On June 1st it stood at 40·3 and on January 1st, 1919, at 60·8 milliard; and the increase of currency in the course of 1918 amounted to 119 per cent as compared with 180 per cent in 1917. But after 1918 inflation proceeded at a disastrously accelerated pace, multiplying three times in the course of 1919 and over four times in 1920.[1]

Inflation enables a Government to procure command over resources by using new paper issues in purchase of what it requires; and to the extent that it does this it leaves less resources available to meet the needs of the rest of the community. Inflation, therefore, acts as a forced levy or tax on the community, forcing other people to "go without," in order that the Government may have a larger share of the available resources of the country. This "going without" is enforced by the rise of prices which inflation produces; and the persons who suffer thereby, and on whom in consequence the incidence of the forced levy or tax rests, are those whose income is in money and is relatively fixed and those who hold reserves of wealth in money form. These persons find their income or their reserves depreciating in purchasing power as inflation proceeds. Under ordinary circumstances wage- and salary-earners are principal sufferers, in so far as revisions of wage-rates lag behind price movements. But under the new conditions in Russia every attempt was made to prevent the industrial worker from losing severely; and it was largely to preclude this that the policy was adopted of giving an increasing part of the worker's

[1] Katzenellenbaum, *op. cit.*, 56–9; Yurovsky, *op. cit.*, 25–6.

wage in kind.[1] The two principal sections, accordingly, on whom the burden of inflation fell were the remaining members of the moneyed class and the peasantry. The former lost in so far as they held wealth in money form; and inflation acted in their case as a means of expropriation of this wealth, as indeed was one of its avowed objects. The peasantry were likewise damaged in so far as, selling their produce for money, they hoarded the money or at any rate held it for an interval of time between their sale and their subsequent purchase with the money of fresh goods. But in their case this was not all. An additional factor which contributed to the burden on the peasant was the grain monopoly, established under the Provisional Government. This was designed to keep the price of grain from rising, and in so far as it succeeded in this, it threw most of the effects of inflation onto the price of manufactured goods. Accordingly, the price which the peasant had to pay for the goods he bought mounted more steeply than the income which he could obtain in return for the produce he sold. In other words, the rate of interchange between products of the town and of the village turned against the village, both at any one point of time owing to the divergence of prices of manufactures and grain, as well as over a period of time owing to the depreciating value of the money for which the peasant sold his produce.

Evasion by an individual of the levy imposed by inflation is possible so far as he reduces the balances which he holds in money form and reduces the interval of time between his receipt of income and his spending of it. This act of his by reducing his holding of money and increasing either his holding or his consumption of goods raises prices still further and so passes on the burden to someone else. In this way

[1] Actually this did not entirely prevent the town worker from suffering. As soon as the peasant began to evade his share of the burden the town worker began to be severely hit by the severe shortage of food in the towns. An I.L.O. estimate makes the average monthly real wage in 1918 only 40 per cent of pre-war, of which ½ was in kind; in 1919, 30·8 per cent, of which over ¾ was in kind; and for 1920–1 between 31–32 per cent of pre-war, 86–93 per cent being in kind (*Industrial Life in S. R.*, 169).

particular individuals may evade their share of the burden of an inflation that has already occurred, but only by means of increasing the burden on others. The burden, once imposed, cannot be evaded by the community as a whole; for the Government has printed paper money and bought things with it, and hence at the moment there must be less of those things left available for the community at large.[1] This applies to an inflationary issue that has already taken place; but with regard to future inflationary issues the community has in a sense a power of evading the burden by making it more difficult for the Government to raise funds by inflation in the future. In so far as the community as a whole increases its total hoarding of goods—holding reserves of goods instead of reserves of money—or in other ways withdraws commodities from the market, it will be reducing the supply of goods coming into the market at any one time, and so will render it more difficult for the Government to repeat its inflationary levy. Since this withdrawal of goods from the market will have decreased the stream of goods coming into the market at any one time as compared with the stream of money-demand, it will have aggravated the rise in prices. This rise of prices will make it progressively more difficult for the Government to acquire real resources by means of inflation, because, in order to buy the same *quantity* of real things, the Government will have to increase the currency issue, not merely by a greater *amount* than before, but in greater *proportion* than before to the total currency circulation. This process will show itself in a decreasing *real value* or purchasing power of the aggregate currency circulation, and a decreasing *real value* yielded to the Exchequer by inflationary issues. The limit to such a process is where no goods are brought on to the market for

[1] The Government, of course, may use the money to buy materials or employ labour which would not otherwise have been employed. This case would require a verbal modification of the argument of the text, which for sake of brevity and simplicity is left in its present form. The modification would not alter the essential fact that to enable the Government to take this action an initial decline of consumption by existing holders of money must take place.

sale against money (but are bartered or hoarded instead), and where consequently the purchasing power of money and the ability of the Government to raise real resources by inflation is reduced to zero. But long before this point has been reached the Government will be faced with the impossibility of raising further sufficient sums by inflation for the requirements of its expenditure.[1]

This was the form of evasion of inflationary levies which took place in Russia, particularly on the part of the peasants. Already in 1916, as we have seen, the peasant was beginning to dishoard money and to throw it on to the market in purchase of industrial goods, thereby causing prices to rise for the first time faster than the increase of paper currency. By the end of 1917 he was beginning to hold reserves in the form of goods instead of money, hoarding grain or industrial

[1] The most satisfactory equation, in its simplest form, is $P=\frac{KR}{N}$, where P = the purchasing power of money (the inverse of the price-level), N = the number of units of money in circulation, R = the total resources in the form of goods, and K = either the *proportion* of those total resources which people choose to keep in money form, or a quantity of "consumption units" (e.g. bushels of wheat) the command over which people choose to keep in money form. Change in the amount of the reserves which people choose to keep in money form will show itself in a change in K. This takes the place of the pre-war use of the somewhat clumsier conception of "velocity of circulation" of money (cf. Keynes, *Monetary Reform*, p. 74 *seq.*; Hawtrey, *Currency and Credit*, 30 *seq.*). If, however, one is treating of a given period of time, one can have $P=\frac{R'}{N'}$, where R′ = the flow of goods on to the market within that period, and N′ = the flow of money-demand in the form of money-purchases (i.e. the "consumers' outlay" in Mr. Hawtrey's terminology). Hoarding of money or of goods will then show itself simply in changes in R′ and N′. In treating of the problem of the incidence of inflation the latter formulation is useful. The aggregate real value of the currency will = R′. But N′ will not necessarily equal the total quantity of currency in circulation, unless the "circulation period" of money (cf. D. H. Robertson, *Banking Policy and the Price Level*, 47) coincide with the period under consideration. If the Government desires by means of inflation to secure command over X quantity of resources, it will have to increase the currency in circulation by more than $\frac{X}{R'}N'$. A change in the hoarding of goods and of money which decreases R′ and increases N′ will make it more difficult for the Government to raise X resources by inflation, until the limit is reached where R′ has shrunk so as to be greater by no more than a small amount than X.

goods if he could get them. By 1918 he was holding back grain in store rather than sell it for paper money, and was beginning to diminish the extent and intensiveness of his sowing. By 1920 the area sown in Siberia was halved, and in parts of the Volga region and the Caucasus it was reduced to a quarter.[1] The result was a catastrophic fall in the aggregate real value of the currency in circulation to less than 10 per cent of its previous value, and a sharp shrinkage of the real values which the Government could raise by inflation, until it could be said that this last remaining source of revenue was virtually exhausted.[2]

This serious fall in peasant sales of grain, combined with transport dislocation and the occupation of some of the most fertile grain regions by the invading armies, faced the towns with famine—literal famine as depicted in Semen Semenov's *Hunger*[3] of the hideous winter of 1919 when the machine-guns of Yudenich could be heard on the Nevsky and men fell dead of exhaustion in the street. Moreover, not merely food was affected, but also important raw materials, which reacted directly on industry, joining with fuel shortage to close down factories and so to aggravate the economic situation in another vicious circle. The cotton crop, affected in addition by the breaking of communication with the cotton areas of Turkestan and Trans-Caucasia, fell in 1918 to 10 per cent and in 1919 to 6 per cent of the 1913 yield; flax, which had already by 1916 fallen to 60 per cent of the 1913 crop, declined further to 42 per cent in 1918 and 18 per cent in

[1] Khalatov in *Yejegodnik Cominterna*, 391.

[2] Prof. Yurovsky (*op. cit.*, 27–8) gives the following figures :—

	Real Value of all the circulating media.	Real Value (in index roubles) of the Revenue extracted by note issues.	
Nov. 1, 1917 ..	2200·6 m. roubles	Nov.-Dec. 1917	163·1 m. roubles
July 1, 1918 ..	488·5 m. ,,	1918	93·3 m. ,,
July 1, 1919 ..	152·9 m. ,,	1919	37·4 m. ,,
July 1, 1920 ..	62·9 m. ,,	1920	20·3 m. ,,
July 1, 1921 ..	29·1 m. ,,		

[3] Published in English in the collection entitled *Flying Osip*.

1919; and sugar-beet by 1920 showed an area reduced to 30 per cent and a crop that had dwindled to 7·8 per cent of 1913.[1]

Shortage of fuel, of materials and of food combined to produce a disastrous fall in industrial productivity. The transport and industrial difficulties, which were almost too great in the existing circumstances for the greatest efforts to surmount, caused congestion and dislocation in the administrative apparatus which reacted on the economic situation and made it worse. Starvation or semi-starvation grievously lowered the intensity of work and the efficiency of the individual worker, increased absenteeism and encouraged petty theft and peculation as means of supplementing starvation rations. Prof. Prokopovitch estimates that by 1920 the number of workers employed in industry was less than one-half that of pre-war, while the average productivity per worker had fallen to 30–35 per cent, and the total output of industry to the amazing figure of 14·5 per cent.[2] Absenteeism in industry ranged sometimes as high as 60 per cent and was quite commonly above 30 per cent;[3] and the workers' monthly wage in Moscow in 1920 was only sufficient to keep him alive for eleven to thirteen days, imposing the necessity for him to supplement it by some other means whether fair or foul.[4]

It was this situation of extremity—the fact that the " incentive limit " of inflationary levies on the peasantry had been reached, and the almost complete " drying up " of all

[1] *Soviet Union Year Book*, 1926, 76 *seq.*; I.L.O., *Co-operative Movt. in S. R.*, 90–1. About the only industrial plant to suffer little reduction in cultivated area seems to have been hemp. Its yield showed a considerably greater fall, but not as great a fall as other crops. The reason for this was mainly that hemp was cultivated less for market than for the peasants' own purposes, and also that its chief centres were in central provinces, namely, Vladimir, Kostroma and Yaroslav, least affected by the civil war.

[2] *Op. cit.*, 24. Popov in *Econ. Jizn*, 31.3.23, gives 15 per cent as the average figure, ranging from 6 per cent in the metal industry (in pig-iron only 2–3 per cent) and in cotton, to 32 per cent in hemp and 35 per cent in linen and wool.

[3] Leites, *op. cit.*, 152, 199.

[4] Khalatov, *op. cit.*, 460.

monetary sources of Government revenue—that was responsible for the system known as " war communism " rather than any desire to apply an *a priori* theory. The holding back of grain from the market on the part of the peasantry led directly—one might almost say inevitably—to the policy of State grain requisitioning, which may be regarded as an attempt to surmount the " incentive limit " by methods of compulsion.[1] Similarly, the exhaustion of all the normal sources of war finance, whether by taxation, loans or inflation, forced resort to the extreme measure of compulsory labour; and the actual process of demonetisation of the currency, which was one of the symptoms of economic collapse, *ipso facto* produced resort to a system of *Naturalwirtschaft*, with payment of wages in kind and State-organised barter.[2] As such, " war communism " indeed had definitely a certain measure of success. Starvation in the towns in the winter of 1919 and 1920 would almost certainly have been greater, had not corn supplies been compulsorily requisitioned from the village, and the army would probably have collapsed.[3] According to the figures of the Commissariat of Supplies,

[1] This system of grain requisitioning was not peculiar to Russia as often seems to be imagined. It was adopted in Austria during and after the war, for instance, with the result that " production was reduced to the point when it barely nourished the farmer's household . . . hay rotted on the fields before it was taken away, cattle stood for days on the railway without food or water, perishing miserably under the eyes of their late owners," and the peasants came to regard " the Government as a band of instruments of oppression " (C. A. Macartney, *The Social Revolution in Austria*, 189).

[2] Cf. The interesting argument developed by Kusovkov in *Soz. Khosiaistvo*, 1925, No. 3, 33 *seq*. Lenin said on April 21, 1919: " War Communism was compelled by the war and the collapse. It was not, and could not be, a policy corresponding to the economic tasks of the proletariat. It was a temporary measure "—quoted by Bronsky (*Soz. Khosiaistvo*, April–May 1923, p. 7), who adds: " Basic facts would confirm entirely the idea that the period of war communism was not a period of conscious socialist construction." Smushkov (*op. cit.*, 16) says that war communism was " conditioned by the pressure on us, first of German Imperialism, and afterwards of our internecine counter-revolution . . . it was not a normal economic policy."

[3] This statement is not inconsistent with the fact that large quantities of foodstuffs actually did appear on the illegal market. But they appeared at prices often 3 or 4 times as high as the regulated prices; and it seems probable that at lower prices, within reach of urban purchasing-power, very little grain would voluntarily have been forthcoming.

grain collections increased, as the collecting apparatus was strengthened, from 107 million poods in 1918–19 to 212 million in the following year and 283 million in 1920–1;[1] and this was reflected in a slight rise in the workers' food ration in 1920 and 1921.[2] At the same time, the relief afforded to the situation by such extraordinary measures could be no more than short-lived. Economic decline had reached such a point that the only resources which extraordinary measures could tap were of a strictly limited and short-period character—existing stocks of grain and fuel and raw material, a certain reserve of human energy which propaganda and military organisation might utilise. When these stocks were exhausted, nothing remained. Attempts to exploit the last ounces of human energy quickly recoiled in the form of physical exhaustion. Compulsion on the peasants produced a further drastic curtailment of the sown area and "the annihilation of economic-individualist initiative to improve the conditions of agriculture."[3] Fixed capital soon reached a stage of depreciation where further depreciation would cause it to fall completely into disuse. By the end of 1920 "war communism," as an extraordinary set of measures to meet an extraordinary situation of economic decline, had come to the end of its tether.

[1] Khalatov, *op. cit.*, 389; Larin and Kritsmann, *op. cit.*, 18.
[2] I.L.O., *loc. cit.*
[3] Khalatov, *op. cit.*, 389–90.

CHAPTER FOUR

THE PERIOD OF "WAR COMMUNISM"

THE Supreme Economic Council (Vesenha) had been set up in December 1917, composed of representatives of the Government departments and trade unions together with technical experts in an advisory capacity, with the aim of bringing some co-ordinating element into the activities of the organs of workers' control and of systematising the process of nationalisation. It was to be the highest economic organisation in the land—a kind of economic general staff—and its functions were visualised as being wider than a mere department of industry, extending to a general supervision of the economic activities of other State departments, of transport, agriculture and foreign trade. Attached to it was a special advisory council of scientists and economists, a commission for foreign trade, and a department of public works; while sub-sections were formed corresponding to the main industries of the country, and local economic councils composed of representatives of local bodies, which should act as local organs of the central council. For some time it remained little more than a co-ordinating body—a general staff, issuing general instructions, but having few direct links with the units in the field. It drew up the general plans for nationalisation and issued general decrees which laid down the guiding lines of economic policy; and it was the body whose sanction was nominally necessary for any act of nationalisation. But its industrial sub-sections were not made directly the administrative boards of the nationalised industries except in cases of special importance.

In the first few months there was little or no co-ordination even of the enterprises within one industry. Nominally, enterprises were supposed to carry on as before; and no single industry was entirely nationalised until May 1918.

Actually, factories were frequently seized on the initiative of the workers or hastily nationalised by the decree of a local soviet, and many of these were administered for some time by their factory committees as virtually independent concerns.[1] The first problem, accordingly, was to introduce some co-ordination among the various enterprises inside each industry. There were three principal ways by which this might have been done. An *ad hoc* government organ for each industry might have been set up and imposed on the industry from above; a representative body might have been constituted within each industry, having a democratic and autonomous character; or by a mixture of both forms an administrative council for each industry might have been organised which was in part representative of the industry itself and in part constituted of members appointed by the State, like an English Trade Board or the war-time Cotton Control Board in Lancashire. In the case of the "heavy industry," which was of such vital importance for war purposes, the first system was adopted. A special Metal Department of Vesenha was organised, absorbing the personnel of the pre-existing Fuel and Metal Council, and this later developed into *Glavmetal*, which concentrated all orders in its own hands and distributed them among the various enterprises. Similarly, in the summer of 1918 *Glavugol* was set up as a controlling body for the coal industry, having "exclusive rights for investigation of new coal resources, control over the private coal industry and its compulsory trustification, for the closing down of technically imperfect enterprises (on confirmation by Vesenha), for the organisation of new enterprises, the working out of a program of nationalisation, the distribution of coal and regulation of the coal trade."[2] But for the light finishing industries the third system was adopted in most cases. Representative boards were formed, to which appointed members were added from various State departments, and these within the limits defined

[1] See above, p. 44 *seq.*
[2] Benediktov, *Tyajolaia Industria S.S.S.R.*, 74–5.

by Vesenha were autonomous. These bodies were called Central Industrial Administrations (*Centres*); and, in contact with the appropriate sub-sections of Vesenha, they exercised at first functions of general co-ordination within the industry, and then gradually extended their functions and strengthened their control over the various enterprises within their sphere. As their functions and their sub-committees multiplied, they tended to create under their control special bodies called *Glavki* to concentrate on the strictly administrative work of controlling the productive enterprises.

One of the first of these Centres to be formed was the *Centro-textile* ; and here the problem of co-ordination was in some respects particularly difficult because the industry still remained predominantly in private hands. The first step in its creation was the summoning of a Congress of the Textile Industry in February 1918, and this set up a Central Administrative Council for the industry to consist of 30 representatives of the textile workers, 15 of the owners, *plus* 20 representatives of various State organs. This in turn appointed a Presidium of 9 workers' representatives, together with a representative each from Vesenha and the Central Council of Trade Unions, together with technical experts. The actual proportions of the representation varied in different cases; but for industries which had been nationalised, where the problem of representation was simpler than in the case of textiles, a Vesenha decree of March 3rd directed that the Centres should be composed, a third of representatives of the workers in the industry, a third of appointed members from Vesenha, the Central Executive Committee of the Soviets, from the Central Council of Trade Unions and the co-operatives, and a third of representatives of the technical and managerial staff of the industry and of technical and scientific organisations (Clause 17).[1]

From the outset these Centres were given fairly wide powers. In the case of an industry that was not yet national-

[1] Labry, *op. cit.*, 62 *seq.*, 142.

ised, it had power to give instructions to owners of businesses, to distribute stocks of materials, to fix prices, to effect the amalgamation of enterprises, and finally to nationalise any firm it thought fit (Clause 22). This presented an interesting half-way house to nationalisation: the State, while not as yet taking over the administration of industry, nevertheless hedged industry about by means of certain powers of general regulation and control, as a bank may do with an industry to which it is creditor, or as the British Ministry of Munitions did with private munition firms during the war. The body, however, through which these powers were exercised was not a Government department, but a predominantly representative body after the manner of an English Trade Board or Agricultural Wages Board. Moreover, these boards had this significant feature: though State nominees were in a minority, yet together with the representatives of the trade unions, who would tend on fundamental questions to act in unison with the State, they formed a firm majority; and so the desired "encirclement" of capitalism was in this way secured.

In the case of a nationalised industry the Centre exercised control by concentrating in its hands the arrangements for the financing of enterprises, and by the appointment of the factory managers or managing collegiates, whose authority was supreme in technical questions, but who were subject on other matters to a factory collegiate composed of representatives of the workers and clerks in the factory (which were not to exceed a third of the whole number), of the technical staff, and also of the local soviet, local trade unions and the local department of Vesenha. The Centre was also granted the monopoly, if it sought to exercise it, of import and export, and the right to concentrate in its hands the supply to the industry of materials, tools, fuel, etc., and the marketing of finished products. Very soon, therefore, the Centre tended to expand its functions and to become the centralised commercial organ in each industry, financing the enterprises with their requisite supplies and taking from them their finished output and assuming responsibility for marketing—like some giant " merchant manufacturer " or *Verleger* of two centuries ago, giving out work and organising the division of labour among numerous dependent producers. Some of the Centres and Glavki, particularly those formed towards the summer of 1918, had wide powers from the outset. They had what in England would be called limited statutory powers. *Centrochai*, for instance, had power to make " regulations touching tea (and associated goods) obligatory for both private enterprises and persons, and also for social and governmental organisations." The Glavki, likewise, were " plenary organs of government," having powers within their own sphere similar to those exercised by Vesenha in the wider sphere.[1] *Centroresin* had power " to increase, to restrain or to close enterprises " ; *Centrokraska* " to procure materials, to elaborate a plan of purchase, to control quality, to arrange a plan for the distribution of products." *Glavsakhar* by Vesenha decree of June 23rd was given authority to " publish obligatory decrees and instructions for all enterprises concerned with sugar, to regulate the increase, the reduction or the closing down of works, to create new establishments and organise new plantations," to establish plans of output, transport and delivery, to supervise the finances of businesses, fix the scale of wages in the sugar industry, to centralise indispensable reserves in its hands and to organise the distribution of labour and materials among the various establishments.[2]

To aid them in this work, the Centres not only formed Glavki to specialise on the administration of factories, as Glav-textile was formed from Centro-textile, and *Glavneft* and *Glavugol* for administering oil and coal production, under the general control of *Glavtop*, which was the commercial organisation ; they also formed local branches, usually as special industrial sections of the provincial equivalent of Vesenha (*Gubsovnarhoz*) ; and these acted virtually as agents of the national centre, transmitting and adapting the orders

[1] L. Kritsmann, *Geriocheskoe Period Velikoi Russkoi Revolutsii*, 199.
[2] Labry, *op. cit.*, 83 *seq.* ; also Zagorsky, *op. cit.*, 22 *seq.*

of the latter to the enterprises of that specific industry in the locality. Sometimes, when the industry was highly localised, or produced mainly for a local market, it was subordinated entirely to the local section, and came within the sphere of competence of the provincial economic council, or Gubsovnarhoz. For instance, attached to the local economic council of the Petrograd district was a Metal Section, which had its sub-departments such as a Technical Committee and the Administrative and Financial Departments; and this Section appointed in collaboration with the trade unions a part of the factory collegiates and gradually concentrated in its hands the financing of enterprises and the distribution of orders. A further stage in the specialisation of sub-departments, as the functions of Centres and Glavki became more complex, was the grouping of localised branches of an industry into *kusts* or groups as sub-divisions of an industrial Glavki, these groups usually having an entirely local character. For instance, the Petrograd Metal Section formed under its control separate boards to control the various divisions of the industry—the automobile group comprising 8 large works, the Avio group comprising 8 factories, the heavy industry group to include the famous Putilov works, the copper group covering 4 establishments, and the medium-sized machinery group embracing about 30 factories.

This early period of the new régime, however, was one of plans and constitutions, of general decrees and instructions in profusion, but a period in which the execution of policy was done on local initiative from below, rather than from the centre, and was done more often without instructions than in conformity with instructions from above. In economics, as well as in politics and military affairs, things had their beginnings in a state of guerilla warfare. The formation of central organs of control introduced some co-ordination and let loose a fresh flood of general regulations and decrees to persuade harassed local officials by their importunity. But it required something more than their mere formation, and something more than a shower of decrees to change guerilla warfare into the campaign of an army corps which moves according to a single strategic plan. Consequently, it was to be expected that a stronger tendency to centralisation should soon succeed the early chaotic period, and that this centralisation should take the form both of closer subordination of individual enterprises to the Glavki, and of the Glavki and Centres themselves to Vesenha. With the coming of the civil war in June 1918 the need for such centralisation was very greatly increased. Already such centralisation had been carried out on the railways, where the extreme urgency of the transport situation compelled the ruthless subordination of every other consideration to the requirements of technical efficiency. The influence of local committees which had exerted such an anarchic influence in the early spring had been severely curtailed, and all local railway officials had been subordinated to orders from the centre. The central railway administration itself was organised on semi-military lines, the various departments being in charge of departmental chiefs, not of collegiates, these chiefs usually being specialists carried over from the old régime. The heads of departments were responsible directly to the Commissariat of Ways and Communications; but to supervise their activities from a political standpoint, political commissars were appointed as in the army.[1] Similarly, in industry in general the iron necessities of civil war demanded that considerations of efficiency should take precedence over democratic forms, where these forms in less critical times might have been desired for their own sake, or for reasons of the class struggle, or as a means of drawing in the masses of the workers to participate in economic administration and so educating them and breaking down the barrier between administrators and administered. The first change was the abolition of the somewhat cumbersome representative councils or boards which constituted the Centres for each industry, and the concentration of authority instead in the hands of a smaller Presidium or Committee. This Presidium now tended to

[1] i.e. until 1920, when the practice began to be discontinued.

lose its representative character and to be appointed wholly by Vesenha, although the latter was careful in its appointments to include representatives of the trade unions concerned, and usually acted in consultation with the latter. The Centres, accordingly, virtually became industrial sub-departments of Vesenha as a gigantic state department of industry. In some cases they disappeared altogether, leaving only the Glavki in direct subordination to Vesenha. These sub-departments consisted of a collegium or board of five to seven persons, of which the president was the chief of the department, and to which was subordinated the requisite staff; and they resembled in form a large trust controlled by a Board of Directors—in this case appointed by the State, not by shareholders—with the chairman of the Board acting as the managing director. For instance, this change occurred in the case of Centro-Textile in August 1918. Similarly, the controlling board of Vesenha was narrowed down from the previous unwieldy representative council, composed of up to fifty persons, to a Presidium of ten to twelve persons. This Presidium was nominally elected at an annual economic congress, drawn from the heads of large enterprises, from the Glavki, from the trade unions, and from the local Gubsovnarhoz; but in practice it appears to have been constituted simply of nominees of the central government.

The local Gubsovnarhoz, in turn, consisted of a small Presidium appointed by the local Soviet authority, as in England an economic council for the area of a county might be an *ad hoc* body appointed by the county council (or, more exactly, by a provincial trades council, if the latter had been made more comprehensive and had been constituted as an organ of government). For purposes of administration industrial enterprises were divided into three categories. First were enterprises of national scale and significance. These were placed immediately under the appropriate Glavki. Second were those which operated for a national market, but whose production was localised. Their administration was decentralised to the extent of being placed under special industrial sub-sections of the Gubsovnarhoz; but these sections of the local body did little more than execute the orders of the central Glavki to which they were directly subordinated, doing little at their own discretion and generally acting merely as channels through which matters were referred to the superior central authority. The third category contained enterprises which were purely local in character, usually both drawing their material and finding their market in the district. These were within the competence entirely of the Gubsovnarhoz; and in their case alone was there complete decentralisation.[1]

In a similar way the administration of production itself was simplified by a narrowing of the controlling factory collegiates, usually to three persons, and in cases where the superior economic organ thought fit by the actual replacement of the collegiate form by individual management, the manager being directly appointed either by the Glavki or the Gubsovnarhoz. By the end of 1920 this process had gone so far that some 85 per cent of enterprises were controlled by individual managers.[2] Moreover, the functions of the factory committees, which in the early days had interfered fairly extensively in industrial control, were now severely curtailed. The factory committee, acting as the unit of trade union organisation (instead of the area branch), concerned itself with welfare work and working conditions and with representing to the management the interests of the workers, their

[1] Larin and Kritsmann, *op. cit.*, 117 *seq.*

[2] Kritsmann, *op. cit.*, 201; Piatakov, *op. cit.*, 342. A typical group of 159 factory managers in 1920–1 was composed as follows:—

Former Owners	16
,, Managers	37
Engineers and Technicians	16
Mechanics	4
Clerks, etc.	30
Workers	48
Peasants	8

Of these 13 per cent had had higher education, and 24 per cent secondary education. It is interesting to note that the investigation found those with secondary education more successful administrators than those with higher or with only primary education (*Econ. Jizn.*, 26.11.22).

The boards of the Glavki were composed as follows:—

Workers	36 per cent
Engineers, etc.	34 ,,
Former Directors	4 ,,
Office Employees	22 ,,

Pasvolsky, *op. cit.*, 43.

complaints and suggestions; and it had power of appeal against the management through the trade union to the higher economic organs. But in the work of factory administration the factory committee was not permitted to interfere, and stood to the management merely in an advisory capacity, with certain rights of appeal to higher powers.

Universally, in fact, this centralising tendency was found—a centralisation in administrative form and also in administrative practice. In the early days, for instance, the initiative in controlling or nationalising enterprises and appointing industrial administrators tended to rest with the trade unions or else with the local Soviet authority. The trade union would make nominations and the State authority merely give formal sanction to the appointment of these nominees. The unions tended to have their own clearly defined views, and these at times conflicted with those of the State economic organs. Of course, in so far as the majority of the heads of the unions were Communist, they were bound by Party discipline to carry out the Communist policy where any definite decision on the point had been taken by the Party—a fact of vital importance in understanding the course of events in Russia, and particularly in appreciating the surprising unity of policy which was so frequently achieved even among bodies which were formally independent and non-subordinate. Nevertheless, before any such Party decision had been taken, the leaders of the trade unions freely expressed and worked for their own distinctive point of view; and on matters which were not considered to be points of fundamental policy, and hence were not covered by any general Party decisions, their own distinctive views exercised strong influence on the framing and the execution of policy. After the summer of 1918, however, the influence of the trade unions over industrial administration declined considerably. Formally, appointments were concentrated in the hands of Vesenha and its organs; while in practice the trade unions, though consulted in appointments and policy and often making their own proposals and nominations, more and more came, apparently, merely to anticipate or give formal sanction to the intentions of the State. The leaders of the trade unions, acting in close touch with the State organs, felt it their duty to co-operate in carrying out the State policy. In practice they became almost subsidiary State departments, making State economic policy palatable to their members, rather than seeking to express and make vocal the interests of the rank and file or to exercise an independent influence on industrial administration and policy in this direction. So much did the trade union apparatus become associated with the State as one of its organs, that by the end of the civil war a serious gulf had begun to yawn between officials and rank and file, and the latter to regard the trade unions, not as their own, but as alien bodies imposing orders from above.

A similar centralising tendency developed with regard to the co-operative movement. With the policy of the grain monopoly, instituted under the Provisional Government, the work of corn purchase and collection was concentrated in the Commissariat of Supply (*Narcomprod*); and in order to counteract the peasants' growing disinclination to market their grain, this body attempted to organise at the same time the supply of industrial goods to the villages. With this latter function the Commissariat was unable to cope in anything like its entirety; and in the spring of 1918 an agreement was made with *Centrosoyus*, the central organ of consumers' co-operation, whereby the State should utilise the latter, selling to it industrial goods from the various Centres and Glavki, and also purchasing from it articles of peasant produce. The co-operative movement as an autonomous body, with its own funds and its own democratic government, was made the principal organ of distribution and supply between the town and the village, much as the British Government during the war contracted with the London Wool Brokers' Committee, the Oilseed Brokers' Association and the Meat Supply Associations, or as it might contract with the C.W.S. for the supply of certain commodities to the army and for the disposal of certain products of State factories. Similarly, the

Industrial Co-operatives, which were societies catering for the town workers and affiliated to Centrosoyus, were made the distributive organisation for the town population, contracting with State organs and Centrosoyus for the supply of village and other products.[1]

The growing acuteness of the food shortage and the withholding of grain from the market by the peasants produced in the spring of 1918 the policy of grain requisitioning. A certain quantity of grain, assessed as the available surplus over the peasants' own requirements, had to be delivered to the State collecting organs; and the poor peasants of the village were organised in Committees of the Village Poor to supervise the collections. Where the required deliveries were not forthcoming, they were to be forcibly collected by military and trade union detachments. Agricultural products were divided into three classes, the first consisting of those subject to compulsory requisitioning, second of goods whose purchase was monopolised by the State but which were not requisitioned, and third of non-monopolised goods open to be sold or bartered freely with State supply organs or the co-operatives or with private persons. The tendency, of course, was for the peasants to cut down their production of the first two groups, and to transfer wherever possible to the production of things in the third group; and this fact caused a continual extension of the number of goods included as State monopolies, until by the end of the civil war scarcely anything of importance remained in the third group at all. The collection of goods of the first category was organised partly by the Commissariat of Agriculture and partly by Narcomprod; and in order to supplement these collections with additional supplies, Narcomprod organised a fund of industrial foods which it supplied to the peasantry in return. Here it made use of the co-operatives—the agricultural and handicraft co-operatives for the purchase of non-requisitioned goods, and the consumers' co-operatives for the

[1] Cf. I.L.O., *Co-op Movement in S. R.*, 20 *seq.*; *Russian Economist*, Vol. II, No. 6, 1935 *seq.*; I.L.O., *Lab. Conditions in S. R.*, 269 *seq.*

distribution of industrial products. In August 1918 it was decreed that industrial goods should only be supplied in the villages in return for receipts for grain deliveries. More and more this exchange, monopolised in the hands of Narcomprod, took on the form of barter, payment being made increasingly in kind and decreasingly in money. The industrial Glavki arranged for the disposal of their output to Narcomprod, which then planned their distribution to the town and village population, mainly through the medium of the co-operatives. The Glavki, being credited with the value of their output at the ruling prices, were increasingly paid in kind in the shape either of foodstuffs and raw materials, collected by Narcomprod, which the Glavki in turn apportioned among the enterprises under their command, or by an arrangement whereby workers were paid in tickets of purchase at their local co-operative store, these purchases being debited to the account of the enterprise and the Glavki in question.

In monopolised goods the co-operatives could only trade by special licence from Narcomprod; and so in this sphere they could do little more than carry out part of the plan of the State organs, acting as the agents of the latter. The non-monopolised articles, in which they were free to conduct their own transactions with their own funds at their own risk, entering independently into relations with the peasants on the one hand and the Glavki and Centres on the other, were being continually narrowed; and in consequence the character of the co-operatives as independent trading organs became increasingly subordinate to their character as commission agents for the State. Transactions which they conducted on order from Narcomprod naturally tended to be financed by the State, the financing often taking the form of the supply to them of a manufactured goods fund which they could exchange direct in the villages against peasant produce, their administrative expenses being covered by a percentage commission. This type of operation tended steadily to increase and to supplant transactions in which the co-operatives acted with their own funds on their own initiative.

But it was not merely in business practice that the taking of decisions with regard to exchange transactions became more and more centralised. Centralisation also developed in regard to the government of the co-operative organisations. Since they played so important a rôle in the distributive machinery of the State, it was clearly important at such a critical period that the co-operatives should be directed by persons who would work in harmony with the economic plans of the State. As it happened, the directors of the co-operatives consisted in 1918 of persons who, while desiring the prosperity of their own organisation, were politically hostile to the Soviet Government, and were loath to allow their organisation to be used to help the new Government out of its difficulties, and still more loath to surrender any of its independence. Though they consented to co-operate with the State as an independent body, their co-operation in practice was of no more than a half-hearted kind. It was as though in England during the war the Government had contracted for a large part of the English food supply with an American firm whose officers were Germans of definite pro-German sympathies. At the end of 1918, accordingly, the Communists were attempting to secure increased control over Centrosoyus. In December 1918 at the Congress of the Industrial Co-operatives the Communists for the first time secured a small majority; and the Industrial Co-operatives as an affiliated body proceeded to place certain demands before Centrosoyus for including on the Board of Centrosoyus sufficient representatives of the Industrial Co-operatives to place the supporters of the Government in a majority. Centrosoyus refused to accede to this request *in toto*, while going so far as to concede a minority of seats on the Board to representatives of the affiliated body. This compromise, however, the Industrial Co-operatives refused to accept, and retaliated by withdrawing their affiliation and setting up a rival trading society, the Centrosection. But the situation thereby created was clearly impossible. The new body could not build up a new organisation overnight to equal in efficiency that of its rival, even if it had had the experience and the personnel. The Government was unable to dispense with the assistance of Centrosoyus, and State departments continued to give contracts to it. Between March and May 1919, accordingly, the Government took the step of appointing to the Board of Centrosoyus a certain number of Government nominees, so that these appointed members, along with the representatives of the Industrial Co-operatives, which now renewed their old relationship with the larger body, constituted a majority on the Board. At the same time the Government made membership of the co-operatives compulsory on the whole working population (such membership to be without entrance fee), ordered a regrouping of the retail shops so that they could serve the whole population in their various districts, and constituted the co-operative organisation as the sole distributive agent of the State, to carry out the purchase and distributive plans of Narcomprod.[1]

This centralisation, together with the system of State-organised barter and requisitioning, formed the characteristic feature of " war communism "; and the centralisation had three principal aspects which it is important to distinguish. First, there was the question of appointments, or of government, which is distinct from the second aspect, which one may define as centralisation in the taking of administrative decisions. The former merely concerns the right of appointment, which may again be distinguished according to form and to fact. This—on which the difference between democracy or autocracy is usually considered to turn—is the question of whether the right of appointment of industrial administrators is diffused widely over the members or constituent organisations of the several industries (a system sometimes known as " direct democracy "), or whether it is concentrated in the hands of a central authority.[2] But this

[1] I.L.O., *Co-op. Movt. in S. R.*, 26 *seq.*

[2] A further distinction is usually made between the case where the

question, though important enough in the determination of the broad general lines of policy, probably does not possess the importance usually attached to it. Certainly, it assumes primary importance when there is reason to believe that the interests and actions of the administrators will diverge from the interests or desires of the mass, and so will produce a policy opposed to the latter. But it probably assumes first importance only when such conditions are present, and it would seem that only in such circumstances is the mass likely to show much interest in the question of where the right of appointment lies, as witness the attitude of the mass of the shareholders of a joint stock company in normal times and on occasions when they suspect the directors of prosecuting peculiar interests of their own. In a class society, where the interests of different classes are divergent, this consideration becomes of prime importance, both in political government and industry and in organisations like trade unions, where elevation to administrative office tends to mean elevation into a different class *milieu* from that of the members whom the administrator is intended to represent. Even so, the mere right of appointment does not ensure that the actions of the administrators shall conform to the interests of the mass. For, in the first place, the judgment of the electors will usually be after the fact, and not before the fact; and, second, either the administrator or some third person, because of the inferior information, organisation and vocalness of the mass, may be able to exert an undue influence over opinion, as a trade union leader may be able to dominate the membership of his union and a Press magnate may be able to turn the scale of an election and make and unmake Cabinets. On the other hand, where specific factors causing a divergence of interest between administrators and administered are absent—for instance, where these do not consist of

central body which does the appointing is indirectly responsible to some body elected by the community at large (e.g. State officials indirectly responsible to an elected Congress or Parliament), which is usually called "indirect democracy," and the case where the central appointing body is, either in form or in fact, non-responsible.

two distinct classes—this question of appointment probably plays a much less significant rôle; for it is only important in practice when it affects the kind of policy pursued. Here a divergence of policy is likely to arise because of the lack of touch of the administrators with the sentiments and condition of the mass, or because the former grow into a separate and exclusive clique, rather than because the framers of policy start on their career with a different policy in mind. Here, accordingly, the question of appointment is dwarfed by the third aspect of the problem of centralisation—the question of contact between centre and periphery, between heads and rank and file.

To some extent the question of centralisation or decentralisation of administrative decisions is inseparable from the question of appointment, since it amounts to a matter of competence; and however democratically elected a body may be, the fact will have little effect on the character of policy if the body has little competence assigned to it. Small matter who appoints a certain personnel, if the power of deciding on policy lies elsewhere. At the same time the two things are distinct, in the sense that centralisation of administrative decisions may coexist with a considerable degree of decentralisation of appointment. For instance, Centrosoyus might have continued to be a democratically controlled body without any Government-appointed members on its Board, while in its actual work it did little more than carry out the orders of Narcomprod. On the other hand, the Boards of Glavki, though appointed by Vesenha, were given fairly wide discretionary powers within their own sphere. From the point of view of policy, what is important is the power of making those major decisions on purely general matters on which the general character of policy depends. The policy pursued may differ according as competence on these matters rests with this or that set of persons, and according to the manner of their appointment. Decisions on minor matters, concerned mainly with detailed execution of a policy already defined, affect the character of policy relatively little; and whether competence in these matters is centralised or decentralised is chiefly a technical administrative question, affecting the efficiency with which a given policy, whatever it may be, is fulfilled.

As we have seen, in the early months of the revolution fairly wide powers of discretion were delegated to local and functional bodies, many of which (such as the Co-operatives, the Centres, and the Trade Unions) were democratically appointed. This decentralisation, however, both of decisions and of appointment, produced a certain disunity and lack of conformity of policy, owing to the heterogeneity of interests and ideas which found expression. When civil war imposed the iron necessity of conformity and unity, a new tendency developed under " war communism " for concentration, not only of appointment, but also of administrative competence in the hands of central bodies, leaving little to the discretion of the local and subordinate organs. In industry there was concentration of all decisions concerning volume of production, funds for wages, material, fuel, equipment, sales in the hands of the Glavki, which exercised discretion, subject to the general regulations laid down by Vesenha and to consultation on important points with the industrial sub-sections of Vesenha. Matters concerned with the internal arrangements of the factory lay with the factory management. But the factory management was not competent with regard to the nature and volume of its production; and in all its relations with the outside world—supplies of materials and equipment, disposal of its wares—it had to refer to, or execute orders of, the appropriate Glavki, with which it communicated directly or through the medium of the appropriate industrial sub-section of the Gubsovnarhoz. Similarly, in the distributive sphere the extent to which the co-operatives could buy and sell and enter into contracts with various persons and organisations was gradually narrowed by the growing State monopolisation of trade; and the decision as to what and how much should be bought and sold and with whom the transactions should be made was more and more concentrated in Narcomprod, while the co-operatives merely carried out the plans of Narcomprod as agents, or merely executed its detailed orders as a subsidiary department.

The third aspect of centralisation is concerned, as we have said, with the matter of contact. A system of centralisation, both in appointments and in administrative decisions, may or may not coexist with a separation of the central administrative organs from contact with the local situation and with the mass. Usually centralisation tends to produce such separation, unless special measures are adopted to prevent it. Most bureaucracies in the past, mainly from the class nature of society, have shown a strong separation of this kind, the official class, at any rate in its higher grades, regarding itself as socially superior to the mass of the populace, and as embodying the dignity of a superior power, which, whether selfish or benevolent, stood in an essentially authoritarian relation to the governed. In Tsarist Russia this was the case to a high degree; while of the Austria of Emperor Franz Joseph a recent writer has said that the bureaucracy, filled "in the higher ranks with youths who had been destined from their childhood up for this career," and having a social standing close to the officer class, "enjoyed a position apart" and "were essentially police, the Monarch's line of defence against the people."[1] In a class society such a separation is well-nigh inevitable, since the higher ranks of the State service are drawn from a superior social *milieu*, with different education, tradition, ideology and way of life from the inferior class; while the lower officials aspire to that superior social *milieu* and imitate its manner and ideals. In post-revolutionary Russia, of course, much of this separation was broken down, in so far as former "high society" ceased to exist, and the workers aspired to a new status and importance, and new proletarian elements were drawn into the State apparatus. Nevertheless, though weakened, the separation continued in so far as much of the personnel of the State service remained the same as before; and the general tendencies of "war

[1] C. A. Macartney, *The Social Revolution in Austria*, 7–9.

communism " certainly emphasised the elements of separation and weakened the elements of contact which had developed in the early days of the revolution.

In a classless society, where a principal reason for the divergence of interest between governors and the governed has disappeared, there seems some reason to believe that the matter of contact is of greater importance than the matter of appointment in ensuring that the policy pursued shall conform to the general interest. For here the most probable cause of any such divergence will be a tendency for the administrators to get out of touch with mass conditions and desires. Russia of 1918 was certainly not a classless society —merely one in which the Party of a new class, the workers, had seized power. To this Party, therefore, the question of appointment was not an unimportant but a pre-eminent one; and, accordingly, it was not surprising that, as the revolution developed, and this Party strengthened its position, it should seek to centralise all important appointments in its own hands —a tendency particularly accentuated under the pressure of civil war. But to ensure that this Party and the administrators under its control should not develop any divergent tendencies, either in actual policy, in way of life and ideology, or even in appearance to the eyes of the mass of the workers and peasants, the matter of contact was of equal importance. This implied a judicious blending of centralisation of appointment with close contact of governors and governed. One factor in such contact was the nature of the Party itself as predominantly consisting of industrial workers and having factory groups as its units of organisation. A further factor at the outset was the drawing of trade unions into close collaboration with the administration. There was also the summoning of congresses of workers and officials in industry to discuss administrative policy, and the linking up of local economic organs with the local workers' and peasants' soviets. But a principal result of the over-centralisation of " war communism," under the exigencies of civil war, was a weakening of these contacts and a certain serious separation between the centre and the localities, and between the State on the one hand, and both the town workers and the peasants on the other hand. Party members tended to be drawn away into official and military work and posts of authority. The trade unions, as we have seen, tended to become parts of the State apparatus rather than organs of the rank and file. The competence of local economic organs became seriously curtailed; and the *smytchka* or union between worker and peasant came in imminent danger of complete rupture under the policy of requisitions.

A certain centralisation of appointment, therefore, was a condition of that leading rôle of the Communist Party during the transition period which was the corner-stone of Bolshevik theory; and one might expect that, as the revolution matured and the new ruling Party strengthened its hold on the "key-positions," this centralising tendency would be applied to spheres which earlier had been left outside Party control. Military needs of civil war, steeling resistance to foes within and without, forced this tendency considerably beyond the point where it would otherwise have halted. Concentration of administrative decisions one would likewise expect to have succeeded what Russian writers call the "elemental" processes of the earlier revolutionary period. For it is a common feature of periods of revolutionary change that in the first stages, when the old structure is being demolished, much is done chaotically and on individual initiative, and later, when the work of planned construction of the new begins, a degree of integration and discipline is shown to be imperative. At the beginning of 1918 in Russia State machinery in the economic sphere was still in process of building; and with an official personnel that was largely hostile, this building was neither rapid nor easy. But as this machinery of central administration was erected, it somewhat naturally tended to take over functions which it had formerly been content to leave to other bodies. Civil war strengthened this tendency; for military necessities at all times impose a high degree of centralisation, partly because they are needs which require speedy satisfaction, and partly because the results of a need not being met according to order are so much more serious than at ordinary times. These military needs require precision and uniformity of policy; and where uniformity is the paramount requirement, centralisation tends to be found.

But while the lack of suitable personnel delayed the erection of centralised machinery at the outset, this lack had an opposite effect once that machinery had been set up: it then favoured a concentration of decisions with central bodies. The reason for this lies in the whole character of the administrative problem and in the peculiar conditions of Russia in 1918 under which this problem had to be solved. Administration usually has three alternatives before it.[1] First, the central authority may lay down the general lines of policy and the general ends to be attained, leaving to subordinate bodies fairly wide discretion in applying the general policy to the diverse conditions of specific cases. This affords the maximum of decentralisation, and, provided it can be achieved, is undoubtedly the most perfect way of the three. It allows the maximum of elasticity, since the details of policy can be adapted to the differing circumstances of each separate case; while reserving to the central authority the power to enforce the broad essentials of policy as is required. It involves the speediest decision and the minimum reference of specific questions from one authority to another. It may take the form either of allowing the subordinate body to act whenever any general guiding lines of policy have been already laid down by a higher body, or else of giving the subordinate body power to use its discretion on any question within its sphere, except in so far as regulations from above set bounds to its discretion. In the former the discretion itself, in the latter the limitation of discretion is confined to the "named cases"; and the latter, representing the greater degree of decentralisation of the two, attains the maximum degree of elasticity, promptness, and initiative. As Mr. E. M. H. Lloyd has said: "It is physically impossible for

[1] Cf. Sir J. C. Stamp, *Current Problems in Finance and Govt.*, 65 *seq.*

one brain to give decisions upon more than a limited number of questions in a single working day. . . . Administration of a large concern must therefore be automatic; but automatism is of two kinds, mechanical and organic. . . . The ideal of administration corresponds to the automatism of a violinist or an expert skater. Conscious direction by the central brain is confined to the essential minimum; the detailed operations are carried out by a subconscious adjustment of subordinate organs, and the central brain is only called upon to intervene when a breakdown occurs or a novel and difficult task has to be tackled."[1]

Second, the central authority may centralise all decisions in its own hands, giving to subordinate bodies the minimum of discretion, and compelling them to refer nearly all matters of interpretation to the centre. This has the effect of accumulating at the centre a large amount of work—an accumulation which may amount to congestion—and it incurs the risk of decisions on detail being seriously at fault because the deciding authority is imperfectly informed of the circumstances of the specific case. Indeed, there is a physical limit beyond which such centralisation cannot go, determined by the "limited number of questions" which it is "physically possible for one brain to give decisions upon in a single working day"; and an attempt to organise anything more than a moderately uniform, simple and small-scale unit on such centralised lines is usually destined to collapse.

Third, a compromise solution is possible, under which, while executive competence is granted to subordinate bodies, the central authorities narrowly circumscribe the decisions of these bodies by issuing elaborate regulations which seek to provide for every detail and to prescribe for every contingency. Where the organisational problem is simple and uniform, then the task of prescribing for every contingency is not a very difficult one: routine execution can be covered by routine regulations. But where this is not so, the task of

[1] *Experiments in State Control at the War Office and the Ministry of Food*, 389–90.

covering every eventuality, every permutation and combination of conditions becomes stupendously complicated; and in such conditions this third administrative method makes for the most wooden and inelastic and cumbersome system of the three. If the regulations are detailed, the subordinate official spends half of his time mastering them, and is turned into a petty interpreter of regulations who answers each question brought to him, not on its merits, but by making it fit into some category or other of the regulations. The framer of the regulations, for his part, is just as likely to lack knowledge of the local situation for which he is legislating as an administrator at the centre giving a decision on a specific case. Initiative and originality tend to be killed, and matters to be dealt with purely mechanically.

As a supplement to either of these, a staff of travelling officials may be employed, to whom all doubtful matters are referred and with whom administrative decisions rest in doubtful cases. Combined with a decentralised system, it may be a useful method of securing greater uniformity of policy than would otherwise be possible, and of securing contact between centre and periphery. Combined with a centralised system, however, it seems to have little power to mitigate the disadvantages of the system. Certainly, such travelling officials are more likely to be *au fait* with the local situation than one who remains in an office in the metropolis; and to that extent the decisions given may be wiser and more flexible. But if this staff of officials is a small one, it can hardly review more than a small percentage of the outstanding issues, and delays and holding-up of business become unavoidable in awaiting an official's arrival for his decision; whereas, if the staff is large, it represents a costly duplication of officials, and the problem of controlling subordinates is merely transferred to the task of controlling the travelling officialdom itself: are they to be given wide discretion or bound by voluminous regulations? Moreover, any system which does not give power of decision to the man (or men) "on the spot"—whether that power rest, instead, with a central office or a travelling staff—suffers from the fact that all appeals and references to, or consultations with, other authorities necessitate a formulation of the situation and the precise issues *linguistically*, as Mr. Hawtrey expresses it,[1] and this involves time, trouble and misunderstanding, and is at best a poor substitute for the intuitive judgment of the man "on the spot."

The first, and ideally most desirable, of these alternatives demands a fairly high standard of education, intelligence, and integrity among the subordinate officials on whom competence is conferred. Further, it depends on these officials being sufficiently "of one mind" to make it probable that they will interpret aright the true spirit of the desired policy in their respective spheres, and that in adapting the general policy to the peculiar circumstances of specific cases they will not introduce any lack of uniformity or any inconsistency. It is in providing this unity of spirit that the question of contact assumes such great importance. Indeed, one can say that a high degree of contact between centre and subordinate bodies is what makes administrative decentralisation possible. Departmental consultations and conferences, cross-representation of different interests on controlling boards, and the association of these representatives in day-to-day administrative work[2]—all measures such as these

[1] R. G. Hawtrey, *The Economic Problem*, 339 *seq.*: "The practical judgment is partly sub-conscious, and, in so far as it is conscious, its mental processes are not *linguistic*. To express in language even the decision itself is an effort; to express the grounds on which it is taken would often be a formidable exercise in psychology and literary composition. And when it has been done with the highest skill and sincerity, the result would probably be only a partial and inaccurate account at the best. This is true not merely of the grave decisions upon which far-reaching consequences depend, but of the trifling decisions taken by average men every day. There is a tendency for an official hierarchy to be limited to those decisions that can be readily communicated in language from one functionary to another."

[2] Sir J. A. Salter attaches considerable importance to this point. Speaking of the war-time Allied "program committees" and of the problems of international joint action, he says: "Contact, and indeed regular contact, must be established between the appropriate permanent officials of the several national administrations. It is important that these officials should (where possible) continue to exercise executive authority in their own departments. . . . These officials must work

harmonise conflicting interests, preclude duplication and overlapping, and by contact of the various parts aid in bringing a unity to the whole. In England this unity is partly achieved by a careful selection of the higher civil service officials, so that they are predominantly the products of a few select schools and of the older universities. In Russia the existence of the Party, with its members occupying the leading positions in the various departments of administration, and at the centre and in the localities, has been a similar unifying element.

In Russia in 1918 none of the essential conditions for the success of decentralisation were present. Russia was still a class society, even if the new government claimed to have dealt class monopoly a death-blow, and hence was an eddy of conflicting social tendencies. Class influences hostile to the aim of the ruling Party tended to exert continual pressure on the administration, and even on the personnel of the Party itself, which tended to be flooded with "post-October" recruits; and these influences might have severely "warped" the official policy, unless the centre had imposed a certain stern uniformity and curbed the administrative system under control. Apart from this, the character of the Russian official personnel scarcely favoured decentralisation. Its efficiency in anything but matters of routine never seems to have been high. Never encouraged to use his initiative, the Russian official had not, on the other hand, any of the German's stolid faith in the regulations by which he was bound. The result was, as visitors to Russia are so frequently heard to testify, that he tended to vacillate in irritating fashion between mechanical adherence to regulations when circumstances demanded elasticity, and unreasoned neglect of

together enough to know each other well, to develop mutual trust and confidence. They must in their own national departments represent the international point of view, and in their international organisation they must represent the national point of view." "The method of direct contact over a wide surface, of linking these departments together by the association of their crucial officers, will prove more effective and successful than any form of external influence or control" (*Allied Shipping Control*, 257 and 254).

them when consistency was most required. Moreover, in economics, where the problems are different in kind from those of legal administration and require greater flexibility, the Russian had had very little administrative experience. Much of the conduct of industry before the war was in the hands of foreigners; while the average Russian was scarcely beginning to learn the discipline and precision and peculiar mental integration which modern industrialism requires. Now the foreigners had gone; while those owners and managers that were Russian had either emigrated also, or remained hostile and suspect. The average intellectual was usually worse than unsuited for tackling industrial questions: he might weave "plans" galore, but execute them never! The old-style *chinovnik* was scarcely less useless. The industrial proletarian, schooled to the discipline of the machine and the division of labour, offered considerably more hope. But of them there were as yet very few, even inside the Party, with the level of education and experience necessary for competent administrative posts. Further, the whole soviet structure was new—actually in the making; it had no tradition or precedents, woven of experience. Hence, even if the personnel had been all that was desired, consistency and uniformity of interpretation would have been unlikely without a strong lead from the centre. As it was, all but a small percentage even of the more trusted economic experts were actively hostile to the new régime; and if given discretion would not have used it in the desired spirit; while, anyhow, they were inclined to be suspect among the workers, and, if given latitude for initiative, would probably have found their way blocked by various proletarian organs in the localities. For instance, Kritsmann gives some very interesting results of a confidential enquiry made among 270 engineers and technicians in responsible positions in Moscow as late as 1922; and these figures, even though possibly subject to some margin of error, give us at any rate an approximate picture, and probably the reverse of an exaggerated one. The engineers in question were divided into two groups: those who had held responsible posts in capitalist industry before the war, and those who had been employed merely as ordinary technicians. The principal items in the enquiry were three: were they sympathetic to the Soviet Government; did they consider their work to be of social value; and was the taking of bribes in their opinion inadmissible? Those answering the three questions in the affirmative of the first group were 9, 30, and 25 per cent respectively; and of the second group, 13, 75, and 30 per cent.[1] Thus, if these figures are correct and representative, nearly 90 per cent of such State officials were unsympathetic to the Government and might even have been actually hostile; a quarter of one group and over two-thirds of another had no faith in their work; while two-thirds were unwilling completely to discountenance bribes. In 1918–19 the proportions of such classes hostile to the Government must have been even greater than in 1922. With an administrative personnel in which it could place little faith, one is hardly surprised that the State allowed little discretion to subordinate bodies, and sought either to bind them with detailed regulations or else to concentrate all important decisions at the centre.

Finally, the high degree of administrative centralisation which developed under " war communism " was also determined by the nature of the economic problem. The existence of the market[2] is, up to a point, a unifying element among all the separate bodies which operate on the market and seek to

[1] Kritsmann, *op. cit.*, 144–5.

[2] The " market " is used here in the sense of an area of exchange transactions in which the rate of interchange is determined otherwise than by the conscious volition of an individual or group of individuals on the market. This implies a sufficient number of free and independent agents operating on the market for the volition and acts of any one to exert a negligible effect on the rate of interchange. Our assumption, therefore, amounts to that of a competitive market where exchange equilibrium is a determinate conception. To the extent that the number of independent agents is narrowed, the influence of any one becomes greater, until, when there are only two—the case of " bilateral monopoly "—the rate of interchange depends entirely on the acts of bargaining of the two parties, and is a theoretically indeterminate conception. Here the " market " in the sense in which it is being used above has ceased to exist.

make a profit. It imposes on them a certain uniformity of action, owing to the fact that certain stimuli, having the form of certain price conditions which quickly spread over the whole market, evoke a similarity of response from similar commercial instincts; just as a music-hall audience listening to a comedian tends to show a certain uniformity of facial expression, or a crowd to show a unity of emotion when listening to an agitator. It was the discovery of this fact that was the chief virtue of the classical economists, even though, to explain the uniformity, they dragged in unscientific assumptions about an unseen Dame Nature as mistress of the marionette show; and even though, growing lyrical about the "economic harmonies," they were blind to the contradictions of the market and its instabilities. This uniformity may be of socially desirable or undesirable features; it may at times suffer a sharp break and yield place to temporary chaos; but the underlying tendency to uniformity remains. Under these circumstances the functions of a central regulative authority are considerably simplified. Since the tendency to uniformity exists among its subordinate organs, the central authority does not have to impose such uniformity itself. Like a human brain which leaves breathing and digestion and walking to automatic reflex actions, it can confine itself to a general curbing and limiting of the forces of the market, steadying its instabilities, "ironing out" its unevenness, and intervening to eradicate specific undesirable features. This it can do by setting bounds to the actions of the subordinate economic organs, intervening where necessary as a seller or purchaser,[1] controlling the volume and distribution of credit, using its monopoly power to influence prices, and so forth—measures which tend to convert the market from a master to a servant. In other words, under such circumstances the centre could control its subordinate organs, not by direct regulations, but indirectly by controlling the conditions of the market. The difference between

[1] e.g. the "goods intervention" which was so much discussed in 1923 in Russia.

the two measures, in respect to the burden placed upon the centre, represents all the difference between the driver of a coach and four who sits on the box and guides the reins and one who has to descend and push the coach himself.

The events of 1917–19 caused a disintegration of any national market for the majority of goods. Transport difficulties hampered the movement of goods and caused the national market to split up into a number of local markets between which prices varied widely.[1] The almost complete demonetisation of the rouble further disintegrated the market, breaking it up into a number of cumbersome barter transactions which had only a small connection with or influence upon each other. Finally, there was the effect of State monopolisation, and still more of State requisitioning, of a large number of agricultural products, which came to represent the predominant part of exchange between town and country. In such circumstances the major part of exchange transactions had to be planned and conducted by the central organs, with subordinate bodies doing little more than handle the goods according to order. At the outset the Glavki made their own transactions with the co-operatives or even with the villages; and the fact that such exchange tended later to be by direct barter did not by itself preclude such independent transactions from being made. But in the case of monopolised goods this could not be done without a licence from Narcomprod; and in the existing shortage this implied an important decision by Narcomprod as to whether the need was sufficiently important for the licence to be given. Then there was the further difficulty of transport facilities, the first claim on which was possessed by the State Commissariats. In the case of requisitioned goods, the Glavki had necessarily to deal with the State collecting organs; and for obvious reasons the planning and direction of requisitioning had to be centralised.

In all matters, accordingly, concerned with the relations of one enterprise with others—that is, all exchange trans-

[1] Cf. Prof. Kondratiev in *Na Novikh Putyakh*, Vol. I, 2–4.

actions—the disappearance of the independent market combined with the urgent demands of civil war and the poverty of personnel to impose a rigid centralisation. This involved a congestion of business at central departments which was completely beyond their capacity to handle; and this led to delays and to confusion. It involved the fettering and mechanisation of subordinate bodies with detailed regulations and orders, which precluded initiative and flexibility, which seldom fitted precisely the circumstances and the particular case, and which not infrequently were contradictory. And when the ending of the civil war in 1920 and the raising of the blockade afforded a new "breathing space" to the exhausted and emaciated country, it seemed as though the administrative machine, with its inflated officialdom, its inertia, flagrant inefficiency and chaos of red-tape, with its local departments seething with discontent at the bonds laid upon them by the congested and harassed central authorities, had very small chance, save by some purgative force from without, of ever shouldering and carrying through the gigantic task of economic reconstruction.

CHAPTER FIVE

THE TRANSITION TO THE NEW ECONOMIC POLICY

NOT until an Armistice had been signed with Poland in October, not until the remnant of Wrangel's army in the South had abandoned its crusade to win back Russia for civilisation at the end of November 1920, and the Don and the Baku oil-fields and the Turkestan cotton belt and the Trans-Ural wheat-area were again under the sway of the Soviet Government, could attention seriously be turned to enquire as to the adequacy of the system of "war communism." Even when attention had been turned to such an enquiry, it was not altogether easy in the circumstances to give an answer. Most people were too close to the problems of the last few years, which had crowded upon them without breathing space or time for reflection, to evaluate the situation correctly. "War communism" had certainly arisen as a necessity from existing circumstances, and in those circumstances had served an important function. To see how far its disadvantages had been merely incidental to it, or an inseparable product of it, was not easy. It was not easy to see how precisely the changed circumstances of peace-time modified this necessity and altered the function required. Ever since October 1917 Russia had in a sense been wandering in strange territory, groping through a gigantic experiment. Before 1917 little detailed thought had been given to the precise nature of socialist construction and its problems. Even in the brief "breathing space" of 1918 there was acute dissension about the road to be pursued. Now, flushed with the immediate military victory, there were many who regarded "war communism" as the embodiment of their ideal, to defend which against criticism was part of their faith.

It can be taken as tolerably certain that the difficulties of "war communism," amounting in some cases almost to disaster, which were so vividly in evidence in 1920, were not merely incidental to the system, in the sense that in happier circumstances they could have been surmounted while leaving the essential features of the system intact. In the main they depended upon the features of the system itself, these features in turn being imposed by the necessities of civil war and the advanced stage of economic decline. In the first place, certain difficulties of the period were directly the product of the transition to a moneyless economy. Since this, combined with the famine in certain staple products, involved State monopolisation of trade in certain essential goods which were most scarce, and hence most likely to soar to famine prices, and the distribution of them by a process of rationing, the central economic organs had piled upon them a host of complicated functions which in other circumstances they would not have had to undertake. With the continuance of an ordinary market—albeit a market narrowed, "encircled," and controlled by the State—much of these functions could have been left to independent initiative. Trade might have been conducted independently by bodies like the co-operatives, and the distribution of goods effected by an ordinary process of sale through retail agencies; and for the details of such a process the central economic organs need have had no more concern than has the human brain for the flow of the gastric juices in the stomach. As it was, under the existing moneyless conditions, goods could only be supplied to consumers on a ration system, while wage-payments themselves had to take this ration form. Hence this distribution had to be planned from the centre and carried out under direct central supervision: since the centre, like the father of a family, held the key of the store-room and parcelled out the fare, all matters of supply had of necessity to be referred to the centre.

Possibly more important, but more frequently unnoticed, was the effect of the demonetisation of the rouble in destroying the common measure in terms of which economic quantities could be equated, and eliminating the market through which such equations could be expressed, thereby sweeping away the basis of economic accounting.[1] Before the advanced stage of demonetisation had been reached, the depreciation of the rouble caused considerable disturbance, such as would be caused to the building of a house if the foot-rule were to change its length overnight. Even when the depreciation of the monetary unit is adequately understood and is allowed for in all calculations, disturbance may be caused, because the stimulus of rising prices and profits operates with unequal force among different industries, and by encouraging some branches of industry to expand too rapidly, thereby produces serious maladjustment. Actually, however, depreciation was not fully understood and allowed for; and as late as 1919 we find officials in the transport administration reckoning costs and expenditure in paper roubles, and without any allowance for changes in the value of money concluding from the figures that "the cost of railway transport has increased 50 times."[2] Generally the correction of monetary calculations by means of an index number of prices seems to have been deficient, if not completely lacking. The former unit of account, because of its instability, was useless and even dangerous as a measure, and no new unit had been found to act in its stead. Not till 1920 did the need for such a stable unit appear to be generally appreciated when a report to a Congress of economic councils in January declared that "in view of the excessive instability of the monetary unit and the unit of account, it should be made incumbent on the organisations entrusted with the keeping of economic accounts to establish a unit of account for the Budget of the country"; and a unit of labour was suggested as a basis.[3] Little that was practical, however, emerged from the proposal; and the New Economic

[1] See Excursus to Chapter Five.
[2] In *Narodnoe Khosiaistvo*, No. 5; *cit.* Bukharin, *op. cit.*, Chap. 9.
[3] *Cit.* Yurovsky, *op. cit.*, 34.

Policy, which followed in 1921, by reintroducing the market and extending the use of money, altered the character of the problem. By decree of November 5th of that year the Council of People's Commissaries (*Sovnarcom*) ordered the Budget estimates for 1922 to be prepared in terms of " pre-war roubles,"—in other words, by dividing existing rouble figures by the index number of prices, as measure of the extent of the rouble depreciation. Ten days later this calculation in " pre-war roubles " was extended to business transactions generally. At first the index number of the Finance Commissariat (*Narcomfin*) was used as the divisor in the calculation, and later that of the State Bank which was based on the rates at which the Bank bought gold. But since these " rates of the State Bank still lagged behind both the prices of gold and the market prices of goods," the system remained unsatisfactory until a completely new unit of value, the chervonetz, began to be issued by the State Bank at the end of 1922.[1]

But apart from the effects of a shrinking unit of account, the pricing of various things, relatively to one another, in terms of this unit ceased to have any basis in reality. The requisitioning and State monopolisation of various staple goods caused their prices to be no longer determined by the market, and rendered them purely arbitrary, according to whatever figure the State organs chose to fix. In numerous cases this monopoly was not completely enforced, and the trade of " bagmen "—persons travelling between village and town with grain—assumed huge proportions; and the prices prevailing on this illegal " free market " showed wide divergence from the official prices in which the State organs calculated.[2] The estimation, consequently, of the relative

[1] *Ibid.*, 70 *seq.*

[2] One estimate maintains that for 1918–19 of the grain supplied to the towns only 40 per cent was supplied by the State and 60 per cent by illegal " free " trade ; while of food as a whole the town population received over two-thirds of its supplies from the " free " market (Kritsmann, *Geroicheske Period*, 134–5). The extent of divergence of State prices from those on the free market is illustrated by the fact that the prices fixed in August 1919 established a 2:1 average ratio

importance and costs of various things, in terms of their prices on the market was abandoned, without the adoption of any alternative principle for equating or " pricing " things in terms of the unit of account. If on the cost side of a balance-sheet there were certain figures of the cost of raw materials, these figures really were meaningless, being based, not on any objective reality, but merely on the arbitrary decision of some board or official that the raw material in question should be priced at that amount. Hence, to compare the cost of one thing or one process of production with the cost of another had little meaning, and to concentrate the limited potentialities of production on things which cost least relatively to their social importance, and to eliminate costly and inefficient processes became impossible. As a result, the State authorities " endeavoured to achieve the greatest quantity of goods without consideration of the cost of their production, or whether the limited resources were being used economically or not," which meant that resources were dissipated in " putting into activity an immeasurably large number of enterprises of an extremely low economy of labour."[1]

Similarly, on the demand side, to calculate the relative importance of various commodities in supplying social needs was equally difficult. The partial disappearance of the market and of market price as an index left the calculation of the relative importance of needs to be based on other criteria or by generalisation from a selected " sample "; and where such criteria were non-existent, as in a very large number of cases they were, and a given " sample " of social needs displayed large internal variation, as it tended to do in all but the most elementary wants, the calculation had to be entirely *a priori* or based on blind guesswork. It was like estimating the character of public opinion in the absence of a plebiscite: it could only be done by taking a " sample "

between industrial and agricultural goods, while prices on the " free " market in September represented a ratio of 6:1 (Larin and Kritsmann, *op. cit.*, 22).

[1] G. Krshishanovsky, *Khosiaistvennie Problemi R.S.F.S.R.*, 64.

of opinion or by drawing inferences from indirect criteria. In respect to consumable goods the circumstances of war-time actually made the position considerably simpler than, under more normal circumstances, it would have been. For the stringent conditions of war-time prevent the satisfaction of more than a few primary wants. The choice is, therefore, narrowed to a few alternatives; and these few are precisely those things for which the demand is least elastic—least variable according to the price—and most uniform as between individuals, so that examination of the preferences of a given small sample of consumers is more likely to give results which are representative of consumers' needs as a whole. Moreover, during the Russian civil war, to the extent that dealings on the "free market" still represented a large proportion of the whole, prices which consumers were willing to pay there afforded some index of the urgency of their need. Even so, war-time supplies generally bear witness to the considerable chance of a misjudgment of demand, with consequent supply to satiety of bully-beef and plum and apple jam at a time when other essential wants are left unsatisfied. In this case supply to consumers was done on a ration system; and in some instances the most elementary data for an estimate of demand seem to have been lacking. In a certain local department of supplies in Tambov gubernia the distribution of different commodities was in the hands of different officials. Each of these officials made his own estimate of the population of the gubernia, and these estimates varied as widely as 20 per cent.[1] So if the number of consumers was not known within 20 per cent, and different commodities were supplied according to different estimates, it was unlikely that supplies would be adjusted to the relative importance of different needs or to the more complex preferences of individual consumers.

This particular case can probably be regarded as illus-

[1] Kritsmann, *op. cit.*, 119. One official indeed, in charge of household utensils, confessed to having no information at all on which to base an estimate. Whether he was more honest or merely more indolent than his fellows history does not record.

trating an incidental rather than an essential difficulty. But when one comes to the supply to different industries and enterprises of various requisites of production, one meets a problem that is more complex still than the supply of finished goods; for here one has the complication that many things are jointly demanded together in proportions which cannot easily be varied, while other things stand in a relation of rival supplies or substitutes to one another, preference for one over another depending mainly on its relative cheapness. The system under "war communism" was that each enterprise submitted to each of the departments responsible for each branch of supply a statement of the quantity required and the purposes for which the supply was needed and the urgency of the need. Clearly, a department faced with several thousands of such statements had no means of determining the order of importance of the numerous requests; and the proportions in which it allocated the limited supplies between the enterprises could be based on little more than guesswork. Even if the department had had fairly detailed information about the enterprises, in the absence of some quantitative measure of cost, on the one hand, and of the state of the demand for the particular product of the enterprise on the other hand, and a means of comparing the net result with other enterprises, it could not have decided satisfactorily which of two requests for fuel or raw material deserved priority. In certain clear and extreme cases, of course, such a decision could be made. But in the majority of cases, where the differences were less noticeable, it was quite likely to happen that the less efficient and more costly enterprise was given priority over the more efficient, and the concern that was producing for a partly satisfied want over one supplying an unsatisfied need. Moreover, it came about that various needs that were of a joint character were supplied by different departments in different proportions. An organisation needing lamps would receive from one department 100 per cent of its need for lamp glasses, from another 60 per cent of containers, and perhaps 20 per cent of its request for burners from a third.[1] One enterprise might have sufficient raw material, but insufficient fuel; or sufficient of both, but not enough supplies to pay its workers rations, and so to prevent them from emigrating to the village. This latter difficulty could, of course, in part have been remedied by a better co-ordination of the work of the supply departments. But this might have involved such a further degree of centralisation as would have proved too great a burden on the administrative machine; and, at any rate, the central difficulty of the situation—the difficulty of estimating the relative importance of different requests—would have remained.

Since any adequate planning of production was rendered impossible for lack of data, the only alternative was to single out certain branches of production which were clearly most important, to concentrate all resources upon them, and to leave other less important industries to struggle on as best they could. This was done under what came to be known as the " shock " system. Certain enterprises of special importance, usually from the immediate military point of view, were settled on and declared to be " shock " industries. On their administration were concentrated all the best administrators available. They were given priority in the supply of fuel and materials and of food rations for wages. Applied as the system at first was to industries of outstanding importance, such as transport and then enterprises serving the needs of transport, its effect was distinctly beneficial. It merely applied the common-sense principle of concentrating on what is most clearly essential, while having all the additional psychological advantages associated with a " drive." But as soon as it began to be applied very widely or very vigorously, its concentration of resources on the " shock " industries tended to starve all " non-shock " industries of essential supplies; so that the comparative plenty of " shock " products was only purchased at the price of a famine in other commodities, of which in many cases a small quantity at least was a prime necessity. This provoked an agitation for

[1] Kritsmann, *op. cit.*, 117–19.

a widening of the " shock " industries, so as to include other products in the category. Each such extension made the situation of the " non-shock " enterprises more critical; and it raised again the whole question of estimating the relative importance of different products. Which of the many claimants were to be judged worthy of inclusion in the " shock " category; and inside the ever-broadening category how was the order of priority to be decided? The widening went so far as to embrace the manufacture of minor office equipment such as pens and pencils. The Commissariat of Health at one time appealed for the inclusion of mineral waters; at another time the inclusion of the production of carbolic was considered.[1] How choose between mineral waters and carbolic? Which of them was most likely to repay the expenditure on it of the terribly limited supplies? Moreover, there were all sorts of pitfalls in such a choice. For instance, in concentrating resources on a " shock " industry, one was liable to find that one had thereby helped to starve a " non-shock " industry which was really an essential subsidiary to the former—in other words, as Kritsmann quaintly puts it, " solving " a problem by applying the " shock " to its head, only to find that in doing so one had " tied up its tail."[2] And when the war period came to an end, which had given some objective to the system by singling out certain military needs as undoubtedly pre-eminent and almost insatiable, the impossibility of continuing the system became only too clear.[3]

The second feature of the period, the high degree of centralisation, had also by the autumn of 1920 produced a serious situation of administrative chaos. An enterprise which required some elementary thing, like a spare part for machinery or a set of hand tools, could not itself get into direct touch with the Glavka, still less with the enterprise concerned. It had to apply to the technical department of its own Glavka through the technical departments of its Group

[1] Prof. Dolgov in *Sozialisticheskoe Khosiaistvo*, March, 1923, p. 21.
[2] Kritsmann, *op. cit.*, 122.
[3] Cf. Krshishanovsky, *op. cit.*, 65.

Administration, and possibly also as a third stage through the appropriate sub-section of the Gubsovnarhoz. Then the Glavka of the industry in question would apply to the Glavmetal, and it in turn to the appropriate factory, and the spare parts or the tools would in due course be delivered. At the same time, metal concerns might be handicapped by inability to procure ore and fuel, even when there were mines close at hand in the neighbourhood, because they were in a separate departmental section and were not allowed to obtain supplies except through application to the centre. The whole process not only involved intolerable delay, if not the actual " pigeon-holing " of the request in one office or another on the way; it also involved a multiplication of documentary work at the various stages and a serious overloading of officials at the centre with documents about trivial local details. Such overloading increased delay in the transaction of business, increased progressively the possibility of mistakes, and prevented the attention of central officials from being devoted to more important matters—for the mental concentration needed for the giving of decisions is exhausting, and there is a definite limit to the number of decisions which even the best administrator can give in a day.

Some Glavki, which controlled several thousand enterprises, were quite unable to deal with the mass of business that passed through their hands; and the problem of organisation was made considerably more difficult by the sweeping character of the nationalisation which developed: of the 37,000 enterprises nominally belonging to the State at the end of 1920, 18,000 had no mechanical power, while over 5000 were businesses with only one employee.[1] In consequence, the central economic organs performed only a fraction of what in theory they were supposed to do. Some of the first essentials of good organisation were lacking, and the most urgent matters failed to get attention because no one had the time or the initiative to give a decision. A committee of investigation set up in June 1920 reported that

[1] Kritsmann, *op. cit.*, 62, 127–9.

many Glavki not only "do not know what goods and in what amounts are kept in the warehouses under their control, but are actually ignorant even of the number of such warehouses." The storing, receiving, and delivery of goods was quite unsystematised; inventories of stocks were the exception rather than the rule; and pilfering and looting of warehouses and secret sale of their contents on the private market was not uncommon.[1] In textiles, even when stocks of raw material were available, they were not utilised because they lay in the warehouses undistributed. With but a few exceptions the Glavki were quite in ignorance of the technical equipment of enterprises under their control, or of the existing stocks in the factories. The Petrograd metal section, for instance, though it had started to take an inventory of stocks at the factories and in warehouses, did not possess any complete inventory in 1920.[2] Indeed, in all respects the information available at the centre about the enterprises which it was supposed to administer was, as one writer says, "quite miserable" and "purely formal in character."[3] In 1920 the program of Narcomprod was so little based on actual possibilities that the department utilised only half of the cargo space assigned to it by the railways, with the result that in June there were 35,000 wagons and 329 locomotives lying idle.[4] Consequently, in the first five months of the year Narcomprod was able to fulfil only 90 per cent of its program of supplies to the army, 70 per cent for transport, and only 40 per cent for factories and workshops.[5] Vesenha itself failed completely to fill the proud rôle originally intended for it—an economic general staff surveying and co-ordinating all economic activities of the State—and became so obsessed with special problems as to constitute in practice merely a Commissariat of Industry. Accordingly, in the relations between it and Narcomprod, which was independent

[1] *Cit.* Pasvolsky, *op. cit.*, 215.
[2] *Brit. Labour Delegation Report*, 1920, 102–3.
[3] Rosenfeld, *Promishlennaia Politika S.S.S.R.*, 123.
[4] Pasvolsky, *op. cit.*, 109, 209.
[5] Larin and Kritsmann, *op. cit.*, 208.

of it, and with transport and the war industries which came under the control of separate commissariats, there was no co-ordinating body, until later the Council of Defence was widened into the Council of Labour and Defence (S T O) designedly to fill this co-ordinating rôle.[1] Meanwhile the multiplication of officials resulting from this top-heavy administrative hierarchy considerably inflated the overhead costs of industry at a time when the output per worker had fallen catastrophically. In July 1920 one out of every four adults in Petrograd was said to be an official; and in industry in general the ratio of administrative employees to the total workers employed had risen from the pre-war figure of 6·4 per cent to 13·5 per cent.[2]

If it be true, as Dr. Rivers has suggested,[3] that "red-tape" is a psychological "defence-mechanism" of harassed administrators faced with a problem beyond their powers, there seems much reason to suggest a connection in this case between the two things. Fearful of letting events pass completely beyond its control, each department tended jealously to guard its prescriptive rights, to resent fiercely any intrusion of another department on its sphere, and to exact inelastic obedience to the letter of its ordinances and decrees. Unable to give the time for careful decision on details, departments tended to settle everything by rule-of-thumb procedure in mechanical fashion, in neglect of individual peculiarities of a specific case. The result was a number of demarcation disputes, in which each side tended to maintain its rights in rigid and unyielding fashion, and which were often settled most uneconomically, according to the letter of the regulation, as when the tanker fleet was separated from the oil industry, and subsidiary enterprises were claimed by another administration from that of the concerns which they supplied, and hence were isolated by departmental barriers.[4]

[1] Kritsmann, *op. cit.*, 208.
[2] Kritsmann, *op. cit.*, 194.
[3] In *Psychology and Politics*.
[4] Kritsmann, *op. cit.*, 207, who refers to "the stupidly crude documentary officialism." Cf. also Rosenfeld, *op. cit.*, 124.

Such demarcation wrangling and the general red-tape were reflected in two popular jokes of the period. One was the legend told by the popular versifier, Demian Biedny, of the dead mare in the streets of Petrograd surrounded by the representatives of the fifty odd Glavki, disputing within whose sphere the disposal of the carcase came. The other was a " turn " of the two famous Moscow clowns, Bim and Bom. Bim appears laboriously dragging a large sack. " Been gathering wood? " says Bom. Bim nods and holds up half a match. " Then what's that in the sack? " asks Bom. " Oh, that," Bim replies, " that contains the necessary permits."

The localities, meanwhile, were in no less confusion. Since the central authorities had neither the time nor the necessary contacts to render them *au fait* with the local situation, it followed that the orders which they sent out " did not correspond to the actual situation in the districts, or arrived late and caused only confusion."[1] A " program " of production for an enterprise would be drawn up which bore no relation to possibility in the shape of existing fuel and material supplies. Sometimes the instructions which came from the various Glavki to the corresponding departments of the local Gubsovnarhoz did not agree (like the orders of separate union executives to their local branches during the English General Strike of May 1926), or were actually in conflict; which involved interminable correspondence and negotiation with many separate departments before the necessary adjustment could be achieved. When finally, if at all, adjustment was achieved, the whole situation had probably altered. Krshishanovsky points out that the merely *formal* execution of the letter of orders from the centre was often adopted as the line of least resistance; while, on the other hand, heroic individual attempts to clear up the mess by improvisation on individual initiative often ended in worse confusion; and he refers to the " heaps of useless report sheets," " the maintenance of numerous agents," and " docu-

[1] Dolgov, *op. cit.*, 22, who adds: " Absolutely no centralised apparatus could have coped with it satisfactorily."

mentary circumlocution " as characteristic of the period.[1] The net effect of the whole situation was the paralysing of action, the stifling of initiative, the desire of everyone to shift responsibility by an interminable process of reference, only to reach in the end a competent authority—if ever it did so—who, because of his ignorance of the case, probably gave a decision that was wrong.

Revolt against this situation came from the localities so soon as the civil war was at an end. Already in the spring of 1920 the question of decentralisation had been raised at the 9th Congress of the Communist Party; but the continuation of the war made further consideration of the matter impossible. At the 8th Soviet Congress in November and December severe criticism of the Glavki was voiced by provincial delegates. Particular complaint was made of the difficulties of enterprises of that second category which came under the control both of the Glavki and the Gubsovnarhoz, and in practice acted on orders from the former passed down through the appropriate sub-sections of the latter. Here it was that the links in the chain of vertical subordination were most complex; here the separation of the enterprise and the competent authority was greatest; and here the possibility of conflict and confusion between the orders of the various Glavki and the local situation as seen by the Gubsovnarhoz was at its height. The Party Congress earlier in the year had characterised the Glavki system in no mincing tones. " In view of the hugeness of the country," the statement ran, " and the inexactitude of the methods and results of accounting, these centralised methods, which inevitably produced an isolation of enterprises in the localities, led to the monstrous forms of procrastination which are causing so much incurable harm to our economy." The criticisms voiced in November were even more strongly worded than this; and much discussion raged on the question, with the effect of placing Glavkism and the Glavki in deservedly bad odour (though it was their situation rather than their personnel that was most

[1] *Op. cit.*, 67.

to blame). The outcome of the discussion was a modification of centralisation and the introduction of a degree of decentralisation—as much as could be introduced while the general features of "war communism" remained. The Gubsovnarhoz was subordinated to the provincial soviet authority entirely, and its industrial sub-sections were subordinated to it and not to the respective Glavki. The enterprises of the second category, which had caused so much of the trouble, were taken out of the hands of the Glavki and placed under the local body; while instructions were given that even the first category—enterprises of national significance, coming directly under the Glavki—were to be cut down. For instance, the major part of the textile industry was transferred from central to local control.[1]

But though this afforded important partial relief, the relief was as yet no more than partial. There was now less crowding at the centre, less circumlocution, and the competent authority was nearer to the local situation which it sought to control. Nevertheless, the change was in some respects merely equivalent to a splitting up of a few large Glavki into a number of little Glavki, to which many of the evils of the larger bodies still pertained. There were still vertical barriers shutting off allied enterprises from one another. There was still "red-tape" and departmental jealousy, and the enterprises themselves still lacked sufficient independence. What was really required was not merely a geographical devolution, but a separation and specialisation of function, drawing a clear line between the organs of general direction and control and planning, which laid down the main lines of policy (but no more), and organs of industrial administration, which should have executive competence on all matters of detailed interpretation of policy. For this competence to be at all considerable, it would have to include competence (within certain limits) in matters of sales and supplies. Indeed, the 8th Congress fully realised that decentralisation once begun

[1] Piatakov, *op. cit.*, 342–3; Krshishanovski, *op. cit.*, 11; Dolgov, *op. cit.*, 22.

would have to proceed further and be accompanied by a more thorough refashioning of the whole administration. The Congress itself emphasised the need to differentiate between what it called the *direction* of the economic system and the actual administration of industry itself, and stated it as a principle that the former should be centralised and the latter decentralised. But this more far-reaching change was not accomplished—and, indeed, lacked an important condition for its practicability—until N E P, by reintroducing the market, made it possible to form new administrative units in the shape of " trusts," as financially independent, competent groups of enterprises, free to conduct commercial transactions of purchase and sale on their own initiative.[1]

The third result of " war communism " which by the end of 1920 called for radical action was the rupture of social contacts which it produced. In some ways this was the most important result of the three, if for no other reason than that the effects of the other two reacted on it and accentuated it. We have already seen that the obsession of each department with a mass of details tended to isolate them from one another, and to render ineffective the arrangements which had earlier been made for co-ordination and *liaison* between the departments. But in fact a rupture of contacts occurred that was much more fundamental than any break in departmental *liaisons*, and one not to be cured by a mere change of administrative technique. This consisted, on the one hand, in a sharp break in the *smytchka* or union between workers and peasants and an ever-sharpening antagonism between village and town; on the other hand, in a widening gulf between the masses of the workers and the State.

The breach with the peasant was, of course, almost the inevitable result of the policy of requisitions, imposed as a means to overcome that evasion of further taxation which had taken the form of withholding grain supplies from the market. At first this requisitioning policy imposed the obligation to hand over the whole of the surplus produce above a

[1] Rosenfeld, *op. cit.*, 148 *seq.*

minimum necessary for the peasant family—a minimum calculated at so much per head. But this was subject to wholesale evasion, and was replaced later by purely arbitrary levies on the initiative of the local collecting department. The system undoubtedly saved the towns and the armies from starvation during the civil war; but it could serve no more than as a short-period method of supply. The evasion of the levies assumed in many cases surprising proportions; and the fact of evasion moved local soviet authorities to more forcible and inquisitorial methods of collection; and this in turn accentuated the hostility of the peasants progressively. According to the figures of the Central Statistical Bureau concealment of actual sowings amounted in 1920 to over 9 million dessiatines, or about 14 per cent of the sown area; while Strumilin gives a higher estimate of 20 per cent. With regard to the gross harvest, the amount concealed apparently reached the surprising proportion of about 33 per cent.[1] Nominally, the grain which was compulsorily handed over to the State in this way was balanced by an equivalent distribution of manufactured goods through the co-operatives in the villages, the receipt for grain deliveries serving as a voucher for purchases at the co-operative store. Larin, indeed, writing in 1920, goes so far as to maintain that the peasant actually gained out of the exchange, and secured between 1917–20 for each pood of grain supplied to the State twice as much manufactured goods as he received pre-war.[2] But this statement is clearly a statement about the *values* of manufactures received by the peasant—the value being calculated at the fixed prices of the period—and this is not a direct index of the *quantity* of manufactures received for each pood of grain, since industrial prices had risen twice or three times as much as agricultural produce. From other estimates

[1] Kritsmann, *Geroicheskoe Period*, 131–3.

[2] *Op. cit.*, 20–1. Speaking of 1918–19, Larin says that industrial goods to the value of 4 milliard roubles went to the peasants of the producing districts. "This sum was sufficient according to the fixed prices of the time for the collection of 216 million poods of grain. Meantime, the State only managed to collect a half of this, or 107 million."

it would appear that, while the towns received from State collections about one-third of their pre-war agricultural supplies, the villages received of manufactured goods little more than 12 or 15 per cent of the pre-war amount, and certainly no more than 20 per cent.[1] To take one important item of manufactures: Larin himself states that in pre-war days a pood of rye exchanged for about eight arshines of cheap cotton goods. For the rate of exchange of the civil war period Kritsmann[2] gives the following figures:—

	Grain collected.	Textile goods supplied.	Ratio of one pood of grain to Arshine of Textiles.
1919	108 million poods	325 million arsh.	1 : 3
1920	212 ,, ,,	(app.) 180 million arsh.	1 : 0·85

Even when all allowance has been made for the fact that the quality of cloth referred to in this latter estimate may have been higher than in Larin's estimate, it seems clear that the real rate of interchange between agriculture and industry moved *against* the village, not in its favour. Figures given by Strumilin for the relative prices of rye and of certain staple manufactures further confirm this view, and indicate that the relation between the prices of these manufactures and the price of rye stood in 1920 at about 2 : 1 as compared with pre-war.[3]

Further, as Kritsmann, writing some five years later than Larin, points out, a large part of the manufactured goods supplied to the villages went to the village poor, who supplied little or no agricultural produce in return; while the more well-to-do peasant, who supplied most of the grain, received no more in return, and sometimes even less, than his poorer neighbour. Moreover, Russia is divided into the so-called

[1] Rosenfeld, *op. cit.*, 165; also cf. Prokopovitch, *op. cit.*, 110–11.

[2] *Geroicheskoe Period*, 173–4.

[3] S. G. Strumilin, *Na Khosiaistvennom Fronte*, 211. Strumilin gives a lower pre-war equivalent of cotton piece goods to rye than does Larin, namely, 5·5:1. Presumably he is dealing with a higher quality than Larin.

"consuming areas" and the "producing areas"—the areas of the centre and north which usually have to import grain, and the areas of the south, south-east, and the Urals and Siberia which customarily produce a surplus above their own requirements. It was to the former that the major part of manufactured goods tended to go, while it was from the latter that the bulk of the grain supplies for the towns and the army were drawn. Hence, as Kritsmann puts it, the exchange was not so much an exchange between industry and agriculture as an exchange of industrial goods with the services of the poor peasants in extracting produce from the richer farms;[1] and the middle and richer peasants, particularly in the "producing areas," were receiving a rate of interchange considerably more unfavourable, as compared with pre-war, than was the village as a whole.

Driven by the failure of the grain deliveries in the spring of 1918, the Government had instituted the system of Committees of the Village Poor, which were to serve as the organs for enforcing the requisitioning policy in the villages. Later, military and trade-union detachments were organised, and were despatched from the towns to aid these committees wherever the richer peasants were suspected of failing in their obligations. Sometimes the division became geographical, and it was a case of sending peasant detachments from the "consuming areas" to requisition the surplus of the "producing areas." By organising in this way the poorer peasants on the side of the State as instruments of the State policy it was hoped, in spite of the requisitioning, to preserve the *smytchka* between worker and peasant, and use it to wage the class struggle in the village against that capitalist-in-embryo, the *kulak* or rich peasant. But the poor peasants often constituted no more than a small minority in the village; and they were from the point of view of food production quite negligible. Accordingly, the result of the requisitioning policy was to arouse the hostility, not merely of the *kulak* element, as might anyhow have been expected,

[1] *Op. cit.*, 174.

but also of the " middle peasants," who formed in most cases the backbone of the village, and from whose ranks the Red Army was very largely recruited; and in the " producing areas " this hostility was particularly keen and widespread. Apart from mere evasion of the levies, the hostility took the form, first of a change in sowing from produce which was requisitioned to produce that was still free; and second, of a serious reduction in the total area sown; since, deprived of any incentive to produce more than a certain minimum for his own requirements, the peasant naturally tended to exert himself as little as possible. In 1919 and 1920 the area under potatoes and millet increased considerably at the expense of grain, because these were still free from requisitioning; while the total area sown, which had already by 1916 declined by 7 per cent, by 1920 had commenced a catastrophic fall of nearly 30 per cent, by 1921–2 reaching the level of scarcely more than half of pre-war.[1] Draught cattle had meanwhile declined since 1916 by 30 per cent, horses by 25 per cent, and sheep and pigs by over 50 per cent.[2] Moreover, the decline was greatest in the large producing areas of Central Russia and Siberia on which the towns relied. The " short period " within which extraordinary methods of compulsion might extend the " squeezability " of the peasant had by 1920 definitely come to an end.[3]

[1] Farbman, *Bolshevism in Retreat*, 230 *seq.* Mr. C. Roden Buxton mentions a certain village near Samara where the area usually sown was 3000 dessiatines and in 1920 had fallen to 900. The special cause adduced in this case was the mobilisation of carts and horses for government transport of supplies (*Report of Brit. Lab. Delegation* 1920, App. XIX). The following table for all Russia (excluding Turkestan and Trans-Caucasia) shows slightly different results from those cited in the text:—

	Av. 1909–13	1916	1920	1921
Harvest (m. poods)	4078	3955	1738	1617
Area Sown (m. dess)	81·2	82·5	56·8	49·1
Yield per dess. in poods	50	48	30·6	32·6

(L. of N., *Report on Econ. Condits. in Russia*, 20–1.)

[2] *Russian Information and Review*, 1.1.22.

[3] Trotsky wrote in Feb. 1920 from the Urals that the policy of requisitions was provoking " the progressive decadence of agriculture, the dispersion of the industrial proletariat, and threatens complete disorganisation of the economic life of the country " (Trotsky, *Novy Kurs*, 53).

In this situation the only logical thing to do, short of abandonment, was to extend compulsion from the surplus available for the State to the actual area sown, just as compulsory requisitioning of one article had created the need for its extension to prevent the peasants' evasion by transfer to other crops. Such an extension was actually proposed by Ossinsky of Narcomprod—a proposal to fix for each peasant a minimum area which it was compulsory for him to sow—and though regarded coldly by the Commissariat of Agriculture and opposed by most of the peasant delegates, this was carried in a modified form at the 8th Congress of Soviets. But this measure was to prove the high-water mark of " war communism ": it was almost that system's *reductio ad absurdum*. When the acute necessity which had imposed extraordinary methods was passing with the civil war, these measures of military compulsion were seen to be both intolerable in peace-time and an actual danger. It was by now becoming apparent that the " kindling of the class war " in the villages had not in general led to the strengthening of the proletarian influence, but had actually strengthened the *kulak* elements; and this had come about, not merely because the " middle peasant," angered by the forcible requisitioning, had been driven into alliance with his richer neighbours against what they both deemed to be " robbery," but also because the *kulak* had actually extended his influence over the poor peasants as well by secretly lending to them land and grain and cattle and instruments on easy terms as a means of evading the requisitioning.[1] Peasant delegates at the 8th Congress of Soviets began to make outspoken complaint of the multitude of officials and committees, of which " there are in a *Volost* almost as many as there are households. If the committees were put one on top of the other, they would almost reach the sky. They are standing on the calloused neck of the toiling peasant and his legs are tottering and will soon break down."[2] And even while these words were being

[1] Cf. Report of Skvortsov at 10th Congress R. Comm. Party.
[2] *Cit.* Farbman, *op. cit.*, 251–2.

spoken, a wave of peasant risings was sweeping over the Volga region and West Siberia, and in Tambov gubernia and Saratov officials responsible for the food collections were being attacked and tortured and killed.

It was not only the peasants who were at this time estranged from the Government. The masses of the town workers were beginning to feel a separation between themselves and the State apparatus, and between themselves and the Communist Party itself. This showed itself in that antagonism between the " centre " and the " provinces " which was characteristic of this time—that grumbling in the provinces even among Communists at smartly-booted, cake-eating Commissars " at the centre," which Jury Libedinsky in *The Week* puts into the mouth of Simkhova, or the musings of his Martuinov as to whether the ordinary rank-and-file members of the Party could not " do more responsible Party work and deal with it with more Communist tact than certain intellectuals " at the top, were it not that " the mechanism of the Party pushes forward those who know how to speak eloquently, preside at meetings and manage them." It showed itself in the factory workers' growing distrust of the higher economic authorities, who deluged them with orders and regulations, and then left them idle for want of materials or fuel, who forbade them to buy food on the " free market " while failing to supply them with even their meagre bread ration. It showed itself in a growing feeling of suspicion of the trade-union apparatus as a body designed to secure acquiescence by the workers in the Government's designs, rather than an organ of the rank and file upholding the interests of the masses in State counsels: the trade unions had come to be looked upon as little different from any ordinary State department.

To counter the decline of labour productivity and to accelerate the mobility of labour, Trotsky, flushed with his success in organising the Red Army, had inaugurated at the beginning of 1920 the project of labour conscription and the organisation of a labour army. Special " shock battalions " were formed to supply a driving force for the " shock " enterprises; while units of the Red Army, released from the military front, were turned on to the "economic front," instead of being demobilised, to deal with the fuel and transport crisis, which was at this time at its height. A certain measure of success was achieved: the gathering of wood fuel was accelerated, and important repair work in the railway shops and on the permanent way was carried through. But against a flagging incentive and physical exhaustion military organisation and compulsion could not avail very much; and after the stimulus of propaganda and "drive" associated with it had exhausted its initial response from tired nerves, as it did within a month or two, little effect remained except to accentuate the feeling of separation between the masses who received orders and those high above them who issued orders like any Government of old and brooked no disobedience. In the second half of 1920 strikes became a fairly frequent occurrence, appearing in six months of 1920, according to one authority, in over 70 per cent of the medium and large enterprises; while absenteeism continued to increase.[1] Factory meetings passed opposition resolutions, protest street demonstrations took place, and Government speakers were not infrequently shouted down; and when the temporary improvements in the fuel situation, due to the return of the Baku oil-fields to Soviet control, showed signs of passing, fresh discontent blazed forth, fanned by sudden disappointment of hope. This time it reached even to Kronstadt, the naval station outside Petrograd, which ever since the early March days of 1917 had been "the pride and glory of the revolution." A mass meeting of the garrison adopted a resolution calling for the abolition of the grain monopoly, and for the formation of a new government based on new Soviet elections; and when these demands were rejected, the Kronstadt sailors, under the lead of a handful of Tsarist officers, broke into armed revolt. Never, even when the Czecho-Slovaks had captured Kazan, or when Yudenich was at the gates of Petrograd, had the star of the Bolsheviks

[1] Leites, *op. cit.*, 195.

fallen so low. But on the Government, which had always placed its ear close to the murmurings of the crowd, these signs and portents were not lost. Almost before the last Kronstadt gun had been silenced, Lenin was proclaiming to the 10th Congress of the Communist Party the urgent need for the " scrapping " of " war communism," and was outlining the principles of the New Economic Policy.

But this new policy, adopted by the 10th Party Congress, was not born from the head of Lenin overnight. It was not delivered without several weeks, even months, of feverish discussion in Party circles and in the Party Press. Already on February 9th the Central Executive Committee had ordered all provincial Soviet executives to summon immediately meetings of the local Soviets and to restore to them their full powers where these powers had been suspended during the military period;[1] and *Pravda* some time before the 10th Congress had inaugurated an open discussion of the whole situation. As early as November of the previous year an important discussion had started on the rôle of the trade unions: a discussion which developed into a general argument about the administration of industry, and out of which five separate " platforms " were born, each of the five being represented in the Central Party Committee. The discussion on the trade unions arose from Trotsky's régime on the railways as Commissar of Ways and Communications, and had its first stage in a disagreement between Trotsky and Tomsky at the 5th Congress of Trade Unions. To deal with the transport chaos, Trotsky had introduced strict military discipline, and had abolished the powers which remained to local workers' committees. In certain important areas the territory immediately surrounding the railway was even removed entirely from the competence of the local Soviet authorities and placed exclusively under the rule of the railway administration. Democracy in the railway union was abolished and the heads of the union appointed by the administration; and this system, which Trotsky would have

[1] Farbman, *op. cit.*, 266.

extended, aroused strong opposition at the 5th Congress of Trade Unions. When the issue was raised for discussion at the Central Committee of the Party on November 9th, it at once became the centre of a complex eddy of crossing opinions. Trotsky produced a thesis in defence of the policy which came to be known as the " State-isation " of the trade unions, with Lenin and Tomsky leading a resolute minority of opposition. Between the two a " buffer " group of ten, including Bukharin and Zinoviev, sought a compromise. At the 8th Soviet Congress Trotsky on December 25th presented a policy of his own, independently of the Central Committee of the Party; and in the ensuing discussion the vacillating " buffer " group divided and went different ways, Zinoviev joining Lenin, and Bukharin, while presenting to the Congress a separate resolution, inclining towards support of Trotsky. Rudzutak meanwhile outlined a policy which was closely similar to that of Lenin. Finally, in January the Trade Union Commission which the Central Committee had appointed, and on which Trotsky had refused to serve, published the so-called " platform of the ten," signed among others by Lenin, Zinoviev, Stalin, Tomsky, Kamenev, and Rudzutak, which was eventually to become in essentials the official policy of the Party. This opposed the " State-isation " of the trade unions, and advocated the restoration of internal democracy within the unions, and the rejection of any reconstruction of the unions from above. The rôle of the unions should be to form a link with the non-Party masses, drawing them into collective activity, and defending their interests against bureaucratic tendencies of the State. At the same time the leaders of the unions should participate in the organs of economic administration, and put forward candidates from among the workers for State economic posts.[1]

This conflict of views, which started from the discussion on the trade unions, and then from the publication of the various " platforms " in January up to the 10th Party Congress widened from specific to more general issues, provides

[1] Cf. Lenin in *Pravda*, 21.1.21; also *Pravda*, 18.1.21.

interesting evidence of the considerable variety of ideas which still persisted as to the direction in which the road to Communism lay. There still survived strong elements of that " leftism " which in the first eight months of the revolution had sought to hasten the pace of events. This " leftism " was characterised by an under-estimation of the importance of the peasantry, an imperfect appreciation of the real nature of the economic factors which they sought to handle, and by the possession of a purely formal conception of what the nature of the desired society was to be. It was natural for them to think of " war communism," not as a deviation from the normal line of development, not as a set of special measures and methods imposed by the emergency of war, but as a partial embodiment of their ideal.[1] The abolition of money—was not that a feature of true communism ? State barter between town and country—was not that merely the " higher form of economy " which was to replace the anarchy of the market ? The " kindling of the class war " in the villages—was not that the wholly desirable " next step " of eliminating bourgeois influence from the countryside as it had been eliminated in the towns ? Even those who did not argue thus from first principles, since they had become accustomed to the system for two and a half years, tended to identify its main features with the very stuff of the revolution, and so could hardly conceive, let alone countenance, an alternative. " Any retreat from the system which for long seemed to be the primary essence of socialist construction was regarded as an abandonment of conquered positions."[2]

This conception of " war communism " shaded off both to the " left " and to the " right " into two other distinct doctrinal tendencies, which in practice came to clash sharply with one another. On the one hand was a syndicalist tendency which believed in decentralisation on principle,

[1] Lenin, on the other hand, characterised war communism as a " mistake " and a " jump," " in complete contradiction to all we wrote concerning the transition from capitalism to socialism " (Speech on N E P reported in *Isvestia*, 19.10.21).

[2] Rosenfeld, *op. cit.*, 144.

desired the minimum of State control from above in economic affairs and the maximum of democratic control from below to stimulate the " initiative " and " creative impulses " of the mass. On the other hand was that group of opinion, of which Trotsky was representative, which believed above all things in organisation, and so favoured centralisation and extolled the dictatorial methods of the war period as an instrument of order and authority. Moreover, according to Trotsky's famous " theory of permanent revolution," revolution was regarded as proceeding from the seizure of power by the workers, in alliance with the peasantry, to its next stage of a new class war between the workers and the peasants, in which the former would stand for order and organisation against anarchy and Asiatic backwardness, and for the higher economic stage of socialism against petty-bourgeois individualism. Accordingly, the application of compulsion, as under the requisitioning system, with its logical outcome in Ossinsky's compulsory farming scheme, appeared as proper steps on the road to socialising the countryside; and the fact that it brought estrangement and actual revolt among the peasantry seemed merely part of the inevitable march of history.

It was only natural that at this critical juncture these different trends of opinion should give rise to different diagnoses of the situation and to different prescriptions for a cure. Trotsky had previously been responsible in the main for the schemes of compulsory labour; and now it was rather natural that he should see a solution for the existing *impasse* in further organisation along military lines to liquidate the prevailing chaos, and in an extension of the system of " the labour army." Discipline, organisation, work—this to Trotsky was the tonic which the " backward," " Asiatic " Russian temperament required. " What does militarisation mean, if not organisation, strict execution of orders, war against idleness ? " he said in a speech in the first week of February. " Misery engenders avarice, famine, epidemics, which at all times have devastated Russia. All this was a thing of the past with the arrival of the workers and peasants in power. We shall lift our country out of the dirt, misery and poverty. The basis of our State is the rule of universal labour. It is time to put this principle into practice."[1] Trotsky would have made the trade unions generally into the brigades of his industrial army, with the local officials as its N.C.O.'s and the national officials as the higher command of each brigade. And, as in ordinary military practice, these officers of the industrial army were to be appointed by the State from above. The best organisers which the Party possessed would be marshalled into *cadres* and kept at the service of the centre, and then sent to take charge of this or that brigade, according as one part or other of the economic front required some special " cleaning up."[2]

Diametrically opposed to the program of Trotsky stood the policy which the syndicalist element was advocating with much vigour. This group was hostile first and foremost to centralisation; and its members had hitherto accepted individual management in industry and appointment from above only as an emergency war measure: its general application they had keenly resisted at the 9th Party Congress in the spring of the previous year. Most of the evils of the present were traced by them to the over-centralisation of appointments and the excessive favour shown to bourgeois " specialists," which caused a gulf to yawn between the State apparatus and the masses. They desired instead a return to what they termed " workers' democracy," based on local initiative and free election from below. In the realm of industry they wished to see restored the democratic and independent character of the unions, in whose hands the whole control of industry should be placed, with a democratic congress of trade unions as the sovereign body in the economic sphere. Madame Kollontai accused the Party leaders of being suddenly overwhelmed by " wise caution,"

[1] *Cit.* I.L.O., *Lab. Condits. in S. R.*, 150–1.

[2] Cf. Trotsky in *Econ. Jizn*, 13.2.21 and 17.2.21, and in *Pravda*, 29.1.21; also Stalin in *Pravda*, 19.1.21, and Rudzutak, *Ibid.*, 30.1.21.

of showing " a dangerous digression from the class line toward ' adaptation,' " and by admitting bourgeois specialists to economic posts of " bringing decay into our Soviet institutions, breeding there an atmosphere altogether repugnant to the working class." " Who shall develop the creative powers in the sphere of economic reconstruction? " she asked. " Whether purely class organs directly connected by vital ties with the industries—that is, whether industrial unions shall do the work of reconstruction—or shall it be left to the Soviet machine which is separated from direct, vital industrial activity and is mixed in its composition? . . . Our Party leaders in a fit of distrust in the creative abilities of workers' collectives, are seeking salvation from the industrial chaos—where? In the hands of scions of the bourgeois-capitalist past-business-men and technicians, whose creative abilities in the sphere of industry are subject to the routine, habits and methods of the capitalist system." She called upon the Party to cease " the process of identifying itself with Soviet State institutions " which was causing its " clear-cut policy to be gradually transformed into an upper-class policy," to expel from the Party all non-proletarian elements that joined the Party in recent years, and to transfer the administration of industry to the trade unions.[1] The exponents of this doctrine formed themselves into a group which they styled the " Workers' Opposition," headed by Shliapnikov of the Metal Workers' Union and Madame Kollontai;[2] and even after the 10th Party Congress had taken its decision in favour of N E P the more uncompromising members among the group continued to agitate against the official policy and in favour of its own syndicalist scheme.

[1] Alexandra Kollontai, *Workers' Opposition in R.*; also Platform of Workers' Opposition in *Pravda*, 25.1.21; Kollontai's speech at 10th Congress in *Pravda*, 11.3.21, and Shliapnikov's speech in *Pravda*, 17.1.21.

[2] Kisiliev, Medvediev and Kutusov were also of this group. Shliapnikov had formerly been Commissar of Labour. Madame Kollontai had been Commissar for Social Welfare, and was subsequently Russian ambassador to Norway and then to Mexico.

Two other groups adopted a position which shares points of similarity with the " Workers' Opposition," while declining to go so far in committing the control of economic affairs entirely to mass organisations. Bukharin, who at this time still retained elements of his " Leftism " of 1918, having inclined towards Trotsky at the 8th Soviet Congress, now turned his efforts as a " buffer " towards the Workers' Opposition, and made the avowedly compromise proposal that democracy in industry should be restored to the extent of giving to the trade unions the right to nominate candidates for all economic administrative posts, and making the acceptance of these candidates obligatory on the State. Once appointed, however, these persons were to be subject to the control and orders of the State organs in the ordinary way; but in certain cases this strengthening of union participation in industry was to be carried " right down to the handing over to an individual union of the administration of a given sphere of economy on the basis of an obligatory program."[1] Ossinsky, however, turned from devising methods of compulsion for the peasant to be a champion of democracy, and together with Sapronov gathered some small popular support for what came to be termed the group of " democratic centralism." Ossinsky declared that most of the evils of the existing situation were due to the extreme centralisation of all decisions on policy in the hands of the Political Bureau of the Party and the Military Revolutionary Committee. As in other countries the real control of affairs had been concentrated in an inner " war cabinet," so in Russia control had in practice passed out of the democratically elected Committee of the Soviet Congress, and even out of the hands of the Council of People's Commissaries. This, he declared, was the reason for the divorce of the State apparatus from the masses, and for the sentiment among the latter that they were being governed by an alien body. The cure for the situation lay in restoring the normal working of the Soviet

[1] *Pravda*, 16.1.21. Bukharin was supported by Larin, Preobrajensky, Serebriakov, Sokolnikov and Madame Yakovleva.

Constitution and in lessening the influence of the Political Bureau of the Party on affairs. Of economic proposals he had little to contribute. Sapronov referred to the " bureaucratic deadness of the unions and their lack of contact with the local needs and the broad masses," and suggested that the right of nomination of candidates for Vesenha should rest with the Central Council of Trade Unions, while actual appointment should remain with the Central Executive Committee of the Soviet Congress.[1]

What is particularly noticeable about these " platforms " is that for the most part they failed to estimate the full significance of the existing situation and the issues which it raised. In so far as the discussion centred on the trade unions, it was, of course, dealing with the urgent matter of contact between the masses and the State and the need to repair that contact, and its very urgency gave this issue the place of honour in the discussion. But the disputants as a whole showed few signs of distinguishing this problem of contact from the issue of centralisation or decentralisation of administrative appointments in industry and centralisation of administrative competence or decisions. Moreover, there was such a distinct danger that the problem of the trade unions might obscure more general economic issues, that *Economicheskaia Jizn* on the eve of the Party Congress had to remind its readers that " the question of economic policy of the coming year, and not the trade unions, is the key question."[2] Most serious of all was the almost complete neglect of the problem of the peasantry. Trotsky, although in February 1920 he had already pointed out the harmful results of requisitioning, gave no indication in general that he regarded the peasants as anything but " backward " elements to be organised into Socialism. Kollontai lumped them together with the many hostile influences which were " perverting " the Soviet State. In general the disputants tended to regard the problem of the towns as the primary

[1] *Russian Economist*, Vol. I, No. 3, 601 ; also Farbman, *op. cit.*, 270 *seq.*

[2] *Econ. Jizn*, 8.3.21.

consideration, the solution of which by increasing the output of industry would *ipso facto* solve the difficulties with the village. Actually, however, the towns were at the moment paralysed by the crisis of supplies, and the problem of supplies depended on the peasants. Moreover, any discontent in the countryside soon spread its infection to the town workers and the army, who were frequently separated by no more than a year or two from the village, and sometimes by less—a connection which was very evident in the case of Kronstadt; and the relations of the State with the urban masses could hardly be settled apart from the *smytchka* between village and town.

Almost alone, Lenin, with his quite extraordinary capacity for grasping the essentials of a situation, saw the one course that it was possible at the moment to steer. And here again, as in 1917, it was not merely a case of different reading of the facts or different emphasis on different elements in the situation. Nor is it adequate to say, as Western writers are wont to say for lack of better understanding, that he was a clever opportunist who, seeing that one plan would not work, quickly dropped it and tried another. The significant difference was that he held an entirely new conception of the character of the problem and of the road to be travelled; and this conception many of his colleagues had not yet learned to understand. To him Socialism or Communism was not merely a formal structure, with its plan woven of one's subjective desires and then given shape in the human materials which were to hand. Communism was not a poem born of the cool night wind, nor was it a quest of the mythical land of Cathay. It was a realistic problem of the search for a new social equilibrium; and this, according to the Marxian analysis, consisted in the abolition of the conditions which produced a division into classes. The starting point—the *sine qua non* itself—was the seizure of power by the Party of the workers, and the dealing of a blow at class monopoly by the nationalisation of the banks and large industry. So long as the Party held these "key positions," it would in this degree have effected an "encirclement" of capital, and by having its hands on the main institutional factors could shape the course of social development in the direction of the classless state: with the new pilot at the helm the ship could start its career on the new course. But this did not mean that any ready-made Utopian plan of social organisation could be imposed at will. It did not absolve the Party from the need to manœuvre appropriately within its given social environment; and the particular forms of organisation which were adopted were not to be devised *a priori* from first principles, but were to be built consistently and in harmony with the basic relationship between the Party and its environment at the existing time. But this basic relationship would alter as the Party managed to modify the environment in the desired direction; and as it altered, the form of the society in adaptation to it would change too, until final equilibrium was reached in the classless society.

The environment within which the Communist Party at this time manœuvred was a predominantly peasant country, backward industrially and culturally, with the towns essentially dependent on the countryside. Hence an appropriate relationship had to be found with this environment, and the forms of economic organisation of the transitional stage had to be such as harmonised with this foundation. Later, when the Party by its hold on the reins of social development had modified this environment, the foundation and the superstructure would be altered as well. But to design the superstructure without regard to the foundation, or to deal with the problem of either in isolation, was a dangerous waste of time. The basic relationship at present which alone furnished temporary equilibrium was the *smytchka* between worker and peasant; and the form of organisation alone consistent with this foundation was what Lenin called State Capitalism—a system centring round a process of market exchange between Socialist industry in the towns and the backward individualist peasant economy of the countryside, the former necessarily having largely to adapt its own character to the requirements of the latter.[1] As a means of modifying this environment progressively, Lenin relied on two things: electrification and co-operation. The first of these would change the economic face of the country, village and town alike; while the second would tend to draw the peasant into closer community of interest with the workers of the town, and by bringing an ever wider range of the peasants' activities within the sphere of collective administration would gradually transform rural individualism into rural collectivism. Further, to achieve such a transformation of the economic basis of society, the economic problem—the problem of industrial production and organisation—had first of all to be solved. In view of the technical and cultural backwardness of Russia, this solution of the economic problem could not be reached without " learning from the capitalists " and also using them—using them as advisers, as experts and managers, even as independent *entrepreneurs* —anything so long as they were sufficiently harnessed to ensure that they should be used as servants, and had not opportunity to take the bit between their teeth and drive their own course!

Lenin, accordingly, opposed the Ossinsky platform, in so far as it aimed to weaken the hold of the Party over the course of events. To relax that hold would be like liquidating the general staff in the midst of an engagement: it would merely relax it in favour of bourgeois and petty-bourgeois influences which would deflect society from the desired course. By all means bring the Party in closer contact with the masses to

[1] Lenin stated at the 10th Congress: " The question of substituting a tax in kind for requisitioning is primarily a political one. Its essence lies in the relations between the workers and the peasants. The interests of these classes do not coincide: the small farmer does not desire what the worker is striving for. Nevertheless, only by coming to an agreement with the peasants can we save the socialist revolution. We must either satisfy the middle peasant economically and restore the free market, or else we shall be unable to maintain the power of the working class. . . . If certain Communists were inclined to think it possible in three years to transform the whole economic foundation, to change the very roots of agriculture, they were certainly dreamers; and we must confess to having a few such dreamers among us."

ensure that it adequately represented their interests and was leading them! But in so far as the Party represented the most conscious and enlightened sections of the workers its hegemony was essential to ensure that the general lines of policy followed the correct road. Moreover, the fact that the State had to manœuvre so skilfully in the environment of a backward peasant country made a clear central lead, infusing some uniformity into a heterogeneous State apparatus, particularly important. The syndicalist proposals, whether of the "workers' opposition" or of Bukharin, he attacked with special severity; since these would lead back to the disintegrating "elemental" tendencies which held sway in the early month of 1918, and were so detrimental to production; since they would elevate the influence of the more backward sections of the workers, who did not see the way clearly and could not see the whole for the part, over the more advanced; since they would tend to create in the workers of each factory a sectional, proprietorial sense, which harmonised ill with the social interest as a whole.[1] Trotsky's proposals, on the other hand, underestimated the importance of contact with, and democratic self-activity of, the rank and file. They would serve to separate the trade unions entirely from the masses and merge them in the State machine, and so to widen the gulf which was beginning to yawn dangerously between the masses and the State.

Lenin's own cure went direct to what he conceived to be the fundament of the problem: it aimed to re-establish the proper relationship between the State and its environment which had been rudely broken in June 1918 by the needs of civil war. This consisted in the re-establishment of the *smytchka* between peasant and worker, without which any progress at all in the towns was impossible. The method of "permanent revolution," or "kindling the class war" in the villages by military means would not achieve this—it

[1] Lenin declared: "Hitherto the chief in the controversy has been Trotsky. Now Bukharin has overtaken him"; and Bukharin's mistake is "an hundred times greater than all Trotsky's mistakes put together" (*Pravda*, 21.1.21).

would widen the breach and starve the towns. What was necessary was to restore and develop market exchange between the town and the village ; and this involved the abolition of the State grain monopoly and the substitution for requisitioning of an ordinary tax—a tax in kind.

This was the basic change—a re-establishment of the relationship broken in June 1918. From it many other important changes logically ensued, although they were not outlined by Lenin at the 10th Congress. With the abolition of State trade monopoly, the extreme administrative centralisation, which was the corollary of centralised supply, could be abolished. Separate industrial departments or groups of enterprises could furnish themselves with their supplies from the market and even arrange their own sales. The co-operatives need act no longer as mere agents for a State supplies department, but could operate independently. To facilitate such market dealings, a new lease of life for the monetary unit, and eventually its stabilisation, was implied, thereby affording a solution of the problem of a unit of account. These changes in turn suggested an important rôle for the trade unions. With administrative decentralisation in industry to State organs which manœuvred on the market on their own, it was particularly important for the trade unions to remain independent of the State as organs of the masses, even while retaining their close participation in administrative affairs ; thereby serving as a link between the masses and the State organs, educating the former and stimulating their initiative, curbing the latter from tendencies which would remove them from the masses and militate against the workers' interests.

The crucial phase of the discussion scarcely extended over more than three months ; and Lenin's proposals came to crown a discussion which had mainly dealt with narrower issues. Now, as in October 1917, it was a matter of urgency —of acting at once at risk of losing the conditions which rendered action possible at all. Lenin's proposals were adopted unanimously by the 10th Party Congress, despite the grumblings of the Workers' Opposition : in face of Kronstadt and the catastrophic shrinkage of peasant sowings, no less drastic change seemed adequate; and the two cornerstones of the New Economic Policy—the replacing of requisitioning by a tax in kind,[1] and the legalising of the free market for peasant produce—were forthwith laid. Perhaps if the full implications of this change of policy—changes in the organisation of industry to the system of financially independent organs operating freely on the market, the growth of private trade, the restoration of a stable monetary unit and credit system—had been fully realised at the time, concurrence in the change might have been less ready, and fondness for the methods of " war communism " might have stayed the innovator's hand.

Nevertheless the New Economic Policy was only new in so far as it represented a return to peace after three years of war. It was a return to the path which was being trodden in the spring of 1918. But the return to the path had a surer tread and less encumbrances. The chaotic, disintegrating elements of the " localism " of the early months were gone. A State machinery of administration was no longer entirely lacking. The bourgeois experts had for the most part ceased to " sabotage," and the personnel had improved. Much of the flexibility of decentralisation under the new trust system could, therefore, be achieved, while retaining the necessary cohesion, the necessary harmony between the parts in a designed policy by a centralisation of appointment and of general direction. The task of rebuilding still remained a gigantic one; but some of the litter and refuse left by the war period had been cleared away.

[1] The tax was to be assessed as a proportion of the produce, over and above the minimum required for the peasant's family, and graduated progressively against the rich peasant ; and it was directed that the amount of the tax should be adjusted to what was sufficient to supply the minimum needs of the army and essential national enterprises, such as fuel and transport. At first the tax was of a multiform and complicated character, taking a proportion of each different kind of produce. Later it was simplified into a single tax, assessed in money ; and after 1923 it was paid entirely in money and not in kind.

EXCURSUS TO CHAPTER FIVE: ON MONEY AND ECONOMIC ACCOUNTING

ECONOMIC accounting depends on the possibility of equating, say, a ton of feathers to a certain weight of lead, and then on reducing them both for accounting purposes to a common standard, or equivalent. Of course, one can arrive at any number of purely arbitrary equations between feathers and lead, and on this basis work out accounts which bear on the surface every appearance of adequacy: one could equate one ton of feathers, or ten or twenty tons, to one ton of lead, or ten tons of lead to one ton of feathers, according to one's whim. But such equations would have no objective basis in reality; and for economic accounting to have any meaning such equations must reflect something real and actual. The common unit to which one reduces both feathers and lead need not be anything which is used as a concrete medium of exchange: it may be simply an " x " or " y." But whether the unit be actual or imaginary, it will be serving the function of a measure or a " unit of account "; and the matter of predominant importance—more important than the character of the unit—is that the equating or " pricing " of commodities in terms of this unit should have an adequate objective basis.

In an ordinary competitive society based on the market such pricing is effected by the play of forces on the market itself, and accounting is accordingly based on this as an objective factor. At one end the pricing of finished goods is influenced by what consumers are willing to pay for the quantity of various goods available; and here the pricing of one commodity is affected by the buyer's choice and his power of substituting the purchase of one thing for the purchase of other things if he thinks he can get more satisfaction for his money that way. Hence, relative prices tend to express the relative scarcities of various goods—scarcity compared to consumers' money demand—whatever the reason may be determining the scarcity, or whatever the reason for consumers' preferences as shown in the amount they will pay for one thing as compared with another. At the other end is the pricing of all those essentials of production which enter into the formation of costs. Here, again, the competition of sellers of these essentials to get the most that they can by the sale, and the competition of buyers of them to get those essentials cheaply, brings it about that these things get priced according to their relative scarcities (as compared with the demand for them), whether they be fuel or raw material or supply of electrical power, a convenient land-site in the centre of a town, a form of technical ability or labour-power in general—again, whatever the varied causes of the differing scarcities may be. Moreover, the pricing of goods in this way acts as an automatic " rationing " : it cuts out lesser demands, and so equates the amount of demand *at that price* (for it will vary according as the price is high or low) to the available supply.[1] Reduce the price of taxicabs until they are virtually free, and one would never see one empty on the streets of London. Raise the price to 5/– a mile, and only a few of the richer or those in most urgent need would ever engage one.

It follows that on a free market the working of the economic system is governed by this pricing of things according to their economic scarcity. This governs what things are produced and in what relative proportions. There will be a tendency for those things which show the largest margin between their sale-price and their cost to be increased in supply, and for economic resources to be directed towards the production of those things, rather than of others which are more costly to produce and are less sought after by consumers. In practice this system fails to produce the most desirable arrangement of production, because money-demand is not synonymous with real need (because there are rich consumers and poor, and because demand can be influenced and " created " by

[1] G. Cassel, *Fundamental Thoughts in Economics*, 83 *seq.*

advertisement), and money-cost is not an adequate measure of real social cost: luxury cars will be built at a time when bread is scarce and poor persons are starving, and things will be produced at the high human cost of intense sweated labour to meet quite unimportant luxury wants which are not "worth the candle." Moreover, the equilibrium of the market periodically breaks down, and a crisis results, in the course of which maladjustment of economic resources occurs and consequent wastage. But it is to be noticed that these failures are due to the existence and results of specific conditions present in capitalist society rather than to the character of market exchange itself.

Nevertheless, it still remains true that there are certain objective quantities which should be represented in prices to provide the basis for an adequate social accounting. Indeed, it is only the existence of such quantities which provides a "plumb-line" for testing the imperfections of this or that particular system. The chief aspect of any economic planning must be the regulation of the relative *proportions* in which different things are produced, and, arising therefrom, the proportions in which economic resources are distributed between the various branches of production. It is the question of producing the right things in the right quantities, and of putting economic resources (machinery, materials, fuel, labour) in the right places. The principal factor in the social importance of the different things will be the extent to which they are *needed* by consumers, this being the basis of their social utility.[1] This is not always so easy to determine as appears at first glance. It is probably more important for

[1] Cf. Bukharin: "Our economics exist for the consumer, not the consumers for the economics. This is a point which must never be forgotten. The 'New Economics' differ from the old in taking as their standard the needs of the masses" (Report to 15th Conference of Moscow Dist. of C.P.S.U., Jan. 1927). The word "need" is used in the text in preference to "want," since a person may "want" a thing when it will not really add to his welfare (e.g. patent medicines). Of course, it may be disputed in specific cases how much a thing adds to welfare, and how far it is really a "need" as distinct from a "want" (cf. Pigou, *Econs. of Welfare*, 23 *seq.*; P. S. Florence, *Econs. and Human Behaviour*, 69 *seq.*).

people to have bread than boots, and more important to devote attention to producing the former rather than the latter, if scarcity of resources makes it a question of "either . . . or." When, however, everyone has one loaf of bread, it then may become more important for them to have a pair of boots rather than a second loaf of bread. And if in these circumstances so much of the available economic resources has been concentrated on the making of bread (in the form of skilled labour, milling-machinery, bakehouse, etc.) as to leave none available to turn to boot production, part of these resources will be wasted: they will be serving a less important want (the second loaf) instead of making the pair of boots which under the circumstances is the more important.

In certain standard commodities of mass consumption, for which the demand is fairly inelastic, it may not be very difficult to determine the order of importance of needs for various things, and hence not very difficult to distribute them on a ration system. But for things outside the main standard necessaries the position is more complicated, and it will usually be impossible to determine their relative importance except by the system of trial and error upon the market—selling them at certain prices and finding how much of the various things consumers buy. For instance, one could not estimate the relative importance of a book, a picture, a seat at the opera, a piece of furniture, a bottle of wine, a pair of gloves, etc., without definite observation of the facts of the market and the use of this as an *approximate* guide. Moreover, one could not secure a complete answer merely by enquiring how much of these things was being asked for in the shops, or by sending round a questionnaire; for, to the extent that the demand for these things is elastic, the quantity wanted will vary with the price: if the price were halved, the consumption of one thing might increase three times, of another four or five times; while, if they were given away free, certain things might be demanded in quantities a hundred times greater than the present available supply.

In addition to social needs, it is also necessary to take into account the social cost involved in producing different things, and it is clearly desirable that the pricing of the essentials of production should represent this social cost. If these essentials of production were sufficiently abundant to meet every use for them, there would be no problem of social cost in this sense, and no problem of pricing. It is because they are not abundant, but limited, that there arises the problem of applying them to the most important uses: the problem that if land or machinery or labour is applied to one use there is less of it available for other uses. Hence, one can say that, if one thing requires for its production twice as much of society's limited supply of economic resources (labour, materials, fuel, plant, etc.) as another, the former imposes on society twice the social cost of the latter, and its production should only be undertaken if it is twice as important. The scarcity of various economic resources, as compared with the productive uses for them, should be the fact on which the "pricing" of them should be based as constituent elements of "cost price."

In a socialist society where economic inequality has largely disappeared it would seem as though the *main* influences which make the system of pricing established by the market a false index would have disappeared. At any rate, the pricing of goods on the market according to their scarcity would afford *some* indication of the real needs and real social costs which any adequate economic accounting should measure. Even though such an indication were no more than approximate, it could be used as a basis, to be modified and corrected by such additional considerations as were available, and it would almost certainly be better than no indication at all. There would then be two sets of prices as a basis for economic accounting: on the one hand, selling prices, expressing the order of importance of various things in meeting social needs; on the other hand, cost prices, representing the burden or deprivation imposed on society by that production. A commodity which had a high importance in meeting needs while imposing a small cost to produce would be manufactured in preference to the commodity with a low selling-price and a high cost-price. The proportions in which essentials of production were allocated to different uses would be governed by the differences in the various cases between these two sets of prices. The *optimum* allocation of resources would be where this difference as a proportion of outlay was approximately equal everywhere;[1] since then, and only then, would there be no gain from shifting certain resources at the margin of one use and applying them to another use. Moreover, in order to plan ahead into the future, it would also be necessary to have some idea of the differing rates at which selling-prices of different things fell as the supply of them increased, reflecting different rates of satiety, or elasticity, of various wants; and on the other hand to know the differing rates at which the cost of different things increased or decreased as the production of them was extended. This implies the construction, on the one hand, of demand-curves for various articles, showing the amounts demanded at various prices, and on the other hand of supply curves showing the cost per unit at various scales of production.

To the extent that the market disappears this objective basis for economic accounting will disappear also. There will no longer be actual prices as established by the market to which to refer. The pricing, or equating, of commodities in terms of the unit of account will, accordingly, have to be done either arbitrarily (in which case it will have no meaning) or by guessing at the real social needs and costs which various commodities represent. Without the invention of some sound method of guessing these needs and costs, an adequate economic accounting, as the necessary basis for adequate economic planning and the utilisation of economic resources to their fullest advantage, would be impossible; and the practicability of a system of *Naturalwirtschaft* depends

[1] This does not necessarily imply that profit on *turnover* should be equal everywhere, since the *rate* of turnover tends to differ in different industries; but rather the profit on a given outlay of resources necessary to finance production.

either on such a system of pricing being invented, or on arrival at such a state of plenty that the problem does not arise.

This elimination of the market may come in various ways, partially or wholly. The abandonment of money and transition to barter will partly, but not entirely, have this result. There may still be a market for various barter transactions in which regular rates of exchange are established. But these markets are likely to be narrower and more local: what used to be one market will now tend to be sub-divided into several markets for specific barter transactions, in each of which different rates of exchange reign, having, perhaps, no very direct influence on one another. For instance, the purchase and sale of coal by various enterprises may still take a market form; but instead of forming one single market for sale of coal against money, it will tend to split up into numerous markets for separate transactions, in one case cloth being bartered against coal, in another iron, another leather goods, another food. In so far, however, as the elimination of money involves the direct rationing of consumers, this retail market completely disappears.

But to the extent that monopoly displaces competition, the market (in the sense in which we have used it[1]) will tend to disappear, even where money still remains enthroned. The monopoly may be of a capitalist trust or of the State. Price will then be partly determined by the arbitrary actions of the monopolist, and will to that extent give no expression of social need or social cost. If the monopolist is only on one side of the market, while competing sellers or buyers still exist on the other side, then the market will be only half eliminated. For instance, if the State or a capitalist firm as monopolist sells goods retail to the consumer, the prices it can charge will be partly dependent on the demand of consumers, the monopolist only being able to affect it permanently by altering the quantity he offers for sale. Hence, if the State as monopolist does not exercise its powers to restrict supply

[1] See above, p. 125.

and raise prices, relative prices of various things will still tend to reflect relative demands. But if there is a monopolist on both sides—a syndicate selling coal to a metallurgical syndicate—then the price becomes wholly dependent on the actions of the two or their respective bargaining powers.

Under " war communism " in Russia the market for a large number of commodities either disappeared or was considerably narrowed, partly by the demonetisation of the rouble and the transition to a barter system, partly by the monopolisation (not always enforced successfully) of trade in the hands of the State. For this reason the objective basis for equating commodities in terms of a unit of account disappeared; and in its place purely conventional values were assigned, which were purely fictitious and had no meaning. Hence any adequate economic accounting was rendered impossible; and economic planning, which depends on such accounting for its index, had to give place to the " shock " system.

The New Economic Policy partly restored the market, and restored the function of money as a medium of exchange. Though the market was " encircled " and " controlled " by the influence on it of semi-monopolist State organs, it retained sufficient elasticity to give market prices an objective reality, and make them an approximately adequate basis for economic accounting. On the one side was the retail market with the demand of consumers as a constituent element in governing price, and even with a certain degree of competition (at certain times a considerable degree) among various retail selling organs. On the other side was the market for raw produce with the peasant sellers in competition with one another, faced by State-buying organisations with a certain degree of (but not complete) monopoly power. The existence of these two markets at the two ends of the productive process provided objective price equations which enabled more adequate economic accounting to be undertaken; and this provided a basis for the economic planning of production and the allocation of resources which occupied such a prominent place in the economic policy of the State in the new period.

. . . . . .

There remains the final question: Should capital costs be calculated in economic accounting, or should only costs in human effort, or labour costs, be taken into account? Hitherto the problem has been treated as though all things which are scarce should be priced according to their scarcity and calculated as costs on this basis. This method would place "opportunity-cost" or "deprivation-cost"—the loss of alternative opportunities or uses involved in employing a scarce agent of production in a particular use—on a par with effort-cost. It may be urged against this method that the creation of capital does not involve a real cost that is at all comparable to the real cost involved in the expenditure of labour-power. True, the creation of capital goods requires an expenditure of labour some time in advance of the reaping of the fruits of such effort, as in the sowing of a crop; and for the period of this creation there is involved a lowering of consumption, or at least a refraining from immediate enjoyment of the full fruits of effort. Resources, for instance, are being devoted to building a railway or machinery for future usefulness instead of to producing food or clothing for the immediate present; and hence at the moment there is less of the latter than there might be.[1] And economists have tried to describe this fact from time to time by such terms as "abstinence" and "waiting," seeking to make such "sacrifice" commensurate with the "effort" involved in labour.[2] A social burden of some kind, certainly, is involved

[1] This, for instance, was the burden referred to by Rykov in the following passage: "For the construction of the Dnieprostroy (electrical scheme), the railway between Turkestan and Siberia, the Volga-Don canal . . . we shall have to spend some hundreds of millions of roubles. In our economic scheme for the next five years this outlay is a 'minus' as regards the achievement of immediate results: as long as the works mentioned are not completed the country will have no actual profit from them, (and) this, of course, imposes a considerable burden on the country" (Report to 4th Union Soviet Congress).

[2] Economists of the liberal school have endeavoured to maintain that this social cost is borne by the investor, who "abstains" from

in the creation of capital; but it seems to be of a distinct character from the social cost involved in the expenditure of human effort of brain or muscle. It would disappear if it were assumed that for society as a whole needs of the future and needs of the present had equal weight, while the nature of the burden (if it is psychological) alters with the expectedness or unexpectedness of what is " saved "; and it seems better placed in a separate category and accorded separate treatment. But though there is ground for the contention that the social cost involved in the accumulation of capital is not commensurate with effort-cost, this is not directly relevant to the purely accounting question of whether capital costs[1] should be calculated or not.

In a socialist society the problem becomes solely a technical question of accounting, to be settled according to accounting convenience, and no more. The charging of interest on capital here loses its wider class significance as a payment to a *rentier* class without the rendering of any equivalent effort-service in return. For instance, if the State Treasury or State Bank advances capital to industrial departments and charges interest, this payment of interest merely provides a fund with the Treasury or the Bank for State purposes or

consumption in order to accumulate capital instead. But against this contention Marx's caustic references to the " abstinence " of a Rothschild still remain valid—a validity unaltered by any verbal change from " abstinence " to " waiting." Only in a classless individualist society could this social cost be said to rest in the last analysis on the actual investor. In capitalist society it rests on those whose relatively low standard of life makes possible the large income of the capitalist class, and hence creates the possibility of capital accumulation by the capitalist class. The " abstinence " or " service " of the latter can only be said to be the creator of capital in the purely limited sense that the " abstinence " of the Pharaohs in lending their slaves for the purpose was the true creator of the pyramids. Those who try to use the statement in any more significant sense than this remind one of the rider of the donkey in the fable, who placed a sack of corn across his knees and maintained that it was he, not the donkey, who was carrying the sack.

[1] By this is meant a charge of interest as a price for the use of capital. Ordinary wear and tear of plant and buildings is, of course an ordinary cost, like the use of stocks of raw materials, to be covered by assignments to a depreciation fund and included in commodity prices.

for further provision of capital: it does not serve to swell the consumption of a *rentier* class, and so is not " at the expense " of, or does not represent " exploitation " of, the working section of the community.

The principal reason in favour of making such an interest charge (proportioned to the scarcity of capital) and including it as a cost in economic accounting is that it is a *convenient means of " rationing " capital*, so as to allocate it between the various uses for it in the *optimum* proportions and prevent wasteful use of it. If no interest were charged, the housing department might well put in a claim for an excessive amount of capital (*excessive*, i.e. in view of the important *alternative* demands for the limited capital resources) for installing electric cooking apparatus in all buildings, when there existed more important uses for capital in supplying electricity to agriculture and in developing railway termini and port facilities for shipping grain. If the capital were used for the former instead of the latter, it would be considerably less " productive " in satisfying social needs. If, however, an interest-charge were made, the housing department would have to calculate whether the advantage of new cooking apparatus were sufficiently important to " afford " the payment of the price; and if the interest-charge was proportioned to the scarcity of capital, the housing department would not be able to " afford " it unless capital were sufficient to satisfy first all more important uses for it. Capital would in this way be rationed by " cutting off " the less important, in favour of the more important, wants.

Against this may be set the consideration that the charging of interest, and the calculation of this in output policy, may *limit the intensive use of capital.* Mr. Hawtrey gives the instance of a hall or a road: it is desirable that the hall should be full and be used as constantly as possible throughout the week, and the road used as much as possible, since this involves no extra cost, and if used less intensively would lie idle and be wasted part of the time. In such a case, if full interest-charge is entered into the price, " a price must probably be fixed which will deter a certain number of people from using it." Similarly, "the royalties of an inventor or an author tend to diminish the use made of their work, while the payment does not represent any extra cost on each occasion when it is made."[1]

Where it is possible for the producer, instead of selling at a uniform price, to discriminate in his charges between different groups of consumers, no difficulty is here involved. By "charging what the traffic will bear," the proprietors of the hall might charge a high price for Saturday night while attracting users on "off nights" by charging a price which did little more than cover the "prime costs" of lighting, cleaning, attendance, etc. This discrimination, however, is only possible where the consumers constitute distinct groups, like the rich and poor patients of a doctor. Where it is not practicable to charge discriminating prices, either because of the presence of keen competition in the market where the higher price is charged, or because the essential conditions for successful discrimination are not present—for instance, the users of the Town Hall might have no preference as between different nights of the week, or the users of a bridge or a road might not fall into easily identifiable groups—then the problem arises in two ways. First, where the cost per unit decreases as the supply is enlarged, the amount of capital which it is "profitable" to apply to this use will be less than the social *optimum*: an electric power station sufficient to supply light to 15,000 buildings might not be profitable if a uniform price had to be charged, even though the *extra* cost involved in a station to supply 15,000 instead of only 10,000 was covered by the *extra* utility it yielded. As a result *too little capital* will tend to be invested in this use.[2] Second, when, owing to a miscalculation or any other reason, a larger

[1] R. G. Hawtrey, *The Economic Problem*, 233; cf. also J. Maurice Clark, *The Economics of Overhead Costs*, 23, 448.

[2] Prof. Pigou has expressed this by saying that under conditions of "increasing returns" or "decreasing cost" the curve of marginal supply prices will be below the supply curve (*Economics of Welfare*, App. III); cf. also D. H. Robertson in *Economic Journal*, March, 1924.

amount of capital has been invested than can be fully used at a price which will cover capital costs, part of this capital will lie idle if the attempt is made to fix a price which will cover the interest charge; and a wastage will be incurred through the idleness of the machinery, buildings, etc., in question. This may occur in a particular industry, or even in all industries simultaneously.

In the first of these two cases there will be a social loss because capital is not distributed in the *optimum* proportions: it will tend to hold back from certain uses where there would be a net social gain in its extension. The second case arises where capital has already been sunk in these uses *beyond* the point where it can be fully employed and still cover overhead costs; and here there will tend to be a short-period social loss through under-employment of that fixed capital. Economists have often been at some pains to show that even when this latter situation does arise no necessary wastage is involved, since it will be in the *entrepreneur's* interest to neglect overhead costs at the moment, and under the pressure of competition to lower his prices towards the level of "prime" or "direct" costs, so as to extend the utilisation of his fixed capital.[1] How far in practice this happens in a competitive society is difficult to say. There seems to be a fairly permanent state of over-capitalisation (*real*, not monetary), at least in certain industries;[2] while capitalist *entrepreneurs* will always govern their price policy by a *desire* to cover overhead costs if they can, and they seem fairly frequently to be restrained by fears of "spoiling the market," even where no tacit or formal agreements to restrict "cut-throat competition" exist.[3] In capitalist society, therefore, some waste due to under-utilisation of already existing capital

[1] Marshall, *Principles*, 374 *seq.* "Prime costs" involve labour, materials, and direct "wear and tear" of machinery.

[2] Partly owing to mistakes arising from the uncertainty of industrial forecasts, partly owing to imperfect divisibility of capital equipment, partly owing to "a definite tendency for the supply of productive capacity to exceed the average demand, being governed largely by the peak" (J. M. Clark, *op. cit.*, 465).

[3] Cf. A. C. Pigou, *Industrial Fluctuations*, 168 *seq.*

in this way occurs, and probably a quite considerable waste.

A socialist system would, on the one hand, probably have the advantage of being better able to employ the method of price-discrimination, in order to attain the *optimum* supply and *optimum* employment of capital in a particular use, than would be possible under a competitive régime.[1] On the other hand, where price-discrimination was not practicable, and where a larger amount of capital had been sunk than could be profitably utilised, the absence of competitive pressure might hold a greater danger of under-employment of the existing capital than in capitalist conditions, because the higher price and smaller output was preferred to the larger output marketed at a price which only just covered marginal "prime costs." To the extent that the producer was under the necessity of charging a price which would cover capital costs, he would tend to prefer the higher price to the lower, so that sales and output were restricted and part of the existing capital equipment was being under-utilised and wasted. *If* interest charges were never too high to allow all the existing capital to be profitably employed, if capital were always distributed in the right proportions (e.g. if the Town Hall were just large enough, and no more, to hold the people who wanted to use it at the price which covered interest on the capital), and if price-discrimination were possible, then the problem would not arise. But if only by reason of the uncertainty of all economic forecasts, the ideal allocation of capital cannot in practice be attained; and where it was not reached, the danger of waste from under-utilisation of existing capital might be even greater than the danger of waste involved in the fact that capital was in the wrong places. Provided that a means could be found of arranging the allocation of capital without the device of charging an interest-rate, there might be a definite advantage in conducting this allocation of capital outside the pricing

[1] Cf. Edgeworth, *Papers Relating to Political Economy*, Vol. I, 106–7.

system, so as not to include capital charges in economic accounting. Whether on balance this course would be the more desirable depends on the administrative question whether an adequate allocation of capital could, or could not, be achieved independently of the pricing system. No more dogmatic principle than this seems possible.

There is, however, an additional consideration which makes such a system more practicable than appears at first sight. Even though no interest charge were levied, industrial enterprises would still tend to show varying degrees of profit (or loss); and this would provide some *index* of the relative importance of different uses for capital. Each enterprise (unless it were restricting output like a private monopolist) would tend to extend its production and the use of its capital equipment up to the point where the marginal prime costs —the cost in materials and labour, etc., of producing further units of output—rose to the level of selling price and so made further extension undesirable. For instance, the traffic over a railroad would be extended until the increased terminal charges, the increased congestion, delays and danger of accidents at junctions, etc., made further extension of traffic unprofitable. In so far as this marginal cost—the extra cost involved in extra output—and hence selling price, was greater than average cost, a profit would accrue, and this would afford a presumption that an extension of capital equipment in this industry would be desirable.

Under the New Economic Policy in Russia the original capital assigned to the industrial trusts carried no interest charge, and accordingly no such charge entered into business accounting. The depreciation of such capital, however, was covered by an amortisation allowance which, by the terms of the trust's statutes, had to be covered out of current receipts. Such capital assignments as were made to industries out of the Budget likewise carried no interest charge; and their allocation between various industries was largely decided by the advice of the State Planning Commission (*Gosplan*) according to an estimate of the relative urgency of different demands for capital development. Similarly, funds accumulated in reserves out of profits by the trusts, and then capitalised, carried no interest charge into the accounts of the trusts. On the other hand, credits granted to industry by the banks, usually in the form of bill-discounting, and used by industry for purposes of circulating (or turnover) capital, were made at a certain rate of interest in the ordinary way. This had both the effect of limiting the demands for credit to the amount of resources available, and also of affording to industry and trade an incentive to accelerate their goods-turnover. But, in addition, the banks used the method of deliberate "rationing" of credit by discriminating between the bills offered for discount, and so exercised a partial influence at their own discretion on the allocation of circulating capital between alternative uses.

CHAPTER SIX

THE BEGINNING OF RECONSTRUCTION

A COUNTRY in an advanced stage of economic decline usually finds a chief cause of its weakness in an extreme shortage of circulating capital. What started as a symptom has become in turn an aggravation of the malady. In the body economic this adrenaline deficiency appears in the form of inadequate fuel and material supplies to keep industry in operation and inadequate means of subsistence available to keep workers in employment. The weakness may even be cumulative, the deficiency once started sapping the power to repair the deficiency in the future. To restore the patient's vitality requires a current supply of fuel and materials and food (including utilisable reserves held over from the past) sufficient and available to facilitate the production of the finished goods which are needed; and if this current supply be insufficient, there is required such an initial economy of consumption of finished goods as will set free resources to increase the output of the primary requisites of production. Presumably a decay of productive capacity must have some limit: at some point before it reaches zero and threatens complete starvation, people are likely to be stimulated to make the initial effort to restore the shortage of circulating capital. But to do this will require an initial increase of fuel and material supplies and available labour power—an increase of these things *in advance* of any increase of finished goods; and this will demand a further economy of consumption by some section of the community in the present, in order to advance subsistence to peasants and workers employed on producing materials and fuel, and later to workers engaged in working up those materials into the form of additional supplies of finished goods. The nearer to the zero point the decline has previously gone, the more difficult will it be to make this initial effort, and the less likely that this effort will be made on any scale sufficient to restore the system to normal health.

When, as usually occurs, the process of economic decline has been accompanied by currency inflation, the real acuteness of the situation does not tend to show itself until inflation has been stopped and stabilisation attempted. The reason for this is that inflation itself, so long as it proceeds, provides a means of supplying circulating capital to industry in the shape of the forced levy upon persons of fixed money income which inflation imposes.[1] Inflation acts as an instrument of compulsory accumulation: it imposes reduced present consumption on those persons on whom the levy falls, and so sets free resources for use as circulating capital. Business men, for whom selling prices rise more rapidly than their costs, can accumulate from the difference liquid funds for purchasing the requisites of production, and so create a demand for the continued production of these things. But as soon as inflation stops, this difference tends to disappear and probably to be replaced by its opposite—a deficiency of selling-price to cover costs; and a shrinkage of the scale of production accordingly sets in. At the same time persons no longer find their consumption restricted by the lag of their money income behind the rise of prices; and their consumption being restored to a higher level (unless incomes are forcibly kept down to a greater extent than productivity has fallen) tends to swallow up resources in providing for immediate needs, and so depletes the amount of free resources available for use as circulating capital to facilitate expanded production for the future.

In Russia in 1921 inflation had not as yet come to an end, and the currency was very far from being stabilised. But inflation had come to play a very minor rôle in supplying real funds to the State treasury, for the reason that the rôle of money as an exchange medium had been so considerably narrowed. The yield of currency emission was, accordingly,

[1] See above, pp. 90–3.

too small to give much relief to the general shortage of resources either with the State treasury or the State economic organs. The abandonment of requisitioning involved the surrender of the power to procure raw materials for industry and subsistence for industrial workers at the expense of the peasants. These things could now only be procured (apart from the agricultural tax) in exchange for the products of industry; and this involved for the immediate present a reduced supply of such industrial products to the towns. The production of fuel, at which the civil war had dealt a heavy blow, had fallen nearly, but not quite, as much as had that of industry on the average; but the amount available for industry after providing the minimum needs of transport had declined considerably more than industry in general; while heavy industry, largely employed in catering for the needs of transport and the rest of industry, was on a lower level than the lighter finishing trades. Certain stocks of fuel and materials still remained to be drawn upon; but they were seldom appropriately distributed, and were often not readily available for lack of proper inventories of stocks and by reason of transport difficulties. In many cases such stocks were almost exhausted; and where the productive process was at all complex the shortage of one requisite alone sufficed to suspend activity, even when other stocks were at hand.

During the civil war period the engineering factories had been living on reserves of pig-iron, and by the middle of 1920 these had dwindled to half a million poods. Engineering was only saved from complete stoppage by the discovery of considerable reserves in the Urals when this area passed back into the hands of the Soviet Government during that year.[1] Reserves of iron ore, however, amounted to some 100 million poods; and the difficulty of smelting consisted, not in lack of ore, but in scarcity of fuel. Stocks of copper were also estimated at some 40 million poods.[2] The reserves of

[1] Larin and Kritsmann, *op. cit.*, 65.

[2] Prof. Dolgov in *M. G. Comm.*, *Reconstruction Supplement*, 6.7.22, 218.

raw cotton in 1920 were actually quite large, being equivalent to about four months' pre-war supplies, and sufficient at the existing level of production for a year or so. But these reserves were almost entirely in Turkestan, whence they could not be moved for lack of rolling stock, even after the area had been cleared of bandits; while there was inadequate storage accommodation, and cotton-dressing factories were closed down for lack of fuel. At the beginning of 1920 there were only 350 thousand poods of these reserves at the factories, a figure which rose by about a million in the course of the next year as stocks were moved from Turkestan.[1] Flax and wool reserves were in a somewhat healthier position, amounting to about 5 and 4 million poods, or respectively 3 and 1½ times the amount collected during the first ten months of the year. Reserves of hides, on the other hand, were considerably lower.[2] The fuel crisis which grew so acute in the early months of 1921 reacted on transport and delayed the movement of grain and material supplies; and in the second quarter of 1921 cotton mills received no more than 7 per cent of their scheduled requirements of fuel, and linen factories only 44 per cent.[3] In August, 35 out of 56 woollen mills were idle, over a third of these for lack of fuel, 4 owing to shortage of food rations, and most of the remainder on orders from Glavtextile. Of 64 cotton factories 51 were idle; and the cement industry was producing only 1 per cent of pre-war output by reason of lack of fuel.[4] The fuel situation, in turn, was aggravated by the large migration of hewers away from the Donetz mines back to the villages in the summer of 1921, owing to the non-arrival of food supplies for rations in the mines;[5] and similar food shortage was responsible for a reduction in the output of Grozny oil. Labour generally was exhausted and demoralised by the underfeeding and strain of the hunger years; and the limit

[1] *Russian Economist*, Vol. I, No. 4, 1140–1.
[2] Kritsmann, *op. cit.*, 184–5.
[3] *Narodnoe Khosiaistvo Rossii*, 1921, 18.
[4] *Russian Economist*, Vol .2, No. 5, 1616.
[5] *Narodnoe Khosiaistvo*, 1921, 7, 12; Benediktov, *op. cit.*, 107.

beyond which additional effort no longer adds to total output had almost certainly been reached, if not already passed. Further, the shortage of skilled labour began to be acute. At the same time, the administrative system was in such disorder as to be incapable in many cases of planning the proper distribution and utilisation of fuel and materials, even where supplies of these were at hand.

Very few countries in such a plight are likely to find a means to break the vicious circle without resort to foreign aid. By means of short term credits and loans or more long period investments, circulating capital can be supplied to industry and the deficiency of fuel or food or materials repaired by imports from abroad. In this way Austria in 1922 drew back from the gates of death; and Germany in 1924, under the ægis of General Dawes, started her phenomenal recovery. Russia in 1921 was in worse plight than either of these; and since she had relied so considerably even in normal times on imports from abroad financed by foreign loans, reconstruction in her case appeared all the less conceivable in the absence of foreign aid. It was to secure such foreign capital that the policy of concessions was devised, and to mobilise internal reserves of capital in private hands that the policy of leasing small enterprises and of " mixed companies " was instituted. But under the circumstances no more than minor help could be expected in this way. Since Russia was surrounded by a hostile capitalist world, aid from outside, even in the form of short term credits, was not likely to be forthcoming with ease; and, as transpired, the conditions which the Government exacted and the hostility or shyness of foreign capitalists prevented the policy of concessions from securing on the average more than some 10 million roubles (gold) per annum in the first few years of the concessions policy. Ordinary business credits were virtually unobtainable until 1924, and then only in comparatively small quantities. Certain sums (amounting to about £21 million, gold) flowed in during 1921–2 in relief of the famine sufferers; but these were small as compared with the added results of that appalling disaster. Long-term loans were sought at Genoa, and then in London in 1923 and 1924; but the quest was in vain. A part of the now dwindled gold reserve could be shipped abroad to pay for imported goods; but this quickly reached its limit. These methods combined sufficed to permit an import surplus equivalent to about £20 million (gold) in 1921 and about £37 million in 1922, about three-fourths of which consisted of food. But that was all. And in 1923 and 1924 the requirements of currency and exchange stabilisation necessitated the rigorous reduction of imports again below the 1921 level, and the replacing of an import by an export surplus. How insignificant were these figures of external aid as compared with the magnitude of Russia's problem may be judged if we contrast them with an estimate made in 1922 of the sum required to reconstruct Russia's transport system alone. This estimate stated a figure of £75 million as the minimum expenditure necessary to restore the main lines of railway to working order; while £100 million would be required to restore the secondary lines and the principal seaports as well.[1] In main part, therefore, the means of reconstruction had in Russia's case to come, if they were forthcoming at all, from her own efforts and resources; and the process of reconstruction had to be correspondingly more painful and more slow.

It was necessary first to liquidate the fuel crisis, a step which by solving some of the transport difficulties would quicken the movement of stocks of raw materials and foodstuffs to the industrial towns. This, in turn, by prompting some recovery of output of essential manufactured goods to be placed upon the village market could induce the peasant to increase his sales of raw materials and grain, and ease the famine in the towns and in the stricken Volga region. All this required an initial effort, and an initial further "squeezing" of the consumption of certain sections of the population, in advance of any relief to the situation which

[1] *M. G. Comm., Reconstruction Suppl.*, 6.7.22, 224.

these measures might later afford: the seeds of revival which were sown would not sprout for several months; but the effort and parsimony had to be at once.

The immediate problem consisted in mobilising existing supplies of food and fuel and concentrating them on the strategic points; and this could not fail to be at the expense of cutting down supplies to persons and institutions that were for the moment of secondary importance. Railwaymen and Don miners had to be given preference in the allocation of food supplies over teachers and office workers, and even over workers in textile mills and leather factories. Fuel had to be supplied to the railways to quicken the movement of grain from the Urals, of coal from the Don, and of raw cotton from Turkestan, even though for lack of fuel this might mean the closing down of cotton mills in Moscow and Ivanovo Vosnesensk, and the reduction of output for the immediate present of yarn and finished cloth. Present needs had to give way to the urgency of restoring the productive resources required to meet the needs of the future.

The first task was to reduce the number of persons directly supplied by the State. The yield of the new agricultural tax was at first estimated at over 200 million poods; but as a result of the famine this estimate had to be reduced to 140 million poods, which was scarcely more than half what had been collected by requisitioning in the previous year. The reduction of State supply obligations had, accordingly, to be drastic. A beginning had been made by the leasing policy, which handed over to private owners and co-operatives most of the smaller enterprises that during 1920 had been swept into the net of the nationalised system. In numbers these leased enterprises were large; and for this reason the release of them from the purview of the State greatly eased the State administrative problem. In economic importance they were relatively insignificant. By September 1922 some 4000 enterprises had been leased (or more than were organised in State trusts at the end of 1922); but these had on the average no more than 18 workers per enterprise and covered in the aggregate no more than 5 per cent of industrial production.[1]

More important than the results of leasing was the economy effected within State industry itself. The State drastically reduced its obligations to supply the light industries with their food and material requirements, leaving them wholly or in part to procure these for themselves as best they could on the market; and at the end of 1921 only 150 enterprises, covering 140,000 workers, were left wholly dependent on supplies by the State;[2] while workers in enterprises partly covered by State supplies were reduced from 1·5 million in October 1921 to 1 million in February and to 400,000 in June 1922.[3] The result was to force numerous factories to close down or to reduce the number employed, and this was reflected in a lowering of the level of production of several of the light industries, such as wool, linen, hemp and paper, in 1921 as compared with 1920. Later, as the administrative reorganisation proceeded, there was a drastic economy of Government staffs. The numbers employed on the railways, which had previously reached an abnormally high figure, was reduced from 1,230,000 to 907,000 in the course of the year, and to 720,000 by autumn 1922.[4] In textiles the number of productive workers per 1000 spindles in operation was halved between 1920 and 1921–2, and the number of administrative workers was reduced to a third.[5] The Commission on the Reduction of Staffs under the chairmanship of Larin made proposals to reduce the employees of State departments by 50 per cent. As a result, in spite of the fact that migration of workers back to the village had reduced the number of industrial workers to less than half the pre-war figure, unemployment in Moscow and Petrograd began to increase considerably during 1921 and to continue

1 Kritsmann, *op. cit.*, 127–9; Rosenfeld, *op. cit.*, 211–12.

2 *Narod. Khos.*, 1921, 17.

3 I.L.O., *Organisation of Industry and Labour Conditions in S. R.*, 54–6.

4 *Narod. Khos.*, 1921, 6–7; S. Strumilin, *Na Khosiaistvennom Fronte*, 86.

5 L. K. in *Na Novikh Putiakh*, Vol. 3, 14.

its rise, until the total number of registered unemployed stood at half a million at the end of 1922; while the real wages of those employed, which in 1920 had risen a little over 1919, were slightly lower again for the average of 1921, and in the summer months, when the fuel crisis was at its height, fell to an appallingly low figure. In these months, indeed, real wages in Moscow were less than a half what they had been in December of the previous year. By the end of 1921 they had risen again with sudden steepness, only to fall once more in the early months of 1922. The average wage of this critical period did not suffice to give the minimum of subsistence for more than a few days in the month, and life was only sustained by petty thieving of property or peddling in the streets;[1] while the death-rate in that year reached the figure of 60 per thousand.

Meanwhile, to deal with the fuel crisis a persistent "drive" was made. Propaganda by printed and spoken word and poster rang out the call to turn from the military to the industrial front. The whole energies of the Party organisation and personnel were mobilised to this end. A new system of wage payments was introduced in September and October, under which in the essential industries still supplied by the State the wages fund paid to an enterprise was adjusted to its output relative to the minimum number of labour units required in the circumstances to produce a standard output; while a new scale of seventeen gradations of wages was introduced, which widened the differences of remuneration between skilled and unskilled.[2] The central fuel adminis-

[1] *Ibid.*, 7–8. Strumilin estimates that such additional income amounted to about 40 per cent of the wages received at this time. The practice had, indeed, been common throughout the civil war period.

[2] The ratio between highest and lowest was widened from 1 : 3 to 1 : 5. Categories 1–9 covered workers, 10–17 covered technical and administrative personnel. The ratio 1 : 3 existed between the 1st and 9th categories, and 3 : 5 between the 9th and the 17th. The payment at normal rates was made conditional on attaining a minimum of productivity in order to discourage absenteeism. The Sovnarcom decree of Sept. 16th declared that " equality of remuneration (in wage payments) must be abolished " while " issue of funds for wages must be made, not in accordance with the number of workmen engaged, but in accordance with the quantity of product turned out by the concern."

tration was subjected to drastic reorganisation. The Fuel Distribution Board (Glavtop), the Mining Council, and the separate Boards for oil and wood and coal were merged in a single organisation under a single head who was a member of the Presidium of Vesenha.[1] To deal with the "key" situation of the Donetz, a special Commission under Smilga was despatched by S T O to introduce a wholesale reorganisation of the mining industry in that area. The available supplies of food in State hands, the lack of which had been the chief cause of the summer migration of hewers, were largely concentrated on the Donetz, and distributed among the various mines on the new system of collective payment by results. A ruthless concentration of production and closing of the less efficient mines, proposed by the Smilga Commission and authorised by S T O, was also carried into effect. In place of the 920 mines under exploitation in January 1921, resources had been concentrated on 471 by the end of the year, and the remainder closed, with the result that the average number of workers per mine was nearly doubled. In particular, measures of reorganisation were introduced into the new State coal trust, Donugol, which was left with only 360 mines under its control, of which only 288 were to be put into immediate operation: a concentration which proceeded further until this figure was reduced to 202 in October of the next year and to 179 in October 1923.[2] Certain of the smaller "peasant" surface mines were leased out, and others were placed under the control of outside institutions, such as the Chemical Trust or certain State and municipal departments. The result was a sharp improvement in the Donetz situation in the final months of the year. The number of workers in the mines increased considerably in the fourth quarter, while at the same time output per hewer doubled and in November was four times the very low figure of July. The total coal output in the fourth quarter rose to 183 million poods, as against 130

[1] Benediktov, *op. cit.*, 96.
[2] *Ibid.*, 105, 107–8.

million in the relatively favourable first quarter, this leading to a considerable accumulation of pithead stocks.[1]

This improvement had an important reaction on the transport situation. The transport breakdown of the spring and summer had been mainly a matter of fuel, since the extreme acuteness of the railway situation of the previous year, due to disorganisation and shortage of rolling stock and locomotives, had by now been passed. Trotsky's military régime on the railways in 1920 had cleared up much of the prevailing disorganisation. Orders for a large number of new engines had been placed in Germany and Sweden; and the work of the railway repair shops was improved by the application of special "shock" methods to them. Much repair work to bridges and permanent way destroyed by the civil war was also effected. Djerjinsky had succeeded to the head of Narcomput in 1921, and carried out a severe reduction of staffs, and a decentralisation of administration by a grouping of the railways into regional administrations with fairly extensive powers of independent initiative, each line being placed in the hands of a line superintendent. Towards the end of 1921 the transport situation was somewhat eased. The number of railway pood-versts per month in the fourth quarter rose to 90,000 as against 35,000 at the beginning of the previous year; and the existing rolling stock began to be more intensively used.

However, at the same time as the fuel situation was showing improvement, conditions were placing greater demands on the transport system; and this prevented the movement of goods from showing an equivalent recovery. The occurrence of the famine in the Volga area not only required a large proportion of railway facilities to be devoted to bringing seed corn and famine relief to the stricken areas, but made it necessary for Moscow and the consuming region of the north-west to draw their supplies of grain from more distant areas across the Urals. In the spring of 1922 a considerable

[1] *Nar. Khos.*, 1921; Smilga in *Econ. Jizn*, 6.11.21; P. Bogdanov's Report to 9th Soviet Congress.

part of grain supplies had to be drawn from West Siberia and the Altai region, a railway haulage of 3000 versts: a transport problem which was accentuated by the dependence of these Siberian railways on fuel from mines some 1300 versts away. Consequently, each pood of foodstuffs arriving in Moscow in 1922 represented a larger proportion of transport costs than before; and transport facilities at the beginning of 1922 were not immediately adequate to move coal from the pithead as fast as stocks accumulated. The metallurgical industry continued at its amazingly low level, with an output of pig-iron less than 2 per cent of pre-war and with only a tenth of the blast furnaces in operation. Complaints continued to be heard of lack of fuel. We find the Yuzovsky and Petrovsky metal works in the south and the Yekaterinoslav works, which produced railway materials, having to limit their production for this reason. In the spring the Petrograd Leather Trust closed several of its factories owing to lack of materials and working capital.[1] The Donetz coal industry suffered its usual seasonal decline in the summer months, owing to the migration of hewers into the country, and food difficulties were again reported; although even so, output between July and August never fell below double that of the same months of the previous year, and in October improvement again took place, so that the total output of coal for 1922, standing at a third of the pre-war figure, showed a 27 per cent rise on 1920, with the average monthly output per hewer actually reaching 97 per cent of 1913. At the same time the movement of coal from the Donetz by the railways gradually improved. In June 1922 it was 26 million poods as compared with 10 million in February; and pithead stocks, which were 121 million in April, were reduced to 90 million in August, after which the movement of coal kept pace with the new production.[2]

By the autumn of 1922 the position was sufficiently eased for the textile trades, whose production had been restricted

[1] *Industrial and Labour Information*, 9.6.22.
[2] *Ibid.*, 1.9.22, 29.9.22, 8.12.22.

in 1921, to show a marked leap forward. The cotton industry in November began for the first time to report adequate supplies of fuel, and in December reported six month stocks of fuel in 38 per cent of the factories.[1] Cotton spinning increased three times over 1921, reaching 19 per cent of the pre-war level, and woollen and linen yarn rose to 27 and 36 per cent of 1913; while rubber and chemicals also showed improvement.[2] The more favourable harvest of 1922, yielding some 60 to 70 per cent of the normal pre-war amount, and the check to the shrinkage of peasant sowings lightened the food position of the towns sufficiently for real wages to show a marked advance in the course of the year: in Petrograd in October they were double that of the previous November; while in Moscow by December they had reached 76 per cent of the pre-war level.[3] The development of the finishing industries was now limited, not by fuel or transport, but by supplies of raw materials. The cotton industry had always relied for half its supplies on imports. These were for the moment unobtainable in any adequate quantities; and cotton cultivation in Turkestan during the civil war had shown the most catastrophic shrinkage of any agricultural produce, the acreage in 1921–2 being only 7 per cent of 1916 and the yield per acre less than half. The crop for 1922 was no more than eleven thousand tons, and the plans of the cotton committee for extending the yield, involving as they did the expenditure of capital on irrigation work, were not likely to show much result in the immediate future. In the meantime available stocks in Turkestan were being depleted. Flax and hemp had not suffered so severely; and the linen industry in January 1923 possessed as much as six months' supplies of flax.[4] But the cultivation of tobacco and sugar beet had suffered a reduction of crop in 1921 to less than 5 per cent of pre-war; while the supply of hides was deficient owing to the reduction of cattle and horses by 40 per cent.

[1] *Ibid.*, 16.3.23.
[2] P. Bogdanov in *Russkaia Promishlenost*, 1922, VI.
[3] *Ind. and Lab. Information*, 16.3.23, 13.7.23.
[4] *Economic Review*, 9.2.23.

Since a period of time had to intervene between any extended cultivation and the ensuing increased yield, the supply of these things was of necessity slower to recover than was the output of fuel or the activity of the light industries. By the middle of 1923 the deficiency of raw materials had spread even to the languishing metal industry; and the south was complaining of a famine of iron ore and Yugostal of a shortage of pig-iron.[1]

Nevertheless, by the end of 1922 the most serious phase of Russia's economic collapse had been passed, and the basis for recovery had been laid. For the first year since 1916 economic conditions had shown an unmistakable advance. Industrial activity had struggled some distance above its lowest point, where production had sunk to below 15 per cent of the pre-war level; and a definite revival of peasant agriculture had begun. To continue the upward process still required an immense effort, a faith and a determination, even a certain ruthlessness. But given such qualities, the stage had been set for the more rapid reconstruction and the currency stabilisation of the next eighteen months.

[1] Istomin and M. Ivanov in *Econ. Jizn*, 25.9.23.

CHAPTER SEVEN

THE NEW FORM OF INDUSTRIAL ORGANISATION

THE use of stocks already sorely depleted and the ruthless reduction of consumption already stringently narrowed by war requirements were not the only " reserves " upon which Russia at this time could draw. Perhaps of equal importance were the potentialities of the new forms of organisation which N E P had introduced or made possible. The revival of the market, the dissolution of Glavkism and its replacement by administrative decentralisation afforded considerable prospect of banishing some of the disorder of " war communism " and preparing the way for a more efficient utilisation of the resources which were already at the disposal of the State. There was a hope of lightening the burden on central economic organs and setting them free for calmer thought and more efficient planning of the tasks before them. There was hope that the process of unshackling industry would lessen the delays and the circumlocution, awaken the initiative of subordinate organs and give to the whole system a greater flexibility. There was hope that the restored free trading in grain and the abolition of the wartime restrictions on labour, together with the new rôle of the trade unions, might have the added psychological advantage of reviving confidence among the masses of the village and the town.

The crucial flaw in the Glavki system was the absence of any commercial competence on the part of industrial enterprises. All matters of supply and disposal of product had to be referred to the central Glavki, with a resulting accumulation of business at these narrow " bottle-necks." The keystone of the new form of organisation which replaced Glavkism was the formation of *Trusts*, or groups of enterprises, which were to have independent powers of operating on the market, both as purchasers of supplies and sellers of their produce, and to operate with their own capital. In the trust was created a unit of commercial competence, endowed with rights of initiative and of independent action except in the " named cases " reserved by Vesenha or covered by some regulation or decree. A division of function was established between what Russian writers call the function of " regulation," or of laying down the main lines of policy and intervening in specific cases only, and the function of " administration," or the executive task of carrying out a given policy and of taking decisions on all " unnamed cases " and on detailed matters arising in the day-to-day work.[1] Such a distinction loses any significance if the " regulative " functions encroach too greatly on the " administrative," and regulations become too voluminous and too careful of every detail; and under Glavkism the division disappeared on all commercial matters, " administrative " functions resting with the Glavki and competence being conceded to the enterprises only on internal " productive " matters. But under the new system as it developed the distinction was able to be a real one; and the central industrial departments of Vesenha undertook no more than those powers of general direction and control which the Centres at the beginning of their career had exercised in the early part of 1918. Indeed, in many ways the system marked a return to the period of the first eight months, with the difference that the bourgeois personnel was now more docile, the centripetal tendencies of that period had been largely eliminated, and industry was now more completely nationalised. In practice it achieved a fairly successful combination of administrative decentralisation with unity of general policy, and certainly it marks one of the most interesting types of organisation in recent economic history.

The trust, composed of a number of factories grouped

[1] The importance of this distinction was first explicitly emphasised at the 9th Party Congress at the beginning of 1920.

together according to some plan, consisted of a Board appointed by Vesenha (in consultation with the trade union concerned), which played the same administrative rôle as the Board of Directors of a private company, and conducted the affairs of the trust as a commercial unit. Each member of the Board had charge of a department of the trust; and the Board appointed the managers of the various factories, these managers having no competence, save in special cases, in commercial matters of buying and selling, but only as regards the internal administration of their works. Contracts of sale and purchase were freely made on the market by the trust; wages and working conditions were fixed by collective agreement with the trade union; production plans in the factories under the trust's control were arranged by the Board according to ordinary commercial principles, subject to the sanctioning by Vesenha of their annual program of production, and subject to the power of some superior organ for special reasons to fix a maximum price for their produce.

The Sovnarcom decree of April 10th, 1923, by which the legal status of the trusts was finally formulated, gave to the trusts legal personality as bodies capable of entering into independent contracts, not as owners of property, but as trustees of the State, endowed with terminable powers by the State in the form of a charter. This charter, by which the trust acquired its legal personality, had to be confirmed by Vesenha and reserved to Vesenha the right to determine the allocation of profit, to liquidate the trust for certain named reasons, and to terminate the appointment of members of the Board at the end of any year. The charter was to contain a valuation of the foundation capital, which was divided into two parts, fixed or basic capital, covering the plant, buildings, and immovable property generally, and the circulating, working, or turnover capital, covering stocks of goods, currency, and securities; and the former could not, while the latter could, be pledged as security for loans and attached for debt. A trust might issue bonds, but without power of binding the State thereby; and the State was not liable for any debts incurred by the trust, and had no obligation to make good any deficit on the year's working. As a check on the financial operations of the trust, Vesenha was to nominate an Audit Committee of three, one of them selected to represent the trade union of the industry, this committee being given power to inspect all accounts, books, and documents.[1] This Audit Committee was forbidden to interfere in the practical work of the trust, and had no power of overriding any decisions of the trust Directors; but it filled the very important rôle of keeping the superior organ informed by periodic reports and consultations of the work of the "Trustees," and, without narrowing the competence of the latter, made effective, as an organ of control after the fact, the supervision of policy by the former.

The trust, therefore, differed from the old Centres and Glavki in possessing no statutory powers to bind third persons: they "were not organs of State government, but organs of State economy,"[2] having such powers over other parties as they secured by contract, like any chartered body, and no more. It differed from the *kust* or group of enterprises under "war communism" in its financial and commercial independence. It differed from the "mixed company" or "concession" in having no private capital: in the event of its desiring such private participation, it had to be re-chartered as a "mixed company." Clauses 2 and 3 of the Decree safeguarded the commercial independence of the trust by excluding the right of any State institution to acquire any property or products of a trust save by contractual agreement, with the exception of an emergency, and then only by permission of S T O or Vesenha. On the other hand, a State preference clause (Clause 50) decreed that "in all buying and selling transactions the trust must give preference, whenever terms and conditions are equal, to State departments and co-operative associations." Clause 29

[1] Apparently this was usually a financial and not an efficiency audit; but the latter took place where the trust showed signs of insolvency.

[2] Rosenfeld, *op. cit.*, 251.

stated that "Vesenha does not interfere in the current administration and managerial work of the Board of the trust." Clause 44 provided for the establishment of an amortisation fund at a given percentage of the basic capital, which is now made a charge on the gross receipts before the declaration of net profits and enters into the costing calculation of the firm.[1] Of the profit, 20 per cent must be put to reserve until the reserve fund reaches a half of the chartered capital, when with the consent of Vesenha it may be capitalised. The remainder of the profit accrues to the Treasury, after the deduction of sums for bonuses to the Board and employees and for workers' welfare, in proportions which may be redetermined each year by Vesenha in consultation with the Finance Commissariat. Clause 47 made the trusts "liable to all forms of taxation, including income and property tax, on the same basis as private undertakings, except where otherwise established by law."

These trusts were rapidly formed and chartered in those industries which were freed from dependence on State supplies and from the collateral obligation to hand over their products to the State—in other words, as soon as financial independence was conceded. Prior to the autumn of 1921 the State still obliged enterprises to hand over a certain quantity of product in return for the supply to them of a definite fund of materials and fuel and food. Beyond that State quota of output they were free to operate on the market, provided that the amount subject to free disposal did not exceed 50 per cent of their output. This gave to the enterprises in question no more than partial financial independence: to at least 50 per cent they were still subject to State supply and obligatory State orders. But by the decree of October 27th a further step was made towards devolution of responsibility. Enterprises were divided thereby into two classes: those still dependent on State supplies, and those endowed with complete financial independence, free to procure their supplies on the market by sale of such

[1] *Ibid.*, 250.

stocks as they had, and free of obligation to hand over produce to the State. Fuel and metal were the principal industries which remained in the first category. By the further decree of February 6th, 1922, this first category was narrowed and confined to those enterprises "the products of which can only be used by the State and cannot be placed on the open market, or else undertakings delivering the greater part of their production to the State." In other words, it was confined to war industries, army supply establishments, certain municipal enterprises, locomotive factories, and certain metal works; and these were to be administered by special State organs, similar to the former Glavki, and conducted on similar lines to the English Post Office or government dockyards. At the same time a resolution of the 9th Soviet Congress decreed that "all State undertakings, whether supplied by the State or not, must be managed on a commercial basis."

It was to enterprises of the second category, which now embraced the main part of industry catering for the general consumer, that the new form of trust organisation was applied. By the end of 1921 the former fifty-nine Glavki had passed away and given place to sixteen new central boards, which were charged with planning and carrying out the new organisation and which then proceeded to curtail their own functions and became mere organs of general regulation and control as industrial sub-departments of Vesenha. The directors of enterprises and the local economic departments seized upon this new-found freedom eagerly, and rapidly began to federate enterprises locally into trusts. Some enterprises, in reaction against the former centralism, plunged off on the market rejoicing as independent units, and like guerilla warriors succeeded for several months in evading any "rounding up" under disciplined control. But this only applied to concerns which were fairly well placed in the matter of stocks: others which had no means with which to procure supplies on the market for continued production were forced to join their fortunes in a group, and to apply to the State, as a penniless son to a father, for a certain modicum of working capital to start them on their new career. Even so, it was found that in the haste to take advantage of the newly-won independence, federation into trusts was often effected on inconsistent and faulty principles. Frequently they clashed or overlapped; and there tended to be a plethora of small local trusts—" trustlets " as Rosenfeld dubs them—without particular *raison d'être* save the desire to be independent. Accordingly, in December 1922 a central Commission for the Revision of Trusts was set up; and this proceeded to co-ordinate their formation, and to reorganise some of those already formed.

The basis on which enterprises were federated into trusts varied considerably, and much flexibility was allowed according to the varying technical and market conditions of different branches of production. In many cases the trusts followed the line of the former *kusts*[1] (to which, indeed, the name " trust " had once or twice been somewhat loosely applied), although in their administrative character the two were entirely different. In the case of a homogeneous process of production conducted on a national scale for a national market, the whole branch of an industry might be combined in a single national trust, as with rubber and sugar. Where an industry was localised in several districts, each of which had special local peculiarities, the industry might be divided among several local trusts, each of which combined horizontally similar enterprises in that area. For instance, in the coal mining industry a large number of the Donetz mines (though by no means all) were combined in Donugol and those of the Moscow area in Moscugol; while Grozneft, Azneft, and Embaneft controlled oil boring and refining in the three oil districts, Grozny, Baku, and Emba. Sometimes these district trusts would be of a vertical character where successive processes were localised together in the district and subsidiary enterprises had grown up closely associated with the industry in question; as, for instance, Yugostal,

[1] See above, p. 103.

which embraced three of the largest engineering works of the south along with coal mines, coke ovens, and auxiliary undertakings, and Chemugol, which was based on a union of chemical works in the Ukraine with glass and coal and timber. Finally, there were a few trusts of national scope which were created on a vertical principle, even though the constituent enterprises were separated geographically, if the concerns in practice represented successive stages of a single process of production, and so as a group constituted a "balanced process." The flexible variety of principle on which this grouping was based is seen particularly in mining and textiles. Some mining enterprises, as has been mentioned, were linked vertically with manufacturing industries to which they were essential subsidiaries, while the remainder were federated horizontally in district trusts. The textile trusts were numerous and all of a local character, since the textile industry in Russia had always been grouped in several districts. These were in all cases vertical, since textile firms in Russia, unlike Lancashire and Yorkshire, had usually embraced both spinning and weaving and even finishing and dyeing. In wool the trusts were organised according to the various branches of the industry; for instance, the production of fine cloth in the Moscow, Petrograd, and Klintzovsky districts was grouped in a separate trust; similarly coarse cloth in Tambov, Penza, and Simbirsk; the long staple industry of Moscow district, and felt production in Yaroslav, Nijni-Novgorod, and Kazan. By the end of 1921 there were 8 wool trusts, covering 78 per cent of the yarn, 64 per cent of the coarse cloth, and 93 per cent of the finished goods production. In cotton the chief were the Moscovsky Trust, covering 7 Moscow factories with 340,000 spindles, 6700 looms, and 17 printing machines; the Orekhovo-Zuyevka, combining 8 factories with 535,000 spindles, and 11,000 looms; and the Bogorodsk of 10 mills with 690,000 spindles and 7700 looms. In a few cases local trusts embraced mills of different branches of textiles, as the largest of the cotton trusts, the Ivanovo-Voznesensk which, in addition to 29 cotton mills with 788,000 spindles and 19,000 looms, also comprised 6 linen mills in the district.[1]

The first of these trusts to be formed were in July 1921 the Northern Timber Trust, or *Severoles*, and a federation of linen factories in Kostroma and Muromsk, near the sources of raw material, covering 40 per cent of linen production from the purchase of flax up to finished piece-goods. The most intense period of trust-building was between December and the following March; and by the summer of 1922 there were 478 trusts chartered with Vesenha, federating 3561 enterprises with some million workers, or 75 per cent of the workers employed in nationalised industry. Some of these which were national in scale came directly under the control of Vesenha; while others which were purely local in character were handed over by " mandate " from Vesenha to the control of the provincial economic departments, the Gubsovnarhoz. Later, with the formation of the federal Union, there was created a triple classification into trusts of Union, of republic, and of local significance, the trusts in each category being subordinated respectively to the All-Union Vesenha, to the federation or republic Esenha, or to the local Gubsovnarhoz. The size of these trusts varied greatly, both in different industries, and according as they were national or local in scale. Of the total production of trusts, some 60 per cent came from all-Union trusts, and some 15 and 25 per cent respectively from those which came under republican or provincial control. The average number of workers covered by enterprises in national or regional trusts in 1922 was about 440, while in enterprises in purely local federations the figure was only 85. On the average each trust covered 2218 workers. But whereas over half of these were quite small trusts covering only 10 per cent of trustified industry and employing an average of 360 workers each, 62 per cent of the workers concerned were covered by 41 trusts, with an average of 12,500 workers per trust and

[1] Rosenfeld, *op. cit.*, 214 *seq.*; *The Russian Economist*, Vol. 2, No. 6, 2020–1.

over 900 in each constituent enterprise. These large trusts were principally to be found in textiles, metal and metallurgical, sugar, rubber, and wood. At the other end of the scale were 41 very small trusts, federating not more than 5 or 6 enterprises, each with only 10 to 20 workers.[1]

In similar manner the revival of the market under NEP was immediately followed by the restoration of financial and commercial independence to the co-operatives;[2] and by a General Agreement of May 25th, 1921, between Narcomprod and Centrosoyus, the latter was granted temporarily the sole right among State organs of trading in foodstuffs and raw materials. Narcomprod agreed to hand over to Centrosoyus all stocks of manufactured goods in its possession, which were to be used for purposes of direct barter against agricultural produce. These foodstuffs and raw materials, in return (less a certain commission), were to be supplied to Narcomprod for purposes of distribution to that part of industry which was still dependent on State supplies. But although " by this agreement the co-operative system became no longer a distributive agent of the State, but an independent contractor, as it were, negotiating on a footing of equality,"[3] the transactions of Centrosoyus were still bound by certain conditions. One of these was that all the barter-exchange which it conducted through its local organs should be carried out at a " fixed equivalent." This condition circumscribed very considerably the independence of local buyers to manœuvre on the market at their discretion, and imposed a wooden rigidity on the system which did not correspond to market conditions on the average, let alone to the widely varying conditions in different districts. Partly for this reason the system was a failure; and after seven months of the agreement (and those the harvest months) the co-operatives had fulfilled only 35 per cent of their program of purchases. Towards the second half of 1921 the prices of

[1] Rosenfeld, *op. cit.*, 216–20; *Russkaia Promishlenost*, 1922, X.
[2] By decree published in *Econ. Jizn*, 9.4.21.
[3] I.L.O., *Co-operative Movt. in S. R.*, 136.

agricultural goods on the market rose sharply, and the " fixed equivalent " established by Narcomprod undervalued grain and overvalued manufactures. Consequently, the co-operatives, bound to the " fixed equivalent," could find few customers, the peasants selling their grain instead to the private trader from whom they could obtain a better price. " The traders would barter a scythe for one pood of wheat, while the co-operatives asked two poods in accordance with their instructions."[1] A further, and in a sense more fundamental, cause of failure was the inability of Narcomprod to supply the co-operatives with the agreed quantities of industrial goods, and the consequent deficiency of a barter fund for the co-operatives to use in procuring grain and raw materials. The fact that scarcely 25 per cent of the required fund could be mustered is a particularly eloquent instance of that general absence of circulating capital which was the crucial feature of this period—a fact which was probably more responsible than *a priori* theory for the haste with which the State placed industries on an independent basis and cut them adrift from State supplies. At the time that these concessions were being made to industry, a new decree of October 26th, 1921, did the same for the co-operatives, terminating the May agreement and placing the co-operatives finally on a basis of commercial independence. Centrosoyus was no longer to be financed by the State, and its position of sole State purchaser from the village was abolished. Gone also were binding conditions such as the " fixed equivalent " ; and there remained merely the preference clause giving to the co-operatives preference in the wholesale contracts of Government departments and State trusts. Such funds of goods as the co-operatives already possessed, plus a small additional contribution from the State, were assigned to them as working capital, and with this they were now free to trade at their own discretion in the peasant market, on the one hand, and with State institutions on the other. At the same time the right of formation

[1] *Pravda*, No. 193, 1921, *cit.*, I.L.O., *op. cit.*, 142.

of agricultural co-operatives on a voluntary basis, and of co-operative organisations for peasant home industries was recognised, and legal sanction was given to the hiring of labour for auxiliary work by the industrial co-operatives up to one-fifth of their membership.[1]

This same shortage of resources available for use as working capital showed itself also in the extreme inadequacy of the funds which the trusts found at their disposal. When a trust was chartered, it was usual for the State to assign to it a certain fund as "turnover capital." In practice this usually amounted to little more than the stocks of materials and fuel and finished goods which the enterprises already had in their possession. The State, as we have seen, had very limited supplies itself, and what it had it wanted to concentrate on the fuel industry and transport and those metal works which were dealing with railway repairs. Funds of paper roubles were of little use with the existing narrow sphere of circulation of money. Commercial paper had as yet no currency. In theory, the trusts were supposed to supplement their turnover resources by bank credits; and the State Bank, which had lost its function during the moneyless period, was reopened on November 16th, 1921, as a necessary complement to the restoration of the market, and with the express aim of "aiding the development of industry, agriculture and trade by means of credit and other banking operations." But for several months it was not in a position to make more than trifling advances to industry. At its foundation the only capital assigned to the Bank by the Treasury was a fund of paper roubles amounting to about 50 million pre-war gold roubles, which "by the time the bank began business and the money was brought to its coffers was only worth about 14 million."[2] As a result of this shortage of resources, and also to guard itself against losses on credit operations through rouble depreciation, the

[1] I.L.O., *op. cit.*, 132–146; A. Orlov in *Russian Economist*, Vol. 2, 1935.

[2] Katzenellenbaum, *op. cit.*, 156.

Bank proceeded to charge rates of interest as high as 12 to 18 per cent per month, and later, while still keeping its rates fairly high, proceeded to base its loans on a gold standard, so that repayment had to be made by a sum of paper roubles equivalent to the given gold value.[1] This removed for industry the difference between what Professor Irving Fisher has called the "real" and the "nominal" rate of interest—a difference which would ordinarily have made credit-borrowing a profitable thing for industry. As a result, the rouble-credits advanced to industry, unless they were instantaneously converted into goods on the market, rapidly depreciated, but at the same time had to be repaid to the bank at their original, not the depreciated, value; and the losses from rouble depreciation were in this way shifted on to industry. Accordingly, even when the Bank's branch system had been developed—which was not for some months—the aid which the State Bank was able to give to industry was so small and on such onerous terms as to be insignificant in helping the trusts to overcome their difficulties.

It was natural that, with production at between a fifth and a quarter of the normal level, the proportion of the turnover resources to the fixed or basic capital of the trusts should have been very much less than pre-war. For Russian industry as a whole in 1911–12 the proportion of turnover resources of all kinds to basic capital was roughly in the proportion of 3 to 2. At the beginning of 1922 it was estimated at rather less than 1 to 2. These turnover resources consisted of 90 per cent of stocks of goods and of less than 1 per cent of currency and commercial paper, whereas the pre-war proportions had been respectively 41 and 11 per cent; while credit-borrowings of all kinds constituted less than 5 per cent of the turnover resources in 1922, as compared with 60 per cent in 1911 and 1912.[2] But even

[1] *Ibid.*, 157–8. Unless this had been done, of course, the real resources of the Bank would have dwindled to insignificance within a few weeks. Later, deposits were also credited to depositors in terms of gold.

[2] Barin in *Sozt. Khos.*, 1926, No. IV, 175–83.

for the lowered production of 1921–2 these resources were quite inadequate.[1] A contemporary estimate concludes that in place of 1000 million gold roubles of turnover resources necessary to finance the production program for 1921–2, industry as a whole (including those industries still supplied by the State) possessed on January 1922 no more than some 550 million roubles of resources. A special commission of Vesenha, making a more conservative calculation, stated that the deficiency of turnover resources amounted to 300 million roubles at very least;[2] and we may conclude that the newly formed trusts in the first year of their existence were faced with a deficiency of working capital of at least 25 or 30 per cent. As the year proceeded, the rise in the wages bill which the trusts had to pay, due to the rapid improvement in the wage-level in the course of 1922, and the delay in the payment for goods delivered to State departments were added embarrassments to their situation; so that in October 1922 industry actually had "less turnover capital than at the beginning of the year."[3]

Given favourable market conditions and an adequate commercial apparatus, the financial plight of the trusts would not have been so bad as it was. By realising existing stocks of finished goods in their possession they might have procured means to pay wages and purchase fresh supplies of materials and fuel, at least sufficient to keep production at a constant level, even if insufficient to raise it until materials

[1] A production of a quarter of the normal level involves turnover resources of considerably more than a quarter of the normal, since costs per unit will be greater for the small than for the large output. For instance, many of the fuel and staff expenses will be constant items of cost, independent of the output. The proportion of fuel used per unit of manufacture in 1922 was in cotton spinning nearly 3 times and in wool 2½ times that of pre-war; while even raw material costs were anything up to 30 per cent greater (Dolgov, *op. cit.*, 29). Apart from this, the number of workers in proportion to plant had been swollen as compared with pre-war: in textiles, for instance, there were 12·1 manual workers per 1000 spindles against 9·6 in 1913–14, while there were 14 workers of all kinds (including clerical) against 10·5 pre-war (L. K. in *Na Novikh Putyakh*, Vol. 3, 14).

[2] *Ibid.*, 14–16.

[3] P. Bogdanov, *op. cit.*, VI.

and fuel had grown cheaper or the market for finished goods improved. As it was, the trusts found themselves like small craft cut adrift in the ocean, isolated and helpless. Old-time commercial connections were broken, and no new ones had as yet been developed in their stead. All wholesale trading institutions, other than the co-operatives and the organs of Narcomprod, had been abolished during the period of " war communism." Centrosoyus, on which the new trusts were intended to rely for their wholesale transactions, was in similar plight to industry in having depleted resources with which to trade; while even the resources which it had were mainly industrial goods which had yet to be exchanged in the village for the agricultural produce of which industry stood in need. On the contrary to their being able to pay " cash down " to industry for goods received, either in currency or in materials and foodstuffs, the co-operatives, by the Decree of October 26th, 1921, were given the right to receive from the trusts goods to the amount of 10 million gold roubles on credit, to supplement their turnover resources. The co-operatives, accordingly, at the moment could lend the trusts little aid.

The only way in which the trusts could exploit their new commercial freedom was by hastily improvising a marketing apparatus of their own. Such an improvisation could not be very far-reaching or much more than primitive; and the result was what came to be known as the *rasbazarivania*—the " bazaar system " of marketing—of the end of 1921 and the early months of 1922. To secure the resources which they lacked for continuing production, the trusts opened small shops or set up stalls in the streets in the immediate locality of the factories, or employed itinerant pedlars to barter their products direct with the peasants in the village for materials and food. Sometimes they even paid wages in kind, leaving to the workers the task of reselling the products for food. Inability to reach a wide market with their products, and the need in their eagerness to sell to unload them in the local market, caused industry to sell out at a much lower figure than they would otherwise have done, often even at less than prime cost. In centres, such as Moscow, where several trusts opened shops in the same line, there was acute cut-throat competition which depressed selling prices still further and aggravated the financial position of the trusts. Much of this trade still had a barter form, which increased the complication of selling and narrowed the market of sale for a trust still further. The Sugar Trust, for instance, produced in 1921–2 over 3 million poods of sugar, of which a considerable part was bartered direct with the peasants for beet. Of the 740 thousand poods which were marketed 480 thousand were realised by direct goods exchange, most of the proceeds of which had in turn to be resold in another market because they were not what the trust required.[1] In the Donetz area certain trusts put on sale a number of their products, as for instance window glass in boxes and textile goods in the piece, but found the goods were unsaleable, until finally the Gubsovnarhoz opened a trading department to purchase the goods from the trusts and set up numerous booths where they could retail the goods to the peasants in much smaller units.[2] Another case, by no means exceptional, was that of the Glass and Pottery Board, which in the spring of 1922 was in process of reorganising the industry on a trust basis. The Board was still under obligation to supply part of its products to the State, which marketed them through Centrosoyus ; but since September it had received in return no supplies of raw materials. Lacking stocks and money it was unable to pay its workers ; and accordingly it applied to the State for permission to enlarge the proportion of its output which it could market itself. It then proceeded to establish its own undertakings for supplying clay and sand, and to negotiate with Centrosoyus a direct barter of its products against food. But Centrosoyus failed to supply more than 20 per cent of the agreed amount ; and the trust had finally to open numerous

[1] L. K. in *Na Novikh Putyakh*, Vol. 3, 20.
[2] Dolgov, *op. cit.*, 27–8.

shops in Moscow, putting in charge of them shop managers to whom it supplied goods on commission.[1] Often in such cases the goods would be bought up by the private trader and then resold in another area at a handsome profit. Bronsky, indeed, declares that the private trader at this period provided about 50 per cent of the market for the trusts' product in this way, thereby playing a not inconsiderable rôle in supplying some of the turnover resources which industry lacked.[2]

But the real cause of the plight of industry in the first three-quarters of 1922 went deeper. The central State departments, the co-operatives and the trusts were all alike, as we have seen, in lacking stocks of food and raw materials, and in depending for their continued existence on being able to market in the villages such industrial goods as they had, and procure agricultural produce in return. It was the old problem of the economic relation between the town and the village, which we saw as so important in 1916 and 1918 and which will recur continually until our final page; and this was the real fact that expressed itself financially in the deficiency of circulating capital, common to State, co-operative, and trust alike. As a result of the famine of 1921 the rate of exchange between manufactures and foodstuffs changed violently to the disadvantage of the town, the value of foodstuffs rising and that of industrial goods falling, until the extreme point of the movement was reached in April and May, 1922. One arshin of cotton piece-goods, which had exchanged in 1913 for 4·33 lb. (Russian) of rye flour, exchanged in May, 1922, for no more than 1·68; while a pair of boots which in 1913 had been worth 283 lb. of rye flour was worth in May no more than 133. Thus, a unit of industrial goods in the spring of 1922 could procure no more than 65 per cent of the pre-war equivalent of agricultural produce, and in some

[1] *Cit., Ind. and Lab. Information*, 26.5.22.
[2] *Sozt. Khos.*, 1926, No. V, 18–19.

cases less than half.[1] This it was that was responsible for the "sales crisis" of the spring which caused so much surprise and alarm to the leaders of industry, and prompted writers outside Russia to announce "the breakdown of NEP":[2] the paradoxical phenomenon appearing of industries unable to find buyers even though production was less than a quarter of pre-war, and even though currency inflation was still proceeding at a rapid rate. The reason of the paradox was that the high prices for agricultural goods did not spell increased, but rather decreased, incomes for the peasants on account of the famine; and while the surplus income which the urban worker had available to buy industrial produce had shrunk to insignificance on account of the increased amount he had to spend on food, the purchasing power of the village was at the same time diminished rather than expanded. The situation was not

[1] Rosenfeld, *op. cit.*, 428. The general index numbers of agricultural and industrial prices are given by Strumilin (*Na Khosiaistvennom Fronte*, 212) as follows:—

	Agricultural	Industrial
1913	100	100
Jan. 11, 1922	104	92
Feb. 1 ,,	105	90
March 1 ,,	109	82
April 1 ,,	111	77
May 1 ,,	113	74
June 1 ,,	106	89
July 1 ,,	104	92
Aug. 1 ,,	100·5	99
Sept. 1 ,,	94	112
Oct. 1 ,,	89	122
Feb. 1, 1923	92	138

Of course, the lowness of industrial prices in the spring was largely influenced by the unloading of stocks by the trusts and the cut-throat competition to which we have alluded. But this latter was itself in large part prompted by the fall of the market for industrial goods which had already begun at the end of 1921.

[2] e.g. M. V. Braikevitch in *Russian Economist*, Vol. III, No. 9, 3195: "The policy has broken down . . . Russia is bound very soon to discard her present communist oligarchy and establish a democratic capitalist regime." Miliukov, writing at this time, said: "This is the beginning of the end." "The end is near" (*Russia to-day and to-morrow*, 230, 295). "Russia is doomed to economic stagnation, local famines, and the actual dying out of the population of whole regions, and to terrible misery" (A. Orlov in *Russ. Economist*, Vol. III, No. 9, 3140).

due merely to monetary or financial causes: it consisted in the fundamental fact that the agricultural produce necessary to continued industrial production was scarce and limited; and no amount of unloading of industrial stocks upon the market could transcend those limits and procure at present for industry increased agricultural supplies. The "sales crisis" was an expression of a disproportion between agriculture and industry, under which the marketed surplus of the village was insufficient to supply the requisites of expanded production in the towns.[1]

The acuteness of the crisis first became apparent in March; and Lomov in *Economicheskaia Jizn* for March 30th stressed the extreme gravity of the position and advocated a contraction of production and the development of exportation of surplus stocks. The problem of the right course of action for Vesenha to pursue quickly became the subject of fevered speculation. In April and May Vesenha reduced the output program for certain spheres of industry—mainly the light finishing industries such as glass and porcelain, textiles, leather, chemicals, paper, salt, and some branches of engineering—and directed the trusts in those spheres to reduce production.[2] But there were many who argued that this curtailment was wrong, or at best only a temporary expedient; and a special report of the State Economic Planning Commission (Gosplan) expressed the conviction that the real solution lay, not in this, but in more liberal grants to industry from the State Budget to supplement the trusts' turnover resources, and in more prompt payment by State departments for purchases from the trusts.[3] But in the circumstances of the case the policy of curtailment of production seems to have been the correct one, for, since the essence of the situation was the scarcity of agricultural produce, affecting not merely the trusts, but all the activities

[1] In more general terms: the real demand of the village for industrial products had, on account of the famine, become smaller and for the moment very inelastic. See Excursus to Chapters Eight and Nine.

[2] Cf. *Russian Economist*, Vol. II, No. 6, 2021.

[3] *Ind. and Lab. Information*, 23.6.22.

of the towns, it was better to make industry "cut its coat according to its cloth." No amount of juggling with credit and financial grants would have surmounted this basic fact, and to have increased grants from the State to the trusts would have been merely to rob brother Peter to pay brother Paul. It would have placed more turnover resources at the disposal of the trusts merely at the expense of less resources in the hands of the central State departments; and since it was on the latter that transport and the fuel and metal industries still relied for their supplies, such robbing of brother Peter would have been suicide for brother Paul. It was clearly much better that the lighter finishing industries should suffer some contraction, in order that such resources as were available might be devoted to maintaining the activity of fuel and transport; and the policy that was actually adopted was probably responsible in part for the easing of the fuel situation which showed itself in the late summer, and which reacted so beneficially on the light industries towards the end of the year.

It was partly to avoid the "cut-throat competition" arising from this "sales crisis," and partly as a logical step beyond the improvised *rasbazarivania* methods of marketing that the trusts in the spring of 1922 began the formation of commercial syndicates. This formation of syndicates represented the first serious attempt to deal with the problem of a commercial apparatus under the new organisation; and it has particular interest as being the spontaneous creation of the trusts themselves. When formed, the syndicates were, of course, legally registered, and received the sanction of Vesenha for their commercial activities; but apart from this they were the product of independent initiative on the part of industry, not of a plan of organisation imposed by the State from above.

In constitution these syndicates were similar to any ordinary Syndicate or Cartel, being founded with a share capital subscribed by the various trusts which joined in their foundation, and being charged with such commercial functions on behalf of the member-bodies as these latter chose to give. The precise functions of the syndicates varied. In a few cases they were merely industrial bureaux partitioning the market among the trusts and agreeing upon minimum prices to avoid "cut-throat competition." In other cases they combined this with the function of purchasing-societies for material and fuel supplies. But in the majority of cases they were definite commercial organisations, purchasing supplies and marketing at least an agreed minimum proportion of the output of the constituent trusts; and in one or two instances they inherited much of the property and some of the apparatus and personnel of the old liquidated Glavki.[1] Only in two cases did a syndicate have a complete monopoly of the market in its product; namely, the Salt Syndicate and the Oil Syndicate, the latter uniting Azneft, Grozneft, and Embaneft, and being legally endowed with a monopoly position in the marketing of oil. In other cases there were usually a number of trusts and enterprises outside the syndicates, marketing their goods independently; and in some cases different syndicates themselves competed in certain lines. But while, like capitalist Cartels, these syndicates exercised considerable powers over the fixation of market price, there was one fundamental respect in which they differed from ordinary Cartels: the syndicate had no power to regulate industrial output by *quota* arrangements, since the fixing of the industrial programs of enterprises rested with Vesenha. Moreover, even in the matter of sale prices, the State had powers—and later regularly exercised them—to override the syndicates' prices with officially fixed maxima of its own.

The first syndicate to be formed was the Textile Syndicate, which was legally registered with Vesenha on February 28th, 1922. It had a capital of 20 million pre-war roubles, divided into 10,000 nominal shares which were allocated among the participating textile trusts or autonomous factories; and among the objects stated in its statute of incorporation were: " (*a*) the co-ordination of trade activity; (*b*) the unification of

[1] Rosenfeld, *op. cit.*, 230.

storage and purchases; (*c*) the co-ordination of financial activities, especially by organising credit for the members of the syndicate and by taking measures to facilitate the settlement of mutual accounts among the members of the syndicate." The governing body was a six-monthly delegate meeting of shareholders, which elected a Managing Board and a President. This meeting had authority over the admission of new members, and to fix the minimum proportion of their output which member firms must hand over to the syndicate for disposal; while the Board had control over all current business and the fixing of sale prices. Among those bodies eligible for membership of the syndicate were: "(1) All textile federations, autonomous enterprises, raw material societies, companies and committees, expressing the desire to enter the Syndicate at its establishment, or afterwards, on condition of submission to the Statute and of buying the necessary number of shares in conformity with the Statute. (2) Those joint stock companies and State undertakings which by the nature of their activities are connected with the textile industry and are accepted members by the delegate meeting of the Syndicate." Later the syndicate entered the foreign market in purchase of raw cotton and wool, establishing agencies in U.S.A. and Britain; and by 1924–5 it was composed of 50 shareholding members, covering 146 cotton, 86 woollen, 56 linen, 20 silk, 23 hemp and 11 hosiery mills with a total of 535 thousand workers, some 8 million spindles, and 240 thousand looms, and had 127 wholesale trading branches at home and abroad.[1]

In the metal industry there were, at the outset, three separate syndicates, the Yugometal of the southern area, the Uralmetal of the Ural area and the Agricultural Machinery Syndicate. These conducted sales on a commission basis, paying the trusts partly in cash, and partly in materials purchased and supplied to them in return. The agreement in the case of Uralmetal was for the constituent trusts to hand over to it 50 per cent of their output. But actual

[1] *The All-Union Textile Syndicate* (Vesenha, Moscow), 4 *seq.*, 11, 15.

practice varied, some trusts marketing as much as 100 per cent of their output through the syndicate and others failing even to deliver the agreed proportion.[1] Owing to the existence of vertical metal trusts, however, which were self-sufficient in materials and fuel and had their own marketing apparatus, and owing to the prevalence of work done to order of State departments, only about a half of the trusts in the metal industry were members of the syndicates, the remainder working to State order or doing their marketing independently outside. In the majority of the larger industries by the end of the year at least half of the trusts in the industry belonged to syndicates, and in nearly all cases more than half, and more often three-quarters, of the workers were in syndicated enterprises. By the end of 1922 there were 17 syndicates in existence, federating 176 trusts and covering 54 per cent of the total workers in trusts; while at the end of 1923, 189 out of 360 industrial trusts were syndicated, and nearly 80 per cent of the workers in State industry were in syndicated concerns.[2] About the only failure among the syndicates was apparently the Coal Syndicate, which laboured under special difficulties owing to the delay in payment by its chief customer, the railways. In a few months it found itself uncomfortably lodged between the opposing criticisms of the coal trusts and the coal consumers. Moscugol attacked it for failing to defend the interest of producers and as a " bad, dragging commission-office, of no use to anyone "; while the railway administration accused it of the rather natural sin of supplying outside consumers, who could pay " cash," in preference to the State. Accordingly, in the spring of 1923 the Syndicate was liquidated, and the various coal trusts proceeded to form trading organs of their own; Donugol organising a wide network of some 300 commission-agencies for the disposal of its coal.[3]

[1] Benediktov, *op. cit.*, 120 *seq.* In 1923 the three metal syndicates set up a common bureau. Finally, in 1925, after some discussion, a Congress of the metal industry agreed to reorganise in two syndicates, metallurgical and metal working.

[2] *Russkaia Promishlennost,* 1922, XII; *Narodnoe Khosiaistvo S.S.S.R.*, 1922–3, 136.

[3] Benediktov, *op. cit.*, 117–18.

Indeed, this initiative of industry, awakened by its new-found freedom, went even so far as to produce a certain tendency to a kind of new "syndicalism." At a Congress of Industrial Bureaux in July 1922 an influential body of opinion from the side of industry proposed the creation of a Council of Syndicates, to which the existing functions of Vesenha in controlling production programs, sales, finance, and economic legislation should be transferred; and Vesenha received some criticism as a "bureaucratic interference." To this sweeping proposal the State representatives, needless to say, did not agree; but they went sufficiently to meet the views of trusts and syndicates to institute regular joint congresses of representatives of industry and trade and representatives of Vesenha, to create a permanent advisory council, attached to Vesenha and representing trusts and syndicates, and further to reduce the regulative functions of Vesenha so as to give it in practice the status of a Commissariat for Industry and Trade.[1]

The controlling measures taken by Vesenha, and later the steadying influence of the syndicates on the market eased the situation of industry from May onwards. Prior to this the "cut-throat competition" of the *rasbazarivania* period had undoubtedly depressed the exchange value of industrial products farther than they would otherwise have gone purely by reason of the harvest; and meeting as it did an inelastic demand, the competition possibly decreased, and certainly did not increase, the values which the trusts were able to realise by the sales. Indeed, the extent to which this unloading of industrial stocks on the market influenced industrial prices, in addition to the effect of the famine in

[1] *Cit.*, *Ind. and Lab. Information*, 29.9.22. A report of a sub-commission of Gosplan about the same time had recommended (*a*) the creation of a Commissariat of Industry and Trade to combine all the controlling functions formerly in the hands of Vesenha, the Comm. of Foreign Trade, etc.; (*b*) to increase the independence of the trusts and syndicates so as to give them as much freedom as well-managed capitalist undertakings in respect to control of production; (*c*) to constitute S T O and its sub-commissions, such as Gosplan, the supreme co-ordinating and legislative body in the economic sphere.

making agricultural products dear, can be judged from the following fact. Professor Kondratiev has pointed out that it was usual for the inflationary rise of general prices to meet with a check between June and September owing to the expectation of the harvest and the accumulation of currency funds for grain purchase. This year this seasonal break in the price-index occurred two months earlier—in April[1]—presumably on account of the increased flow of industrial goods on to the market in the *rasbazarivania* period, this increased flow of goods countering the increased emissions of paper money. Accordingly, the slackening of this "cut-throat competition," as the syndicate apparatus developed and as the trusts' need of supplies, with diminished industrial programs, became less intense, was bound to ease the position of industry. Nevertheless, no real solution could come until the real resources which industry lacked were more plentiful; and the fundamental factor which brought improvement was the better harvest in the summer of the year. In the summer months the prices fixed by the syndicates still tended to be both lower than cost price and at the same time higher than the economic price at which the current production could be absorbed by the market. But by September the new harvest had lowered agricultural prices, relatively to industrial, so that for the first time in the year the relative exchange value of the former was less than pre-war. This prepared the way for the revival of production in the finishing industries which took place in the last quarter; and in spite of a steady increase of industrial output this relative cheapening of agricultural products continued, until at the close of the year the position of May had been more than reversed. The continuation of the process into 1923 constituted the famous "scissors" problem, and ushered in a completely new, and more advanced, stage of the reconstruction process.

[1] *Na Novikh Putyakh,* Vol. I, 7–8. Up to then, between October and May, general prices (on account of the failure of the harvest) had been rising particularly fast—considerably faster than the growth of currency emission.

CHAPTER EIGHT

THE "SCISSORS" CRISIS OF 1923

IN 1921–2 reconstruction had suffered from the very small volume of agricultural produce available for purchase on the market. The legacy of the war period in the shape of shrunken cultivation, both in area and intensiveness, aggravated by the failure of crops in the Volga region, fettered industry in its efforts toward recovery by starving it of the supplies of food and materials which it required. For the moment agriculture could not be wooed by the offer of more favourable terms of exchange by industry, however much the trusts might lower prices and unload their stocks; and the result was the crisis of circulating capital in the first half of 1922. But by the turn of 1923 the wooing had won some favour. The more favourable terms of trade had begun to evoke response in extended cultivation, and Nature, relenting, had yielded an improved harvest. So much, indeed, had the recovery of agriculture proceeded in the 12 months that its restoration by then had greatly exceeded that of industry. Industrial recovery had been retarded by the crisis of the spring of 1922; and even though the end of 1922 witnessed a progress that in the illusory form of percentages appeared phenomenal and 1923 continued steadily the upward trend, this recovery, depending on more complex factors, was appreciably slower than that of agriculture. Moreover, the trusts had ceased their hectic liquidation of stocks, and were even accumulating stocks again, so that the flow of goods on to the market was actually slower than the rate of output from the factory. Further, by the formation of syndicates industry had achieved some success in limiting competition between the trusts, and in improving the terms of exchange between itself and its customers. The result was that the rate of interchange

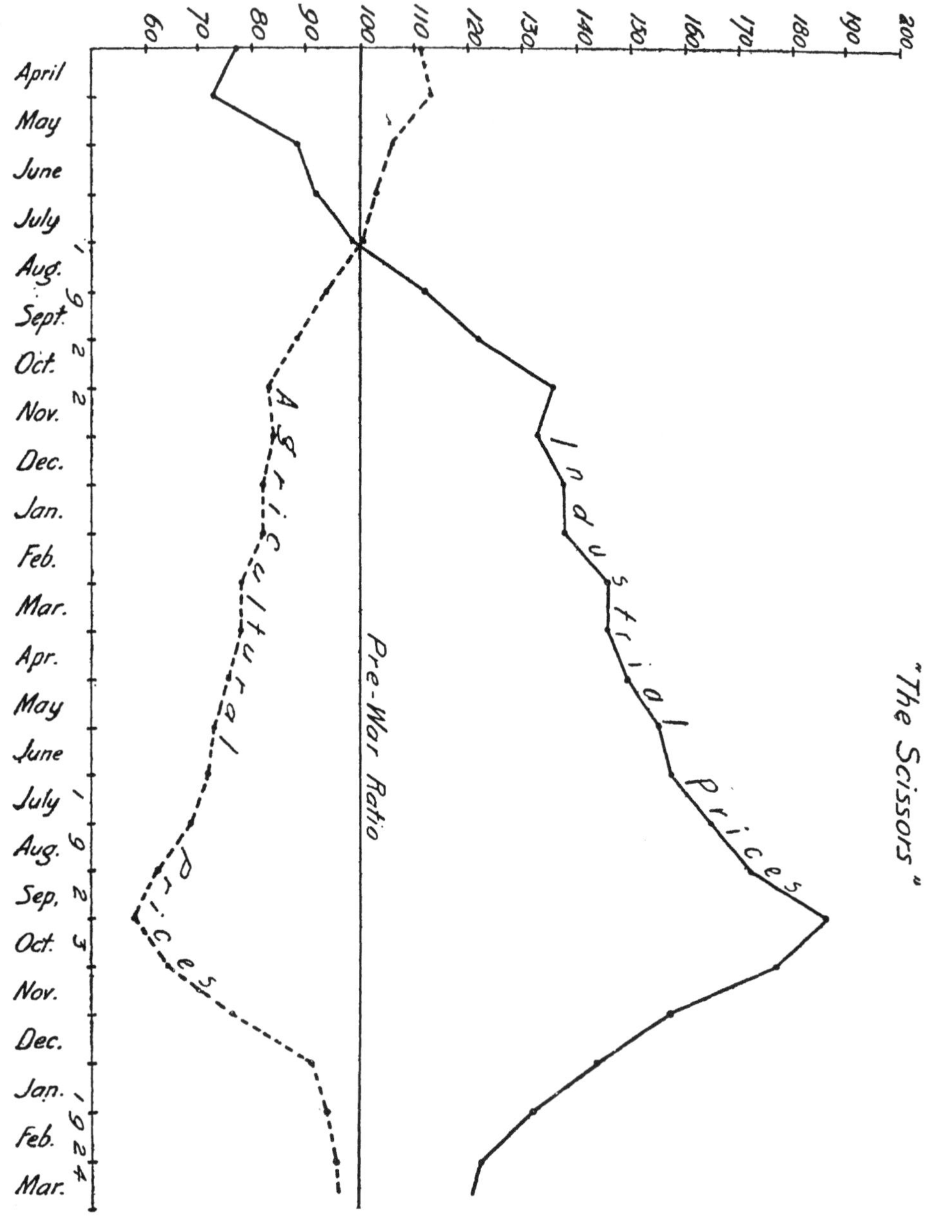

Diagram of the Relative Movements of the Retail Prices of Agricultural and Industrial Goods, according to Gosplan. General trend removed. 1913 ratio between agricultural and industrial prices=100. Based on figures in S. Strumilin's *Na Khosiaistvennom Fronte.*

between the products of the town and the village, which in the spring of 1922 had heavily favoured the latter, now changed in industry's favour, until in September 1923 it attained the surprising ratio of over 3 : 1.[1] It was this which constituted the great problem, the " scissors " crisis of 1923.

The recovery of industry had proceeded from a level of about a quarter of pre-war production at the beginning of 1922 to about a third at the beginning of 1923. According to official estimates, gross industrial production, which had stood at about 18 per cent of the pre-war level in 1920–1 (October 1st–September 30th), was raised to 27 per cent in the following year and to 35 per cent in 1922–3. In the fuel industry, which had shown a large advance in the previous year, the progress made in 1923 was proportionately small, coal and oil production advancing some 10 to 14 per cent over 1921–2. The metal industry showed the large percentage improvement of 70 per cent, but still remained at a level of some 10 to 12 per cent of pre-war. The finishing industries, however, profiting from the earlier progress in the fuel and transport situation, showed a more substantial growth than the average, chemicals and rubber attaining nearly half their pre-war level, linen some three-quarters, other textiles between 30 and 35 per cent and the paper industry over 40 per cent.[2] On the other hand, the area sown with grain in 1923 had recovered to about 80 per cent of the area of 1916 (for U.S.S.R. as a whole) and the gross yield

[1] i.e. compared to a 1:1 ratio pre-war. Cf. Strumilin, *op. cit.*, 220 *seq.*; Rosenfeld, *op. cit.*, 431 *seq.*

[2] Cf. Groman in *Narod. Khos.*, 1922–3, XII–XIII. The figures given by Groman are as follows :—

	No. of Workers.		Gross Production.		Output per Worker.
	in th.	%	in m. roubles (pre-war)	%	%
1913	2599	100	5621	100	100
1920–1	1480	57	994	18	32
1921–2	1243	48	1493	27	55
1922–3	1452	56	1949	35	62

The figure of production for 1913 is an estimate only, and subject to a margin of error.

of grain to over 70 per cent of 1916.[1] The quantity of agricultural produce placed upon the market, since it represented a surplus over peasant home-consumption, had not recovered as greatly as the total yield. In pre-war days this marketable surplus, according to the estimate of Professor Prokopovitch, had amounted to about 32 per cent of the gross agricultural yield. In 1923 it scarcely reached a quarter of the total yield; and in quantity it amounted to nearly 60 per cent of the pre-war figure.[2] Compared with the pre-war proportions, therefore, agricultural produce on the market was some 70 per cent more plentiful than were industrial goods. Strumilin, on a rough estimate of effort-cost, concluded that each unit of industrial produce represented an 80 per cent greater cost than a unit of agricultural produce, when compared with pre-war.[3]

Some increase, accordingly, of industrial prices over agricultural was to be expected from the fact that industry in its recovery lagged behind agriculture. It is possible that this fact warranted as much as a 2 : 1 change in the terms of trade between town and village—that is, a rise in industrial values until each unit of manufactures was worth twice as many units of agricultural produce as pre-war. But a 2 : 1 change was almost certainly the maximum change that could be attributed to this cause; while probably this factor was responsible for no more than a considerably smaller rise. The much greater widening of the "scissors" which took place in the summer of 1923 cannot, therefore, be attributed to the disproportion between industrial and agricultural development. This disproportion, while it constituted an important cause, was probably not the main cause; and the principal explanation of the "scissors"—at any rate for the full extent of their widening—must be sought elsewhere.

The unravelling of the "scissors" phenomenon was for

[1] *Abrégé des Données Statistiques de U.R.S.S.* (Admin. Cent. Stat. U.R.S.S., 1924), 54–69.

[2] *Khosiaistvennie Itogy, 1922–3*, 8–12.

[3] Strumilin, *op. cit.*, 209.

some time retarded by the overshadowing problem of the rapid rise of the *general* price-level in the course of the year; and discussion of the latter tended continually to take precedence and to obscure the discussion of the former. Rapid increase in the price-level through rouble depreciation had now, of course, become a commonplace of ten years' standing. But in the last two years it had happened that the rate of depreciation of the paper rouble relatively to the rate of emission had actually slowed down; and with an increase both in the total goods turnover and in that part of the turnover exchanged against money, the total real value of the currency circulation had increased. Further, in the course of 1922 the first steps had been taken in the direction of budgetary stabilisation—a process continued and strengthened in 1923—by an increase in the revenue from taxation and a decreased reliance by the Treasury on the yield of currency emission. In order to provide a stable unit of account, even while revenue was still being secured by paper rouble inflation, a Sovnarcom decree of October 11th, 1922, had authorised the State Bank to issue bank-notes in a new denomination, called the *Chervonetz*, which were made legally equal to the gold content of the pre-war 10 rouble coin (though not immediately convertible into gold), had to possess a minimum "cover" of 25 per cent in precious metals or stable foreign valuta, but were endowed with no fixed relation to the depreciated paper rouble. The issue of the new chervontsi began at the end of 1922, and made 1923 notable in monetary history for the highly interesting example of the circulation of two unrated paper currencies, the one limited and prized for its hoarding-use as a means of holding values in stable form, the other still subject to inflation and continually depreciating, but still assured a range of currency by the fact that the chervonetz was only issued in large units, and paper roubles were still required as a means of payment for small change.[1]

The fact which attracted discussion in 1923 was that

[1] Cf. Yurovsky, *op. cit.*, 86 *seq.*; Katzenellenbaum, *op. cit.*, 101 *seq.*

not only did the rate of depreciation of the paper rouble proceed at a greatly accelerated speed in the course of the year; but the purchasing power of the chervonetz itself began to depreciate. The aggregate real value of the rouble currency in circulation, which had risen to 95 million pre-war roubles in January 1923, rapidly fell to 76 million in July and to 34 million in October; while the rise in prices in terms of paper roubles rapidly increased from 23 per cent per month in the first quarter of the year until it reached 104 per cent per month during the last three months of the year. Once again the rouble depreciation was proceeding progressively faster than the rate of emission, and the possibility of Government revenue by inflation was being rapidly narrowed. Moreover, the chervonetz, which at the beginning of the year had exceeded the pre-war purchasing power of 10 roubles gold,[1] itself depreciated until by October it had lost more than 25 per cent of its January value.[2] Once disentangled, the causes of this phenomenon are not very obscure; but it was not unnatural that at the time the phenomenon should have come as a surprise and that its explanation should have seemed complex. At any rate, it became the principal subject of discussion of the late summer and autumn; and almost daily for several weeks the *Economicheskaia Jizn* invited the opinion of some economist or financial expert or some leader in the commercial and industrial world.

In the analysis of the problem various distinct tendencies showed themselves—tendencies of interpretation which later

[1] It acquired a premium which may be said to have been roughly equivalent to the saving of depreciation losses which the holding of chervontsi afforded—a special value created by the special demand for it as an investment or hoarding medium superior to the paper rouble.

[2] According to the Gosplan Wholesale Index Number its purchasing power on Jan. 1 represented 11·08 pre-war gold roubles, by Oct. 1 only 7·47. The latter, of course, was no lower than the *existing* value of the gold in 10 pre-war roubles (owing to the fall in the world value of gold). But, in terms of retail prices, its purchasing power was nearly 20 per cent lower than this (owing to the widening gap between wholesale and retail prices since pre-war). At the same time the foreign exchange value of the chervonetz was actually appreciating (cf. Yurovsky, *op. cit.*, 94–6).

gave rise to differences in the choice of a solution. Not until later in the discussion did the specific problem of the "scissors" secure considerable attention; and even when *Economicheskaia Jizn* indicated the significance of this specific problem by running a symposium under the title of "Why Industrial Prices are Rising," many of the contributors to the discussion failed to disentangle this specific issue from the more general monetary question.

One trend of opinion, represented principally by Professor Falkner, assigned chief importance to monetary factors as causes of the price phenomena of 1923. He pointed out that in previous years the inflationary rise of prices had always shown a slower pace in the second quarter of the year, which even tended to become an actual fall in the third quarter. The reason for this was a seasonal influence in the shape of the accumulation of money-funds in the spring and early summer for purposes of grain purchases and the increased flow of goods on to the market consequent on the realisation of the harvest. This year, however, no such seasonal break in the rise of prices had taken place. On the contrary, the rise, which had been comparatively slow in the first quarter of the year, started its sharp upward turn in April and continued its career at an accelerating speed. This peculiar feature of 1923 was not to be explained by any seasonal influence: a change in the harvest was quite inadequate to account for the phenomenon; and the difference between this year and previous ones must lie in a change in the conditions of currency emission. "When we have to deal with a rise, not in units, but tens of percentages in the course of a short period, provided there have been no catastrophic phenomena in the industrial process itself, then *a priori* the explanation of this phenomenon by material causes on the side of production and of commodities cannot be regarded as satisfactory"; and in support of his statement that "we have to come to the conclusion that the decisive cause is to be found on the side of money," he adduced figures to show the parallelism of rising prices and increased currency emission. By July the quantity of chervonetz and paper roubles in circulation had increased seven times over January and wholesale prices six times. By October they had increased by 52 and by 34 times respectively.[1] This inflation had mainly taken place in the course of a liberal financing of trade and industry, in order to supplement inadequate turnover capital, and this had exerted its principal influence on the prices of industrial goods.[2] Among others, Tamarin of the Salt Syndicate also supported this view, declaring that the State Bank had directed its policy, not to adapting the supply of bank-notes to prices, but to adapting bank-notes to foreign currency; while it had supplied Moscow and the central area too liberally with chervontsi issues, to the neglect of the villages.[3]

This emphasis on the influence of currency inflation certainly served as an adequate explanation of the main part of the rapid rise in prices in 1923 in terms of paper roubles. But it hardly sufficed to explain the rise of prices in terms of chervontsi as well, still less to explain the " scissors " rise of industrial prices at a more rapid rate than agricultural. The direct influence of the chervonetz issues was transferred almost entirely to the paper rouble, causing a depreciation of the latter by displacing it and narrowing its sphere of circulation. Since the chervonetz now provided a new investment or hoarding medium, it exerted the additional influence on the paper rouble of depriving it of any function except that of a medium of exchange, and so caused any existing rouble holdings or balances to be disposed of rapidly, and paper roubles to be held in future only for the brief

[1] How chervontsi and paper roubles are equated for the purpose of this estimate is not stated. Paper roubles alone had increased by July five times and by October only twelve times over January. The reason for the very much higher *percentage* increase of chervontsi was that in January the issue had only just begun, and the amount in circulation was relatively insignificant.

[2] *Econ. Jizn*, 1923, 179, 181, 182; also *Sozt. Khos.*, Nov.-Dec. 1923, 33–52.

[3] *Econ. Jizn*, 15.9.23. Groman in *Narod. Khos.* 1922–3, refers to the abnormal rise of prices in June and July, " in which is revealed the effect of credit inflation " (XXXVIII).

interval of time necessary to effect an exchange transaction. "An industrial or trading concern which had received payment in Soviet money tokens (paper roubles), anxious to avoid the losses consequent upon their depreciation, would hasten to buy chervontsi even at the higher rate likely to rule on the morrow, rather than keep the money tokens in the safe overnight."[1] This was the factor which accounted for the enhanced rate of depreciation of the paper rouble after April; but its effect on the chervonetz was to raise rather than to lower its value. Possibly by the summer chervontsi had been issued in sufficient quantities to satiate the investment-demand or hoarding-demand for stable currency; and in so far as this was so, one might have expected the special premium placed upon it in the early months of the year to have disappeared. By August chervontsi constituted a half of the real money values in circulation, and in that month there actually developed a small change famine and a certain tendency to sell chervontsi holdings and buy paper roubles. This may have signified that the range of circulation of the new currency unit was limited (owing to its large denominations), and that this range was not extending as rapidly as was the supply of chervontsi. But this hypothesis does not seem to be very adequately supported. The new unit was only just beginning to penetrate into the countryside, and demand for it was still expanding steadily. In June and July there certainly were signs of too rapid issue owing to over-crediting of industry, but this was quickly checked in the following months; and the issue, even so, was rapid only relatively to a goods turnover which had unexpectedly declined.[2] On the whole,

[1] Yurovsky, *op. cit.*, 114. The introduction of the chervonetz had the same effect on the old paper rouble as the adoption of foreign currencies as investment media in other countries which caused the "flight from the krone," from the mark, etc. In terms of the formula cited on p. 93, it caused K to dwindle almost to zero in the case of the paper rouble, while in the case of the chervonetz K stood at a correspondingly high figure.

[2] Cf. Kondratiev in *Econ. Jizn*, 26.9.23, and Scheinmann, *Ibid.*, 9.9.23.

the issue of the new bank-notes had not been incautious; and it would seem unreasonable to attribute more than a small part of the chervonetz depreciation to an excessive rate of issue.

The rival interpretation placed principal emphasis on changes in the goods turnover. There was, of course, no question that the general downward trend in the value of the paper rouble was due to inflation; although the acceptance of this point, which constituted the main part of Professor Falkner's contention, was not made clear by all the disputants. The point at issue was concerned with the cause of the variations in the rate of depreciation about the general trend, and particularly with the cause of the depreciation of the chervonetz. One of the contributors to the discussion, Bierbrauer, was concerned rather to rebut Professor Falkner's view as to the predominance of the monetary factor than to advance a complete explanation of his own. The so-called "summer stabilisation" of previous years, he declared, had been due to the anticipation of the harvest, rather than to the harvest itself. This anticipation at a time of high grain prices caused the peasant to throw existing reserves of grain on to the market before prices fell, and their action accordingly "swallowed up new currency emissions" and counteracted the effects of inflation. In the current year, however, grain prices were already low at the beginning of the year, and peasants were less inclined to unload reserves of grain in the spring, with the result that the seasonal influence on prices was much weakened; while in the case of rye the prospect of a poor harvest in the central and northern area had caused a withholding of rye from the market. The price of industrial goods, on the other hand, was enhanced by the growing raw material shortage and the consequent rise of costs.[1] Professor Kalinikov of Gosplan, while attributing the rise of prices both to financial and to goods causes, gave major importance to the latter, particularly to the growth in the cost of raw materials.[2] Rising raw

[1] *Econ. Jizn*, 6.9.23. [2] *Ibid.*, 18.9.23.

material costs was similarly emphasised by N. Kutler of the State Bank, who attributed it to the influence of the world price of these materials, which had risen owing to the fall in the world value of gold and was beginning to influence Russian prices now that import of these commodities was being developed. Thirty per cent of the rise of industrial prices he attributed to the change in world gold prices, and the rest to the enhanced burden of other costs, as, for instance, increased wage-cost per unit of output.[1] Professor Dolgov of Vesenha also stressed the fact that between January and August raw material prices had risen more rapidly than prices of finished goods, flax rising to 16, cotton to 13, and hemp to 24 times the January figure. But at the same time he attributed the depreciation of the chervonetz to its "excessive introduction into wholesale and retail trade." With regard to the "scissors" he had no more to say than a reference to the "disintegration of industry and the relative over-production of agricultural goods."[2]

The most convincing exposition of the view that it was factors on the goods side which constituted the most important cause of the specific problems of 1923 came from Professor Kondratiev. This writer expressed agreement with Professor Falkner that the unusual increase in the tempo of rouble depreciation which began in April was not due to unfavourable reports of the harvest: in 1922 the harvest prospects had been worse when a converse price movement had appeared in the spring and summer. Quoting the formula of Professor Irving Fisher, he agreed that the change must be explained, not by any seasonal influence, but by some "unfavourable conjunction of changes in money circulation, in the level of the goods turnover and in the speed of circulation of money." But he dissented from Professor Falkner in the prominence assigned to inflation as cause of the changed rate of depreciation subsequent to

[1] *Ibid.*, 12.9.23.
[2] *Ibid.*, 14.9.23.

April. The primary cause of this changed tempo was a decline in the goods turnover, and hence in the supply of goods coming on to the market for exchange against money. Prior to March this turnover had been growing. In March the turnover on the Moscow Goods Exchange reached 172 million gold roubles, and the turnover of Moscow trusts reached 287 million. By April these figures had fallen to 106 and 140 million respectively—in the latter case a fall of 50 per cent. A similar fall was reflected in the volume of railway loadings. In June there was considerable recovery, which corresponded to a slackened rate of rouble depreciation in that month; but in July and August a fall in the goods turnover again took place. Accordingly, a rate of issue of chervontsi which would not have been excessive if the goods turnover of the early months of the year had persisted caused a depreciation in its value in view of the fact that the goods turnover not only failed to show an expansion as was reasonably anticipated, but suffered an abrupt shrinkage in the spring and summer months. The depreciation once set in reacted on the speed of circulation of money—in other words, induced industrial and trading institutions to reduce their holdings even of chervontsi—and thereby aggravated the depreciation.[1]

What was the reason for this decline in the turnover of goods? At first sight it might seem tempting to attribute the decline to the rise of prices itself, causing trading organs to hold back stocks from the market in anticipation of a further rise. But this explanation seems hardly adequate for two reasons. It is scarcely consistent with the fact that the turnover was steadily rising prior to April and then very abruptly showed a fall; while the break in the turnover preceded rather than followed the changed *tempo* of prices in April—a change which was the reverse of what was anticipated. Moreover, with the chervonetz as a new investment medium, it was precisely at this time that the urgency of reducing money holdings and investing instead only in

[1] *Ibid.*, 26.9.23, also 13.9.23.

stocks of goods was removed.[1] Once the chervonetz had begun to depreciate, the desire to reduce chervontsi holdings may have had an aggravating effect on its decline and also on the goods turnover—a probable contributing factor in July and August. But for the initial change in April some additional explanation is clearly required; and it is in the search for this that we come back to the "scissors" problem and find it the more fundamental. For this reason Professor Kondratiev's conclusion is particularly interesting and brings us at once to the heart of the matter. "The basic cause of the depression of the goods turnover" he saw in the fall of agricultural prices and the narrowing of the village market. Towards the spring peasant purchasing power usually declined. This year, with the low prices of grain which had ruled since the previous September, it had fallen more than usual; and he accordingly advocated the adoption of measures to raise agricultural prices and to reduce industrial costs.

Already by April, therefore, the worsened terms of exchange between town and village had caused a shrinkage of the volume of exchange transactions between the two. The more favourable terms of trade in 1922 had induced the peasant to expand his sowings and to increase his offers of grain; and in turn the market for industrial goods had expanded. Now the response of the village was receiving a harsh rebuff, and the violent swing back of the terms of trade in favour of the town and against the village was reducing the willingness of the peasant to come to market, and might even, if it continued, induce him to restrict his sowings again for lack of adequate incentive, or at any rate to refrain from further effort to intensify his cultivation. Indeed, such a restriction of sowings was very likely; for the peasant was beginning to be in as bad a position as he had been under "war communism." Retail prices for commodities in the

[1] Cf. Barin in *Sozt. Khos.*, 1926, IV, 174, who points out that the introduction of the chervonetz actually created favourable conditions for increasing the turnover of goods.

village often showed a much greater rise than the retail prices in the towns. The exchange-value of salt and of textile goods had risen more than four times over 1913, but in villages much more, sometimes ten times.[1] A peasant often had to give "nearly the whole harvest of seven or eight dessiatines to buy a pair of boots," while "a pood of salt cost as much as a pood of meat."[2] Moreover, it was the peasant who bore the main burden of inflation, owing to his tendency, having sold his crop, to hold the proceeds for a time in money form, holding it in this way, probably, for a considerably longer period than the town worker or a trading institution. By the autumn of 1923 experience seemed to have made the peasant fully aware of this fact; and in October the cotton-growers in Turkestan, for example, were refusing to part with their crop except against chervontsi.[3]

A certain difficulty, however, attaches here to Professor Kondratiev's explanation. If this factor had operated alone, one might have expected the initial check to the transactions between town and village to have quickly brought its own remedy. Trading organs, faced with a slackening market and accumulating idle stocks, might have been expected to reduce their prices, and agricultural prices to have shown a recovery or at least to cease their fall. A slight break in the "scissors" actually did show itself in wholesale prices in May and June, but did not appear at all in retail prices; and after July the "scissors" (both retail and wholesale) continued to widen at an accelerated speed. The curious situation is presented of industrial prices continuing to rise steeply in the face of what was, according to Professor Kondratiev's explanation, a decline in demand owing to deficient agricultural purchasing power. This decline in peasant buying, therefore, though it undoubtedly existed as an underlying factor, can hardly be treated as the operating

[1] Kondratiev, *loc. cit.*, 26.9.23.
[2] Editorial in *Econ. Jizn*, 20.9.23.
[3] Yurovsky, *op. cit.*, 91.

cause of the fall of industrial turnover in April.[1] Rather did it become operative only at the climax of the "scissors" in September, when the rise of industrial prices had gone so far as to cause a "sales crisis" in industry. Cries were then heard from all sides—and heard in most cases then for the first time—of insufficiency of markets, and of goods accumulating in store unsold and unsaleable. In Baku there was talk of closing down of oil refineries because of accumulation of reserves sufficient to exhaust the tankage accommodation.[2] In the Ukraine, Chemugol and Yugosol (salt) were experiencing a depression of sales, and were complaining also of a "tightness" of credit; while the Ukrainian Agricultural Machinery Trust had stocks in the warehouses to the value of 3 million roubles.[3] Sales difficulties were also reported in the case of tobacco.[4] Centrosoyus on October 1st had a debit balance amounting to 10 million chervontsi,[5] including bills of exchange for 3·5 million, and had undisposable stocks of goods to the amount of 3·6 millions.[6] For large scale State industry in general Djerjinsky estimates the total unsold stocks in October to have amounted to some 400 million roubles, or 40 per cent of annual industrial production.[7] The features of an ordinary capitalist crisis of overproduction appeared to be present in full; and on all sides the urgent gravity of the position was brusquely challenging attention.

The principal cause, both of the decline in goods turnover in April, which was chiefly responsible for the summer depreciation of the chervonetz, and also of the extreme widening of the gap between industrial and agricultural prices in the summer of 1923 seems undoubtedly to have

[1] True, in the case of the textile and sugar industries there were some complaints of sales difficulties in June and July (cf. *Econ. Review*, 13.7.23). But this was scarcely as yet serious or very general.

[2] *Econ. Jizn.*, 20.9.23. In August these reserves had already reached double the normal pre-war amount.

[3] *Ibid.*, 21.9.23.

[4] *Ibid.*, 19.9.23.

[5] 1 chervonetz = 10 roubles.

[6] I.L.O., *Co-op. Movt. in S. R.*, 169.

[7] Djerjinsky, *Promishlenost S.S.S.R.*, 13–14.

lain in the monopoly position of State industry on the market and the extent to which that monopoly power was being used. NEP had restored market exchange between the village and the town; and the play of forces on the market, working through the actions of the various agents engaged in market operations, once again attained supremacy over the movement of prices and the volume of exchange transactions. State industry faced across the market the millions of independent units of small-scale peasant agriculture, facing it on the one hand as purchaser and consumer of foodstuffs and raw materials, facing it on the other hand as a seller of industrial products. The general process of exchange between industry and agriculture was divided into two sections, in one of which State industry figured as a buyer and in the other as a seller, with money as the intermediary which linked the two. But though divided into two sections, the whole exchange process of agricultural produce against manufactures was fundamentally a single whole. The price which the peasant received for his grain, measured against the price which he had to pay for town products, represented his return to each unit of the effort he expended; and if the price of manufactures was high, relatively to the price of grain, he would probably reduce the effort he exerted and reduce the supply of his own produce which he placed upon the market.[1]

In the early stage of NEP competition was fairly free on both sides of the market in both of these sections. At the outset the co-operatives had been given the monopoly of all grain purchases on behalf of the State; but this in practice broke down, the peasants preferring to sell to the host of private traders which was springing into being, and it was abolished in October 1921. The trusts in their newly gained independence seem to have refused in the

[1] Unless his demand for income in terms of effort were very inelastic, which there is reason to think it is not, *a priori* for reasons given above, p. 79 footnote, and *a posteriori* from the experience of "war communism." For analytical treatment of the whole matter see Excursus to Chapters Eight and Nine.

majority of cases to deal through Centrosoyus, in spite of the preference clause in their charters, preferring to purchase their supplies from private merchants or even through their own agents; and in 1923 Centrosoyus relegated dealings in agricultural produce to the background. Of the total sales of State industry in 1922–3 the co-operatives handled only 16 per cent, and of its total commercial turnover only 9 per cent.[1] The urban consumers' societies which supplied the town workers purchased in 1922–3 about 30 per cent of their supplies through private organisations, another 30 or 40 per cent through various State organs, less than 10 per cent through Centrosoyus, and between a quarter and a third from various provincial co-operative unions; while with regard to the supply of manufactured goods to the peasants the rural co-operatives supplied no more than 16 per cent of the total in 1922–3.[2] At the end of 1921 Vesenha set up a central commercial department to act as a wholesale intermediary between various State organs; and this proceeded also to go into the market as purchaser of supplies required by industry. In addition, provincial governments proceeded to set up commercial organs (*Gubtorg*), often without the knowledge of Vesenha;[3] while various central government departments, such as Narcomprod, and the Commissariats of Health and Agriculture instituted their own buying departments. These various bodies all tended to compete with one another on the market, at the same time

[1] I.L.O., *op. cit.*, 153, 157, 163, 167, 255.
[2] *Ibid.*, 190, 253.
[3] These often developed into financially autonomous bodies working for local industry or on their own account, e.g. Mostorg, Petrotorg, Ukraintorg. Some set up branches in other towns, and some even engaged in foreign trade. In the sphere of foreign trade numerous bodies operated, subject to licence and the approval of their trading program from the Comm. of Foreign Trade (*Narcomvneshtorg*). The latter body itself operated through an autonomous trading body, *Gostorg*, which traded on its own account and on commission for other bodies and possessed specialised sections such as *Metaltorg*. Narcomvneshtorg also operated through Trade Delegations in foreign countries. Centrosoyus, certain provincial commercial organs, one or two syndicates, such as the Textile Syndicate, and also mixed companies, like the Anglo-Russian Timber Co., the Russo-German Company, and Derumetal, also engage in foreign trade.

as each of them clamoured for monopoly rights in its own particular sphere; while in the *rasbazarivania* period the trusts launched out on the market on their own, frequently dealing with the peasants direct, and often even setting up their own retail agencies for the sale of their produce. In the first eighteen months of N E P, therefore, competition on the market was almost as keen from the side of State industry, both as buyer and seller, as it was from the side of the village.

In the spring and summer of 1922 the position began to change; and measures began to be taken to limit competition between industrial organs, and to give to State industry a greater degree of control over the market. Syndicates were established in nearly all industries with the aim of limiting competition between trusts, both in sale and purchase; and although these seldom had a complete monopoly, being still subject to the competition of trusts which remained outside the syndicates or of private bodies, they controlled in most cases a sufficient proportion of the transactions of the market to exercise a considerable degree of control over price. Moreover, as frequently happens when large units on one side of the market face a much larger number of small units on the other side (as in the case of employers bargaining with workers), the State organs were in a stronger bargaining position for securing terms of exchange favourable to themselves, since they had usually a wider choice of alternative markets, possessed better information and had greater resource. In the matter of grain and raw material purchases, a conference on the regulation of grain prices in September 1922 had discussed measures for co-ordinating the work of various organisations engaged in grain purchasing, and certain agreements were arrived at between purchasing organs which had the effect of lessening competition between them.[1]

As a result, State industry by the beginning of 1923 was in a position to face the peasant buyer and the peasant

[1] *Russian Economist,* Vol. III, No. 9, 3195.

seller across the market as more or less of a monopolist, with the result that it could turn the terms of exchange with the village in its favour—could turn them, that is, to a much greater extent than was warranted by the relative plentifulness of agricultural produce. This, however, it could only do by restricting its own sales on the village market, or at least by restricting them relatively to the expansion of agriculture: like any monopolist it could secure more favourable terms of exchange by restricting, and only by restricting, the supplies which it offered for sale. This showed itself in the decreased flow of industrial goods on to the market subsequent to April, and in the resulting increase both of the general price index in terms of chervontsi and of the gap between industrial and agricultural prices—namely, the "scissors." To the resulting accumulation of stocks the trusts and syndicates were not particularly averse: many of them welcomed an opportunity of replenishing stocks that had been depleted in the previous year. They looked forward to expanded village sales after the realisation of the harvest; and they were provided with the means of holding larger stocks by the relatively generous crediting of industry in the spring to meet the insistent complaints from industry of deficient working capital, which had been voiced particularly at the 10th Soviet Congress in the previous December.[1] But such accumulation of stocks necessarily had an upper limit, which began to be reached by August; and when, partly through alarm at the depreciation of the chervonetz, and partly through the need for the seasonal transfer of credits into the channels of grain purchase, credits to industry began to be restricted again in August,[2] loud complaints were heard from industry of acute financial difficulties; and it was

[1] e.g. in the Report on Industry by P. Bogdanov, who particularly stressed this point, prophesying a repetition of the 1922 spring crisis in the spring of 1923 and advocating an expansion of credit advances to industry as a remedy for this.

[2] While credits to industry were restricted, there was no *general* deflation of credit at this time, discounting by the State Bank actually rising from 83 million cherv. roubles in August to 103 million on October 1 (*Econ. Jizn*, 8.1.24).

realised that current sales at existing prices did not suffice to cover current production, let alone to clear accumulated stocks. " Portfolios of undiscountable bills " and warehouses full to overflowing became the general order of the day. The root of the whole crisis was that State industry had been using its monopoly power to turn the terms of exchange with the village in its own favour, and such terms of exchange could only be maintained at a smaller scale of industrial production. For instance, the Odessa Leather Trust for the year 1922–3 was reported to have made a profit of nearly 30 per cent on its turnover, and the Moscow Silk Trust as much as 175 per cent on its capital.[1] For the first year industry as a whole showed a profit instead of a deficit, net industrial profits increasing from 52 million roubles (gold) in the first quarter of 1922–3 to 100 in the second quarter and 110 and 116 million in the third and fourth quarters of the year.

Several of the contributors to the discussion on the cause of the " scissors " had already stressed this point, although few had given it the prominence it deserved. Professor Kondratiev mentioned it among several causes of the relative depression of agricultural prices.[2] Professor Weinstein of Narcomfin referred to the use of their monopoly power by the syndicates to replenish their turnover capital from the proceeds of higher prices.[3] Vladimirov, who preceded Sokolnikov as Commissar of Finance, cited the effect of increased credits to industry in enabling trusts to hold up goods and to raise prices. " The weak purchasing power of the population," he declared, " and the price policy of industrial enterprises are in contradiction."[4] At an Economic Conference of the Ukraine in September, in reply to complaints of credit shortage, the official representative of Narcomfin declared that the existing sales crisis was due to the trusts themselves in having held back goods from the market and raised prices to an unduly high level.[5]

[1] Chubar in *Econ. Jizn*, 11.9.23 ; and report in *Econ. Jizn*, 2.9.23.
[2] *Ibid.*, 26.9.23. [3] *Ibid.*, 12.9.23. [4] *Ibid.*, 13.9.23. [5] *Ibid.*, 21.9.23.

As soon as this explanation of the crisis became heard, the representatives of industry, being thrown on the defensive, hastened to refute the accusation that the blame for the rise of prices rested on themselves, or at least they sought to plead extenuating circumstances; and as discussion about interpretation of the problem passed over into discussion of appropriate remedies, two main tendencies of opinion began to appear. On the one hand, what one may, perhaps, call the "industrial" tendency was inclined to attribute the crisis to the relative backwardness of industry, and to prescribe, accordingly, as a cure the strengthening of industry, improving its credit position, mending the system of industrial planning, and increasing the subsidies to it from the Budget to enable it to overhaul depreciated plant and lower costs and expand production. On the other hand, the group of opinion which attributed the crisis to the market policy of trusts and syndicates sought a remedy in curbing the activities of State industrial organs in conformity with the requirements of the peasant market.

The former opinion found support, not merely among the heads of trusts and syndicates, but also among an influential section of the State Economic Planning Commission (Gosplan).[1] Strumilin strongly attacked Kondratiev's proposal for a raising of grain prices, arguing that the existing relation between agricultural and industrial prices corresponded to the existing relation between the productivity of labour in agriculture and in industry.[2] Professor Kalinikov of Gosplan ascribed the high industrial prices to high costs, such as labour and raw material costs, overhead charges and the need for industrial enterprises to insure themselves against losses due to currency depreciation.[3] Nogin of the Textile

[1] S T O was the supreme executive body in the economic sphere, filling the rôle of an Economic General Staff which Vesenha had aimed, but had failed, to fulfil in the earlier period. Gosplan was an advisory permanent sub-commission of S T O, undertaking detailed investigations and providing the expert recommendations on which S T O based its decisions. It remained, however, though very influential, no more than an advisory body.

[2] *Op. cit.*, 208–9. [3] *Econ. Jizn*, 15.9.23.

Syndicate actually denied that a real sales crisis existed. The cause of the financial difficulties among the trusts in his view lay in the sudden restriction of credit by the State Bank; and the high industrial prices were due to the various middlemen organisations which "sometimes raise the price of textile goods by 100 per cent."[1] From the concerns which fulfilled orders for Government departments came complaint of financial embarrassment through delays in payment. From various quarters the burden of State taxes on industry, the charges for social insurance and the statutory allowance for the amortisation fund aroused keen lament.

Across this main issue lay several subsidiary issues, partly complicating it, partly falling along the same general lines. Chief of these was the question of currency stabilisation. As in other countries where the question came to the fore, opinion tended to be divided between those who desired immediate stabilisation and those who desired to postpone this drastic measure till a more favourable time. Already at the 10th Soviet Congress in December 1922, when Sokolnikov had outlined the policy of budgetary stabilisation and cessation of inflation, considerable opposition had been voiced, particularly to the credit stringency and the increase of taxation which stabilisation involved. Larin, for instance, declared that taxation was unfairly distributed between industry and agriculture, the former being retarded by a tax burden amounting to 30 per cent of its wages bill, together with an additional 35 per cent in social insurance charges. The same view now tended to be held by that group of opinion which saw the cause of the "scissors" in the under-development of industry, and sought a remedy in easier credit and subsidy facilities to trusts and syndicates. On the other hand, those who had their eyes on the position of the peasant saw that it was the peasant who was the principal loser under inflation, while industry, on balance, stood to secure from inflation an unfair gain. Ossinsky declared that Russia could not at the moment

[1] *Ibid.*, 29.9.23.

afford the luxury of a gold standard. Surely it was better to put resources into industry rather than into amassing a reserve of barren gold? To which Shapiro replied that the cost of a gold reserve was a necessary overhead charge to secure the advantages of the development of trade with the world market.[1]

Linked with this issue went certain criticisms of the State Bank and of Narcomfin, on account of the policy of credit stringency and economy of State expenditure enforced by these two bodies. Krasnoshchekov hotly protested against industry, when it was starved of circulating capital, being "supplied with the stone of the theory of credit inflation"; and appealed for the curtailment of the functions of the State Bank to a bank of issue, and the concentration of all financing of industry in the hands of the Bank for Industry and Trade (*Prombank*).[2] At the 10th Soviet Congress suggestions had been made for withdrawing the financing of industry from the charge of Narcomfin and the State Bank and handing it over to the Prombank under the control of Vesenha; and it was not long before an influential body of opinion had formed, which urged that the interests of industry would be better served if, at least, the Prombank were strengthened, so as to make it the leading institution in the country for long and short-term credits to industry. It was for the express purpose of financing industry, and freeing it from complete dependence on the State Bank, that the Prombank had been established in October 1922. The major part of the share capital had been subscribed by trusts and syndicates and by Vesenha, and accordingly industrial interests had predominant control.[3] But at present this institution was unable to supply more than some 16 per cent of the credits to industry; and the dominant position was still held by the State Bank, which had now

[1] *Ibid.*, 12.1.24.

[2] *Ibid.*, 7.9.23.

[3] Other shareholders were: mixed companies, co-operatives, private persons, and certain State departments. The State Bank had subscribed a small part, but only a very small part, of the share capital (cf. Levin in *Econ. Oboz.*, Nov., 1925, 142–3).

courted severe unpopularity by its curtailment of industrial credits in September and October. Before the war the State Bank had been moving more and more into the position of a bankers' bank; and between 1912 and 1914 nearly a half of its loan and discount operations had been with other credit institutions. In 1923–4 barely a tenth of its credit operations had been with other credit institutions, the remainder consisting of direct dealings with industrial and trading organs;[1] and of the total credits to industry and transport nearly 80 per cent were supplied by the State Bank and of trade credits some 55 per cent.[2] The State Bank had, accordingly, a direct and powerful control over the credit situation—a control which it was now exercising in the direction of deflation. If it were to withdraw to the position of a bankers' bank, crediting industry not directly but by crediting intermediary institutions, it would still exercise some control over the credit situation through its control over the rediscount operations of the other banks.[3] But the representatives of industry, no doubt, secretly hoped that this control would be a weaker one, and that the Prombank, operating with the collective reserves of industrial and trading institutions, would be able to adopt a more liberal credit policy, free from the " tight-laced " influence of the Commissariat of Finance. Along the same lines went a strong departmental rivalry between Gosplan and Nar-

[1] Cf. Katzenellenbaum, *op. cit.*, 195. Most of the other credit institutions which rediscounted with the State Bank in pre-war days were " commercial banks " on the German model (cf. Epstein, *Les Banques de Commerce Russes*, 12 *seq.*, 45 *seq.*). The intention apparently was to make Prombank a socialist equivalent of these " commercial banks."

[2] *Russ. Inform. and Review*, 20.9.24. In supplying trade credits the Co-operative Bank played a large part. Of all loan and discount operations in 1925–6 the State Bank was responsible for 55·8 per cent; and of these operations of the State Bank 50 per cent were with State industry, 10 per cent with State trade, 12·5 per cent with the Co-operatives, and only 13·5 per cent with other credit institutions (Sobolev in *Planovoe Khos.*, 1926, No. 12, 66 *seq.*).

[3] On the other hand, control through discount rates would probably be considerably less effective under the circumstances than under a competitive system, owing to a more inelastic demand for credit: if discount rates rose, monopolist industry might seek to add the amount on to selling price rather than to curtail its operations.

comfin. Those who criticised the credit policy of the State Bank declared that the errors were due to " the practical autonomy of the State Bank "[1]—or, rather, what was worse in their eyes, its untimely obedience to Narcomfin. This led to imperfect subordination of credit policy to " a single economic plan." When in the autumn there came to be talk of improving the system of " economic planning," proposals were mooted for increasing the powers of Gosplan to make it in practice the supreme regulating body in the economic sphere. In its hands, instead of in the hands of Narcomfin, was to be placed the control of the crediting of industry and of capital allocations from the Budget.

This complicated issue, in which rival interpretations of the " scissors " crisis, the question of currency stabilisation and deflation, departmental questions of the State Bank *v.* Prombank and of Gosplan *v.* Narcomfin were interlaced and confused, had become by the end of the year a dominant political question. In the discussion which preceded the 13th Party Conference it held the fore-stage. It caused the appearance of a definite minority opposition within the leading organs of the Party. It proved to be the most important issue by far since the 10th Congress; and it evoked a contest more bitter than that of the spring of 1918. In retrospect one sees that it marked a parting of the ways between two fundamentally different views of N E P and of the whole transition period. Had its outcome been different, Russia would have travelled by to-day many leagues down a road into territory far distant from where she now is. To the historian who looks back over ten years it stands out as a landmark surpassed only by October 1917 and March 1921.

[1] Ossinsky in Resolution submitted to a Meeting of Party Nuclei of Moscow Dist., Dec. 29, 1923.

CHAPTER NINE

THE CLOSING OF THE "SCISSORS"

THE policy which the Government adopted to meet the autumn crisis of 1923 was far from winning unanimous approval. It showed too little care for the clamour of industrialists to gain much favour in that quarter; and its opponents regarded it as the dark child of Narcomfin, born in departmental exclusiveness, and nourished on financial parsimony. Small sympathy was shown in the official diagnosis for the view that the weakness of industry was the root of present difficulties. On the contrary, the monopoly of State industry on the market was singled out as the principal cause of the trouble. The medicine prescribed, designed to exert pressure on industrial organs to reduce industrial prices, could hardly fail to be unpalatable to the heads of trusts and syndicates; while ground for much complaining of undue favour to the peasant was afforded by the official efforts to raise agricultural prices from their existing low level, partly by altered price-policy in grain purchase and more liberal credits to grain-purchasing organs, and partly by a development of the export of grain. But no policy of sufficient vigour to overcome the sales crisis could have avoided hurt to some departmental interest; and the leaders of the Government pursued their policy in the confident hope that a direct attack on the problem from both sides in this way would gradually close the blades of the "scissors." If industrial prices were reduced while at the same time village purchasing power was increased, the sales crisis in industry would inevitably be abated.

The pressure on trusts and syndicates to secure a lowering of their prices was exerted in three ways. First, and probably most important, was the drastic rationing of credits to industry by the State Bank. This forced industrial and trading organs to unload their stocks on the market, in order to realise the turnover resources in money form which they could no longer secure by discounting bills. Second, definite regulative measures were taken in the shape of maximum selling prices through the new Committee for Internal Trade (*Comvnutorg*). Third, the policy, known as "goods intervention," of importing finished goods at the lower world prices and using them to undercut the syndicates and so force down their price, was adopted in special cases. But this latter policy of "goods intervention" was confined to special cases, rather than used as the general method that *prima facie* might have been expected. The possibility of importing finished goods and so extending this policy was limited for two reasons: first, by the need to curtail imports and create a favourable trade balance in the interests of currency stabilisation, and second by the desire to import machinery and essential raw materials, like cotton, on as large a scale as possible. Indeed, those who saw the main cause of the "scissors" in the under-development of industry, and desired to meet the shortage of manufactures by import of finished goods, brought the additional argument against currency stabilisation that it made a policy of "goods intervention" on any considerable scale impossible.[1]

Although in several cases large profits had been made by industry in the preceding months, it was true that in many cases price-reductions could not be carried very far without turning profit into loss. At least, this was true of many "marginal" enterprises and trusts which were operating under least favourable conditions. On the face of it this seemed a vindication of those who saw in the under-development of industry, and not its monopoly position, the root-cause of the trouble. But closer analysis shows the matter to have been less simple than this. The high level of industrial costs at this time could be traced to a number of factors. According to Strumilin, taxes and excise amounted

[1] e.g. Ossinsky, *loc. cit.*

in October 1923 to 10–12 per cent of the value of net industrial production, as compared with 3 per cent a year previous and 13 per cent in pre-war times. High credit costs he estimated to affect cost price by 5 per cent; whereas in the previous year industry had enjoyed a minus real rate of interest of 8 per cent owing to rouble depreciation;[1] while railway tariffs were some 20–25 per cent above pre-war. He estimated that these three items combined added 18 per cent to industrial costs.[2] Other items of cost, such as materials, fuel, labour, and administrative expenses, varied widely between industries and between enterprises. For the first half of 1923 raw material costs, on account of the lowness of agricultural prices, were generally lower than in 1913, often substantially lower, as in the leather industry where they were little more than a half the 1913 figure per unit of output. Increase in labour costs over pre-war varied between 18 per cent in leather and about 60 per cent in textiles to 80 per cent in cement and matches, and over 200 per cent in iron. But the greatest rise of all was in fuel costs and in "general" and administrative expenses. Fuel costs in cotton spinning were some two and a half times the pre-war burden, and in the production of cast-iron they were four times as heavy. More remarkable still, "general" expenses per unit of output had increased over four times in matches, over five times in yarn and calico, and seven times in iron.[3] An estimate made by Kaktyn for the previous year showed that overhead expenses represented a considerably greater proportion of total productive costs than in 1913—that is, a greater proportion even of the higher costs of the post-war period. In a pood of pig-iron such overhead expenses represented 37 per cent of total costs as against 22 per cent in 1913, in a pood of coal 39

[1] It is not clear whether Strumilin here allows for the fact that the State Bank adopted the policy of demanding repayment of credits at their gold value.

[2] Strumilin, *op. cit.*, 225–6.

[3] *Ind. and Lab. Inform.*, 21.1.24; also Dolgov in *Sozt. Khos.*, March, 1923, 29–30.

as against 32 per cent, in cigarettes 22 as against 10 per cent; while in the manufacture of goloshes overhead expenses had risen from 17 per cent of total costs to 57 per cent.[1] These figures are significant enough. But it is to be noticed that "overhead expenses" do not here represent a cost-accounting category, and so do not include several things which would be covered by such a category. If we include that part of fuel costs which could be regarded for accounting purposes as "overhead," we arrive at figures which are even more significant than those given by Kaktyn.

This great increase in the burden of overhead costs could to some extent be attributed to increased unwieldiness and inefficiency of the administrative apparatus. The ratio of administrative to manual workers in industry was in 1923 slightly more than double the pre-war figure.[2] But this could account directly for no more than a small part of the increased burden. By far the most important cause was the fact that industry was still operating at a small proportion of its full capacity, thereby rendering constant overhead expenses a very heavy burden per unit of the reduced output. This fact in itself was, in part, responsible for the high ratio of administrative to manual workers, since the administrative personnel does not need to expand proportionately with expanded production, and a larger scale of output and employment would *ipso facto* tend to reduce the ratio. It was, therefore, precisely the pursuit of a monopoly policy of high prices by industry that was most likely to augment the burden of overhead costs, since such a policy involved a restriction of the volume of output which could be marketed. Whereas, conversely, a reduction of prices and an expansion of output would tend correspondingly to lighten this burden.

But with the existing curtailment of industrial credits and the possibility of losses to the trusts from sales on a falling market, progress along the line of extended output

[1] Kaktyn in *Econ. Jizn*, 31.3.23.
[2] Kaktyn, *Ibid.*, 18.9.23.

showed signs of being slow. The very expansion of output which was necessary to relieve the burden of overhead costs required increased circulating capital in order to set in motion additional supplies of raw materials and labour. With the expansion of credit in the course of the year, the position of industry in this respect had been considerably improved, circulating capital as a percentage of total industrial resources increasing from some 32 per cent in January to 46 per cent in October, 1923.[1] Now there was a danger that the position would worsen again. Some more immediate means of reducing the burden of overhead costs was clearly required; and it was to provide this immediate economy that the policy of "concentration" of industry, already proclaimed at the 12th Party Congress in the spring of 1923, was pushed forward with vigour. On the wisdom of this policy there was no serious difference of opinion. Those who opposed the official policy on other points were equally insistent on the need for industrial "concentration." The difference was that the industrialists would have applied such measures of economy independently of price-reductions, while the official policy insisted that price-reduction should have precedence even over economy of costs. To reduce prices, it was urged, was the measure most calculated to force the heads of industry to apply their energies to an economy campaign, whereas to leave their monopoly untouched would tempt industrial organs to "conceal their defects of organisation" behind profits won at the expense of high prices and to shun the harsh work of economy.[2]

The problem of high overhead costs was not merely that industry was working at reduced capacity in the sense that a number of plants were idle: it was also the case that factories actually in operation were working at a very small "load." Consequently, there was a wide margin for economy in concentrating production on the better-equipped factories, and in increasing the "load" of these, while temporarily

[1] Barin in *Sozt. Khos.*, 1926, IV, 175–6. The pre-war percentage was 60.

[2] Kaktyn, *loc. cit.*

closing down less efficient plants. In the 20 leading trusts of the metal industry in 1923, 39 per cent of the factories were idle, yet the average " loading " of the 113 which were in operation was only 50 per cent of pre-war. In the Southern Steel Trust blast furnaces were working at only 17–20 per cent of capacity, marten furnaces at 10–17 per cent, while rolling mills varied between 17 and 50 per cent.[1] In the textile industry the " loading " of factories was seldom above 70 per cent and not infrequently below 30 per cent. The Vladimir Trust stood in the best position with a 55 per cent " load " in its spinning branch, 71 per cent in weaving and 89–95 per cent in printing and dyeing. On the other hand, the Moscow Trust had only 40 per cent in spinning and less than 15 per cent in printing and dyeing, and the Yaroslav Trust only 25 per cent in its spinning section.[2] Already at the beginning of 1923 concerted action had been taken to promote concentration of production under the influence of the Commission for the Concentration of Industry which had been formed in February and which in April was transformed into the Commission for the Revision of the Trusts. At the beginning of the year the " load " in the Leningrad Machine Trust was as low as 12 per cent, in the Gomza 20, in the case of the Ukrainian Agricultural Machinery Trust it was actually only 6 per cent and at the Putilov works under 5 per cent. In the cotton industry as a whole it was 46 per cent, while the active factories of the nine chief cotton trusts in February had only 38 per cent of their spindles in operation. In the glass industry it was 42, in sugar and rubber 33 and 40, in paper 60, flax 62 and leather 69; while tobacco and chemicals were the only industries to approach a 70–75 per cent " load."[3] Even by the end of the year a great deal remained to be done.

But by the spring of 1924 the policy of concentration had begun to achieve quite considerable results. In face of the autumn crisis the number of active cotton mills was

[1] *Russ. Inform. and Review*, 24.11.23.
[2] *Ibid.*, 15.12.23. [3] Rosenfeld, *op. cit.*, 222, 225–6.

reduced from 131 to 104 and in wool from 64 to 55. In leather the number of active factories was halved; and in metal the number was reduced from 69 to 39. In the case of cotton and leather this was accompanied by a small reduction in the number of workers, in wool and metal by an actual increase.[1] As a result, a considerable fall in the burden of overhead costs soon began to be felt. In the case of salt this economy amounted to 35 per cent, in coal to 21 per cent, in iron to 24, and in cotton spinning to 18.[2] By the end of 1924 a general fall in industrial costs had been achieved which amounted on the average to nearly 20 per cent.[3]

The second pillar in the official policy was currency stabilisation. The depreciation of the new chervonetz in the summer of 1923 and the final plunge of the old paper rouble, rendering possibility of future revenue by emission almost insignificant, had made the question of stabilisation a pressing issue. The fact that the peasant was beginning to insist on receiving payment in chervontsi and to refuse to part with his produce in return for paper roubles was probably a decisive influence in the matter; and there was the additional consideration that the peasants' impoverishment by past inflation had lent acuteness to the " scissors " crisis. It seemed clear that the experiment in two parallel unrated currencies provided no promise of stability to the chervonetz; and without such a stable unit of account all economic accountancy became distorted, and the danger remained ever present of industrial organs holding back stocks in anticipation of a rise of prices and so evoking a recurrence of the " scissors " difficulty. Plans were accordingly made at the beginning of 1924[4] for replacing

[1] *Econ. Review*, 14.12.23.

[2] Djerjinsky, *op. cit.*, 44. In addition there were economies in labour costs amounting in Donugol to 21 per cent, in low-grade tobacco to 29, in oil to 12, in cotton spinning 6, and in salt 12 per cent.

[3] *Ibid.*, 43; Rosenfeld, *op. cit.*, 443–4.

[4] The policy was definitely announced by Sokolnikov, the Commissary of Finance, at an *ad hoc* conference on Dec. 5th, and outlined in Memoranda by Sokolnikov in January. A decree of Feb. 5 provided

the depreciated paper rouble by a new issue of Treasury Notes in denominations of five, three, and one roubles gold, to be issued under the control of Narcomfin as legal tender, subject to their quantity being limited to half the quantity of chervontsi in circulation.[1] This implied certain measures which were bound to place a temporary handicap on industry. Restriction of credit had to be continued: indeed, the reduction of credits for grain purchase and export caused a slight relapse of grain prices in March and April 1924. The Budget had to be balanced by means of a rigid economy of State expenditure, including grants to industry, and an increase of taxation. Further, imports had to be reduced in order to create a favourable balance and place a fund of gold and foreign valuta at the disposal of Narcomfin and the State Bank.[2] The problem was crowned with particular difficulties from the fact that the "scissors" crisis and the virtual breakdown of the experiment in two parallel currencies forced the introduction of the currency reform before the deficit on the Budget had completely disappeared. Nine per cent of State expenditure in the final quarter of 1923 still had to be covered by the proceeds of currency emission; and 15 million gold roubles had still to be raised each month by this means at the beginning of 1924.[3] It was hoped, however, that such inflation as this necessitated in the early months of the new Treasury Note would be at a slower pace than the expansion of production and of the goods turnover, and so would not produce any further depreciation; while in the financial year 1924–5 it was

for the issue of Treasury Notes, and that of Feb. 14 announced the discontinuance of the old rouble. Finally the decree of March 17 established a fixed rate of redemption for the old paper roubles in terms of the new Treasury Note, namely, 50,000 roubles of 1923 notes for 1 rouble gold.

[1] Chervontsi were Notes of the State Bank, which according to the Decree of October 11th, 1922, had to have cover of not less than 25 per cent in precious metals and stable foreign valuta. These were also legal tender, but were issued only in large denominations of 10 gold roubles or over.

[2] Cf. Editorial in *Econ. Jizn*, 10.1.24.

[3] Yurovsky, *op. cit.*, 124–5.

anticipated that reliance on revenue from currency emission would have completely disappeared.

The opposition to this official policy began to voice its criticisms within the Party in November and December 1923.[1] The criticisms were not necessarily homogeneous, and the persons who came to group themselves in a loose opposition *bloc* did not necessarily agree on all points of their several complaints; while the economic issues in the Party discussion came to be interwoven with political issues concerning the measures to be taken for reviving internal Party democracy. But their economic critique had this much in common: they all tended to make the strengthening of the position of State industry, rather than the curbing of its monopoly power, the centre-point of their proposals, and to give more liberal financing of industry at least precedence over the campaign to reduce industrial prices.

The clearest expression of this criticism came from Ossinsky in a memorandum which was to constitute the banner of the opposition attack. The criticism itself fell under ten heads; but the ten points of the indictment formed a planetary system around a single sun. The flaw which he found in the whole gamut of official policy was a misreading of the events of the past year. These events, with their disastrous culmination in the autumn, had been due to "the lack of a plan uniting the work of all the branches of State economy," particularly in respect to the crediting of industry and agriculture—a defect which showed itself in "the attempt, instead of aiming at a general economic plan, to regulate economy from the financial centre" (i.e. from the State Bank and Narcomfin). Thus the autumn crisis had been "a crisis of disparity"; and it was this imperfect planning, and not "objective factors," which bore responsibility for "the disparity between industrial and agricultural production." During the spring and

[1] Already on Oct. 15 the "Declaration of the 46" had voiced criticism of the official policy in purely general terms. The principal signatories of this Declaration were Piatakov, Preobrajensky, Sosnovsky, Sapronov, Serebriakov, Rosengoltz.

summer of the year " the financial means of the State Bank were totally engaged in operations of industry and wholesale trade on unsound bases, without retaining a reserve for the autumn period of the grain crop "; while in the autumn credits to industry were as ruinously deflated. The appropriate remedy was to bring all economic organs, including those of finance and credit, more closely under the control of a single economic plan and a single planning organ; while at the same time reining the trusts, " which are at present virtually autonomous," into closer connection with Vesenha. In the official declaration of policy such an improvement in the work of co-ordination and planning had been promised after the introduction of a stable currency. But this, according to Ossinsky, was to invert the proper order; it was both " incorrect and dangerous." Co-ordination " of finances with the other elements of the State and national economy " must precede the currency reform; since without it " there can be no talk of securing a really stable currency," or of avoiding a repetition of the autumn " crisis of disparity."

In addition, Ossinsky had three subsidiary points of criticism. First, the leaders of the Party had postulated " a totally incorrect task " in directing that the price policy of economic organs should be to calculate in price only " the necessary minimum profit." This " excluded the possibility of basing the State Budget on incomes derived from industry," and ought to be replaced by the principle of " obtaining the maximum profit with a given average price, and with the obligation of striving to reduce price by means of enlarging and perfecting the working capacity." Second, the official policy did not do full credit to the successes of private capital which had " already come into possession of 14 per cent of the wholesale trade, 15 per cent of the whole-sale-retail and 80 per cent of the small trade," and had " also accumulated large sums in goods and stable values." To combat this danger it was necessary to pay particular attention in the near future to " the fight against private commercial capital," by aiding the co-operatives and affording them more liberal credit facilities. Finally, Ossinsky opposed the policy of creating a "positive (or 'favourable') trade balance." It was inadmissible that Russia should "allow herself the luxury of spending means for the transition from bank-notes to metal currency":[1] these resources should be spent "for productive purposes" instead. In place of "the abstract slogan of a 'positive trade balance'" should be set a policy of "goods intervention" ("i.e. partial importation from abroad of goods which we lack and of those of which the price has particularly increased"). For import of capital goods reliance would have to be placed on foreign loans, making possible a "negative trade balance."[2]

A similar diagnosis of the autumn crisis had already been advanced in more general terms by Trotsky in a Memorandum to the Central Committe of the Party on the 8th of October. This placed the blame for the present situation on an insufficient enforcement of the decisions of the 12th Party Congress at the outset of the year with regard to the concentration of industry and a plan of production. In a brochure issued at the beginning of 1924[3] and devoted mainly to the discussion of democracy within the Party, his economic proposals received more explicit formulation—more explicit even than in Ossinsky's resolution. Crises under N E P, according to Trotsky's chapter on "The Economic Plan," were attributable to imperfect anticipation of the changes of the peasant market and imperfect adaptation of industry in its various parts to the existing situation. Since errors of forecast were inevitable, imperfect adaptation to the

[1] This had not in fact been proposed as an immediate measure (except for the issue of metal coins as token money of less than 1 rouble); but it had been proposed to increase the gold reserve which acted as "cover" for the chervonetz.

[2] Resolution on "The Immediate Tasks of Economic Policy," submitted to a Meeting of Moscow Party Nuclei, Dec. 29th, 1923.

[3] This was a reprint of articles published in *Pravda* in December as part of the Party discussions which had been officially opened by Zinoviev in the middle of October.

market was bound to show itself, now in insufficiency of production, now in sales crises. " Nevertheless it is obvious that such crises will be less acute and prolonged, the more seriously planning is applied to all branches of State economy. Even if the doctrine of the disciples of Brentano and Bernstein that the domination of capitalist trusts would regulate the market and make market crises impossible were radically false, yet it is entirely right when applied to the Workers' State considered as trust of trusts and bank of banks. In other words, the intensification or weakening of crises will be in our economy the clearest and most infallible barometer of the advance of State economy over private capitalist elements. In the struggle of State industry for conquest of the market the plan is our principal weapon. Without it nationalisation would become an obstacle to economic development, and private capital would inevitably undermine the foundations of Socialism." In the application of such a plan the dominant organ should be Gosplan. " Gosplan ought to control all the fundamental factors of State economy, to co-ordinate them with one another and with peasant economy. Its central work should be to develop State industry. Precisely in this sense I have had occasion to say that the ' dictatorship ' ought to belong, not to finance, but to industry. . . . In other words, not only foreign trade, but also the re-establishment of a stable currency ought to be strictly subordinated to the interests of State industry."[1]

With the 13th Party Conference which opened on January 16th, 1924, the discussion reached its final stage. Krassin in the previous year had urged the impossibility of reconstructing industry with sufficient speed except by the attraction of foreign capital, and had criticised Trotsky's Theses on Industry on the ground that his plans for industrial development were on too small a scale. He now attributed the difficulties of the past year to the attempt to carry through reconstruction solely by internal resources, and proposed

[1] *Novy Kurs,* 70–1 ; trans., in French as *Cours Nouveau.*

a modification of the concessions policy and the attraction of a foreign loan of 300–500 million gold roubles.[1] Piatakov followed Ossinsky in emphasising the large rôle played by the private trader, particularly in village retail trade, and the need to combat this development by bringing the trusts, transport, trade and the banks under the control of one single organ and into one planned system. The " scissors " he attributed to the under-production of industry and the relative surplus of grain: " the basic method of struggle with the ' scissors ' is an expansion of production," and this requires State grants and credits to remedy the shortage. His comment on the Narcomfin policy of an " active trade balance" was caustic: "we need, not gold, but the quickening of our industry, and this we cannot do by piling up gold in the hands of comrades Sokolnikov and Scheinmann." Even more stress was laid by Preobrajensky on the growth of the Nepman or private trader. Of some 600 million gold roubles profit of trade and industry (excluding transport and taxes) in the course of the year, 200–300, he estimated, had been accumulated by the Nepman. The question, therefore, was urgent whether the Nepman would strengthen his position and influence with the peasant, and form an economic alliance to stem the drift to socialism, or whether the Workers' State would be able to break such an alliance and convert the private trader into a mere dependent and subsidiary distributive organ for State industry. Separately and in competition with one another, the trusts would be weak and liable to be beaten in the struggle. Linked together in a united State organisation, they would be in the same strong position as a capitalist combine in competition with rival smaller fry. The proposed monetary reform he did not explicitly oppose; but contented himself with criticising the " planless " policy in the past which had hastened the death of the old paper rouble before the Budget deficit had been abolished, and with prophesying for the

[1] Krassin did not, however, associate himself with the opposition on other points of criticism.

future a stormy passage in attempting stabilisation while this Budget deficit still remained.[1]

This "dictatorship of industry" which formed the common platform of the opposition only appears in its true perspective when one stands back from the details of the immediate situation and surveys it against the background of the whole New Economic Policy. Moreover, one is hardly disposed to appreciate the significance of this important parting of the ways in Russian economic policy until one has discarded those crude and facile categories of "moderate" and "extreme," "opportunist" and "doctrinaire" in which writers outside Russia usually delight to interpret the issue.[2] Such classifications, the product either of stupidity or a superficial approach, are purely obscurantist. The real issue is both more interesting and more fundamental than this; and the full importance of the decision which the 13th Conference had to face is difficult to appreciate until we find the opposition standpoint formulated in terms of a general theory. Although it had no explicit connection with the 13th Conference discussion, the relation between the policy of the "dictatorship of industry" and a theoretical study by Preobrajensky of the transition period to socialism which appeared in 1924 is quite plain to see.[3] In this study Preobrajensky was concerned to analyse the sources and methods of capital accumu-

[1] *Econ. Jizn*, 17.1.24, 18.1.24; *Pravda*, 18.1.24, 19.1.24.

[2] For instance, Sir Bernard Pares can see in these 1923–4 discussions merely a contest between "fanatics" and "opportunists," with Trotsky as the representative of the latter (*A History of Russia*, 487). *The Economic Review* (22.8.24), quoting from *Wirtschaftsdienst*, described the defeat of the Trotsky-Radek opposition as "a reaction from the New Economic Policy, and the repression of private trade and capital, in other words a return to the early days of the Revolution." "A Correspondent" in *The Economist* (*not*, I think, its usual Russian correspondent) declared that in 1924 "the more extreme elements in the C. P. gained the upper hand" (15.11.24). On the other hand, the Special Correspondent of the *Observer* (29.8.26) declared that all the major opposition movements in the Russian Party since 1917 had been "revolts of the doctrinaire and uncompromising Left Wing against a conciliatory policy."

[3] *The Fundamental Law of Socialist Accumulation* in *Viestnik Komm. Akadem.*, Vol. 8.

lation for State industry under the conditions of the New Economic Policy. In this transition period, to which Lenin gave the name of State Capitalism, large-scale State industry would exist as an island towering above a sea of small-scale private enterprise of various kinds. In the towns there was the private lessee of a factory, the concessionaire, the Nepman trader, in the villages the vast mass of peasant producers. The less developed economically the nation might be at the time of the workers' seizure of power, the smaller the island and the greater the expanse of the surrounding sea. Socialism would develop according as large-scale State industry grew and developed, increasing its productivity and taking over functions previously performed by small-scale private economy. If State industry failed to expand and develop, it might well be submerged in the encroaching sea.

The growth of State industry depended primarily on the accumulation of capital to finance industrial development; and the fundamental economic question of socialism became the question of the source and the forms of this socialist accumulation. Leaving aside capital from abroad, the two sources of such accumulation consisted in the surplus production of State industry itself and the " exploitation " of this weaker small-scale private economy. The less advanced was the country on the road of industrialisation, the greater the need of accumulation by industry to strengthen its position and the more reliance would it have to place on the second, in the absence of the first, source of accumulation.

In dealing with the origin of capitalism Marx had used the term " primitive accumulation " to describe the accumulation of capital at the expense of the expropriation of small producers, directly or through the gradual pressure of monopoly in some form.[1] This " primitive accumulation," " playing in Political Economy about the same part as original sin in theology," when it had laid the basis of class division

[1] Marx, *Capital*, Vol. I, pp. 736 *seq.*; also cf. the writer's *Capitalis Enterprise*, 204–314.

and inequality, gave way to normal accumulation out of the "normal profits" of industry. Preobrajensky transferred the term to his own problem, and used "primitive socialist accumulation" to refer to "the accumulation in the hands of the State of material means obtained chiefly from sources lying outside the State economic system. In a backward agrarian country this accumulation is bound to play a very great rôle. Primitive accumulation predominates conspicuously during this (transition) period; and we must therefore designate this whole stage as the period of primitive or preparatory socialist accumulation." These outside spheres of economy he termed "colonies"; and the necessary economic basis of the transition period was a relation of "exploitation" between the "metropolis" of State industry and its surrounding "colonies," the former drawing in "surplus-value" from the latter, whereby it expanded the basis of industry, its productivity and the possibility of living on its own surplus, until finally petty private economy was crushed out and "engulfed" in socialist economy, as the rise of capitalism had crushed out the peasant and the small craftsman and turned them into proletarians.[1]

The methods of this accumulation were two in number. First, the "colonial" areas might be subjected to direct taxation. But this had very definite limits: it might be evaded; it was more easily felt and more likely to cause political complications. Second, and more important, was the method of market exchange between State industry and the "colonies." Through the monopoly position of State industry on the market and by measures of "Socialist Protectionism" adopted by the State for the express purpose of encouraging socialist industry, the rate of interchange between State economy and its "colonies" could be turned to the advantage of the former. Since this would operate by "altering and partly cancelling the law of (labour)

[1] Preobrajensky, *op. cit.*, 59 *seq.*, 69–70, 78 *seq.* It seems distinctly misleading for Prof. Karlgren to imply that this theory of "colonies" was the official theory of the Government in its dealings with the peasantry (*Bolshevist Russia*, 163).

value "—that is, by causing the product of a unit of labour or effort in State economy to exchange for the product of several units of labour in the colonies—it involved an " exploitation " of the latter by the former, and the creation of " surplus-value " for the benefit of socialist accumulation. In other words, the " law of socialist accumulation " implied for Russia a monopoly price policy for State industry;[1] and socialism would develop according as the monopoly position of State industry and measures of State Protectionism succeeded in turning the rate of exchange between town and village in the former's favour. The only limit to this policy was the necessity for State industry, because of its backwardness, to make use of private capital for the time being and the necessity not to kill the goose so long as gold eggs were essential to socialist accumulation. " Monopolist capitalism," wrote Preobrajensky, " leads to the creation of monopolist prices for the products of industry in the home markets, gains a surplus profit in consequence of the exploitation of the small producers, and thus prepares the ground for the price policy of the period of primitive socialist accumulation. But the concentration of the whole of the big industries of the country in the hands of a single trust, that is, in the hands of the Workers' State, increases to an extraordinary extent the possibility of carrying out such a price policy on the basis of monopoly, a price policy simply signifying another form of taxation of private production." The " dictatorship of industry " became the Appian Way to Socialism; and a return to the conditions of " war communism " was only postponed in favour of the expedient of placing china eggs in the nest to encourage the goose to continue laying.

Here one is at the very core of the 1923–4 discussions.

[1] Preobrajensky wrote: " I deliberately avoid saying ' increased prices,' since taxation in combination with sinking prices is not only possible but would in our case certainly attend sinking or unaltered prices. This is possible for the reason that when the cost price of goods is reduced the selling price is not reduced by the whole amount of the reduction of cost price, the difference being added to the funds of socialist accumulation " (*Ibid.*, 80).

Presented with an abstract chart of the road to socialism, one can see the crucial significance of that dividing of the ways which the " scissors " presented, and which to first glance seemed a trifling issue of administrative forms. It is always a favourite topic of academic socialism to discuss whether the transfer of power to the workers, instead of being the harbinger of a classless society, may not result rather in a mere inversion of an exploiting system, with the workers as the new ruling class. The usual answer of the Marxist is that the workers will constitute the majority of the community, at least when they have absorbed in their ranks the former lower middle class (salariat, intellectuals, small business men, etc.), and will have no substantial section of society which they can exploit. The seizure of power by an " aristocracy of labour " which like a mediæval gild closed its ranks to new-comers might have this result; but a movement basing itself on the working class as a *whole* would have no others to exploit: it would merely absorb them into itself. Such a retort, however, is not valid for a backward agrarian country, where there exists the important " third class " of the peasantry, constituting a majority of the population. Moreover, it is possible for the working class of an advanced industrial country, if it has " colonies " in backward countries, to turn and exploit, as the former masters have done, the weaker colonial peoples : palace slaves often incline to ape the manners of their masters and to swagger over the humbler plantation slaves outside. In this way the old exploiting system might merely be transformed into a new one, and the previous capitalist class struggle yield place to a new, more violent struggle of town *v.* country, of industrial Europe *v.* agricultural Asia. History would have completed a turn of a dismal spiral, with the exploitation of the countryside by the mediæval towns and of colonies by Mercantilist nations of the Atlantic seaboard reproducing itself in 20th-century terms.

True, Preobrajensky envisaged this exploitation of " colonial areas " as lasting for no more than a season, and as merely providing the means for that expansion of industrialism which would ultimately absorb the inhabitants of these backward areas into the ranks of the working class. But it does not need an abnormal scepticism to doubt whether history would actually take this road. Is it not equally possible that in a decade or two, when revolutionary traditions have faded into a legend, the industrial workers who have tasted the fruit of " original sin " will desire to continue the eating of it? When they have had their cake made for them by others under duress, to expect them to turn and share it with its makers might well be a little utopian. If the goose will continue to lay golden eggs while it lives, what motive has its master to kill it in order that its soul may transmigrate and become a member of the master's family? Why should the working class, having become a ruling class for a season, alone fail to become exclusive, possessive and gild-like as has every other nascent exploiting class in history?

Moreover, there is a further consideration which Preobrajensky's theory of " primitive socialist accumulation " fails to take into account. The possibility of " squeezing " the peasantry was shown by the experience of " war communism " to be very definitely limited. Such a limit to his policy Preobrajensky recognised; but he pursued the matter no further. Peasant " squeezability " is probably smaller than that of an urban proletarian, because the former has his subsistence requirements safeguarded, while the proletarian's desire for income (in terms of effort) becomes more intense the further he is pushed towards or below the subsistence level. The peasant's desire to trade with the town is consequently fairly elastic, and becomes very elastic as soon as the terms of exchange are pressed appreciably against him. Hence, the town can only press its advantage against the village at the expense of diminishing fairly sharply the volume of trade between them. Conversely, to the extent that peasant demand (in terms of effort) for the products of industry is elastic, every improvement in the terms of exchange offered to him by the towns will encourage him to extend his efforts in producing for market and will considerably increase the volume of trade between village and town.[1] It follows that, if industry were to pursue a monopoly policy in the market, it could only do so at the expense of a restricted market for its products, as the " scissors " crisis showed, and also at the expense of a restricted volume (even though at an improved *rate*) of foodstuffs and raw materials. Accordingly the expansion of industry would necessarily proceed at a slower pace than otherwise: its expansion would be limited (and also the possibility of enlarged supply of food and raw materials) to the economies of cost obtainable from the exploitation of inventions and the sinking of new capital in industry. And such economies over a given period of time might well be considerably smaller than the " increasing returns " to be gained by extended sales and extended production, facilitated by a much smaller investment of capital—advantages which would be augmented by the more plentiful supply of foodstuffs and raw materials which the more favourable terms of exchange called forth from the peasantry. In other words, with a larger total production of industry and agriculture combined, the town workers as a class would in the long run get a greater aggregate income of utilities, even though their share of the whole and the *rate* of income in terms of their labour might be less; and with this greater income the objective possibility of capital accumulation would be greater. If the elasticity of peasant demand were considerable, and also the " internal " and " external economies " to be gained by industry from an expanded scale of production, then the town workers, while securing a greater aggregate income, might even receive a better rate of income in terms of their effort than if they had relied on a monopoly policy of restricting the scale of production and securing an improved rate of exchange between industrial and agricultural products.

[1] Cf. above p. 79 footnote, and the fuller treatment of this argument in the Excursus to Chapters Eight and Nine.

Thus, whereas under an individualist system it would be in the interests of a group of capitalists, or in the short-period interests of the working class as a whole to pursue a monopoly policy of exploiting "colonial areas," such a policy would actually be contrary to the long-period interests of the working class as a whole. Only on the assumption that peasant demand for industrial products in terms of effort were inelastic, which there is strong reason to believe it is not, would Preobrajensky's policy on economic grounds hold good.

This was in substance the argument which Bukharin advanced in a vigorous criticism of Preobrajensky's policy.[1] Lenin had demonstrated on political grounds that a monopoly, exploiting policy by the proletariat towards the peasantry was contrary to the workers' interests. Since the workers standing alone were too weak to seize and to hold the reins of power—and the less industrially developed the country, the more was this true—they must treat the poorer and "middle" peasants as equals and as partners, even while the workers remained the active partner and senior partner in the enterprise. This was the very fulcrum of his controversies with German Marxists, such as Rosa Luxemburg, before the war, and the reason for his elevation of the *smytchka* to be the first principle of political strategy. It was for this that he had scrapped "war communism" and made of the *smytchka* the corner-stone of the New Economic Policy. The town workers must lead the way along the road to socialism; but they must take with them the peasantry as fellow-travellers.

[1] Printed in *International Press Correspondence* (Vienna), Vol. 5, No. 5. Bukharin denounced Preobrajensky's theory as "completely trade unionist and gild-like in character" (p. 40). "It would be nonsense," he wrote, "on our part to renounce the advantages of our monopolist position. But while utilising these advantages we must take care not to diminish the powers of absorption of the home market, but to increase these powers. This is the most important point. The next is: we must utilise every advantage gained in such a manner that it leads to an extension of the field of production and the cheapening of production, to the reduction of cost prices, and consequently to ever cheaper prices in each successive cycle of production" (p. 45).

Now came the evangelists of "dictatorship of industry," admitting the force of the argument on political grounds, but arguing that on economic ground the opposite policy was desirable, and that the "dictatorship of industry" should be pressed so far as political considerations would allow. Moreover, Trotsky was suspected of never having accepted even the political argument for the *smytchka*, save as a temporary expedient at the moment of revolution and to provide a "breathing space" in the subsequent reconstruction period. In his theory of "permanent revolution" some years previous he had expounded the view that the road to socialism lay across a second revolution, in which the workers having seized power in the towns would then have to wage a fresh class struggle against the reactionary individualist tendencies of the peasantry; and this second struggle could only be carried to success in a backward agrarian country if the workers could lean on the support of a workers' revolution in the industrialised West.[1] Thus, the methods of "war communism," even if they had been pressed too violently and had come too soon in 1919 and 1920, must sooner or later be taken up again if socialism were to be achieved. Not "war communism," to this view, but N E P itself appeared as an expedient and a deviation. Clearly this political theory of "permanent revolution" of Trotsky had a strong affinity with Preobrajensky's "law of primitive socialist accumulation"; and Bukharin hastened to denounce them as sinister half-brothers, destined to bring down the New Economic Policy about the ruins of the *smytchka* on which Lenin had built.

To this general critique Bukharin added the more special argument that a monopolist policy by industry would tend to lead to stagnation and "parasitic decay." Capitalism in its heyday was rendered progressive by the pressure of competition; but under monopolist capitalism this spur to progress largely vanished. If, then, industry under a Workers' State, with its much enhanced monopoly power, were to

[1] Trotsky, 1905, pp. 4–5.

content itself with living on " easy " surplus profits, what was to prevent the natural tendency to rest upon the oars? What spur was there to industrial progress? Only by the State imposing on industrial organs a policy of constant lowering of prices as output expanded would the necessary pressure be applied to industrial administrators to compel them to seek out ways and means of cheapening production.

At the 13th Conference the cleavage between the two policies had not as yet been formulated in such clear-cut general terms. Nevertheless, the deeper issue was evident as a strong undercurrent beneath the discussion of more commonplace details of immediate policy. Rykov had already on behalf of the official policy made an extensive reply to the criticisms of the opposition. The " scissors " crisis had been said to be due to an insufficient carrying out of the resolution of the 12th Congress, drafted by Trotsky, concerning the " concentration " of industry and industrial planning. But " if we examine the actual practice of our economic organs during the past year," Rykov replied, " we see that the interests of the peasantry were taken too little into consideration, and that if any reproach can be made against the Party Centre at the present time, it is that though it has proved fully equal to its task in the industrial question, and in suitably adapting Comrade Trotsky's draft resolution, it has not taken sufficient care that the alteration provided for in the peasant question should be fully and completely realised in the activity of our economic organs."[1] The insistence on a " plan " as the sovereign specific he dismissed as mere worship of phrases which glossed over the real problem. " When I was in Vesenha," he said, " nothing was easier than to see plans. In every Glavka and Centre there was a literary person. One rang him up on the telephone, and literally in three hours a plan was ready with all its lines and circles and so forth. But this plan could in no way take into account the conditions of our market." To talk of

[1] Speech at Meeting of Moscow Party Nuclei, 29.12.23, reported in *Econ. Jizn*, 2.1.24.

plans and to make them was easy; to understand the facts of the market position was not. The real cause of the autumn crisis was that industry had failed to adapt itself to the peasant market: it was "principally due to the disparity in price of agricultural products and the products of factory industry," owing to the misuse of the monopoly power of trusts and syndicates. Hence the adaptation of industrial price policy to the village market was the primary remedy; and "there are many capital outlays which must be postponed until such time as industry has won the possibility of increasing its revenues on the basis of an extended peasant market and increased mass production." "Every kopeck which can be applied for the reconstruction of industry must be expended for this purpose without the slightest delay. But this must be done by forming an alliance with the peasantry, and not by fixing prices which the peasantry cannot possibly pay. The conquest and satisfying of the peasant market will bring about socialist accumulation, and the effect of this accumulation must be expressed in the steady growth of our industry and economics." True, the private trader played a considerable part in village trade—in retail trade a predominant part.[1] This indicated the need to pay special attention to developing the co-operative apparatus; but it was no ground for alarmist views. Hitherto the State had been unable to afford the capital to engage in trade on any considerable scale; and the private trader had accordingly performed a definite service to State industry which was considerably greater than any profit he secured. In some rural districts "the conditions obtaining are so Asiatic that there are not only no retail shops, but not even pedlars. Where such a state of affairs obtains, the private retail business is naturally a step forward in comparison with present conditions, and it is manifestly impossible that 'State capitalism' should set itself the task after only

[1] According to Rykov's figures the State and co-operatives controlled 85 per cent of wholesale trade, but private enterprise 83 per cent of retail trade.

three years of N E P of attaining a state of affairs where only a small number of State organs are required, forming an immediate connection between the factory and the consumer." Moreover the best way of displacing the private trader was precisely the way of lowered prices: State and co-operative trading organs winning the custom of the peasants by cheaper sales.[1]

Rykov's reply to the discussion at the 13th Conference was less general in character and was devoted to a reply to the specific points raised in the opposition speeches. The whole analysis of the autumn crisis by the opposition was in his opinion incorrect. Piatakov had called it a crisis of under-production and had even denied the existence of a sales-crisis altogether. But this was contradicted by the figures of Bourse turnover which showed a sharp fall in the figures of turnover in October and an accumulation of unsold stocks. Import goods which were not available at home, by all means. But what use to import commodities to repair a supposed deficit when there were eighty million roubles-worth accumulated in the warehouses? The key to the crisis was the peasant refusal to buy at the existing high prices; and the remedy was to carry through a strenuous campaign to reduce the price of industrial goods.[2]

The 13th Conference rejected the opposition proposals and endorsed the official point of view, and the policy of lowering industrial prices which had been commenced in October was continued. In March the currency reform was introduced, and the career of the paper rouble was brought to its close. The issue of the old rouble was discontinued, and in its place the new Treasury Note, convertible at a fixed rate into chervontsi, was issued by Narcomfin; with the old rouble redeemable up to May 10th at the rate of 50,000 paper roubles (1923) for one rouble of the new denomination. Meanwhile the "scissors" had begun rapidly to close. The over-valuation of industrial goods against agricultural, as compared with pre-war, which on October 1st had reached

[1] *Ibid.* [2] *Pravda*, 19.1.24.

a ratio of more than 3 : 1 on the wholesale market, by the end of the year had fallen to 2 : 1, and by October 1924 had fallen to less than 1·5 : 1.[1] The index number of agricultural prices had risen in the former period from ·56 to ·74, while the industrial index had fallen from 1·72 to 1·47.[2] In the course of 1924 the closing of the " scissors " continued. Rye, which in August 1923 was priced at 49 kopecks a pood, by August 1924 sold for 100, and wheat in the same 12 months rose from 92 kopecks to 164.[3] By February 1st, 1924, industrial prices on the average had fallen by some 14 per cent, and by October 1st, 1924, they showed a reduction of 29 per cent over the high point of the previous October, accompanied by a 30 per cent increase in output; this reduction varying from some 40 per cent in textiles and 35 per cent in the food industry and 28 per cent in mining to 15 per cent in metal and 6 per cent in woodworking.[4] To the extent of about two-thirds this price reduction in industry was covered by economy of costs—an economy achieved not by a lowering of wages, but in face of a rise. For the rest, it was at the expense of lowered profits to trusts and syndicates; and industrial profits for 1923–4 were substantially lower than the previous year, although when expressed in terms of goods the decrease disappeared.[5] The " scissors " to-day still persists and remains an important problem; but its acute stage, when it threatened a crisis for industry and a growing wave of peasant discontent, has passed.

When in the summer of 1924 Russia faced again an inferior harvest, she had already turned her back on the " dictatorship of industry," and had passed the parting of the ways. The successful currency reform in the spring had

[1] A. K. in *Econ. Jizn*, 9.1.24; Krumin in *Econ. Oboz.*, Dec. 1924, 8–9.

[2] *Econ. Jizn*, 16.1.24. In both cases 1913=1.

[3] *Econ. Review*, 7.11.24. Rosenfeld gives different figures for retail *uyezd* prices between Oct. 1923 and Oct. 1924: namely, rye 37 and 80, wheat 62 and 113, oats 35 and 74, barley 29 and 89 (*op. cit.*, 449).

[4] A. Grintser in *Econ. Oboz.*, May 1926, 50–1; *Econ. Review*, 7.11.24.

[5] Djerjinsky, *op. cit.*, 41.

done something to symbolise the ending of the critical stage of reconstruction and the vindication of the *smytchka* as the sovereign principal of N E P. But though his solution had been rejected, the problem which Preobrajensky had presented of the source and method of socialist accumulation still remained. For 1924 it was not a matter of immediate import, since reserves of unused capital capacity were still to hand. But by 1925 this reserve had approached exhaustion, and the question of capital accumulation became the vital problem of Russia's future.

EXCURSUS TO CHAPTERS EIGHT AND NINE: ON TRADE BETWEEN INDUSTRY AND PEASANT AGRICULTURE VIEWED AS A SPECIAL CASE OF EXCHANGE BETWEEN "NON-COMPETING GROUPS"

1. LET the two lines A′ and B′ in Diagram One represent the terms on which A and B, two groups of traders on opposite sides of any market, are willing to transact exchange; and let it be supposed for the sake of simplicity that the exchange is carried on by direct barter without the intervention of money, and that A desires to exchange a certain commodity (or group of commodities) *a*, and B to exchange a certain commodity (or group of commodities) *b*. The quantities measured along A and B respectively represent *total* quantities of *a* and *b* which are offered for sale; and the *rate* of exchange is represented by $\frac{a}{b}$ or its inverse.

The fact that the lines A′ and B′ are both straight lines and are parallel to B and A respectively implies that the two groups of traders have a rigidly fixed supply of goods of which they desire to dispose, *whatever the rate* at which they can sell them: however unfavourable or favourable to themselves the rate of exchange may be, they are willing to offer the same quantity for sale. In other words, the elasticity of demand of both parties is constant for all rates of exchange, and the elasticity is equal to Unity. The short-period situation will in practice tend to approximate to this imaginary case to the extent that commodities are perishable, costly to hold in stock, and take some time to reproduce.

It will follow that if the groups on the two sides of the market are equally placed in bargaining strength, the equilibrium point at which market transactions will settle down will be the point X, where the lines A′ and B′ intersect.

For, if, travelling left to right and upwards along A′ and B′, exchange takes place at any point before X is reached, the best rate which A will offer and the best rate which B will offer will overlap, and it will be in the interests of both to extend their dealings up to (but not beyond) X. At this point the rate of exchange will be represented by the slant of the dotted line XO (or more exactly by the tangent of the angle between XO and line A or B), and will be the rate which under conditions of competition will best satisfy both parties.

Let it further be assumed that *a* and *b* are produced by persons A and B by their own efforts, and that at the rate of exchange OX the amount of *b* that is sold costs its producers

Diagram One

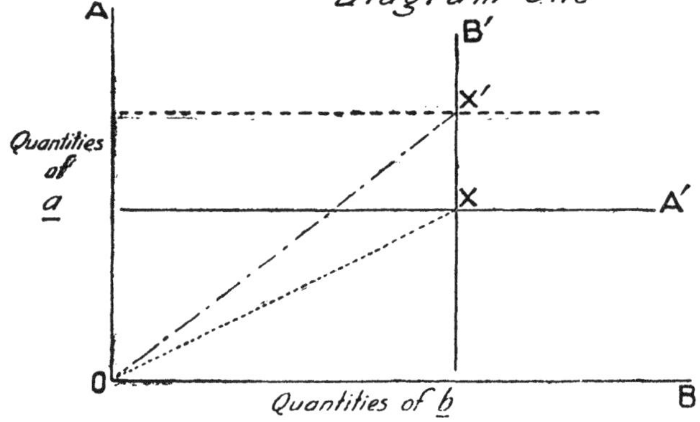

a greater quantity of effort or labour than the amount of *a* that is sold. Then, other things being equal,[1] a tendency will arise for a certain number of persons, formerly belonging to group B, to *cross over the market* and to become producers and sellers of the more profitable commodity *a* instead. If this were to occur, then the line A′ would tend to rise to a new position, owing to the influx into that side of the market of new competitors willing to offer more favourable

[1] This assumes the absence of such complicating factors as (*a*) different conditions of natural scarcity expressed in production under different rates of diminishing returns, in which case the labour expended at the *margin*, or under least favourable conditions, would be relevant; (*b*) different quantities of capital required to produce *a* and *b*; (*c*) hindrances to perfect competition and to perfect mobility, both from one side of the market to the other and along each side of the market.

terms of trade to B; and as a result a new rate of exchange, OX′, would tend to be established.[1] Consequently, the long-period equilibrium in the market would be where the rate of exchange OX′ represented the real cost, or the expenditure of labour or effort, of producing the relevant quantities of *a* and *b*.

2. If, however, conditions should be such that this movement from one side of the market to the other were impossible or were difficult (e.g. because A represented an exclusive gild, or because A and B were different nationalities or social classes), this tendency would not operate. This would be a case of what Cairnes called "*non-competing groups.*" As a result, the rate of exchange OX might be such that the quantity of *b* sold represented several times more units of labour than did the quantity of *a* which B secured in return; and because of the hindrance to crossing from one side of the market to the other, there would be no tendency at work to alter this equilibrium. The reason of B's willingness to accept such relatively unfavourable terms of trade (i.e. the reason for the position of the line B′ in Diagram One) would be her inability to produce *a* herself any cheaper, owing (i) to unfavourable natural conditions governing production, (ii) to relatively backward conditions of productive organisation and technique.[2]

[1] Actually, of course, B′ would at the same time tend to move to the left; but for simplicity we have left this out of account in our diagram.

[2] In so far as (ii) is due to B having a smaller fund of capital resources than A, and in so far as this fact involves a greater burden, past or present, to A in the creation of that capital (*apart* from the direct effort-cost of building the capital goods), allowance for this fact will have to be made and a modification introduced in the ensuing argument. In this case since the two types of "real burden" will be incommensurable, "units of real cost" cannot be postulated, and instead the assumption of the values ruling in an ideal state of free competition and absence of "non-competing groups" (under which values will tend to represent real cost) will have to be made. For this reason the simpler form of analysis has been used in the text as a "first approximation."

Actually, however, the modification which has to be made in the analysis by reason of this consideration is probably very small; for the reason that the burden involved in the creation of capital (even if it be regarded as a "real cost") does not fall, except for a small fraction

This is likely to be the nature of exchange between a propertied class and a propertyless class (in this case the exchange is of income against labour-power). It is also likely to be the characteristic of exchange between an advanced industrial country and a backward country, or, more generally, between developed industrial communities and agricultural peasant areas. In this sense the former, possessing certain differential advantages, both natural and acquired, may be said to " exploit " the latter, or at least reap from them a " differential surplus." This was the fortunate relation in which European nations, and Britain in particular, stood in the 19th century in their trade with backward countries outside Europe. From this trade Britain was able to acquire a differential surplus which gave to her *entrepreneurs* what may be termed a *super-profit*—a profit which would not have been acquired except from these conditions of foreign trade.[1] This in turn raised the *entrepreneurs'* marginal demand price for the factors of production; and it became the primary aim of British trade unionism to share in this super-profit through wage-advances, first under the " Old Unionism " by gild-like restrictions in

of it (the marginal units), on the persons who possess and invest it (see above, p. 174, footnote). The additional capital used by A is probably in main part the fruit of previous monopoly or differential advantages, in which case the " burden " of its creation has fallen, not on A, but on those " exploited " by A. In so far as A's capital is merely accumulated out of super-profit gained at the expense of B, B (not A) bears the burden of the accumulation. A man who puts out £1 at compound interest till it becomes £10 can hardly be said (except in a limited and special sense which is not comparable to the " real cost " involved in effort) to suffer any " burden " greater than the initial £1; and if he has inherited the £1, and is not abnormally poor, he does not even suffer that much " burden."

[1] Cf. Marx: " Capitals invested in foreign trade are in a position to yield a higher rate of profit, because they come in competition with commodities produced in other countries with lesser facilities of production, so that an advanced country is enabled to sell its goods above their (labour) value, even when it sells them cheaper than the competing country. . . . These higher rates of profit realised by capitals invested in certain lines and sent home by them . . . enter as elements into the average rate of profit and keep it up to that extent . . . (and) so far as the rate of profit is higher it may go hand-in-hand with a low level of prices if the natural conditions are favourable " (*Capital*, Vol. III, 278–80).

favour of an " aristocracy of labour," later under the " New Unionism " by collective bargaining on behalf of the unskilled. This found a parallel in other leading European countries, " chained up the Malthusian devil " and provided the objective basis for the rise of Reformist Socialism.

3. Finally, let it be assumed that in our imaginary case the condition of free competition between sellers on both sides of the market is replaced by a degree of deliberate monopoly, partial or complete, on the part of A. (This might take the form merely of a customary desire " not to spoil the market " or to avoid " poaching," or of a cartel agreement.) This would be equivalent to a lowering of the line A′ to a new position, so that the rate of exchange, OX, was moved to a new position more favourable to A and less favourable to B. The fact that in Diagram One we have assumed B's desire to trade to have a constant elasticity no greater than Unity means that B is " squeezable " to an indefinite extent. Under these new conditions A secures a monopoly gain at the expense of B; but only by restricting the sales of *a*. The end may be achieved either by directly restricting the supply of *a* offered for sale, or by agreeing upon a price or rate of exchange below which no offers of trade will be accepted. Both have the same effect, equivalent to lowering the line A′ and diminishing the total trade between A and B.

In the relations between a propertied and a wage-earning class, this may come about in the form of a tacit or open agreement between employers as to the level of wages they will offer, or by the growth of combines and trade associations among producers and sellers of commodities consumed by the wage-earning class. This will tend to increase the surplus which the former class can acquire at the expense of the latter.[1] In trade between an industrial community and an agricultural area, it may come about through the former fixing minimum prices for its own products and maximum

[1] If this results in a lessening of the national income it will not necessarily lead to an absolute increase, while producing a relative increase, in the share of the propertied class.

prices for agricultural products, or by limiting the possibilities open to agricultural producers to find alternative markets in which to sell, as was done by the mediæval towns;[1] or, again, if the agricultural country is a "colony," by forcing it to buy certain manufactured goods only from the Mother Country and to refrain from making them itself, and to export certain agricultural produce only to the Mother Country, as was done by Mercantilist England in the 17th and 18th centuries. A modern instance is afforded by the transition from the ordinary mid-19th century forms of colonial trade to modern Imperialism—a transition which was characterised by the adoption of deliberate measures of a monopoly character to increase the acquisition of super-profit by turning the rate of interchange in colonial trade further in favour of the Imperialist country than it would otherwise have been. These measures fall under two heads. First are those which in Diagram One would be represented by a lowering of A's demand curve; for instance, the growth of large trading organisations, combines, associations, or cartels having partial or complete monopoly in specific colonial markets and the consequent limiting of competition in buying from petty colonial producers and selling to colonial buyers. Second are those measures which would be represented by an extension of B's demand curve to the right. For instance, the attempt to annex colonial areas and convert them into more or less of a "private market" for the Imperialist country,[2] and so to exclude or limit alternative sources of sale and purchase for the colonial country. Again, the levying of land or poll taxes on native producers or the reduction of native "land reserves," as in the case of certain African colonies, will increase the native's desire to gain income, either by marketing his produce or selling his labour-power for wages, and so will increase his willingness

[1] Cf. the writer's *Capitalist Enterprise*, 204 *seq.*

[2] Principally by means of special business connections and preferences in the matter of "concessions," orders for constructional work and materials, loans, etc., in virtue of the political influence exerted, demarcation of "spheres of influence," etc.

to trade on less favourable terms.[1] The first group of methods will give increased super-profit to the Imperialist country accompanied by a decreased volume of trade, but in the second accompanied by an increased trade. Finally, in the case of Russia in 1923 the "scissors" phenomenon was evidence of the use of its monopoly power by State industry to turn the rate of interchange between itself and the village in its own favour, and so to derive a "super-profit" at the peasants' expense; and the "sales crisis" of the autumn showed that this could only be done at the expense of reduced trade between village and town.

4. On the other hand the exploited group may take deliberate monopolist measures to turn the rate of exchange in its favour and so lessen its exploitation. A trade union can fix a minimum price for its labour; a less advanced country can place an import duty on products from a more advanced country; a group of peasant producers may form a co-operative agency for purchase and sale. But these measures, so long as existing underlying conditions remain, cannot bring any immediate gain to the weaker party, unless the effect of the measures is merely to counteract and defeat the superior bargaining power of the other party; and if the demand of the latter has an elasticity greater than Unity the improved *rate* can only be achieved at the expense, in the first case of lessened employment, and in the second case of lessened trade, and hence of lessened aggregate income of utilities.[2] If, however, the measures taken by the weaker country have the "protective" effect of increasing its acquired "productive powers" in the future, then the immediate loss may be offset by a future gain, when its reliance on foreign products is less intense. The industrialisation of former "backward" countries to which the export

[1] For the country as a whole this will also apply if it is indebted to foreign capital (cf. Marshall, *Money Credit and Commerce*, App. J., 349).

[2] The lesser income of utilities, however, depends on the demand of the other group having an Elasticity greater than Unity, which is the usual case (see below, Sections 5 and 7). Though the total trade and total receipts will be lessened, the *profit* on the trade may not, if the fall of costs is greater than the fall of receipts.

of capital leads encourages this tendency, and by lessening the inequality between nations in foreign trade tends to diminish the super-profit which the more advanced countries can acquire and so to bring about a relative, and even absolute, decline in their position.

5. In actual practice the desire to trade on the part of individuals and groups in a market in the long period is unlikely to have an elasticity equal to Unity, or to have a constant elasticity for all rates of exchange. In other words, in Diagram One the lines A′ and B′ will not be parallel to B and A, and they will not be straight lines, but curves. In the ordinary case these curves will tend to have an elasticity greater than Unity, and an elasticity which for a small volume of trade starts by being considerable, and then

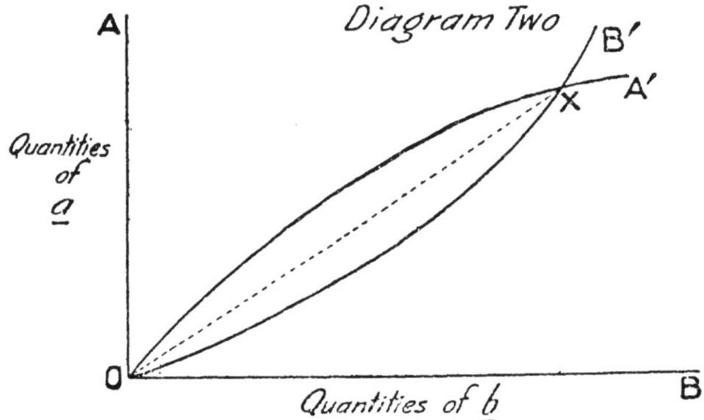

diminishes as the desire to trade approaches satiety. This is shown in Diagram Two. Only in exceptional cases is either curve in any relevant portion of it likely to show an elasticity as small as or less than Unity.[1] Nevertheless these special cases are found, and are most likely to be found where the two groups in question trade for the most part exclusively with one another.[2] For instance, a wage-earner exchanging labour-power for income may, in the region of the subsistence-level or an accustomed standard of life, have a desire

[1] Cf. Marshall, *Money Credit and Commerce*, App. J. When Marshall stressed the exceptional nature of such cases he was referring to conditions of international trade.

[2] Cf. *Ibid.*, 358.

for income in terms of effort that has an elasticity equal to or even less than Unity. In trade between town and village the town will tend to start with a very inelastic demand for foodstuffs—a demand which then becomes more elastic when essential subsistence is obtained. The more self-supporting the group, the more elastic its desire to trade; the more dependent it is on supplies from the second group, owing to weakness of its own productive powers and to absence of alternative sources of supply, the less elastic its desire to trade will be, at any rate for a certain minimum quantity. It will follow that the peasant, being assured at least subsistence, will tend to have a more elastic demand than the proletarian.

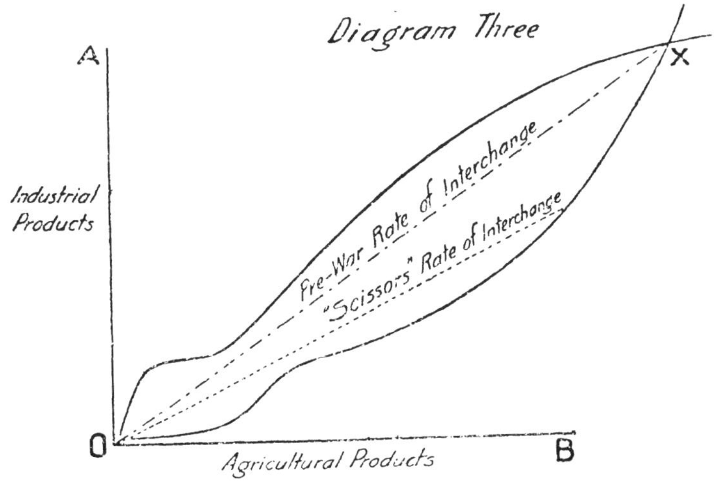

This elasticity of demand for the products of the industry of the home country will be greater if he can secure access to foreign markets for exchanging his produce against manufactures, or if he can procure manufactures from his own village (*kustarni*) industry. For a certain minimum quantity of essential manufactures, such as salt, kerosene, clothing, iron implements, his demand will probably be fairly inelastic, though not so inelastic as the townsman's demand for a minimum quantity of agricultural produce; but for quantities in excess of this it may be very elastic. It seems probable that conditions of trade between State industry and peasant agriculture in Russia approximate to those represented in Diagram Three.

6. In Diagram Two or Three, in place of quantities of produce, *units of effort* involved in producing *a* and *b* might be used as the units measured along A and B. (These units would not be actually measurable, but only theoretically measurable.) If equal units were measured by equal distances along A and B, then the differential gain acquired by one side or the other out of exchange between them could be measured by the divergence of OX from an angle of 45° from A or B. In Diagram Three, for instance, the pre-war rate of interchange probably represented a considerable differential gain to the towns at the expense of the village, owing to the greater productivity of labour in manufacture than in peasant agriculture, and owing to the weaker position of the peasant in the market; and this set up a tendency over a long period for a gradual transfer of population from agriculture to industry and of capital into agriculture, a process which did not, however, proceed fast enough to rectify the initial difference. If production were carried on under conditions of "constant returns," the curves would be the same whether units of produce or units of effort were used; but if under conditions of increasing returns the curve in terms of produce would show a greater elasticity, and under diminishing returns a smaller elasticity, than the curve in terms of effort. Any improvement in the methods of production, increasing the productivity of a unit of effort or labour, will extend the demand curve expressed in produce, and so extend the total volume of trade, even while the desire to trade in terms of effort remains constant. In the case of agriculture a good harvest, increasing the yield of a unit of labour, will have the same effect.

7. It follows that if the curve of peasant demand has an elasticity greater than Unity, any monopolistic attempt by direct measures to turn the rate of interchange to his disadvantage (other than indirect measures designed to extend his demand curve to the right, referred to above in Section 3)

must have the effect of lessening the volume of trade between village and town, and lessening the aggregate income of agricultural goods which the town can secure. The more elastic the peasant demand, the greater will this shrinkage in the volume of trade be. Conversely, every improvement in the rate of interchange offered to the peasant (expressed as raising and making more elastic the curve of the town's willingness to trade) will increase the amount of peasant produce offered on the market and the total income of agricultural produce which the town can secure.

If the peasants' desire to trade has an elasticity *equal* to Unity, a worsened rate of interchange will not diminish, and an improved rate of trade will not enhance his willingness to trade; and the total income of agricultural produce which the towns can secure will remain constant.

If the peasant's desire for trade has an elasticity *less* than Unity, a worsened rate of trade will increase, and an improved rate of trade will decrease, peasant willingness to trade and the aggregate income of agricultural goods which the town can secure by trade. In such circumstances the "squeezability" of the peasant will be at its greatest.

An Agricultural Tax on the peasant which is independent of the amount he places on the market will have the effect of extending the peasant demand curve to the right, and so extending his willingness to trade; since the peasant, having to pay the tax before he can acquire any industrial produce for himself, will have an increased desire to sell his produce. In this case the rate of interchange will move in favour of the town at the same time as trade is increased. But the extension of his demand curve will probably be less than the full amount of the tax (owing to diminishing returns and the increasing disutility of labour); and the *net* gain to the towns in the shape of increased income of agricultural goods will probably be less than the amount of the tax—a net gain which will be smaller relatively to the tax, the greater the tax is. The Agricultural Tax in Russia was actually based on output; but since only some 30 per cent of peasant output is placed on the market, the effect of the tax will tend to be, while reducing the total output, to increase the proportion placed upon the market. Part of the over-estimation of the surplus of grain in Russia in 1925 seems to have been due to a failure to calculate fully the effect of a diminished burden of the Agricultural Tax on the proportion that is marketed.

8. Marx's theory of industrial and commercial crises was mainly what one may term a theory of *disproportion*. In the course of industrial development under an individualist system there was a continual tendency for various industries and groups of industries to develop, not in proportion, but disproportionately. In particular this was true of the two main groups of industry: those producing means of production and those producing means of final consumption; since each technical change and each expansion of the scale of production disturbed the relations between these two groups. If the exchange between these two groups (again regarded as barter, without the intervention of money) were represented as exchange between A and B in Diagrams One or Two, then it would be clear that any expansion of A without a corresponding expansion of B, by raising the curve of A's desire to trade, would move the market rate of exchange in A's disfavour. This would tend to produce a "sales-crisis" in A,[1] and a tendency to closing down of production which might spread the influence of the crisis by the unemployment thereby created. True, industry tended in this way to reach an ultimate equilibrium, where the principle of proportionality was restored. But this was only a tendency which operated in "the long period," whereas the actual world was a succession of "short periods" in which economic change under "anarchic" conditions of production tended continually to disturb equilibrium; and the

[1] If, of course, the expansion of A were accompanied by an equivalent cheapening of production in A, this would not narrow A's profits and would not necessarily have any subsequent effect. Even so, it might produce a situation which for A would appear as a "sales crisis," if the continuance of the higher profits resulting from the economies had been anticipated, and this anticipation had been partly capitalised.

tendency to ultimate restoration of an equilibrium only worked through disappointment of business expectations and through partial or general crises. If *entrepreneurs* in the over-expanded industries cut prices immediately and were willing in face of lower profits to continue production until proportionality was restored by the expansion of other industries, the " sales crisis " might be quickly passed and would not spread in a general set-back to all trade and industry. But operating as isolated units, motivated by profit, it was contrary to their nature to do this.[1]

In addition to this *relative* overproduction, crises might also arise, according to the Marxian theory, from over-production of a *general* character. If we express the exchange of capitalists' outlay against labour-power between the capitalist class and the proletariat according to Diagram One or Two as an exchange between A and B, then it follows that anything which raises the curve A′ will turn the rate of interchange between A and B in B's favour, and so lower the degree of exploitation and the return on his outlay which A can secure from the transaction.[2] Anything which extends the scale of production of finished commodities (unless accompanied by a correlative decrease of labour costs through labour-saving economies) will tend to have this effect, and a " crisis " will tend to ensue before the *entrepreneur* adapts himself to the new situation.[3] This will be an influence in the search for new markets (e.g. in colonial countries) where the rate of interchange between A and B

[1] Cf. Marx, *Capital*, Vol 2, 457 *seq.*, and Max Beer in *The Plebs*, Vol. XIX, No. 6.

[2] This will involve a decline in aggregate profit in terms of money and of effort, but not necessarily in terms of goods in general. We are here assuming that the supply of labour is inelastic. The more elastic the supply of labour the less the rate of interchange will turn to the capitalists' disfavour.

[3] This extension of the scale of production may take place (*a*) through an increased investment of capital, (*b*) by a more intensive use of existing capital. In (*a*) the *rate* of profit will probably decline both in terms of goods and of money (assuming the money supply constant), while *aggregate* profit decreases in terms of money, but not necessarily of goods. In (*b*) the rate of profit will decrease in terms of money, but not necessarily in terms of goods.

is more favourable to A and there is possibility of drawing profit at the old level. Some persons looking at one side of the problem have interpreted Marx's theory as though it attributed crises to " under-consumption." But this was not Marx's view: indeed Marx pointed out that such a theory was either a tautology, or else, if it was meant to imply that crises could be cured by raising wages or by inflation, was false,[1] since such a cure would not alter the basic fact of lowered profitability of production. Lack of " consumers' purchasing power " is merely equivalent to the level of prices and profits being too high for the existing level of production, and a " crisis " is merely the travail involved in bringing the two levels into adjustment.

9. In Russia one of the chief economic advantages of a socialist system was considered to be the replacing of " anarchy of production " by a system of " planned " production. It was natural, therefore, that when the " sales crises " of spring 1922 and autumn 1923 occurred, they should both be attributed (as the opposition in 1923 attributed the 1923 crisis) to the absence of an adequate " planning " of productive development as a single whole, leading to " lack of proportion " in production. As Trotsky said: " Mistakes are inevitable, if only by reason of harvest variability. These errors will show themselves on the market under the form of insufficiency of products, stagnation, and crises. Nevertheless it is obvious that these crises will be less acute and prolonged according as a plan is seriously applied in all branches of State economy."[2]

The official policy, however, emphasised the relation between industry and agriculture as the cause of the autumn crisis of 1923. But this was not an ordinary crisis of disproportion. A " sales crisis " from the side of industry would be expected to arise from a disproportionately large development of industry relative to agriculture. Actually, the reverse was the case; and some members of the opposition even denied the existence of a general (as distinct from

[1] Marx, *op. cit.*, 475–6. [2] *Novy Kurs*, 70.

a partial) sales crisis of industry, asserting that the root cause of the "scissors" was the *under*-development of industry. The "sales crisis," therefore, could hardly be an ordinary phenomenon of disproportion, but was caused by the price policy of industry, for which the solution was to be found in the revision of that price policy. Even an ordinary "sales crisis" arising from disproportion could as a rule best be liquidated by a policy of continued production coupled with price-reduction; and it was only to the extent that socialist industry put up less resistance to a lowering of prices and profits than its predecessor that crises of general overproduction could be avoided. The spring crisis of 1922 was not a fair parallel with 1923 or with "normal" crises. It was an exceptional case, characterised by an extreme inelasticity of demand by industry for agricultural produce, coupled with a very small elasticity of supply of agricultural produce. Hence in this case a cheapening of industrial prices had no appreciable effect in securing for the towns increased agricultural supplies.

10. Since agriculture and industry represented to a considerable extent "non-competing groups," the ordinary principle of proportionality (which implies a relation of exchange values corresponding to the relation of marginal effort-costs) did not apply. On Preobrajensky's theory the ordinary principle of proportionality would designedly be violated in this case. According to the official theory, on the other hand, the principle of proportionality between industry and agriculture, while not immediately applicable, was to be held as the ultimate aim of economic development. This policy is the one calculated to maximise the production of industry and agriculture combined (relatively to effort), since the condition for maximising production (relatively to effort) is where productive resources are so distributed that relative exchange-values correspond to marginal effort-costs. But this principle only applies in the absence of substantial real costs of moving economic resources from one group to the other. If such real costs of movement exist, the

principle of proportionality must be modified to make allowance for these real costs. For instance, if a unit of labour were less productive in group B than in group A by an amount x, while the total real cost of transferring labour from B to A amounted to y, then total production relatively to effort would only be increased by such a transfer so long as x was greater than y.[1] Therefore, to the extent that such real costs of movement of capital and labour between A and B exist, an " exploitation " of B by A does not prevent the attainment of *optimum* production, so long as it is no greater than the equivalent of such real costs of movement. But if such " exploitation " exists in excess of this, it will offend against *optimum* productivity.

11. " Sales crises," on the one hand, and " goods famines " in industry, on the other, of a purely price character may arise from the effect of harvest fluctuations on the productivity of a unit of effort applied to agriculture. If peasant desire to trade in terms of *effort* remains constant, then harvest variation will cause the curve of peasant demand in terms of *goods* to fluctuate, causing a movement in the rate of exchange favourable or unfavourable to industry according as the harvest is respectively plentiful or scanty. Such fluctuations can be met, without further reaction on industry, by two alternative methods.

First, they can be met by the suitable adjustment of industrial prices to the varying situation, the result being to impose losses on industry at times of bad harvest, to be compensated for by extra gain during good harvest.

Alternatively, however, the situation may be met by so regulating the crediting of grain-purchasing organs as to place a constant aggregate of money at their disposal, whether the harvest be plentiful or scanty, thereby keeping the aggregate *money* purchasing-power of the peasants (and hence their money demand for industrial goods) at a constant magnitude. This alternative method would throw the effect of harvest variations on to agricultural money-prices instead

[1] Cf. Pigou, *Economics of Welfare*, 118–19.

of on to industrial money-prices. This is equivalent to so framing the State grain-purchasing policy as to make its demand in terms of *money* have an elasticity equal to Unity. This policy would not, as appears at first sight, involve a lowered incentive (or a relative " exploitation ") of peasant producers at times of good harvest when agricultural prices fell, since the aggregate return (in money and in industrial goods) to their effort would not alter.

But this division of the problem of exchange between town and village into its two separate parts—a sale against money and a subsequent purchase with money—does not alter the underlying real facts of the situation, namely, that a scanty harvest involves a real loss to the towns. If the town workers' demand for food had an elasticity equal to Unity, he would spend the same amount of income each year on food, and his money-demand for industrial goods would not alter. The loss in a bad harvest would fall on him simply in the shape of his getting less food for his money. If his demand had an elasticity greater or less than Unity the situation would be complicated by the fact that as food prices varied, he would at one time desire to spend more of his income, and at another time less of his income on food; and the remainder of his income which he had available to purchase industrial goods would fluctuate. This element of fluctuation could only be met in so far as the State grain organs followed a Joseph-policy of building grain reserves,[1] and so keeping the supply of grain placed on urban markets and its price constant from year to year, whatever the harvest. The State reserves would then be depleted in years of bad harvest and replenished in times of good harvest; no real cost, other than the cost of warehousing, would be involved to the community in the carrying of such reserves from year to year.

[1] A policy of accumulating a grain reserve was started in Russia in 1926.

CHAPTER TEN

THE PROBLEM OF FIXED CAPITAL

WHEN the Russian snows melted in the spring of 1925 there was a new hope in men's eyes. The past year had been one of hard struggle. Spring of 1924 had blossomed under the cloud of the currency reform, with the credit stringency it entailed and the fight against the "scissors." Summer came beneath the frown of a bad harvest, causing breathless fears lest the currency stabilisation might fail to be maintained. The winter had brought fresh financial difficulties for industry, caused by credit stringency and slackened village sales.[1] But by the spring of 1925 these clouds had gone. Fears for the maintenance of the currency reform, and with them credit stringency, were now things of the past; and by the summer hope, suddenly succeeding apprehension, became almost intoxication. Prospects of a "bumper" harvest led the peasant to unload reserves of grain and so to provide an expanding market for industrial goods. The efforts of the previous year began to bear fruit in a rapid industrial expansion which for the whole year showed an advance of over 50 per cent, bringing the level of industrial production to above 70 per cent of pre-war. Plans were made for a large grain export, and for an import of machinery in return, to fulfil an ambitious program of industrial re-equipment and extension. In outward signs the progress could almost be measured from week to week. Moscow offices suddenly acquired a new youth by an unprecedented "spring-cleaning." Public buildings in August gleamed bright with new paint and renovated stucco; while in the suburbs scaffolding

[1] This appears to have been due to the snowless winter, which, through fears of consequent ruin to the spring crops, caused the peasant to hold back grain reserves from the market (*Narod. Khos.*, 1924–5, 101–2).

climbed around new houses and blocks of flats. The gardens in Sverdlov Square, the Alexandra Gardens, and the Boulevards once again cooled the eye with the green of trimmed grass and the colour of flower-beds. Leningrad was everywhere congested by the activities of street repairers. In Moscow a growing service of new Leyland motor-buses commenced to invade the streets and to relieve the pressure on the over-crowded tramcars; while traffic experts even began to talk about a Moscow "tube." The hum of activity had come to include a new note. The task of restarting the wheels of industry was ending; the task of constructing new wheels had begun.

But it was this very task of constructing new wheels which presented a problem of greater magnitude even than the effort of restarting the old wheels in 1921. And those who dipped beneath the surface of things perceived behind the temporary prosperity of 1925 the gathering of difficulties, greater, if less spectacular, than Russia had so far faced. The spring and summer of 1925 had been witness of remarkable expansion, because the increased demand, based on good harvest expectations, had made possible industrial economies from the utilisation of idle capital equipment: "concentration" of industry in the past and increased "loading" of enterprises in the present had yielded to industry "increasing returns." But in the "loading" of capital equipment there is always an *optimum* point (just as there is in the intensive cultivation of land) beyond which more intensive employment will yield, not "increasing," but "diminishing returns," not economy of costs through lessened overhead, but increased "prime costs" through less efficient working.[1] By 1925 most of the

[1] This *optimum* will be at a point just before average costs (prime and overhead) begin to rise for an additional output. Before this point has been reached, marginal prime costs will have been rising, this rise having previously been counterbalanced by the fall in overhead costs per unit of output. The practicable limit of expanded production will be where marginal prime costs have risen so far as to balance the social utility created by the marginal increment of output (cf. Prof. Pigou in *Econ. Journal,* June 1927). An instance of rising prime costs as existing

economies from increased "loading" of enterprises had been gained. The first half of 1924–5 showed an economy of some 15 to 20 per cent in industrial costs over 1923–4, ranging from 13 per cent in oil to 28 per cent in cast iron.[1] But the "load" had in many cases reached a fairly high figure; while the actual process of concentration had advanced considerably beyond pre-war; so that a slightly greater number of workers were employed in a smaller number of enterprises and the proportion of these active enterprises which were of large size had increased. The enterprises with over 30 workers numbered at the beginning of 1926 5883 as against 8516 in 1913, while the total number of workers employed in them was some 2,339,000 as against 2,296,000 pre-war. But the proportion of these enterprises which employed over 1000 workers had risen between the two dates from 5·5 to 8·4 per cent, while the proportion of workers employed in these large enterprises had risen from 47·2 to 61 per cent. This concentration reached its apogee in the cotton industry, where 90 per cent of the workers were now in mills employing more than 1000 hands, as against a pre-war figure of 79 per cent, and the same number of workers were now employed in 290 enterprises as in 467 enterprises in 1913.[2]

Very largely, of course, this change represented definite "internal economies" to be obtained from organising production in larger units. At the same time it meant that the larger factories, which had not experienced any expansion of capital equipment, but rather a contraction owing to war-time depreciation, were now manned with a labour supply

equipment is used more intensively will be the decreased productivity of labour as the ratio of machinery to labour decreases. After a point it will not be worth while to employ more units of labour with the existing equipment. An American writer has laid down the principle that "the normal balance between fixed and circulating capital is reached when the saving in operating expenses to be effected by the next increase of fixed capital is equal to the fixed charge which that increase will create" (E. D. Jones, *The Administration of Industrial Enterprises*, 31).

[1] Rosenfeld, *op. cit.*, 444.

[2] A. Rashin in *Econ. Oboz*, July 1926, 91 *seq.*

some 25–30 per cent greater than before; and the ratio of capital to labour in industry had, therefore, fallen. Even allowing for a reserve of productive capacity in industry in pre-war times, and even allowing for the possibilities of capital-economising improvements (such as multiple-shifts), it seems clear that the *optimum* point in the " loading " of factories must have been reached, if not already passed. Unless industrial plant itself were expanded, further increase of production involved either a greater "loading" of existing enterprises, or else the reopening of smaller factories which were *ex hypothesi* less efficient. Both of these courses implied production at increased cost. In financial terms this situation would express itself in a rise in productive expenses in the future until they were no longer covered by selling price, and the profits of industry consequently dwindled to zero. From the social point of view, it would approach a *cul de sac* where the extra human effort required to expand production had become so great as to be no longer compensated by the extra utility thereby acquired. Neither inflation nor all the jugglery of financial medicine-men could exorcise this fact.

It seemed probable that this situation would be reached some time before industrial production attained to the pre-war amount. Since 1922 the depreciation of industrial equipment had been met by the building of amortisation funds charged to the current expenditure of the trust. But these funds had been accumulated as working capital in the coffers of the trusts rather than spent on repairs and renewals, and the charges themselves were criticised from various quarters as being too low to cover actual current depreciation.[1] Prior to this the depreciation suffered in the eight years of war and civil war had not been offset, either

[1] e.g. a convincing article by A. Kalmanovsky in *Plan. Khosiaistvo*, 1926, No. 4, 145 *seq.*, in which it is claimed that the amortisation charges covered in 1926 at most 59 per cent of actual amortisation. Another writer, Segal, however, in *Plan. Khos.*, 1926, No. 12, declared that the official amortisation charges fixed by Vęsenha were on the whole too high (pp. 47–8).

financially or actually, to anything like the same extent. During the war very little current repair work or renewals were done, even if private companies continued their customary financial allowances to cover depreciation;[1] while during the period of "war communism" almost all repair work was suspended, and in the military areas direct destruction of machinery, buildings and railway permanent-way was added to the ordinary effects of wear and tear. During the reconstruction period after 1921 a certain amount of leeway was made up: some of the worst ravages of the last few years were repaired, partly by the help of State subsidies from the Budget.[2] In so far as the subsidies expended in this way came from the proceeds of inflation, or later from the profits of the more prosperous industries, the previous decline in capital equipment—the disaccumulation of previous years—was being repaired by forced levies on

[1] Most of these financial allowances were probably later destroyed by inflation, in which case the Government financed its current expenditure directly at the expense of the depreciation of industrial equipment.

[2] Prof. Karlgren maintains that this subsidisation, enabling industry to charge prices which did not fully cover costs, made Russia's industrial recovery in a sense "unreal," and made her problem much easier than that of other countries in similar plight (*Bolshevist Russia*, 98–9). But this seems to be a fallacy. The real burden of repairing industrial plant and providing working capital exists, and falls on the community, whether it is met by subsidies or through industrial prices. It may be argued that the subsidy method was an easier way of shouldering the burden at the moment than any other, but the fact of the burden remains. A similar fallacy attaches to the same writer's claim that Russian industry "had a handicap very greatly in its favour" in inheriting industrial equipment from the past. But this would apply to any country under any circumstances at a given point in time. The real cost of bringing the industrial equipment into being is a thing of the past: the question of the subsequent payment of this (e.g. by a Sinking Fund) is merely a question of imposing a levy on the buyers of the article in question to compensate those on whom the real cost was alleged previously to have fallen. But no *additional* burden is imposed by this payment on the community as a whole: merely a transfer of money from one set of persons to another. The favourable handicap, mentioned by Prof. Karlgren, only exists to the extent that industry is not providing for current depreciation, and so in that sense is "living on its capital." That is done by most countries in times of stress and is a different matter. Similarly, abolition of interest charges lightens the real burden for society as a *whole* (as distinct from *transferring* it from one shoulder to another), only in so far as it lessens the burden of supporting the luxury consumption of a *rentier* class or lessens payments which have to be made abroad.

the community through inflation or industrial prices. But the expenditures on capital repairs between 1921 and 1924 were relatively small, and did not equal the current amortisation charges, which the trusts tended to use at this time to supplement their circulating capital. Estimates of the amount spent on capital reconstruction vary fairly considerably, and estimates of actual current depreciation even more. But it seems probable that between 1921 and 1924 such expenditure in industry (excluding transport and electrification) amounted to not less than 120 million pre-war roubles and not more than 200; and that at very most it did not exceed one-half of the current depreciation for those years.[1] Kalmanovsky goes so far as to maintain that not until October 1926 had the total capital expenditures since the introduction of N E P caught up the current depreciation over those five years.[2] If, therefore, we take the low figure of 5 per cent as a figure of annual depreciation of capital equipment, which is lower than the figure taken by Kalmanovsky and considered by him to be an underestimate;[3] and if we assume that current depreciation was not offset at all between 1917 and 1921, was offset to about a half between 1914–17, and was offset completely between 1921–4, then we arrive at a total depreciation of industrial equipment at the beginning of 1925 amounting to about 25 per cent as compared with 1914. It seems probable that the actual depreciation must have been greater than this, since the depreciation of equipment during the civil war, particularly in the military areas, was certainly greater than the normal, while by the beginning of 1925 capital reconstruction had scarcely as yet kept pace with the depreciation of the previous

[1] Cf. Kalmanovsky, *loc. cit.*, 150; R. Gordon, *Ibid.*, 1925, No. 3, 30.

[2] *Loc. cit.*

[3] 10 per cent is the usual figure taken in England for depreciation of machinery. The Co-operative Wholesale Society, by Resolution of the Co-operative Union in 1926, fixed the rate of depreciation for buildings and shops at 2½ per cent, for fixed stock and plant at 10 per cent, and for rolling stock at 20 per cent. These figures were made intentionally rather too high than too low. The proper figure for factories and plant together would seem to be below 10 per cent, but distinctly above 5 per cent.

four years. Moreover, if a higher percentage of annual depreciation is taken, the resulting total, of course, is equivalently raised. Such *a posteriori* estimates of the condition of plant as are available show, at any rate, that this figure is not too high. The Rubber Trust, for instance, where the depreciation would probably be below rather than above the average, valued its machinery at 29 per cent lower than 1913.[1] Of boilers in use in the central industrial area only 4 per cent had been installed since 1915, and about 40 per cent were in imminent danger of falling into immediate disuse.[2]

For those who realised this situation it appeared clear that industry, far from continuing its rapid progress of 1925, would very soon be reined in and forced to "mark time." It seemed unlikely with capital equipment depreciated by at least 25 per cent against 1913, and probably by considerably more, that industrial production could surpass the level of three-quarters of the pre-war standard which it was now approaching. True, the present might have the advantage of the past in the economies of greater "concentration" and the achievement of systematic economic planning. But at the same time there was the contrary effect on labour efficiency of the exhaustion of the hunger years, there was a probable decline in the efficiency of business management, owing to the suspicion entertained by the technical personnel to the new régime, the greater impediments imposed to their initiative, and the increased intricacy of the administrative machine. Moreover, spheres like transport and housing were in worse plight than industry in the matter of capital depreciation, and the former affected industrial costs directly, and the latter indirectly through its effect on workers' efficiency. There was even some reason to fear that the level of industrial production of 1925 was only the result of the stimulant of a good harvest,[3] and on the morrow was bound to suffer a relapse.

[1] *Russian Inform. and Review*, 15.11.24. [2] Rosenfeld, *op. cit.*, 359.

[3] This acted by giving an increased demand in terms of agricultural produce for industrial goods, even while the effort-demand of the peasants remained the same, thereby rendering an increment of output

The difficulty in Russia's existing penurious condition of restoring capital equipment had already troubled many minds at the time of the Genoa Conference. It was then quite a prevalent fear that even the preliminary stages of reconstruction were impossible of achievement without the aid of foreign capital on a considerable scale; and with this fear in their minds the Soviet representatives at Genoa were willing to make quite considerable concessions in their foreign policy in return for foreign financial aid. But when the winter of 1922 and the spring and summer of 1923 showed an industrial advance which many had not dared to expect, earlier fears were laid to rest, and Krassin was in a small minority at the 12th Party Congress when he urged a policy of liberal concessions to attract foreign capital. At the back of their minds many felt with Professor Hensel, when he wrote at the end of 1923 that since "the transformation of industry demands a swift and grandiose flow of new capital," "the voluntary flow of (foreign) capital, even at the price of sacrifice and the yielding of privileges, is easier than the achievement of a large excess of exports over imports," involving the "pumping out of every ounce of surplus over bare necessaries."[1] But so long as industrial output continued to develop, and economies were possible by means of industrial "concentration," the majority were content to acquiesce in the view that concessions demanded by Western finance in return for its aid would constitute an "auction sale" of Russia[2]—the auction, not now of the Cherry Orchard of a declining aristocracy, but the virgin plantation of the new régime.

Nevertheless, behind much of the opposition proposals in the 1923–4 discussions this apprehension lurked. Those who supported the Preobrajensky theory of socialist

profitable to produce, where in other circumstances the utility it yielded would not have compensated the labour it cost. Alternatively one can regard the effect of Nature's bounty as a temporary increased productiveness (in utilities) of labour, or a lowering of the real cost necessary to maintain a certain standard of life.

[1] In *Sozt. Khos.*, Nov.–Dec., 1923, 70, 75.

[2] Bronsky, *Ibid.*, 28–9.

accumulation, while they rejected the despairing policy of putting Russian industry in pawn abroad, did so only because they relied on an alternative means of reconstructing industrial capital at the expense of the peasant. In 1925 when the question of the renewal of capital equipment began to come to the fore, the old fears revived. Already from one quarter the mistrust of any effective progress without foreign aid had been voiced in quite uncompromising terms. What came to be known as the "Baku group," headed by Medvediev and Shliapnikov, who in 1921 had championed the "Workers' Opposition," issued at the end of 1924 a sharply worded criticism of the official policy in the shape of Medvediev's famous "Letter to Baku." According to Medvediev, under the conditions of N E P the old class differentiation in the village was bound to reappear: the rich peasant would prosper, but the poor peasant would inevitably be ruined and become proletarianised. For this relative over-population in the village, with its increasing misery and discontent, the only solution was a rapid industrialisation of the country to absorb in industry the surplus population. "To conclude that we should be able to extract enough capital for the development of our extinct industry from taxation would be to console ourselves with hollow illusions. To flatter ourselves that we could raise this capital 'out of pennies' would be to add to the old delusion another. . . . The Government should take energetic steps to raise the necessary means by foreign and internal State loans and by granting concessions with greater loss and greater sacrifice than the State is prepared to take on itself for granting credits. Great material sacrifices to international capital, which is prepared to build up our industry, would be a lesser evil than the condition into which we might drift in the next few years."

There were many, on the other hand, who were held by the same fears but drew a different conclusion. Several had thought in 1918, including Trotsky, that politically and militarily the régime could not survive if it were not aided by revolution in the West. Now the active military danger from a hostile capitalist world was for the moment passed. But financial hostility remained. To appease that hostility, it was felt, would involve such sacrifices of principle as to nullify much of the work of October 1917 and of the sufferings of the civil war: sacrifices, not of mere formal things, nor economic sacrifices alone, but sacrifices which would have an essentially political significance, would involve the surrender of important "key positions" or placing them in tutelage to the foe, and would purchase a little economic prosperity at the price, not merely of retarding the march to socialism, but probably of forsaking altogether the socialist road. Those who took this view did not draw the Medvediev conclusion. They held instead that the only hope for socialism in Russia was the triumph of the workers' movement in the West. The whole issue came to be debated on the motion, "whether socialism can be built in Russia alone" or whether for the success of a socialist experiment some economic unit larger than Russia was in practice required. And we find Stalin in 1925 pointing out that the mistrust in building socialism in Russia alone led to two extremes of policy: on the one hand to an excessive nationalism which would stake everything on winning the favour of the surrounding capitalist world, on the other hand to a romantic internationalism which was willing to stake everything—Russian economic progress, trade, and foreign relations—on the chance of a revolution in the West, like the students in 1923 who "were ready to throw down their books and go to Germany, saying that there was nothing left in Russia for a revolutionary to do."[1]

If the immediate possibility either of a social revolution in Western Europe or of a "Dawes Scheme" for Russia were ruled out, the issue narrowed down to the crucial question as to how far Russia could accumulate from her own internal resources the necessary capital to ensure a sufficiently rapid

[1] In a lecture delivered at the Sverdlov University on June 11th, 1925, published as *Bolshevism: Some Questions Answered.*

industrial advance. Capital accumulation involves an initial sacrifice of present consumption,[1] in order that resources may be set free (or procured where they were not previously available) to bring buildings, machinery, locomotives, railways, and roads into being, which lighten the costs of production and increase the productivity of labour in the future. Such an initial sacrifice represents a burden on society, analogous to the burden involved in financing a war, discussed in an earlier chapter;[2] but it is a burden which holds promise of future compensation, to be measured either by the increased utilities, or the saving of effort-cost, which the new capital equipment will untimately bring.[3] In a capitalist country this burden will fall on the proletariat, or on various groups of small producers, or through foreign trade and Imperialist acquisition on other more backward countries;[4] and by virtue of the low consumption of these exploited sections, relatively to their effort or the fruits of their effort, funds can be accumulated and invested by the privileged class. In a socialist society, likewise, the burden would have to fall upon the mass of the population—the workers and small producers[5]—and capital would have to be accumulated out of the difference between the product of their economic effort and what they immediately consumed. The difference in this case would be that the

[1] At least of consumption relatively to effort expended. Capital, of course, could be accumulated out of the results of increased effort or increased productivity of effort, while the standard of consumption remained the same or even rose.

[2] Chapter III.

[3] If the present burden—the sacrifice of present utilities, and the future yield, the extra utilities acquired by the same expenditure of labour—can be reduced to a common denominator, then for purposes of social accounting we can get a fraction, representing the *rate* of return on the initial outlay.

[4] Cf. Excursus to Chapters Eight and Nine, Section 2.

[5] For a time, of course, new resources could be obtained from the reduced consumption of the former privileged class, as much of the resources for waging the civil war in 1918 and 1919 were obtained. It is to be noticed that expropriation, either in a capitalist or a socialist system, though it may add to specifically capitalist accumulation in the one case or socialist accumulation in the other, will not *directly* increase the *total* social accumulation, since it will involve only a *transfer* of property.

accumulation took place mainly in the hands of the Socialist State, not of a capitalist class. The *source* of all such accumulation, accordingly, must be the surplus between the product of effort and the consumption of the workers, of the peasants or of some intermediate group of producers. But the forms of attracting this surplus could be of two kinds. First, each section of producers could be allowed to receive as income the full fruits of their effort (however that were measured), and a part of this income be attracted back by the State through deposits, saving banks, share and loan issues. Second, the State might draw "surplus-value," either through taxation or the profits of State industry, just as the capitalist class had formerly done, by handing over to the producers as the price of their effort only a part of the produce resulting from their labour.[1]

The former method would be severely limited in practice by several considerations. It is a commonplace of modern economic theory that the total voluntary "savings" available out of a certain aggregate of income equally distributed between persons is likely to be much smaller, *ceteris paribus*, than when that same aggregate income is unequally distributed and is largely grouped in a few hands.[2] Consequently this method is likely to produce a considerably smaller accumulation than under a capitalist régime. At the same time the requirements of a socialist society might forbid the granting of the "full fruits of their labour" to each group of producers—all coal (or its equivalent) to the coal miners, all gold to the gold miners, all oil to the oil-workers—in so far as differential advantages of one kind or another would still attach to particular groups, and the income of such groups would contain a differential surplus which might lay the basis of an inequality tending to increase progressively in the future.

[1] Cf. Preobrajensky, *Novaia Economika*, 203 *seq*.

[2] This follows from the law of diminishing utility of income. The millionaire sacrifices less in "saving" half his income than does the man with £200 a year. Consequently there would be a greater *a priori* probability of income being accumulated, instead of spent, if the national income were in the hands of a few millionaires than if spread over a large number of persons with £200 each.

On the other hand, the method might possess a certain equity, both real and apparent: the sacrifice demanded from each family would probably be more equitably adjusted to their several circumstances under a voluntary, than under the alternative method, while each investor would receive in some form of interest an apparent " compensation " for the sacrifice of present enjoyment he had undergone.[1] The second method would have the advantage of a certain simplicity; and there would be the consideration that with the same rate of " surplus-value " relative to mass consumption a larger accumulation would be obtained than under a capitalist system, *ceteris paribus*, since the whole of it could be applied to the creation of capital, instead of part of it contributing to the consumption of a privileged class. The limit to accumulation would then consist in the " incentive limit," below which the present consumption of the masses could not without harm to production be reduced; although in practice accumulation would probably be more narrowly limited than this by considerations of the amount of welfare which it was worth while sacrificing in the present for a future gain.[2] This method might involve friction between

[1] This latter advantage is no more than apparent (save to the extent that there are considerable inequalities in the receipt of interest by different persons) for this reason: If the contributions to capital accumulation were equitably distributed it would make no difference to anybody's real position whether he received interest on his contributions, or whether his contribution was compulsory and he merely gained later from the larger real income made possible by the new capital equipment. The interest would have to be paid from somewhere, and such payments would amount merely to the community as a whole paying interest to itself.

[2] This calculation would be a complex one, requiring quantitative data of the return on various quantities of outlay, and the periods within which this return would mature according as the outlay were devoted to this or that purpose. An ideal plan of capital allocation would require to plot a graph of the different returns at different points of time in the future which would be required to make such outlay worth while. The shape of this curve of returns might be of almost any character, subject to the condition that its general trend was upward into the future; and the decision on its shape would have to be entirely *a priori*.

For instance, if a capital outlay were to be undertaken which would yield economies twenty years hence, this would have to be a *larger* return to make it worth while (except in the eyes of one willing to

the State and the masses, if there were not a close sense of unity between the two; and some have expressed the fear that mass pressure exercised short-sightedly in favour of present enjoyment might seriously narrow the amount that the State could accumulate in this way. On the other hand, where a strong sense of unity existed between the masses and the State, so that the former were possessed of a feeling that they were producing, not for a privileged class, but to increase their own future heritage, an actually greater burden of present sacrifice might well be submitted to by the workers than under a capitalist régime. At any rate an expert planning body might well show more care for the interests of the distant, as against the immediate, future than private investors who are usually eager for "quick returns."

A balancing of these considerations suggests that main reliance would have to be placed by a socialist society on the second method, with the use of the first as a supplementary means of attracting voluntary private savings into State accumulation. The latter could take the form of the State loans which have played some part in Russian finance since 1924, or of attracting savings into bank deposits of various kinds; and this in a country where banking is undeveloped may not only increase specifically socialist accumulation by the attraction of private savings, but may add to the total

sacrifice the present generation entirely—a sort of collective miser) than the return of another outlay which would yield its results inside five years; but *how much* greater—whether 10, 20 or 30 per cent—would be entirely a subjective matter. In calculating various returns certain complicated interrelations would have to be taken into account, e.g. the decision not to build a certain branch railway in the next three years might increase the cost of erection over the next ten years of a large electrical scheme and so decrease the return on that outlay. In such cases a certain order of priority might have to be drawn up. In numerous cases the return could hardly be computed quantitatively, e.g. expenditure on public health, research, education—a reason why sufficient investment in these is commonly neglected. The question, therefore, before the planning body is not simply How much shall be put to capital this year? but also: To what point of time in the future shall it be directed, i.e. to quick or slow returns? and, What is the distribution of the capital between various purposes, both in space and time, which will give the *optimum* results over a period of time?

social capital created by pooling hoards which might otherwise have lain idle, as a reservoir pools numberless rivulets, and making them available to industry through long and short term credits.[1] The first method would take the form of open taxation, of the concealed taxation which lies in inflation, or of the profits of State industry and trade. Of these three forms the latter would represent internal accumulation by industry out of its own resources; while the proceeds of taxation or inflation would be made available to industry by State investments or subsidies out of the Budget, or else, if it were credit inflation, through freer crediting of industry by the Banks. A mixture of these forms would occur if the State redistributed the internal accumulation of different industries by taxing the profits of some industries and distributing the proceeds to other branches of the economic system.

To place the main burden of accumulation on the peasantry—fattening State industry by the exploitation of areas lying outside—was ruled out by the decision in the Party discussions of 1923–4. The means by which the merchants of mediæval gilds had grown prosperous, and the Mercantilist nations of Europe had amassed the funds whereby the industrial revolution was later financed, for a socialist society were deemed, not merely inconsistent in principle, but in the long run inexpedient. Something, of course, could be acquired, and continues to be acquired,

[1] If a bank expands credits to industry no faster than its real deposits increase, such expansion will have no inflationary effect, since it will represent no more than a mobilisation of private savings. If, however, the increased deposits on which an increased crediting is based merely represent money which would otherwise have stayed in private hoards, the credit advances based on these will raise the price level as compared with what the level would have been had the money lain in these hoards unused. This is an important hidden source of credit inflation, affecting the price-level by reducing the total of idle money-hoards. Of course, as Mr. Hartley Withers has shown, "loans tend to create deposits," since a loan to A being paid to B is then deposited by B in his bank and swells his deposit. But this occurs *after* credit has been expanded and after the spending of this fresh purchasing power has influenced the price-level, and it does not increase *real* deposits, i.e. money deposits divided by the index number of prices.

by "super-profit" from trade with the peasantry, but it could not be the main source of accumulation, and must be on the basis of a steady reduction of industrial prices and of profit.[1] As a minimum, at any rate, urban industry could receive the fruits of the higher production of technically-equipped industrial labour over that of the more primitive labour in the fields.[2] But not all of this was necessarily available for socialist accumulation: part might be swallowed up in a higher workers' wage; and the relation between urban wages and industrial productivity came in practice to be the real crux of the matter.

It was this point on which Djerjinsky had already fastened when he succeeded to the Presidency of Vesenha in 1924. Revising the estimates previously made of the relation between wages and the output per worker, he pointed out that up to the end of 1923–4 wages had risen on the whole more rapidly than the output per worker. Between October 1922 and October 1924 wages had slightly more than doubled, while the output per worker had increased only by 45 per cent.[3] In various factories where detailed estimates were made it was found that real wages, as compared to pre-war, were greater than the output per worker; and when to real wages had been added further benefits such as social insurance, the difference became very considerable. A decree of Vesenha had already pointed out that to produce one pood of cotton goods now required 3·2 man-days as against 2·14 before the war; and it was to this rise of labour costs that

[1] A reduction in *aggregate* profit in terms of money, but not necessarily in terms of goods (if peasant labour grew more productive); but a reduction of the *rate* of profit, both on turnover and capital outlay, in both senses.

[2] Since such a rate of exchange represents the *optimum* from the standpoint of economic expediency, for reasons given in the Excursus to Chapters Eight and Nine, Section 10, so long as industry and agriculture represent "non-competing groups," and so long as such a rate of exchange does not hinder the improvement of the technical methods of agriculture—improvements which will tend ultimately to remove the element of inequality in the rate of exchange.

[3] Rosenfeld, *op. cit.*, 352.

Djerjinsky attributed a large part of the high industrial costs and the financial difficulties of industry. The point was particularly relevant to the question of accumulation; and Djerjinsky being quick to realise this fact[1] urged the necessity of slowing up the rise of wages, so that in future wages rose behind rather than in advance of productivity. Once the problem had been framed in these terms, attention was focussed on the influences retarding the rise in the productivity of labour and the methods by which that productivity could be advanced. A special commission of Vesenha was set up to investigate the matter; and in the evidence before the commission the representatives of the trusts and the trade unions very largely advanced opposing views. The former blamed what was termed the "subjective factors"—the activity of the worker himself—and the latter blamed the management and "objective factors" in general. Between the two the commission's report adopted a middle way, and attributed the low productivity to various factors, among which the deterioration of plant, the increased number of auxiliary employees, the reduced skill and intensity of work and relaxation of discipline were the chief.[2] This report and the framing of the problem in this way was of particular importance since it focussed attention on the need for stringent industrial economy; and from the beginning of 1925 a campaign for "rationalisation" of production, both by improved working methods and economies of management, was launched. Towards the end of 1924 considerable economies of labour cost were achieved, and in the three months between October 1924 and January 1925 labour costs, as a percentage of total cost, fell on the average from 17·5 to 15·1 per cent; while in the spring and summer of 1925 productivity per worker achieved a rapid

[1] In his *Promishlenost S.S.S.R.*, published in 1925, he pointed out that when the "load" of industry had reached the normal figure, as it was fast doing, the question of reconstructing fixed capital would arise, without which there would be a "failure of industrial output to meet demand or to swallow up the surplus population of the village" (8 and 11).

[2] Cf. *Econ. Review*, 4.11.24.

advance, while real wages remained constant.[1] A practical treatment of the problem of accumulation had begun.

The profits of industry, which in spite of a campaign for lowering prices were to be achieved by a stringent economy of industrial costs, were partly reinvested by the trusts themselves in their own industries, and partly paid into the State Treasury, which then transferred them for investment in other economic spheres in the form of subsidies to electrification, to transport, and to the metal trades. To this was added a certain extra amount out of the Budget from the proceeds of ordinary taxation. As additional sources of accumulation the State relied on two principal methods: first, on the development of banking to mobilise private "savings," including those of private traders and business reserves, and advance them to industry in the form of long and short term credits; and second, by the floating of various State loans to be earmarked for capital purposes. Both methods were limited to accumulating real savings: at least, the requirements of monetary stability precluded the first method from being used, save in so far as credit expansion (apart from a previous increase of deposits) proceeded at a slower pace than industrial productivity. The funds which could have been raised by means of inflation might well have been less than the funds which were lost through the deterrent effect of rouble depreciation on peasant willingness to entrust their hoards to the banks.

What prospect was there of accumulating by these means sums adequate to Russia's task? In the financial year 1925–6 the total sum allotted to the financing of national economy (excluding transport) out of the Budget amounted to 483 million roubles.[2] This represented partly direct subsidies

[1] Rosenfeld, 361. This progress was checked again in the late summer and autumn of 1925, and in October 1925 labour cost as a percentage of total cost again slightly exceeded the figure of October 1924.

[2] This is the figure given in the Budget statement contained in *The State Bank of U.S.S.R.*, 1921–6, p. 14. Mr. Shenkman in the *Soviet Union Monthly*, Jan. 1927, gave the higher figure of 532 million. Of this, 193 million was assigned to industry, 159 to agriculture, 69 to electrification, and 80 million to commercial organs.

to essential branches of industry, where capital was particularly depreciated and which were unable as yet to show a profit, partly of long term loans to industry made from the proceeds of special State Loans[1] and from a special State Industrial Fund created for this purpose. Of the 483 million, 145 came from State credit operations and 171 from that part of the profits of industry, trade, and banking which went as revenue into the Budget. Some 160 million odd, accordingly, represented allocations to industry out of ordinary taxation. In addition to such contributions from the Budget, industry had available to devote to capital purposes the residue of profits left in its hands, which amounted in all to some 300 million roubles. Part of this 300 million, however, might well have been used to subscribe to the State Reconstruction Loan, a portion of which was subscribed by various State bodies, and not by private individuals;[2] and to add such sums to the total of capital allocations, after including it in payments through the Budget, would involve double counting. But making allowance for this fact we may say that probably about 730 million roubles was available out of the Budget and the internal reserves of industry combined for the current year. To cover current depreciation, industry had its special amortisation funds; and in so far as these charges were insufficient to cover actual depreciation, an equivalent deduction would have to be made in our figure of 730 million to arrive at the *net* sum available for the creation of new

[1] In 1925 a special Reconstruction Loan was publicly floated and placed upon the market for subscription with the express purpose of augmenting the funds available for capital purposes.

[2] Cf. Brukhanov, *Isvestia*, 1.12.26. The internal State Debt in 1926 was only 2·1 per cent of the national income, as against 35·8 per cent in Tsarist Russia. On Oct. 1, 1926 (excluding the Reconstruction Loan), it stood at 413 million roubles, of which a third was held by private individuals directly, another 22 per cent by small investors through savings banks, 23 per cent by various State departments, particularly the State Insurance, and the remainder by the banks and industry. Prior to 1925 State loans had been "forced": trusts and State departments had been forced to invest a certain proportion of their resources in them, which often meant that they were ultimately financed out of bank advances.

capital; and this might reduce the net figure as far as 600 million.[1] The amount of newly created (as distinct from outstanding) long-term credits, particularly from Prombank and the long-term credit banks, is difficult to gauge; but it would probably suffice at least to raise our net figure to 650.[2] For purposes of circulating capital industry had to rely on discounts and advances from the banks, together with part of their own fluid resources. Discounts and advances at the end of 1925–6 for all the banks (excluding rediscounts) amounted to 3830 million roubles, showing a real advance in the course of the year (allowing for a slight depreciation of the rouble) of some 760 million. This increase represents partly the result of mobilising individual savings and making them available to industry, partly of expanding credit proportionately with increased production, and so handing back to industry in the form of circulating capital the fruits of increased productivity.

These figures, however, though they indicate the relative importance of the various methods by which accumulation could proceed, and show that by far the most important source of accumulation at present consisted of industrial profits, do not necessarily indicate the actual capital creation that was possible in that year. In past years a large part of

[1] Kalmanovsky gives 130 million as the figure by which actual annual depreciation exceeds the amortisation allowances of the trusts.

[2] This was a potential source of accumulation which many were stressing at this time, urging that it could be made almost as important a source as the capitalisation of industrial profits. Djerjinsky advocated the establishment of a special fund and special department with Prombank for long-term credits, earmarked for capital construction (*op. cit.*, 49); and such a department was opened on May 1, 1926. Bierbrauer strongly advocated the extension of the rôle of credit in accumulation through the attraction of individual hoards into bank deposits and the "economy of reserves" to be obtained by concentrating them in the banks, thereby making available resources for capital creation (*Plan. Khos.*, 1925, No. 9, 48 *seq.*). Kisiliev declared that it was now time to change the function of the banking system from "pumping out circulating capital" into a source of accumulation, "drawing in savings." He also urged a move in the direction of making the State Bank a banker's bank, regulating the money market through its rediscount rate (*Plan. Khos.*, 1925, No. 11, 25 *seq.*). But unless applied cautiously this method of accumulation may involve a kind of concealed inflation for the reason mentioned above, p. 304, footnote.

the amortisation funds of trusts had been accumulated in reserve, and used to supplement circulating capital, and had not gone into actual renewal of fixed capital. Similarly, part of the subsidies to industry out of the Budget, particularly to heavy industry, might be used as working capital to tide them over a period of stress, instead of being invested in reconstruction of plant. Moreover, to arrive at the total creation of social capital, we must add to the figure given above the net amount invested in transport, the amounts added to housing, local enterprises, and communal construction out of local budgets, and the private accumulation of the peasantry in the shape of live-stock, implements, and buildings. Of these three, the first amounted to some 150 million (allowing for current depreciation), and the second group to about 200 million.[1] Of peasant accumulation there seem to be no very reliable current estimates. But it is probable that it does not fall very far short of the pre-war amount, which was estimated at between 200 and 250 million, and to estimate it at about 75 per cent of this would probably not be an error on the high side.[2] The addition of these items brings the total social accumulation (excluding circulating capital) to about 1150–1200 million roubles, of which about 1000 million represents accumulation in the hands of the State. For purposes of comparison with pre-war estimates, a further addition would have to be made to this figure to include the accumulation of capital in the hands of private traders and small producers, which might raise our total figure by anything between 50 and 100 million.

This estimate agrees fairly closely with a conservative estimate made by Professor Weinstein of Narcomfin early in 1926.[3] Professor Weinstein pointed out that the three

[1] Strumilin in *Plan. Khos.*, 1926, No. 4, 47, 58.

[2] If we were to include in this the increase in peasant grain reserves, which were estimated by the Central Statistical Bureau to have increased from 130 million to 400 million poods in the course of 1925–6, we should probably arrive at a figure that was *greater* than pre-war (cf. Professor Weinstein in *Sozt. Khos.*, 1926, No. IV, 10). But for our present purpose we are probably not justified in including this item.

[3] *Ibid.*, pp. 8–27.

principal sources of accumulation for industry were, first, the "voluntary accumulation" of the population drawn upon through bank deposits, State loans, saving banks, life insurance, etc.; second, "compulsory accumulation" through the Budget; third, "socialist accumulation," or internal industrial accumulation out of the profits of State industry. Of these the first was very limited and much lower than pre-war, partly as a legacy of inflation owing to the destruction of the habits of saving, partly by reason of the higher consumption relative to income which resulted from equalisation of incomes. The second was strictly limited by "the danger of dealing an injury to the source of tax receipts." The third was at present limited by the limited profit-margin of industry, mainly on account of high industrial costs.[1] Agriculture, in addition to agricultural credits supplied by the help of the State or out of the co-operative pooling of peasant reserves, relied on accumulation "in natural forms." From these sources he estimated a possible net accumulation of 1400–1500 million roubles in the course of 1925–6—a figure some 200 million higher than our own estimate which probably errs on the cautious side. Of the national income, which he estimated at about 20 milliard roubles for 1925–6, this accumulation represented between 7 and 7½ per cent. The pre-war annual accumulation (excluding foreign loans) had been estimated by Professor Sobolev at 1490 to 1550 million pre-war roubles,[2] which represented about 9 per cent of Professor Prokopovitch's figure of the pre-war national income. Professor Weinstein, however, considered this figure of pre-war accumulation too high and the figure of the pre-war national

[1] The existing margin of profit in industry was narrower than pre-war. According to Strumilin, in 1925–6 the rate of profit was 6 per cent on turnover and 9 per cent on capital as against 7·4 and 13·1 per cent pre-war. For subsequent years he estimated the rate on turnover to remain constant and the rate on capital to rise to 9 per cent (*Plan. Khos.*, 1926, No. 4, 35). Cf. also Report by Vesenha to S T O in *Econ. Jizn.*, 5.1.27.

[2] Including a sum of 731 million of issues of shares and interest-yielding paper (including State and municipal), and 230–240 million as capitalisation of reserves of joint stock companies.

income a trifle too low; and arrived at a lower percentage of 8½ per cent. Further, it is to be noticed that Sobolev's figure includes 173 million as increase of bank deposits plus one-tenth of the growth of current accounts, and so presumably includes a part of the additions to circulating capital through bank credit. We may safely conclude, therefore, that the relation between accumulation and the national income before the war did not exceed 9½ per cent and probably fell a little below 8½ per cent; while for 1925–6 the comparable figure almost certainly was not less than 6 per cent and may have stood between 7 and 8 per cent—a comparison which is not unfavourable to the latter period in view of the fact that the national income in 1925–6 probably did not exceed 90 per cent of pre-war,[1] while the national income per head stood at rather less.

The actual expenditure on capital repairs and construction in 1925–6 was considerably larger than this. Strumilin at the beginning of 1926 made an estimate of the total capital investments by State bodies for 1925–6, based on the preliminary plans for the year.[2] This amounted to over 1600 million roubles. But the figure apparently excluded investments by private persons, such as increase of capital among the peasantry (apart from investments in State farms and irrigation work and State aid to agricultural co-operation) and among private business men and private capital applied to housing; and if this private accumulation had been included, the total figure would have been raised by at least 200–300 million. About a year later Rykov in his Report to the 4th Union Soviet Congress gave an aggregate figure of 2000 million for all forms of capital investment for 1925–6, out of which 780 million consisted of investments in industry, 110 million in electrification, 220

[1] Professor Weinstein puts the figure at 85–6 per cent, and adds that with a smaller absolute income the amount accumulated should be smaller both absolutely and relatively. No direct comparison of absolute figures of national income and accumulation is possible between 1925 and 1913, since the area of U.S.S.R. is smaller than the area of the Russian Empire by the loss of the fairly rich Baltic Provinces.

[2] *Plan. Khos.*, 1926, No. 4, 33–58.

million in transport, 350 million in agriculture and 300 million in housing. This unexpectedly high figure for industry was largely explained by the expenditure of amortisation funds which had previously been accumulated in reserve;[1] while the high figure for agriculture was doubtless to be accounted for by the peasant prosperity resulting from the good harvest of 1925, and consequently was a figure rather higher than on the average could be expected. By no means all of this figure, however, could be taken as representing net creation of fixed capital in the course of the year: it included expenditure which merely replaced current depreciation and wear and tear. To cover this current depreciation, it seems probable that as much as 350 million might have to be substracted from the figure for industry to arrive at the net accumulation.[2] If allowances were made for depreciation in other spheres of investment, the result might well be to bring down the figure of net capital creation in 1925–6 to 1250–1350—namely, to a figure almost identical with our original estimate. It seems unlikely that this figure errs on the side of being too high an estimate: it may probably err in being rather too low.

Such by no means contemptible achievements in tackling the problem of capital reconstruction were actually lower than had been anticipated and planned in the summer and

[1] It might seem to follow from this that the real industrial accumulation of this year was much lower than 780, because part of the capital expenditure was properly attributable to earlier years and was only by chance instituted in 1925–6. But the allowance to be made on this score is probably not very considerable for this reason: Industry had previously utilised its reserves to supplement circulating capital. This year, owing to increase in circulating capital through bank credits and economies of its use through accelerated turnover, these reserves were set free for investment in fixed capital. If the increase of circulating capital had not taken place some of it would probably have been available for transfer into fixed capital in other ways (e.g. through State loans, long-term credits, etc.), and the result would have been to swell some other item of capital allocation. The spending of reserves on construction work represented a real transfer of funds from circulating to fixed capital through an improved supply of the former.

[2] Strumilin, calculating depreciation on a 5 per cent basis, which is probably too low, makes an allowance of 250 million for this (*op. cit.*, 34). Kalmanovsky takes 310 million (*op. cit.*, 150).

autumn of 1925. These anticipations erred, partly in overestimating the amount of the harvest which would be marketed, and partly in overestimating the surplus which would in any case have been available for accumulation. Plans had been made for a large program of wheat export, which would bring the total exports up to 1·1 milliard roubles, or double those of the previous year. In return it was planned to import one milliard roubles, largely consisting of machinery and constructional materials, showing an advance of some 40 per cent over 1924–5. This import of machinery, financed by large grain sales abroad, would serve to provide the basis for a large program of capital construction for 1925–6, which for industry alone had been planned at 860 million, or some 14 per cent higher than was actually realised.[1]

But by the end of September the optimism of the summer was beginning to be shaken. Owing to late rains the crop in some districts was less than had been expected, and the actual harvest proved to be 3 to 5 per cent less than the earlier estimates. But in addition to this for several reasons agricultural prices, which had reigned abnormally high over the previous year after the poor harvest of 1924, failed to fall as much as had been anticipated, and after September actually rose; while the quantity of grain placed on the market by the peasants proved to be much smaller than was expected. The result was that the buying program of the State purchasing organs had to be reduced in September from 780 to 600 million poods and the program of export pruned even more drastically. A principal reason for this phenomenon seems to have been that the peasant was better supplied with funds than was usual at this time of the year, and was consequently under less pressure to market his grain.

[1] Svetlov in *Econ. Oboz.*, Dec. 1926, 8. Gurevitch in *Vestnik Truda* (Oct. 1925, 4 *seq.*) mentioned a figure of 878 million roubles for industry alone (excluding electrification and war industry), of which 420 million were to come from industry's internal resources, 72 million from the State Industrial Fund, 153 million from the Budget, and 181 million from long-term credits.

The Agricultural Tax had been reduced by 50 per cent from the previous year and placed a smaller burden upon him. His sales of the autumn harvest of 1924 had been postponed for seasonal reasons, and were realised along with the winter crops in the summer of 1925 at the prevailing high prices; and this left him in the autumn relatively well supplied with funds. In the previous year, to prevent an undue rise of grain prices from the poor harvest, the grain collections had been governed by a system of "limiting" or maximum prices, which by their very rigidity served to prevent the State from collecting even the limited program it had anticipated. The policy of fixed maxima was consequently abandoned; and in its place a system known as "directive prices" was adopted: statements of purchasing price were given out from time to time to the buying organs to define the general trend of their buying policy, while the separate organs and their local agents were left free to vary the actual price they offered according to the variation of market conditions. The gist of the new policy of manœuvring on the market in line with general directive orders, instead of relying on fixed maxima, was expressed by Kamenev as follows: "If prices fall, we ought to increase our demand; if they rise, we ought to withdraw our collecting agencies." In 1925 it was a fall in prices that was expected as soon as the new crop came on to the market, and the grain-purchasing policy was consequently directed, not to preventing a rise as in the previous year, but to preventing a sudden fall which would have been unfavourable for the peasantry. In the attempt to counteract this anticipated fall the grain-purchasing apparatus came into the market in August and September with a strong demand, one agency often competing against another in certain areas quite sharply; and this strong demand meeting a smaller supply than was anticipated produced a tendency for prices to rise. Finding in some areas an unexpected rise, the State organs then held back from the market, or at least with the funds at their disposal were unable to fulfil the program of purchase assigned to them;

while the peasants on their side, particularly the richer peasants, were inclined to reserve their produce in anticipation of a repetition of the winter price-rise of the previous year; and the private trader, quicker to manœuvre than the State buyers, took advantage of the exhaustion of reserves and the very inelastic demand in the towns to buy grain and resell it to the towns at a profit. Inadequate co-ordination between the State organs created chaos in the grain market, so that prices fluctuated widely between different districts. Between September and the following February wholesale grain prices according to the Gosplan Index Number rose from 154 to 181; and the high prices obtained by the peasants who had sold their grain had so increased village purchasing power, as to cause a sharpening of the so-called "industrial goods famine" which had already appeared earlier in the year. Meanwhile, in anticipation of a great increase in the goods turnover as a result of the large harvest, credit had been somewhat recklessly expanded, both to finance grain purchase and export, and also to finance the ambitious program of capital construction. The engagement of additional workers for this constructional work, combined with a rise of wages which took place in the late summer and autumn again faster than industrial productivity, helped to swell the demand both for grain and for industrial goods. As a result by the end of the year the wholesale index number, not only of agricultural produce but of all commodities, showed a rise, and all the signs of a fresh inflation and depreciation of the currency had appeared.[1]

Once again, as in 1923, the theory of disproportion between industry and agriculture stepped to the fore; and those who had explained the difficulties of two years ago by the backwardness of industry now explained by this cause the "goods famine" which had developed since 1924 and was accentuated since the autumn crisis. Mistrust in the ability

[1] Cf. Rykov's report to Leningrad Soviet, 9.3.26, *cit.*, *Economist*, 27.3.26; *Narodnoe Khosiaistvo*, 1924–5, 28–37, 102–3; Rosenfeld, *op. cit.*, 450–1; Svetlov, *loc. cit.*, 9 *seq.*; Smilga in *Plan. Khos.*, 1925, No. 9, 10 *seq.*; Krumin, *v. Borbye za Socialism*, 17–19.

of State industry to solve the problem of fixed capital without financial aid from abroad and without pressure on the peasantry now saw in the events of the autumn and winter the worst confirmation of its fears. These events were cited as witness to the impossibility of achieving accumulation and the progress of industrialisation on any sufficient scale; they were a refutation of the official hopes which had built plans of capital reconstruction that were no more than "castles in the air"; they pricked the utopian bubble of complacency which preached the possibility of building socialism in Russia alone, an island in a capitalist sea. Some even saw in these events the beginning of a chronic crisis—an *impasse* for Russian industry from which there could be escape only by extraordinary means. The opposition of the "scissors" period began to furbish its weapons for a fresh tourney, proclaiming that the new crisis was due to the weakness of industrial accumulation and the growth of urban production at too slow a speed. Even some of those who had tilted with the opposition in 1923 and had then stood with the majority, including influential members of the central committee of the Party such as Zinoviev and Kamenev, began to raise the cry that the concessions to the peasantry had gone far enough and must stop. The difficulties of grain collection experienced in August and September the opposition tended to attribute to the undue enrichment of the peasant (thanks to the official policy) and particularly of the rich peasant who was becoming again a power in the village. At the same time as State industry was pinched and thwarted for lack of funds to reconstruct its wasted capital equipment, in the village private accumulation was growing and the private trader and usurer was gaining ground.

At the 14th Party Conference and Congress in 1925 this new opposition began to muster; and Zinoviev and Kamenev, who had previously attacked the policy of Trotsky, Radek, and Preobrajensky with some bitterness, now ate salt with their erstwhile opponents and began to form with them an alliance in common criticism of the official standpoint. By the time of the 15th Party Congress in the following year the new alliance had closed its ranks. It had begun to conduct propaganda and to carry on concerted activities which called down on it the charge of forming a separate fraction within the Party, breaking the unity of the Party in action—a charge which led to the displacement of Kamenev from his post as Commissar for Trade and Zinoviev from his position in the inner Political Bureau of the Party.[1] A new note of bitterness had crept into the discussion, exceeding considerably the bitterness of the discussions of 1923. The new, like the old, opposition did not constitute an entirely homogeneous group; perhaps now less than formerly. But they had in common now as then an emphasis on the position of industry, an insistance on the need for its more rapid development, an unwillingness to countenance concessions to the peasantry, and a mistrust in the possibility of facing the problem of socialist accumulation in Russia except by some extraordinary means.

At the 14th Congress the cloud of future disagreement appeared on the horizon no larger than a man's hand. The policy of industrialisation had then been pronounced in the report of Stalin, secretary of the Party, and with it the problem of the reconstruction of fixed capital was for the first time brought prominently to the fore. The choice which at some period vexes all agrarian countries now lay before

[1] It had always been a cardinal principle of the Party that while there was complete freedom of discussion before a decision on policy was made—forthcoming issues were usually expressly thrown open to discussion in the Party Press—the majority decision once taken was binding upon all, and all had to carry out that policy without reservations. *A fortiori* all opposition groups inside the Party were regarded as inadmissible, the formation of such a group warranting expulsion. This view followed logically from the conception of the Party as an organisation for action—a sort of General Staff—the brain and nerves of the whole workers' movement. Rykov has said: "It is a perfectly natural phenomenon for various shades of opinion to exist on political questions. If differences of views were to expose us to persecution, inner Party democracy would be but an empty phrase. Disciplinary measures only become necessary when groups and fractions rise on the soil of these differences of opinion and a split threatens" (Meeting of Moscow Party officials, 26.7.26).

Russia. Should she remain primarily an agrarian country, exporting agricultural produce and importing industrial goods from abroad? In such a case her chief interest lay in foreign trade and in free trade, and her need of capital, except for transport development, was not very great. Or should she transform herself into an industrial country by accumulating capital and developing her manufacture, so as to supply needs which formerly had been satisfied by import from abroad, and to find an internal market for raw material which had formerly been exported? This policy required an extension of the pre-war system of Protection, to nurse "infant" industries which were as yet unfitted to stand upon their feet, and particularly to nurse, by subsidy if not by the shelter of a tariff, the constructional and machine-making trades which in Russia were particularly backward. It involved a diversion of raw material exports to supply the needs of home industry and a reduction of the volume of foreign trade. It imposed on the present a burden, both in the higher cost of manufacturing at home in place of purchase abroad and in the parsimony required to supply the capital for the development of industry. On the other hand, it promised for the future the benefits of a partial self-sufficiency, and the possibility of maintaining the population at a higher standard of life, or absorbing a surplus rural population, by virtue of the "increasing returns" which industrial development would bring. As to the desirability of taking the road to industrialisation there was never any very serious doubt. The fact that Russia stood alone amid actual or suspected enemies made her averse to any considerable dependence on her neighbours and eager to improve her self-sufficiency. Opinion differed as to the possibility and the methods of achieving this desired aim; and the doubters repined at the fact that the failure of the revolution and the partial stabilisation of capitalism in the West made the task so urgent and at the same time for want of the aid of foreign capital so difficult. Stalin himself admitted that, if Germany went socialist, the self-sufficient protectionist policy would be unnecessary, and a policy based on specialisation within a larger economic unit would then be required. But given the situation as it was, he declared, a policy of industrialisation of Russia was both essential and practicable, and her foreign trade must be confined as far as possible to acquiring from abroad, not finished goods, but the requisites of industrial construction.

Disagreement at the outset assumed rather an academic than a practical form. Zinoviev stressed the danger of the recrudescence of the *kulak* or rich peasant as a result of recent concessions to the village which he characterised as a "retreat," and revealed a certain hankering after the forsaken methods of "war communism" in denying that NEP was a system of socialism and insisting that while it had to be pursued "for a time" it was not to be pursued "for ever." To this Bukharin replied that NEP was not merely a retreat, but constituted a "regrouping of forces and an advance upon a reorganised front line," and that the urgent need of the present lay in "the extermination of the last remnants of war communism," particularly in the policy toward the village. By the end of the year these doubts as to the road which Russia was travelling, fears of the *kulak* danger and mistrust of Russia's ability to solve the gigantic new problem of industrialisation which now towered in front had increased and multiplied. The first rush at the new ascent seemed to have met a sharp rebuff, so that a different angle of approach seemed to be required. Complaints were made that industry was developing and bound to develop under the circumstances at a slower pace than agriculture, which meant a relative growth of private economy and private accumulation and an accentuation of the "goods famine." Said one writer: "The supposition that in the immediate future our industry can develop at the same pace as agriculture is essentially wrong. This problem is insoluble in practice, or at least cannot be solved without a large import of capital or a sudden forcible arrest of the development of agriculture."[1] At the beginning of 1926 Trotsky wrote: "All reports indicate that our industry will meet the harvests of 1926 without any stocks of goods, which may mean a repetition of the present difficulties on a larger scale. In these circumstances the good harvest, i.e. the potential growth of a surplus of agricultural goods, may become a factor which does not accelerate the rate of economic development in the direction of socialism, but on the contrary will disorganise industry and exacerbate the relation between town and country, and in the town itself between consumers and the State."[2] Proposals were advanced for doubling the capital allocations to State industry for the coming year from one to two milliard by means of increasing the burden of the agricultural tax, particularly on the rich peasant, and by raising the factory selling-price of industrial goods. Smilga had already assigned a prominent place to the change in the agricultural tax as cause of the failure of grain collections in 1925. "If the tax," he said, "is not to play a stimulating rôle in encouraging peasant offers of grain, then the only economic means of attracting a surplus of grain from the peasantry is the satisfaction of its needs in town goods." For this reason the sharpening "goods famine" was a more serious phenomenon than previous crises which had been crises of sale. From the high grain prices of the last twelve months not the poor but the rich peasant had profited. About half the grain surplus was supplied from 14 per cent of peasant farms, and these richer peasants, no longer pressed either by the tax or by poverty, could hold back their grain from the market and secure a higher price.[3] Preobrajensky in the summer of 1926 advocated fresh inflation as the only means of securing the funds required for industrial development;[4] and Smilga at the beginning of 1925 had advocated as a remedy for the

[1] Shanin in *Bolshevik*, No. 2, 70. Cf. also Shanin in *Econ. Oboz.*, Nov. 1925, 25–32.

[2] *Cit.* in Rykov's report to 15th Party Congress.

[3] Smilga in *Plan. Khos.*, 1925, No. 9, 10–14; also No. 1, 43, 49.

[4] Preobrajensky apparently later withdrew this suggestion.

" goods famine " a revival of the policy of " goods intervention," this import to be financed by inflation, which for a somewhat unconvincing reason would have no effect on the stability of the chervonetz because it would be balanced by an increased supply of goods.[1] Towards the end of 1926 a section of the opposition began to criticise Djerjinsky's policy of making the advance of wages succeed, and not precede, the progress of productivity, declaring that it was necessary to raise wages first in order to improve labour efficiency. In the sphere of international policy Zinoviev was inclined to advocate less of a policy of adaptation to the requirements of trade with foreign countries and a more uncompromising policy to rally the workers of Europe to seize power in their own countries and bring to Russia both political and economic aid. Some of his disciples even began to speak of a " degeneration " of the Communist leaders from their previous revolutionary rôle, of a " *kulak* deviation " in State policy, and of a Russian Thermidor. But though to the eye the proposals of the opposition formed a strange mosaic, apparently lacking in form and consistency, the mosaic had a spiritual unity. The opposition proposals arose from a common mistrust in the ability of Russia to face the problems of the new phase which 1925 had opened and a desire to hasten the process of industrialisation by special means. Moved by this desire, some looked to strike a bargain with foreign capital; some harked back to the " dictatorship of industry " and to Preobrajensky's " law of socialist accumulation," proclaiming that concession to the peasantry had already gone too far; others even were ready to " lay down their books and go to Germany, saying that there was nothing left in Russia for a revolutionary to do."

But the theory of disproportion between industry and agriculture was scarcely more satisfactory in 1925 as an explanation than it had been in 1923. In the mouths of its

[1] *Ibid.*, 1925, No. 1, 50–1. " Lowering of grain prices and import of foreign finished goods are the main tasks of the coming year."

various exponents it seemed to be capable of different and sometimes contradictory interpretations, so that it almost came to mean all things to all men. The most common form of the theory seemed to amount to the claim that in view of the more backward development of industry than of agriculture, the price relationship between the two was over-favourable to agriculture—over-favourable in view of the relative supplies of manufactures and rural produce available. In other words the position of 1923 had been reversed: now agricultural rather than industrial effort was overvalued; so that the "sales crisis" of 1923 had now yielded place to an industrial "goods famine" and to an inability of the towns because of their poverty to secure agricultural produce in sufficient plenty, either for their own needs or for purposes of export. An interesting variant of this view was that advanced by Smilga, who maintained that while the wholesale price-relationship tended to favour the village, in view of the shortage of manufactures the *real* rate of interchange was insufficiently favourable to the peasant to evoke a supply of agricultural goods at the required level. One of the results of this was to increase the money resources in the hands of the rich peasants, and by swelling the margin between industrial wholesale and retail prices to enrich the private speculator and trader.

The facts of the case seemed to afford no very valid evidence of this alleged outdistancing of industry by agriculture, rather the reverse. In 1923 industry had certainly been the more backward as compared with the pre-war standard. But in the two years since then it had largely made up this leeway: industrial production had grown from about a third to two-thirds or three-quarters of the pre-war standard; while the gross yield of agriculture, though it was still in 1924–5 slightly in advance of industry, being about 73–4 per cent of the pre-war figure, showed very little advance on 1922–3. The immediate increase of agricultural yield in the autumn of 1925 as a result of the harvest certainly exceeded for the moment any industrial expansion;

but for the year 1925–6 as a whole, when agricultural yield increased to 91 per cent and its cultivated area to about 92 per cent of pre-war, it was actually surpassed by the recovery of industry. Moreover, the agricultural surplus available for the market had not recovered to the extent of the gross yield, as was to be expected from the fact that the quantity marketed represents a surplus of gross yield over a not very elastic standard of consumption; while the increased equality in the village had augmented village food consumption and further reduced the marketable surplus. It followed, therefore, that, taking the pre-war ratio as standard, industrial production by the autumn of 1925 was nearly level with the marketable surplus of agriculture, and by the following year had surpassed it. In view of this, one would expect the ratio of prices to have been the same as pre-war, or even industrial prices to be relatively cheaper. During a brief period between April and July 1925, it was true, the wholesale "scissors" (but not the retail) had closed and had actually begun to open in a converse direction. But this was no more than a seasonal movement, due to the exhaustion of grain reserves after the poor harvest of 1924; and with a fall of agricultural prices in August and the beginning of an industrial rise in September, the former margin between the two sets of prices reappeared and continued throughout the next year.[1] There was little reason to think that the price-ratio of the winter and spring of 1925–6 was unduly favourable to the peasant: now, indeed, that industrial growth was overtaking agricultural, it would seem that industrial prices would need to be cheapened still further, relatively to agriculture, if a market in the village were to be found for manufactured goods.

[1] The Gosplan Wholesale I.N. showed the following movement:—

(1913=100)	Agricultural	Industrial	General
June 1925	193	190	191
Aug. ,,	161	190	175
Jan. 1926	169	198	183
April ,,	191	202	196
Aug. ,,	162	204	181

For Smilga's fears there seemed more reason. The lessened pressure on the peasant in the form of taxation certainly meant that he required a greater incentive than before to market his grain, although at the same time it probably encouraged him to extend his total cultivation.[1] Moreover, to the extent that the town worker was now probably consuming a greater share of a smaller aggregate of industrial output than pre-war, the volume of industrial goods supplied to the village was probably smaller relatively to pre-war than appeared at first sight. This fact would tend to show itself in a much larger gap between the village retail price of industrial goods and the price at which the peasant parted with his grain than in pre-war days;[2] and it was this "scissors" that was directly relevant to the real return which the peasant received through the market, and this "scissors" at the moment was considerably wider than the "scissors" of wholesale prices. The town was still living at the expense of the village. But even so, the situation in this respect was not worse, but considerably better, than previously: it was a disproportion that had decreased and was decreasing. At any rate, the existence of such an insufficient incentive to cultivation was clearly inconsistent with the too rapid development of agriculture which other advocates of disproportion claimed to see—at least, inconsistent with a continuance of such too rapid development. Moreover, the widened gap between wholesale and retail prices which was a symptom of the so-called "goods famine" could hardly be attributed to any such disproportion: even if the high grain prices increased village purchasing power for industrial goods, this would tend to be counterbalanced by a decreased urban demand for manufactures, since the town worker had to spend more of his income in

[1] Cf. above Excursus to Chapters Eight and Nine, Section 7.

[2] This is not equivalent to the ratio of retail prices of agriculture and industry, which is influenced by the *village* price of manufactures and the *town* price of grain. Yakovlev, speaking at the 15th Party Conference, mentioned 1·46 and 2·40 respectively as the index numbers of peasant net money receipts and of the village retail price of industrial goods (pre-war = 1·0).

obtaining food. Moreover the gap between wholesale and retail prices applied equally to agricultural and to industrial goods[1]—a fact apparently neglected by the advocates of disproportion theories—and the " goods famine " was as much a famine of agricultural produce as of manufactures. At any rate, if the real rate of interchange were still too unfavourable to the peasant, as was probably true, the appropriate remedy would surely be to reduce industrial prices both wholesale and retail still further rather than to raise either the one or the other.

The real explanation seems to be both simpler and more obvious. The phenomena of the autumn and winter of 1925 were simply the usual phenomena of credit inflation. Credit inflation, by expanding purchasing power faster than the flow of goods on to the market and in excess of any " saving " of purchasing power in the form of money-hoards or bank deposits, produces a rise in the general price level. If some prices are fixed, then inflation exercises its influence more strongly on the prices of others; if wholesale price is fixed, it increases retail and widens the margin between the two; if all prices, including retail, are fixed, it empties the shops, produces a " goods famine," leads to the war-time queue system and the need for rationing to secure equity as between different consumers. In Russia, where wholesale prices were largely under the control of the State and did not rise in response to an increased demand in view of the policy of price-reduction,[2] this expansion of purchasing power expressed itself in a widening margin between wholesale and retail prices. In the grain market the demand was largely embodied in the policy of State grain-purchase and depended on the credits advanced for this purpose; and there was as much evidence here of deficiency of supply

[1] The margin between wholesale and retail prices in 1926 was about 60 per cent, as against 20 per cent in 1913 (Grintser in *Econ. Oboz.*, May 1926, 52).

[2] As Djerjinsky said, between 1923 and 1925 " the policy of lowering prices (was) carried on despite the fact that demand was increasing faster than supply " (*op. cit.*, 9).

relative to money-demand in the relatively high prices of grain in the autumn and winter of 1925 as there was in the case of industrial goods. The appearance of this so-called " goods famine " at the end of 1924 was a symptom of the difficulty of maintaining the monetary reform in face of the poor harvest of 1924 : it was an inflationary symptom. The waning of this phenomenon in the beginning of 1925 was witness to the easing of the situation in view of the rapid expansion of industrial output. Its reappearance at the end of the year in an accentuated form was a result of a fresh credit inflation in the autumn of 1925.[1]

This inflation was the result of an attempt to finance accumulation and construction to a greater extent than the actual economic circumstances warranted—in excess of the real " saving " or economy of consumption which was necessary for accumulation to take place.[2] The miscalculation on which this credit policy was based was partly an overestimate of the actual harvest which would be marketed in the autumn, and partly in the mood of prevailing optimism

[1] Cf. Bronsky : " Credit inflation is the source of the rise in prices both of agricultural and of industrial production. It calls forth a depreciation of the currency, increases the effective demand both of town and of village . . . renders export difficult, and imposes the necessity of reducing imports, and evokes the critical phenomena of a goods famine " (*Sozt. Khos.*, 1926, No. 1, 24). Also Svetlov : " An insufficiently cautious bank emission on the eve and during the first period of the realisation of the harvest, and credit expansion in the sphere of grain collection and goods turnover fed by this emission, gave birth to the phenomenon of a surplus of currency in circulation. We had present all the signs of inflation " (*Econ. Oboz.*, Dec. 1926, 10). Also Guchman, *Ibid.*, 29–30. A Joint Resolution of Sovnarcom and S T O of June 28, 1926, referred to " a considerable excess of effective demand over supply " in the preceding six months, producing a widening " difference between wholesale and retail prices in the markets where there was a shortage of goods."

[2] Cf. Professor Pervushin in *Econ. Oboz.*, Feb. 1927, 10–11 ; Professor Weinstein, *loc. cit.*, 11 *seq.* : " Currency emission would not have evoked economic complications if at the same time the savings of the population had increased in the same measure. . . . (As it was) these currency notes were put on to the market where they did not find an adequate supply in the form of goods for present consumption. This led to inflation. It is interesting to note that inflation, generally speaking, characterises the condition of national economy which consumes more than it produces. . . . The tendency to accumulate more than the national economy can stand leads to a similar economic result."

of the summer an exaggeration of the real " savings " which were available.[1] In addition, apart from specific mistakes of the grain-purchasing organs, the character of the State grain policy itself and of grain-crediting had an important influence. It was pointed out above[2] that a State grain-purchasing policy has two alternatives: to keep agricultural prices steady or agricultural purchasing power. With a fluctuating harvest it cannot achieve both. If it adopts the former policy, as on the whole seems to have been the case in 1925,[3] then this will cause village demand for industrial goods to fluctuate according as the harvest is large or small. Moreover, if the increased crediting of grain purchase required when the harvest is large is not balanced by a cancellation of these credits,[4] or decreased crediting or decreased consumption in some other direction, when the marketing of the harvest is drawing to a close, it will have an inflationary effect; for although the increased credit will at the outset be balanced by an increased supply of agricultural goods, it will give enhanced purchasing power to the village and tend to continue in circulation after the increased flow of agricultural goods resulting from the harvest has come to an end. But in addition to such an expansion of credits for grain purchase, swelling the village demand for industrial goods, the autumn of 1925 witnessed also an expansion of credits to industry for capital construction purposes, thereby swelling urban demand as well. In previous years the majority of such urban credits had gone to swell the circulating capital of the trusts, and so evoked a more speedy response in the supply of furnished goods. Now that they went to

[1] Cf. Krumin in *Econ. Oboz.*, July 1926, 6–11.

[2] Excursus to Chapter Eight and Nine, Section II.

[3] According to Lejava's estimates, in 1925–6 the peasant marketed a quantity of produce larger by 46 per cent than in the previous year, received in money 80 per cent more, and paid less in tax by 60 per cent (*cit.* Bronsky, *loc. cit.*, 22). The State Bank had outstanding credits for grain movement on Oct. 1, 1925, to the amount of 183 million roubles, as against only 57 million the previous year.

[4] A. Blum in *Econ. Oboz.*, May 1926, remarks on the continual danger of grain credits, opened ostensibly for a limited period only, becoming " frozen " (15).

finance constructional work which would yield its fruit, not in months ahead, but in years, increased consumption from the increased wages and increased employment financed by these credits greatly exceeded any expansion in the supply of finished goods.[1] The result was a sharpening of the "goods famine" and a steady rise first in the retail and then in the wholesale prices both of industrial and of agricultural goods.

In face of this situation the State economic organs adopted measures which in effect, if not in aim, limited consumption and brought it within more reasonable bounds of the available supply. The State Bank was given special powers to cut down its credits and its rediscounts; and the official policy was expressed by Rykov in March when he said: "We are keeping an iron hand upon credit issue to individual economic branches, in particular to industry."[2] In the last quarter of 1924–5 the demands on the State Bank for credit had caused an increase in circulation of nearly two hundred million roubles of chervontsi, a sum greater than the increase of the whole preceding three-quarters of the year; and in October there was an expansion of an additional 60 million. It was not immediately possible to cut down advances without causing sharp embarrassment to industry; and in November and the first three weeks of December chervontsi had to be issued to the extent of a further 40 million roubles. But in the final week of December the State Bank was able to gain control of the situation: by January 1st the bank-note circulation had fallen by 17 million, and by the end of May the reduction of a further 80 million roubles had been achieved.[3] In the total currency

[1] Cf. "Shortage of supply is because industry yields the necessary production much later than it creates a demand for the means of production, and so creates a demand for means of consumption" (Shanin in *Econ. Oboz.*, Nov. 1925, 32). Also Djerjinsky, *op. cit.*, 10; and Resolution of Plenum of C.P. of Soviet Union, *cit.*, *Int. Press. Correspondence*, 29.4.26.

[2] Report to Leningrad Soviet, March 9th, 1926.

[3] A. Blum in *Econ. Oboz.*, May 1926, 11–15; *The State Bank of U.S.S.R.*, 1921–6, 24–5.

circulation there was a reduction of 7 per cent between January and May, which by May had begun to show its influence in a fall of agricultural prices, reducing the wholesale price index by 3 to 4, and retail by 2 to 3 per cent—a fall in the general index which continued until in the final quarter of 1926 it was lower than the average for 1924–5.[1] By the second half of 1926 the " goods famine " had appreciably slackened[2] even though in 1927 it continued to be considerable. At the same time the program of capital investment was cut down by 200 million roubles; and the program of imports was drastically curtailed from 1000 million to 685, the reduction falling principally on finished goods and raw materials, while the program of machinery was left untouched and even a little increased.

The preliminary plans of capital reconstruction for 1925–6 were products of that mood of optimism which had come to Moscow in 1925 with the summer winds; and as the winter frosts succeeded the summer, the inflation crisis came as a sharp reminder to Gosplan that in future it should season its plans with a healthier dose of scepticism. Here the opposition critics were justified: Russian industry in existing circumstances was unable to provide out of her own resources as large a capital accumulation as was anticipated by the high hopes of June and July; and the attempt to realise so large an accumulation had placed a strain on the credit mechanism which it could not bear. In future, plans of capital assignment would have to be more modest, and kept within the bounds of the real surplus that was available without the expedient of inflation. But these exaggerated hopes were hopes which should never have been seriously entertained; and their failure gave no reason for flying to the contrary opinion that no appreciable accumulation was possible at all. The actual accumulation realised in the course of 1925–6 was far from negligible; and industrial

[1] Cf. Professor Kondratiev in *London and Camb. Econ. Service*, Vol. 4, Nos. 4, 6, 7; also Professor Pervushin in *Econ. Oboz.*, Nov. 1926, 74–6.

[2] Editorial in *Econ. Jizn.*, 4.1.27.

production in the year showed a growth of 40 per cent and by the end of the year had almost reached, and according to some estimates had actually passed, the pre-war level; while the grain collected in 1926 was actually greater, in spite of a smaller harvest, and at a lower price than in the previous year. For the following year capital accumulation was planned—and this year planned after the previous sharp lesson much more conservatively—so as to raise the figure of net capital creation to some 1800 million roubles, on the basis of which a further expansion of industrial output was estimated of between 15 and 20 per cent.

To find the means for this continued industrial expansion, reliance was placed on a new campaign to secure an increasingly effective utilisation of individual savings and the achievement of economies both in industrial and commercial costs and in increased turnover of working capital. To this end the previous policy of price-reduction for State industry was now extended to the retail prices of State and co-operative trading organs, and was linked with a greatly strengthened economy campaign. Particular attention was now turned to simplifying the commercial apparatus. The margin between wholesale and retail prices either gave large profits to the trading organs, in which case they could afford some reduction of retail prices, or else represented—as was more generally the case—excessive trading costs, eating up in wasteful expenditure resources which should have gone to the expansion of industry or the improvement of the State and co-operative trading apparatus. The Joint Resolution of Sovnarcom and STO of June 28th, 1926, called upon the banks to make the granting of credit to co-operatives conditional on " actual achievement in the reduction of commercial expenses and of retail prices," and instructed Centrosoyus to elaborate jointly with Vesenha plans for the " rationalisation " of co-operative and State trading, so as to secure " the greatest possible economy and the reduction of the total personnel employed in the apparatus of trade." Rykov in his report to the 15th Party

Conference stressed the importance and the great potentialities of increasing the attraction of peasant savings into savings banks, co-operative credit institutions, and State loans, and placed in the forefront of his proposals " the revising of the whole machinery of State and economics with the object of adapting it to the new tasks and of reducing bureaucratism." Vesenha proceeded to form special commissions in each industry of representatives of Vesenha, the trusts, syndicates and trade unions to make recommendations for the raising of quality and the lowering of costs; while the trade unions summoned special conferences of workers in each factory to discuss means for eliminating waste. Among five tasks for the New Year, 1927, the President of Vesenha, Kuibyshev, included " the rationalisation both of the productive process and of commercial work " and " the re-organisation of the administration of industry " on the basis of " centralisation of planning and decentralisation of operative activity." Serebrovsky, the Vice-President of Vesenha, gave the keynote of the tasks of the coming year as the abolition of " the superfluous ink in our day-to-day business which is so dangerous."[1] The old-style smug *chinovnik* was beginning to be hustled by a new race of men in " leather jackets "; and in the tenth year of the Soviet Government " rationalisation " and " scientific management " were probably more talked and written of in the land of Chekhov and Dostoievsky than in New York or Berlin.

[1] *Econ. Jizn.*, 1.1.27.

CHAPTER ELEVEN

TOWN AND VILLAGE

IN the dissensions which held the centre of attention in Russia in 1925 and 1926 detailed questions of economic policy were hardly the essential issues. Questions of price policy and of accumulation were little more than incidental, guided by the bias of more general views. The inner doubts of the opposition concerned the destination of the course which Russia had followed since 1923. Some were anxious lest the course were wrongly set to the map and to the compass, others lest progress on the course were too slow; and since some took the bearings differently from others, while some even used a map which was differently drawn, discussion inclined to be complex and diffuse.

For those who had lingering regrets for " war communism," considering it as holding qualities essential to their ideal, certain doubts about the progress of events were only natural. Quantitatively there was no question of the economic advance. The rate at which that advance was likely to continue was an open matter, and there were some who even doubted its continuance at all. But the qualitative character of that advance was in general a more fevered object of discussion and aroused a more definite mistrust. Was not the quantitative progress being purchased at the price of the strengthening of individualist peasant economy, of the adaptation of capitalist forms in industry, and the development of a " new bourgeoisie " of private traders and even of " specialists " and managerial personnel in State economic organs? Was not the Soviet Government, in the absence of political and economic aid from the workers of the West, having to throw more and more " to the wolves " —to the peasantry to secure its co-operation and its supplies of food, to foreign countries to secure credits and favourable terms of trade, to the ex-bourgeois technician and expert and to capitalist efficiency methods, in order to surmount the difficulties of industrial reconstruction? Was not Russia merely a country of State capitalism, distinguishable by very little from many other European countries during the war—save that the standard of life of her workers was probably lower? And was there really any serious possibility of Russia in the near future being anything else than this? For such a puny offspring the travail of the hunger years might well seem to have been in vain.

Doubts of this kind had already been voiced in 1921 by the Workers' Opposition, when Kollontai and others had fulminated against the " degeneration " of the State apparatus and the deviation of State policy from the proper communist line. Again in 1923 two small opposition groups appeared. The " Workers' Truth " group, with A. Bogdanov as its spokesman, declared that the October revolution had not done more than introduce up-to-date capitalism in Russia, and could not possibly have done more in the existing backward state of economic development and of the proletariat. The " Workers' Group " under Miasnikov charged the Government and the Party with " opportunist deviations "; and both groups proposed to form new rank and file organisations within the Party and the Soviets and the Trade Unions to bring opposition pressure to bear on the State.[1] Many others outside these groups considered the departure from " war communism " to be a very serious " defeat " in which positions essential to socialism were abandoned—a retreat which was forced upon them only by the failure of the revolution to spread to Western Europe and which in fairer circumstances would not have been required. And as those who had visualised socialism in their dreams as wearing the garb of " war communism " now saw how different from their facile dreaming the actual appearance of the new Russia was destined to be, the murmurings among these people increased and multiplied—murmurings

[1] Cf. *Isvestia R.K.P.*, 1923, Nos. 9–10, 14–15.

against the concessions to the peasantry, against the slow advance of social welfare schemes, against the new administrative methods and business personnel. The drab tasks of economic reconstruction were so much less romantic and alluring than the clamour, the shouting and the singing, the banners and the tramp of battalions, the sweat and confusion and the electric tension of the civil war days. Figures of output of ploughshares and pruning-hooks were so much less stirring than figures of Cheka executions.

It was not by chance that the discussions of 1925 were prefaced by apparently doctrinaire disagreements about the character of NEP: whether NEP was a "retreat" in the sense of abandoning positions essential to socialism which would later require recapture, or only in the sense of withdrawing from territory which lay aside from the main line of advance; whether State industry was "socialist" in character or only "State capitalist"; whether the growing prosperity of the peasant was synonymous with the rebirth of capitalism. Thus prefaced, the argument proceeded to place State policy in the balance: to debate the alleged backwardness of State industry, with its danger of a relative decrease in the importance of socialist elements in the economic system and a relative increase of capitalist elements. It reached its conclusion in proposals to place an increased burden on the peasantry for the benefit of socialist accumulation, and to speed up the rate of industrial advance. It attained to flowery peroration in charges of "degeneration" and "*kulak* deviation" against the government, with the proposals of Ossovsky as its logical corollary that an organised "workers' opposition" should be formed within the Party to exert proletarian pressure and "ginger" upon the conservative, bureaucratic State machine which in the conditions of NEP had grown too tender of the interests of the peasant and the "new bourgeoisie."

Partly these fears were based on misunderstanding of NEP and an unreasoning "Eldorado-fantasy" which would have economic realities to be different from what they are. A note of despair was frequently introduced into economic discussions by the complaint expressed by Medvediev that the root cause of the troubles under NEP was the need to adapt industry to the peasant market. Others declared that State industry could not be socialist because it worked on commercial principles for the market. In his " Letter to Baku " Medvediev expressed the opinion that, given this " adaptation to the market " as the basis of policy, the prospects of industrial development were so hopeless as to make it preferable to scrap socialist principles and summon foreign capital to their aid. What precisely this adaptation to the market was intended to mean is not entirely clear. Some appeared to mean by it the abandonment of the attempt to base industrial development on the exploitation of the peasant; although even this could only be done on the basis of a certain " adaptation to the market." As a rule one suspects a less rational interpretation of the phrase. For many it undoubtedly contained a certain mystical significance. If one only gave goods away instead of selling them, and regulated production *a priori* and not according to the desires expressed through the market, economic difficulties would miraculously vanish away! In a system like " war communism " one could be guilty of inefficiency, stupidity and muddle, and without the harsh check of a balance-sheet still cherish the illusion that one was building the millennium. When " planning of production " meant merely composing plans *a priori* in an office, it was easy to produce a dozen alternative millennia merely by burning a little midnight oil. It was so easy for a mere Mr. Preemby to be Sargon, King of Kings. It is natural for the devotee of quick utopias to think that when he has banished the balance-sheet and the money in which it is measured, he has banished also the real economic quantities on which the items in a social balance-sheet are based. But this is the conceit of the cloistered *chinovnik* who thinks that to move mountains requires merely a mountain of decrees. In the world as it is real economic quantities, whether expressed in money and in market form or not, still exist to be reckoned with, and on the apprehension of them through a system of social accounting any successful economic policy must depend.

Partly, however, the fears had a basis in important economic facts. There was always the possibility that NEP as the form of the transition to socialism might be nourishing tendencies which led back to capitalism faster than tendencies which were leading towards the desired socialist goal. NEP was defined by Lenin as a " mixed system "; and to this " mixed system " as a whole he gave the name of " State capitalism," the mixture comprising large-scale State industry which was " socialist " in character, small-scale private industry, State and collective farms and backward small-scale peasant agriculture, the co-operative society and the private Nepman trader. The characteristic feature of this system, sharply dividing it from other countries, was that in Russia a Party of the workers held the " commanding heights " and in storming them had dealt a blow at the foundations of class monopoly. In other countries a form of State capitalism might arise from the needs of war or the requirements of economic organisation: land, mining, railways might be nationalised and conducted on such lines as are the telephone and post office and much electrical and gas supply to-day; industry might be harnessed under measures of State control as are the British railways, or organised under semi-public corporations like the Bank of England or the Port of London Authority.[1] Former captains of industry and former financiers might now receive, in place of an uncertain profit, a steady salary and an assured *rentier* interest, while the State shouldered risks and acted as bailiff and active director of the concern. But this change of form might not imply a change of social substance. The former propertied class might still retain its old privileges, its

[1] Mr. J. M. Keynes in a paper read to the Liberal Summer School on July 30, 1927, stated that in Britain some £3·5 milliard, or two-thirds of the capital in large-scale undertakings, was in enterprises of a State capitalist character, i.e. enterprises either in State hands or subject to some form of State regulation and control.

differential advantages, and its hold on the reins of power: society might still remain on a class basis with the rights of an exploiting class to profit from the dependent position of an exploited class jealously guarded and preserved; it might even approximate in character to Mr. Belloc's "Servile State." Lenin's theory made the forcible transfer of the "key positions" from the capitalist class to the workers the historical watershed between these two systems—systems alike in form but antithetical in substance. As this "mixed system" found its distinguishing birth-mark in the blow which had been dealt to class monopoly, so its success as a transitional stage to socialism was to be judged by the ability of the tendencies towards a classless community to overbear the opposing tendencies towards the revival of elements of class monopoly and the recrudescence of class differentiation; and only the entrenchment of the workers on the "commanding heights," giving them power to control the movements in the plain, gave possibility to the former tendencies to gain the mastery.

To this view, socialist forms of economic organisation and the increase of them were to be valued less for their own sake than as the necessary foundation of a classless society. Class monopoly, of course, could be and was broken by the dividing up of land into small properties, as well as by socialisation of property in the hands of the State. But the former, apart from being a retrograde step economically, also left greater possibility of a revival of class differentiation in the future. Individualist societies of small property owners have generally tended in the past to give birth in the course of time to some form of class monopoly, unless special legal measures were in force to prevent it; and a principal factor in the origins of economic inequality has been the possession of property and the fortunes which the private ownership of property allows individuals to acquire.[1] Consequently, an

[1] Cf. *Capitalist Enterprise*, 153, 235 *seq.*, 271 *seq.*; Dr. H. Dalton, *Inequality of Incomes*, 276: "The greater the scope of private property, the greater inequality is likely to be; the greater the scope of public property, the smaller inequality is likely to be."

increase in the relative weight of socialist forms in this mixed system was regarded as the desirable line of development, and was treated as the criterion of social advance or retreat. Nevertheless, it was not the sole criterion; and a growth in the prosperity of the peasantry, in the absence of class division in the villages, was by no means synonymous with a revival of capitalism—a point which was considerably stressed in the discussions in 1925 and 1926. The question, "Whither Russia?" which Trotsky made the title of his book,[1] depended for its answer on conditions somewhat wider than those which he postulated: it depended, not merely on whether State industry would advance more rapidly in the future than other elements in Russian economy—more rapidly even than industry in other countries—but on whether either in the town or in the village old class differences and privileges were beginning to reappear, or whether the germs of such differences and the environment in which they would flourish were being progressively destroyed.

The method of "war communism" held the charm of simplicity for many in that it dealt with every situation by direct administrative means. If one saw a speculator making money on the Sukharevka, one sent him to kill lice in the Butyrka prison; if in the village one came across a *kulak* with bulging barns, one sent an armed detachment from the *uyezd* food department to requisition his surplus and leave him a poorer and an angrier man. In war time when immediate results are imperative and the short-period is everything, such methods are necessary: the devoutest advocate of Montessori methods pushes and orders people about when the house is on fire. But such inflexibly simple methods could not for long in normal conditions manage a complicated system without creating more strains and stresses than they healed; and the essence of NEP was that it abandoned the attempt to exorcise all obstacles by a volume of decrees, and facing the economic situation as it

[1] Translated into English as *Towards Socialism or Capitalism?*

was, applied the influence of the more subtle and indirect "economic" measures which were in the hands of the State to shape society in the desired direction. It was the difference between the Victorian pedagogue, striving to implant a sense of the beauty of Greek iambics by the influence of the birch, and the modern educationist who seeks to mould development by creating for the child an appropriate environment. The modern school system, while it offers the greater promise, holds also the danger that untutored tendencies may break out and display behaviour which would cause the matron of a Victorian dame-school to raise her arms in shocked alarm. NEP likewise contains the possibility, sharply repressed under "war communism," of the rise of a new class of "Nepman," enriching themselves from the profits of private trade. In the village the redistribution of land after the October revolution had considerably equalised peasant land holdings; but inequalities in ownership of stock and implements still remained; and N E P gave possibility for these inequalities to increase and for the rise of a class of rich peasants, cultivating more land because they had more equipment, and lending stock, implements and seed at onerous rates to their needy brethren. In industry and State departments there was a tendency for the managerial and technical personnel to put on starched collars and adopt the airs as well as the incomes of a new ruling class.[1] Should the Nepman, the *kulak* and the white-collared official combine together by sympathy, social ties or business contacts, the policy of the State might well "degenerate" and become more careful of the interests and differential privileges of this new ruling class than of moulding social change in the direction of a classless society. The State machine in policy and personnel might become estranged from the working

1 "Specialists" are given special salaries, not included in the ordinary wage scales, and ranging up to 500 or 600 roubles a month. "Red directors," however, promoted to managerial posts from among the workers on the nomination of the trade unions, and members of the Party (including Commissars) receive no more than the highest category in the wage scale, approximately 225 roubles a month.

masses, growing to be an alien force imposing orders and coercion from above like any class State of old.

In the autumn of 1924 under the slogan of " The Face to the Village " particular attention began to be turned to the situation in the countryside. The " scissors " crisis and the dying plunge of the paper rouble had left their after-effects in a certain hostility towards the towns among some sections of the peasant population. The richer peasant who could hold his gain for a good price, where his poorer neighbour had to sell quickly at any price he could, had tended to profit from the high grain prices and the stabilisation of money in 1924, and in some districts had attained to something of his old influence.[1] With the question once more to the fore of extending and improving agricultural production, particularly the more intensive cultures for raw material supplies, the need to remove some of the legislative hindrances to peasant production became urgent. The difficulty was that the major part of the grain supplies and also the more efficient production came from the richer peasant, whose growth from a class point of view the State desired to prevent. Many of these had followed the practice, inaugurated under Stolypin, of migrating from the village and taking up farmsteads of their own a few miles outside, where they were free from the cramping custom and routine of the commune. These farms were usually more efficient in every way than the old cultivation under the village commune, where land holdings were customarily scattered in 10 or 20 " strips " in various parts of the village lands, were subject to periodic redistribution and reallotment every few years, and were cultivated on the old 2-field or 3-field system. In the early days of N E P this migration outside the village commune took on considerable dimensions, nearly 3 million acres in the first year of NEP being taken up in farmsteads in this way.[2] These " progressive farmers " naturally tended to

[1] Cf. Smilga in *Plan. Khos.*, No. 9, 13–14.

[2] These farmsteads did not carry any right of individual ownership: they were merely granted by the local land committee on behalf of the State on the principle of " working use "—a rent-free lease by the State

outdistance those who had remained behind in the village: those who took up farmsteads would tend to be originally the richer peasants with animals and equipment of their own. And this more well-to-do peasantry began to constitute a new upper class in the countryside, sometimes playing the rôle of village usurer, either in kind or money, to the poor peasant who cultivated his "strips" without possessing horses or even implements of his own, and sometimes combining the rôle of usurer and trader in buying the crops of the villagers in return for advances of seed or cattle, and then holding and later selling the grain at a more favourable price in a neighbouring town. The more well-to-do peasant could make a speculative profit from a difference of price in time or in space, where the poorer peasant was unable to take advantage of the difference because he had not the same power of moving and waiting.

As long as the law remained that no one should possess more land than he and his family could cultivate, and the leasing of land and the employment of hired labour was forbidden, this tendency to class differentiation could not proceed very far. Nevertheless, inequality in possession of cattle and implements itself led to a certain amount of inequality in land holding, since the peasant with several horses was able to cultivate more land than the peasant who had no horses at all; and the possibility existed of a certain exploitation by him who had of him who had not, which might tend to grow cumulatively as it had in pre-war days, piling up at one end of the village private fortunes and private capital and at the other end creating a dependent proletariat. Moreover, there were ways for the well-to-do peasant to circumvent the law, extending from a system of temporary "marriages" and sham "adoptions" into the

for an indefinite period, but made conditional on proper cultivation. Any peasant had the right to be allotted such farmsteads, where all the land was in one or a few plots and not in scattered strips, and was not subject to the periodic redistributions of the village commune, the size of the farm being based on the number of members in the peasant family (*Dvor*). (Cf. Gubsky in *Econ. Journal*, June 1927, 234–6.)

family in order to increase the claim for land and the number of hands available to the farmer, up to secret agreements on a *métayage* system and actual bribery of local Soviet officials; and by 1924 in some areas a small group of so-called *kulaks*, though excluded from the franchise and from certain other political rights, had in practice attained to something of their old position of dominance in the village.

Much interest attaches to the report of a tour of investigation undertaken by Yakovlev in the course of 1924, and the economic relationships which he describes in a typical volost of Tambov gubernia are particularly illuminating. One peasant in this volost of Znamenka had owned before the war some 150 acres, traded in timber and owned a bakehouse. To-day he no longer had the bakehouse, but trading remained his chief means of support, and he advanced credits to his clients to the sum of 150 roubles monthly. Another trader, Yefimov, who kept a private shop, had added to his own 30 acres another 30 from his poorer neighbours. Another owner of 150 acres had built a mill, employing in it a man who worked 12 to 14 hours a day for a wage of 15 poods of rye flour a month. Another, Skorotchkin, was a trader in horses and spent most of his daytime, not in farming, but in riding to neighbouring towns and villages in the pursuit of his trade. To these persons the poorer peasantry presented a sharp contrast. A certain Denisov, in return for the loan of a plough and horses to plough two-thirds of a dessiatine, gave a quarter of a dessiatine to his richer neighbour. Another after he had hired a horse for ploughing and carting retained only 13 out of a harvest of 35 poods per dessiatine, and of this remainder the agricultural tax took a half. A widow, Vieselova, with no means of cultivating land allotted to her, had to pay 3 poods of grain and 35 quarts of milk to another to plough her two dessiatines for her, for the sowing of it she had to pay 8 poods, and for the reaping of the harvest she had to part with another pood of grain. At the same time 21 poods had to be paid in tax. The result was that by April she was herself destitute of food and had to sell her only calf; while her son who worked for a rich peasant achieved the reward of a bottle of lamp-oil as compensation for two days' work.[1]

Another aspect of the rural problem was that Soviet officials in the village were often of inferior calibre, particularly in outlying areas, to those in the towns. Not infrequently they were drunkards and petty tyrants; some were actually corrupt and took bribes. A large number were stupid and inflexible, still "clinging to the traditions of war communism," bullying like a sergeant-major and imposing commands and regulations at the point of the gun, "fighting the *kulak* danger" as they called it by suppressing every industrious farmer, and doing little or nothing constructive to build up village communal life. "Our comrades in the country," says one communist writer, "are still too much inclined to command, to give orders, still strive too much to become the village 'boss.'" "Some have become bureaucratic," says another, "and 'command' in their district in a most arrogant fashion, whilst a small section have become positively corrupt."[2] Arbitrary methods and appointment from above, which had been in force during the civil war, in many cases continued; so that the village soviets, lacking any real influence or democratic character, became mere dead wood, of no interest to the peasants, in some cases actually boycotted by them. Professor Karlgren quotes the remark of a peasant at a congress: "If they ordered us to elect a horse to the village soviet, we should be compelled to do so."[3] In some cases by means of their influence or by bribery a handful of rich peasants was able to dominate and use the soviets for their own ends. The gulf between the State and the peasant masses and actual discontent and hostility which had reached such a height in 1921 still remained to a considerable extent; while the existing administrative and legal measures for preserving the equality

[1] Yakovlev, *Nasha Derevnia*, 19–25.

[2] A. Martinov in *Comm. International*, (N.S.) No. 9, 55; and article on "Tasks in the Rural Districts of U.S.S.R.," *Ibid.*, No. 12, p. 19.

[3] *Bolshevik Russia*, 14.

of the village were not only in large part ineffective in actual practice, but at the same time hampered the development of agricultural production, particularly when operated through incompetent local officials, and fettered improvements in agricultural technique.[1]

The slogan of the new " Face to the Village " campaign which was pronounced by the 14th Party Congress was " the elimination of the remnants of ' war communism ' in the village." The old " sergeant-major " methods which were antagonising the peasantry and paralysing the soviets must be banished. " Administrative " measures for combating the rise of the *kulak* and the attempt to regiment the middle peasant into socialism by administrative pressure must be replaced by more flexible and more indirect " economic " measures ; and a *modus vivendi* must be found, by which the improvement of agricultural production could be encouraged at the same time as the tendency to class differentiation was held in check. Zealous devotees of " war communism " had placed reliance for improved cultivation on the development of State and " collective " farms, the former consisting of that part of the former estates which were taken over and run as large-scale farms by the State, the latter of land leased to groups of peasants to be cultivated in common. On the development of these the future of agriculture was considered to depend : for the future of backward peasant production one need have little thought or care. But in the course of the civil war these State and collective farms, which at the outset never covered more than 3 to 4 per cent of the cultivated land, had come very near to the point of breakdown through lack of equipment and mismanagement ; and the task of

[1] Cf. Stalin : " Up to the present in a number of districts the elections to the Soviets in the countryside were not real elections, but empty bureaucratic procedures, dragging in ' deputies ' by means of various kinds of artfulness and pressure on the part of a narrow group of rulers, fearful of losing their power. As a result of this, the Soviets risked being transformed from organs near and dear to the masses into organs foreign to the masses. . . . The old electoral practice in a number of districts is a relic of ' war communism,' which must be abolished as a harmful practice, a practice rotten through and through " (*op. cit.*, 37).

reviving and extending them so as to give them any substantial significance in the supply of agricultural produce would have required such large allocations of working capital, and might have caused such hostility on the part of the peasants, who tended to look on them as competitors and as the old landlords' estates in new guise,[1] as to make the task a utopian one. Lenin had outlined a policy which, though less simple to the eye, was more adapted to reality. The issue for him was not a simple issue of State farms *v.* small holdings, with the growth of socialism depending on the triumph of the former and the elimination of the latter, as capitalism in its growth had eliminated the yeoman farmer and the handloom weaver. It was a question of raising peasant agriculture itself on to a higher level, particularly the poor and middle peasants, and then transforming its individualism gradually into collectivism through the influence of co-operation—co-operation at first in commercial matters of sale and purchase, co-operative credit, later co-operative ownership of implements, cattle and machinery, and finally co-operative cultivation itself on intensive large-scale lines. Not by the path of "permanent revolution," not by a fresh class war in the countryside, expressed economically in the mortal rivalry of the State *v.* the peasant farm, but through the intermediate stage of "co-operative collectivism" was urban socialism to extend and envelop the backward countryside. While in form the growth of agricultural co-operation would transform individualism, so also would it combat the growth of class monopoly by differentiating in the aid it gave in favour of the weaker families like Demisov and Vieselova in Yakovlev's report; and the task of raising the prosperity and productivity of peasant agriculture and the task of fighting "the *kulak* danger" were no longer treated as contradictory aims, but were reconciled and combined.

[1] Cf. Maurice Hindus, *Broken Earth,* 205 *seq.*, who gives an account of a soviet farm in the neighbourhood of the village of his birth, of the suspicious attitude of the peasants towards it, and of the difficulties which the manager had to face.

The murder of several " peasant correspondents "[1] in the summer of 1924, who had exposed in the newspapers abuses and cases of corruption in their villages, served to focus the attention of the central government on the situation in the countryside; and after the conduct of special investigations and the examination of various reports on the rural situation, a series of important measures were introduced towards the end of the year. Actually these were scarcely more than the logical completion of NEP, the carrying through in the countryside of changes which had already taken place in the towns. But they constituted an important milestone in Russian development, since they marked the definitive abandonment of the methods of " war communism " and " permanent revolution " in the village and the final adoption of Lenin's policy of rural " co-operative collectivism," as the form of transition to socialism in the backward countryside. Since 1921 there had been an uncertain vacillation between the two policies. Local officials while following the letter of the new had often interpreted it in the spirit of the old; and even the central party organs, failing to recognise at once the full implications of the new policy, had at times spoken with an uncertain voice. Now the position was clarified. The more obvious hindrances to the improvement of peasant farming were removed, while at the same time a campaign for strengthening agricultural co-operation among the peasantry was set on foot. The keynote was the removal of the hindrances on the industrious and progressive " middle peasant " and the effort to break his connections with the *kulak* and draw him into the *smytchka* with the towns.

The first measure was a political one: the " restoration

[1] The system of worker and peasant correspondents attached to the central newspapers had been adopted as one of the methods of contact between the State and the rank and file. These correspondents were purposely chosen from among ordinary peasants in the villages and factory workers in the towns to express the viewpoint and the grumbles of the rank and file. They provided both a reflection of mass opinion and a useful running criticism of official personages and official methods. In 1926 these numbered 160,000 in the villages alone.

of Soviet democracy in the countryside " as it was officially called, designed to " revive the activity of the Soviets from below." The central committee of the Party issued instructions to its members in the villages to abolish forms of pressure on soviet elections and of appointment from above which still prevailed as relics of the civil war period, to restore the responsibility of soviet delegates to their electors, and to attract non-Party peasants into active work in the co-operatives, in peasant mutual aid committees, village libraries and clubrooms, etc. At the same time a certain " purge " of Party members in the countryside and of officials was undertaken, eliminating corrupt elements,[1] drawing in new blood and developing the constructive side of their activities in the direction of educational and economic work and activities among the village youth. Fresh elections were ordered in some 40 per cent of the local soviets which had previously been elected by a small minority of the village population, so that the new soviets might hold a greater degree of confidence among the peasantry and have a greater chance of displaying independent activity and initiative.

But in some respects more fundamental than the political question were the economic difficulties in the village; and these were dealt with by series of special regulations passed by the Central Executive Committee,[2] which modified the land code as it affected peasant landholding and production. The most important of these changes concerned the leasing of land and the right to employ hired labour. Formerly

[1] Cf. Maurice Hindus, *Broken Earth*, 106–8, where the conversation of villagers is reported about chairmen and treasurers of neighbouring soviets and other officials who were imprisoned and shot for corruption. Communists were always treated much more severely for such offences than non-Party persons. One of the peasant grumbles was the number of new offences for which the new authorities inflicted punishment: " If you give someone in the Soviet a gift, no matter how small, maybe just to be nice to him, they put you in jail. If you whip your child they send an agent down to investigate you and threaten to lock you up. If you go to the woods far, far away for a load of wood in summer they put you in jail " (p. 193).

[2] The body elected by each Soviet Congress as the semi-permanent legislative chamber, out of which Sovnarcom is appointed.

a peasant to whom land had been granted on the right of "working use" could lease that land to another only for the period of one rotation of a crop. Now that length of lease was extended to a period of three rotations under a multiple-field system and to 12 years where the three- and four-field system existed. The employment of a certain amount of wage labour was legalised, subject to a maximum working day which was made elastic according to the season; and the "middle peasant" who worked his own land was not to be excluded from the political category of "working citizen" and from the franchise for the reason that he employed auxiliary labour at certain seasons of the year. To encourage *kustarni* industry,[1] home-workers who employed auxiliary labour as well as those who did not were exempted from paying the "business tax," from the income tax if they paid the agricultural tax as peasants, and also from the trading tax if they traded only in their own products. The burden of the agricultural tax, which was considered to bear too heavily on the poor and middle peasant, and to discourage improved cultivation, and especially stock-breeding, was lowered from 470 million roubles to about 300, pending a detailed reconsideration and reconstruction of the whole tax.[2] In particular, the assessment of cattle for purposes of the tax was lowered, and the age when a beast became liable to assessment was raised. Further, a larger proportion of the tax was

[1] The number of *kustarni* workers at this time was about 2 million, or a half of the pre-war number.

[2] Direct taxation at this time (before the change in the tax) represented about one and a half times the pre-war burden and a considerably greater percentage of the farming income per head than in pre-war time. But taking all payments which the peasant had to make, including rent and indirect taxes, the burden was considerably less than the pre-war figure—little more than a third (cf. Bronsky in *Sozt. Khos.*, 1926, No. 1, 19; also *The Economist*, 24.7.26). Professor Karlgren would seem to be unduly influenced by his zeal when, speaking of changes in the agricultural tax, he declares: "In one respect alone these modifications never showed any change, that is on the terribly heavy burden of taxes that rested on peasant shoulders" (*op. cit.*, 171). This misleading statement is contradicted four pages later when he describes what he calls the "capitulation of the Bolsheviks to the peasantry."

assigned to the expenditure of local rural soviets than previously.

When these changes in rural policy subsequently arose for discussion at the 14th Party Conference in the spring of 1925, no very serious opposition was expressed: the political position in the countryside was clearly unsatisfactory, and the need to expand the marketable surplus of agricultural produce, especially of raw materials which required more skilled and intensive cultivation, was becoming imperative. A certain group of opinion, however, represented by Kritsmann and Larin, urged that to meet the *kulak* tendencies which had now been given greater leash, the efforts of the Party should be directed towards the political organisation of the poorer peasantry to fight the *kulak* influence, and that a campaign should be undertaken for strengthening the State and collective farms. If the *kulak* was to be given rope to-day, preparations should be made to expropriate him to-morrow and transfer his land to collective cultivation. This was the first breath of the coming storm.[1] But at this time, though Zinoviev gave signs of some doubts, Kamenev joined with Stalin and Bukharin in stressing the danger of "rekindling the class struggle in the village," and in declaring that such a suggestion, based on "overestimation of the *kulak* danger," was more harmful in the conditions of the moment than the opposite error of "underestimating the *kulak* danger" and desiring to give him still more leash. Kamenev stated in his opening speech to the 14th Conference: "The removal of all obstacles in the way of the development of productive forces in the countryside, the disappearance of every vestige of 'war communism' from the village, the abandonment of those administrative methods which are inconsistent with the development of the productive forces in the rural districts, and finally the finding of honest soviet officials for the village administrative apparatus—these are the concrete tasks now confronting us,

[1] Larin did not, however, join or even support the opposition in their proposals in the following year.

and waiting to be solved by our Conference." In the ensuing discussion Bukharin spoke as follows of Larin's proposal to concentrate attention on the State farms: "Collective economics are a mighty force, but they are certainly not the main road to socialism (in the countryside). We look to a prospective inclusion of the farmer in our total system of socialist upbuilding, but Larin looks to a 'second revolution'— he holds substantially to the old method of 'using our teeth.'"

But by the end of the year, after the experience of the harvest difficulties of 1925, murmurings became extensive against the results of "restoring Soviet democracy in the village" and "banishing the remnants of 'war communism' from the countryside"; and Kamenev and Zinoviev began to oppose the majority policy and to declare that concessions to the peasantry had gone too far. The failure of grain collections to reach the expected level in 1925, with its consequent reaction on the program of industrial construction, was regarded as largely due to the dominant position of the *kulak* in the village, who was able to defeat the State grain purchase policy by holding back his supplies for a higher price; and the benefits of the high price had in turn gone to enrich the *kulak* rather than to benefit the poorer villager. The industrial "goods famine" was said to be evidence of a faster development of agriculture than of industry, involving the danger that the growing prosperity of the individualist peasant would develop the non-socialist elements in the transitional "mixed system" faster than the socialist elements—would give private accumulation precedence over socialist accumulation. Politically this had been shown in the decreased number of communists elected to the village soviets at the previous election. Moreover, the excessive margin between retail and wholesale prices resulting from the "goods famine," on the one hand, and the policy of continually reducing industrial sale-prices, on the other, opened the way for large fortunes to the speculator and trader who were firmly entrenched in the retail—particularly the village retail—market. The point had been reached where the backward currents in the complex eddy of NEP were overmastering the forward ones; and the danger of retrogression threatened, unless special measures were taken to speed up the development of State industry and curtail the accumulation of private fortunes.

Discussion on such an issue was bound to be somewhat vague and general by reason of the absence of appropriate statistics relating to the class composition of the village, still less of comparative statistics by which to measure tendencies over a period of years. Consequently to measure the social tendencies with which the discussion was concerned presented very considerable difficulty. To calculate the profits of the private trader was easier than to judge the number and wealth of the *kulaks;* but estimates even here differed widely. Kutler of Narcomfin estimated that some 950 to 1000 million roubles of private capital was engaged in private industry and trade.[1] On this capital he estimated an annual profit of anything between 320 and 580 million; and Piatakov arrived at a similar figure of between 400 and 500 million. An estimate made by Gosplan, on the other hand, on the basis of an investigation in seven large towns and a number of villages, arrived at a figure that was considerably lower than this; and Bukharin argued that, even if the higher figure were correct, the actual amount accumulated as capital out of these profits was probably less than 100 millions, since the figures of Kutler and of Gosplan represented, not net, but gross profits, which were not concentrated in a few hands but were divided among some 320,000 private *entrepreneurs.*[2] The official reply to the

[1] This figure was arrived at by taking figures of turnover (4 per annum for trading enterprises and 3 for industrial) based on a questionnaire sent by Narcomfin to private traders, together with a figure of 4000 million as the annual turnover of private trade and industry in 1924–5 (3579 of trade and 511 of industry). *Cit.* Bronsky in *Sozt. Khos.*, 1926, No. 5, 24–6.

[2] Bukharin in Report to Meeting of Leningrad Party Officials, July 28, 1926.

opposition criticism, therefore, partly took the form of a denial that the growth of the Nepman and *kulak* was as considerable as the opposition tried to portray. But this was not all. It also denied that the growing prosperity of the peasant was synonymous with or indicative of the revival of capitalism. Here was the basic error of the opposition, their misconception of NEP, their belief that State industry ought to develop at the expense of the small producer, instead of by raising the small producer along with it. Increased peasant prosperity was a benefit to State industry, and was an entirely progressive symptom so long as the prosperity was not confined to a *kulak* minority and accompanied by a growing dispossession of poorer peasants at the bottom of the village. Capitalist tendencies only developed when a class appeared in the village who made their living predominantly, not by cultivating their own land, but by making profit out of the employment of wage-labour or by usury and speculation. The issue was erroneously represented as a competition between the prosperity of State industry *versus* the prosperity of peasant agriculture: the latter might grow more rapidly than the former and still not represent any capitalist tendency; and the growth of that very private accumulation in the hands of the peasantry which was depicted as dangerous might be a source of strength to socialist accumulation, if it could be attracted into Co-operation, State Loans, and Savings Banks.[1] At the 15th Party Conference in 1926 Rykov quoted figures of the Central Statistical Department for 35 provinces to show that, although the more well-to-do peasant with over 10 dessiatines of land and 4 head of cattle had increased in the last three years, so also the number of landless peasants and those with less than 2 dessiatines and no more than 2 head of cattle had decreased at the same

[1] e.g. Bukharin (*ibid.*): " Agricultural economics is confused with capitalist economics, private economics is regarded as identical with private capitalist economics, and there is a lack of comprehension of the fact that there can be such a thing as non-capitalist private undertakings."

time.[1] What had been occurring was a raising of the level of the whole village, including the village poor, not a dichotomy of the village along class lines.

Moreover, it was declared that the opposition, scared by the removal of clumsy administrative barriers against capitalist tendencies in the village, were blind to the important, but less obvious, economic methods which were at work resisting these tendencies more surely and successfully than before. Chief of these methods were taxation and credit, both of which represented strategic "key positions" from which the workers' State could shape the course of social development in line with its conscious purpose. Though the total burden of the agricultural tax had been lightened, in the revised form which was subsequently introduced in 1926 it was made considerably more progressive against the rich peasant, so that 15 per cent of the farms paid about 47 per cent of the tax and about 25 per cent of peasant households were exempt.[2] In pre-war days taxation had always been an important factor which forced the poorer peasant into the hands of the money-lender to mortgage his crops or even his farm; now that burden for the poorest strata had disappeared. Most important of all, the growth of agricultural co-operation and of agricultural credit were stemming any revival of the pre-war tendency for a village bourgeoisie to thrive on the weakness of the poorer peasant, at the same time as it began to transform rural individualism into rural collectivism by drawing individual savings into collective

[1] The percentages quoted by Rykov were as follows:

	1922	1923	1924	1925
No land	6·9	5·3	4·8	4·2
Up to 2 dessiatines .	46	40·7	36·6	33
From 2–6 dessiatines .	40·3	44	46·7	49·3
From 6–10 dessiatines	5·6	7·8	9	10·2
More than 10 dessiatines	1·2	2·2	2·9	3·3

	1923/4	1925/6
No cattle	17	15
Up to 2 head of cattle .	63	60
From 2–4 ,, ,, .	18	22
Over 4 ,, ,, .	2	3

[2] Rykov in Report to 15th Party Congress.

accumulation and giving both to the commercial operations and the working capital of agriculture an increasingly collective form. In pre-war days agricultural societies, particularly credit societies, were mainly composed of the more well-to-do peasants. Now the reverse was the case, and their policy was deliberately framed to give differential support to the poorer as against the richer villager. In the report of Yakovlev a second village, Voronsov, was cited, where conditions were considerably different from the village of Znamenka where Yefimov and Skorotchkin prospered while Denisov and Vieselova were impoverished; and the difference Yakovlev attributed to the existence in Voronsov of a small but flourishing co-operative society organised on the initiative of the local teacher. This not only performed functions which made a Yefimov and Skorotchkin largely superfluous: it gave special aid to the poorer peasant and saved him from the need to resort to the money-lender or to hire his land and his labour to the *kulak*. In the three months between February and April the society had given loans amounting to over 5000 roubles to 34 peasants to buy seed and also to purchase horses and stock, with 150 roubles as the maximum loan which its rules allowed to be advanced to one family. It had also a store which sold cheaper than the private trader, it hired horses to its members, and from its profits it gave subsidies to a number of poor widows. Those benefiting by its credits were mainly poor peasants, and the rest were " middle peasants "; of the 34 who secured credits for seed, a half had no horses, of which 10 had managed to procure horses by means of its credits since the formation of the society.[1]

In the course of 1924 particular attention began to be paid to the development of co-operation of all kinds; and the number of households belonging to agricultural co-operatives increased by some 30 per cent to about 2 million;[2]

[1] Yakovlev, *op. cit.*, 48–9.

[2] This represents about 10 per cent of all peasant farms. The proportion of the population served by consumers' co-operation in 1924 was estimated as 16–17 per cent: in the towns 44 per cent and in the

while the financial resources of such societies were doubled. An agricultural credit bank had been formed at the end of 1922 with a capital of 40 million gold roubles, to which the State now began to assign considerable sums out of the Budget to augment the Bank's fund for long-term credits—sums which by 1926 reached about 100 million roubles. In order to increase the financial facilities of the co-operatives by the attraction of peasant savings into shares and deposits, certain special changes were made. A vertical separation was established between the societies of agricultural, consumers, and credit co-operation; the principle of complete voluntary membership with a small entrance fee and increased responsibility of officials to the membership was established as being more consistent with confidence, interest and initiative among the members; while to minimise the risks of those investing in agricultural co-operation, agricultural co-operatives were forbidden to trade on their own account apart from purchases and sales performed on behalf of their members. At the same time the decree which prohibited rich peasants not enjoying the franchise from being members of co-operative societies was repealed, the undue influence of such elements, which might warp co-operation from its desired function, being prevented by a prohibition of their election to committees and management boards.

" The Face to the Village " involved also attention to the specific encouragement of improvements of agricultural technique. Inside the village commune certain improvements were achieved through the Party influence in the village soviets which now performed most of the functions of the old land committees. In numerous places a considerable consolidation of the scattered " strips " in the open-

country 8–9 per cent (I.L.O., *Co-operation in S. R.*, 245). The extent of agricultural co-operation on Oct. 1, 1926, was officially given as follows: 5000 agricultural societies with 565,000 members, 9500 credit societies with 3·6 million members, 5500 dairy societies with 1·1 million members, 7000 collective farms with a membership of 164,000. In all there were 7·3 million members of all kinds of agricultural co-operatives in U.S.S.R. (*S. U. Year-book*, 1927, 173).

field system and a departure from the old three-field method of cultivation was achieved; while the periodic redistributions of land were now permitted no more frequently than every nine years. Migrations outside the village were particularly encouraged, and special help was extended to such migrations in the form of loans and cheap transport facilities; and the policy was adopted of encouraging these settlements outside the village commune to be of a group, and not an individual, character, so that if rich peasants left the village to take up new farmsteads, they should take with them and assist by means of implements and horses a number of poorer peasants as well. In many of these new farm colonies the old "strip" system had been abolished entirely in favour of concentrated farmsteads; in others the number of strips had at least been drastically reduced; while most of them adopted a modern system of crop rotation and deeper ploughing. Yakovlev mentions a colony of this kind from the village of Pavlovka in Tambov gubernia, where as a result of the migration the number of pieces of land per family was reduced from 20 to 8 and the farthest distance of their land from their homes from 7 versts to 2. Previously in the village "all their day was spent in riding from piece to piece, harnessing and unharnessing; they never had time to plough." The colonists were mainly poor and "middle" peasants, most of them younger and more vigorous men who had served in the Red Army. The land assigned to them had formerly belonged to a Count's estate, and as it had not been ploughed for 20 years it needed 2 or 3 horses to plough it. This necessity had forced them to plough the land at the outset in common, and had instituted the custom which persisted in the colony of sharing horses without payment and of purchasing ploughs and using them communally as the property of the colony as a whole.[1] The Commissariat of Agriculture calculated in 1926 that about 600,000 farms covering an area of some 3·5 million dessiatines—nearly equivalent to the arable area of England—

[1] *Ibid.*, 71–2.

had introduced a system of crop rotation in the last four years. In Kaluga gubernia alone in 1924 as many as 458 villages transferred to crop rotation; and in Volokolamsk district only 83 villages remained on a 3-field system.[1] In the same year special progress took place in the more intensive cultures such as flax, hemp, oil-seeds, beet, and tobacco, so that their relative importance in the total cultivated area considerably increased. In 1924–5 some 5000 tractors were imported and provided either to village soviets to be used communally or to specific groups of peasants or co-operative societies on condition of joint ownership and use. In the following year it was planned to import some 17,500 and to manufacture another 1800 at home, while the total number of tractors in use at the end of 1926 was said to amount to over 50,000.[2] In many respects more significant were the psychological changes which were beginning to appear among the peasantry, stirring the old stagnant inertia of the Russian village. The older *moujik* still retains many of his superstitions, his quaint pessimism, and his *samagonka* : he still tends to place more faith in the sprinkling of holy water than in new forms of tillage to bring a good crop; and for all the alarums and excursions of revolution the new régime often means no more to him than the old Tsardom in new guise. But with the new generation it is different. The younger men who have been in the army now return to the village with fresh ideas and a wider horizon and a groundwork of education—for education plays a prominent rôle in military training to-day. While their elders shake their heads and mutter that the younger generation has gone to the devil, many village boys and girls have shed with their belief in priests and *ikons* the old superstitions and the old

[1] Kamenev in *Plan. Khos.*, 1925, No. 1, 8. Cf. also Tcherchinsky in *Int. Rev. of Agric. Econs.*, Oct.–Dec. 1924, 501, 536 *seq.*

[2] *Narodnoe Khos.*, 1921–5, 14; Krumin, *v. Borbye za Socialism*, 23. There seem to be no reliable figures of tractors in use before the war. Soviet statements put the figure at 500 : probably they did not amount to many more than 1000. These, however, were in use on the landlord's estates, and were usually the large 30–50 horse-power German tractor. To-day the smaller Fordson tractor is the predominant type.

obedience to the past as well. Many of them read books, have their ears open to the towns and the hum of machinery, and think in terms of change and evolution, while in their talk is often interwoven "school buildings" and "club-rooms," hygiene and atheism, "science, tractors, culture, technique, electricity."[1]

But the consolidation of the New Economic Policy gave rise in 1924 and 1925 to discussion, not only in respect to the village, but more widely to the whole problem of trade between the village and the town; and the "banishing of the remnants of 'war communism'" became as burning an issue in the problem of ways and means of handling the private trader as in the policy towards the *kulak*. Until 1923 the question of trade and of State policy towards it had received little serious consideration. Attention had been fully focussed on the elementary tasks of reconstruction and on the problems of industry and finance. Apart from isolated creations like Gostorg and the Gubtorg of certain local authorities, the only serious constructive work in the creation of a trading apparatus came from the trusts on their own initiative in their institution of the syndicates. For the time being the State with its preoccupation in the realm of production was willing to let such trading bodies as existed, including the private trader, work their own sweet will. But at the end of 1923 the State was being forced to give attention to the marketing problem. The "scissors" crisis had transferred attention from industry to the market. It had raised the whole question of the syndicates and their trading policy, and placed on the agenda the much larger issue of exchange between industry and agriculture. To offer more favourable terms to the peasantry was a question not merely of production and factory prices: it was a question of marketing as well; and the improvement of such terms of trade might be hindered, not only by high factory costs, but also by the cost of getting the goods from the factory to the consumer owing to a clumsy and expensive distributive

[1] Hindus, *op. cit.*, 185–6.

apparatus or to the excessive profits of private middlemen. Moreover, the opposition at the 13th Party Conference in January had expressed strong views concerning the dangerous growth of the private trader and the urgent need to combat his influence. It was certainly true that the private trader controlled over 80 per cent of the retail trade, particularly in the village, while his influence in the wholesale market had in recent months been growing. Banks seemed more ready to grant credits to them than to the co-operatives whose security was often poor, and many of the trusts preferred to sell to the private trader since the co-operatives for lack of working capital were seldom able to pay " cash down." Accordingly, while repudiating what it termed the alarmist views of the opposition, the central committee of the Party went so far toward meeting the opposition criticism as to give to the trade question a prominent place in the agenda of the 13th Conference; and the official report to the Conference stressed the urgent need to strengthen and extend the co-operatives as an organ of distribution, and as the essential link with the village and the town.

In the discussion of the matter two view-points were presented. The one, which originated in some proposals of Larin in the autumn, desired to supplant the private trader in favour of the co-operatives and State trading organs by direct administrative means. Larin proposed to prohibit State bodies from delivering goods to private middlemen, except to village retailers who undertook to sell their goods at an assigned price; to restrict the issue of bank credits to private wholesalers; and to apply additional differentiation by means of taxation to the private trader. At first this policy was adopted almost *in toto* by the central committee, who added to it a proposal for an organised boycott by trade unions and factory committees of private firms which charged too high prices, and for the more rigorous enforcement of the section of the Penal Code which applied to profiteering. But this aroused strong protests from those who considered that mere administrative measures were useless so long as State bodies and the co-operatives were unable to perform the function more cheaply. Some considered it definitely inexpedient at the moment for the State to take on the burden of erecting and financing a trade apparatus, particularly in retail trade. The trade unions and some of the heads of industry were particularly loud in such protests, and the journal of the central council of trade unions was quite brutally frank. "When the co-operatives only supply a quarter of the workers' needs," it wrote, "when they are inefficient in trade and fail to consider the needs of their customers, when they are unable to treat purchasers politely, to reduce their overhead charges and get rid of their useless expenditure, does anyone think they will amend their ways for the sole reason that the workers are obliged to make all their purchases at the co-operative shop? . . . Where we have hitherto failed to capture the market, private trade is at the present time not merely tolerable but indispensable. We must not saw off the branch on which we sit."[1]

These protests against what in many quarters was hailed as a "revision" of NEP in the direction of "war communism" succeeded in carrying the day, so that the official proposals presented by Kamenev to the 13th Party Congress in May had departed considerably from the pronouncement of the central committee four months before. It said less about the administrative measures for repressing private capital and considerably more about the measures to develop the co-operative apparatus so that it might adequately undertake what the private trader had previously done. The principal task of the coming year was defined as a campaign under the new Commissariat of Internal Trade (*Narcomvnutorg*)[2] to win trade from private capital for the

[1] *Cit.*, fr. *Trood*, 19.4.24, in I.L.O., *Co-op. Movt. in S.R.*, 310.

[2] This had formerly been a sub-commission of STO, and in the summer of 1924 was elevated to the status of a Commissariat, with Lejava at its head in the early months, and later Kamenev. In 1926 it was merged with the Commissariat of Foreign Trade to form a united Commissariat of Trade (*Narcomtorg*).

State and for co-operation; but the measures taken in this campaign were not to be such as would reduce the total goods turnover. "The basic methods in conquering the market," said the resolution of the 13th Congress, "should be, not measures of administrative pressure, but the raising of the position of co-operation and State trade."[1]

In the discussion of State trading policy the co-operatives came in for a large degree of apparently well-merited criticism. The trusts and syndicates complained that they were bound to rely on the private trader to a considerable extent because of the inefficiency of the co-operatives. "Cumbersomeness of the trading apparatus," "excessive overhead costs," "insufficient links with the consumer" and "inflated charges" were some of the charges made.[2] Rykov wittily remarked that when the co-operatives applied for credits they frequently offered no other security than Lenin's brochure on co-operative trade. Centrosoyus was accused of trying to centralise all commercial dealings in its own hands, of allowing no freedom to the local retail societies, supplying the latter on a system known as "goods credits" with an arbitrary selection of commodities which bore no relation to the requirements of their customers. When this arbitrary supply of "goods credits" meant the delivery of high-heeled shoes and perfumes and volumes of Lunacharsky's plays to a village store, it was small wonder that the peasant found a more congenial assortment at a cheaper price in the private shop. One investigation into the deficiencies of co-operative organisation traced the passage of goods sold by a syndicate to Centrosoyus through five or six distinct stages of the commercial apparatus, at each stage a large margin of profit being added, so that its price to the final consumer had been inflated to about five times its factory price.[3] Larin proposed that the middleman's work of Centrosoyus and the provincial co-operative unions should

[1] Rosenfeld, *op. cit.*, 477; I.L.O., *op. cit.*, 309–12.

[2] Professor Ustinov, *Evolutsia Vnutrennoi Torgovli v. Rossii*, 1913–24, 86.

[3] *Ibid.*, 85–6.

be abolished altogether; and Nogin, President of the Textile Syndicate, in an article headed "Down with the Middlemen," urged that the co-operative movement should be deprived altogether of its wholesale business. In its defence Centrosoyus pleaded the handicap of extreme shortage of working capital which it had suffered since 1921, and blamed the trusts and syndicates for supplying to the co-operatives an assortment of goods regardless of requirements and forcing them to take the whole arbitrary selection on pain of cancellation of credit facilities and the transfer of business to the private trader.

In the early days of NEP an experiment had been made in giving to Centrosoyus the monopoly of State wholesale trade. Later in 1921 this had been abandoned in favour of the preference principle with regard to the co-operatives in the wholesale dealings of State bodies. The new State policy in 1924 still further modified the privileged position of Centrosoyus in wholesale operations, while retaining and strengthening the preferential position of the consumers' retail societies. The principle was adopted that the State should only participate in retail trade in fields which were not covered by co-operative societies, since, in the words of Professor Ustinov, "State trading always contains a certain element of bureaucracy which is specially dangerous for retail trade; and for this reason State trade should tend towards wholesale business, leaving retail operations to the local co-operatives."[1] But in return for continued preference to co-operative societies in retail distribution—preference in the granting of bank credits, preference in taxation policy, preference in terms of supply by trusts and syndicates—Centrosoyus must submit to a decentralisation of co-operative activities. It must abandon the policy of concentrating all wholesale dealings in its own hands and of

[1] *Ibid.*, 96–7. Instances of State retail trade were: a few shops run by trusts and syndicates, principally by the Textile Syndicate; a few universal stores, such as GUM in Moscow, conducted by companies of which State departments held the shares; and shops run by the Gubtorg, or local trading organ of provincial soviets.

forcing all goods to pass through the accepted stages established by itself. Instead the trusts and syndicates must have the right of concluding direct contracts where it was convenient with the retail societies; and the crediting of the retail societies by the banks must be permitted to be direct, and not solely through the medium of the central body. In the realm of wholesale trade Centrosoyus would merely be one of several trading bodies, forming a link between industry and the retail market.[1]

Equipped with these renewed preferences and moved by the criticisms of the 13th Congress to adopt administrative reforms, co-operative activities expanded rapidly in the course of 1924; and for the financial year 1923–4 the participation of the co-operatives increased to 20 per cent of the total goods turnover as against 14 per cent in the previous year. At the same time the share of the private trader fell from 44 to 36 per cent of the whole.[2] Nevertheless, the progress achieved was not altogether satisfactory, and the new trade policy in its actual execution followed lines which were not precisely those laid down by the 13th Congress and were subsequently declared to be serious mistakes. In the first place many trusts and syndicates in their zeal to cut through the old centralised inefficiency of the co-operative apparatus went to the extreme of neglecting Centrosoyus and the provincial unions altogether, and supplied their goods direct to the local retail societies whom they treated virtually as retail commission agents. Certainly it was arguable that the syndicates could constitute the sole wholesale organs for State industry, and that no intervening link was necessary between them and the local retailer. But at the moment this meant a certain duplication of machinery in the shape of new

[1] *Ibid.*, 87–90.

[2] The relative position in wholesale and retail trade in 1923–4 was as follows :—

	Wholesale	Retail
State . . .	61·4	15·7
Co-operative . .	16·7	26·6
Private . . .	21·9	57·7

(Rosenfeld, *op. cit.*, 478–9).

local offices and agencies of the syndicates; and it was a development which had not been intended by the framers of the new trading policy, who wished to balance the monopoly position of the syndicates by a strong and active co-operative movement to represent the interests of the consumers and to interpret consumers' desires in the shape of definite anticipatory orders to State industry. The difficulty of State industry producing what it wanted to produce and not what the consumer desired was not likely to be surmounted if the retail societies were reduced to mere commission agents of the syndicates. The question assumed particular significance because the adaptation of industry to the consumer meant primarily its adaptation to peasant needs, and thereby raised the whole issue of country and town. For production to be adapted to the retail market the co-operatives, representing the consumer, needed to command, rather than to be commanded: otherwise private trade and industry would continue to prove more adaptable to the market and to win more favour. Centrosoyus maintained with some reason that in a large range of goods bulk contracts between it and the syndicates had a distinct economic advantage, and that the decentralised direct contacts should be less between syndicates on a national scale and the retail societies than between the latter and the trusts themselves in cases where geographical propinquity made this desirable.

In the second place the exclusion of the private trader by administrative measures of the kind which Larin had proposed, in spite of the warning of the 13th Congress, had proceeded faster than the growth of co-operative and State trading in its place. According to one rather high estimate, as much as 400 million roubles of private capital was pushed out of wholesale trade—a gap which it was clearly impossible at the moment for the State organs and co-operatives to fill;[1] and in many areas the position had been made untenable for the private trader while no other trading organ had been erected in his place. In Moscow wholesale trade betweer

[1] I.L.O., *op. cit.*, 325.

January and September the participation of private capital fell from 15 to 5 per cent.[1] The net result was to aggravate the marketing problem and to reduce the industrial goods turnover in the summer and autumn, at the same time as credit facilities to industry were being unduly strained by the fact that industry had locked up a large amount of its working capital in its trading operations. Moreover, private capital did not cease to be a competitor of State enterprise: it merely transferred its activities to more favourable spheres where it was less accessible to State control, principally to the meat market where it became predominant at this time, and to the grain market where it competed severely against the State buying organs in the summer and thereby helped to raise the price of grain. As Rykov declared in his report to the 6th Trade Union Congress, only one half of the recommendations of the 13th Congress had been observed in the execution of policy, and that the destructive half.[2]

At the end of the year, accordingly, the policy of eliminating private capital from trade by administrative measures was checked. It was clear that neither State organs nor the co-operatives had the funds at the moment to take over all wholesale trade, still less retail; while even had they possessed the funds, the building of a suitable organisation would have taken some time. Larin's proposal to have a State shop in every village was at the moment quite utopian. A considerable sphere was left where the private trader remained essential, and the State, realising this fact, began to direct its policy, while placing the co-operatives in a preferential position, to limiting that preference so that

[1] Ustinov, *op. cit.*, 92.

[2] Rykov, *Osnovnie Voprosi Khos. Pol. S.S.S.R.*, 29–30: "In the struggle with private trade methods of administrative pressure have often been applied, and then it has been said: 'On the economic front we have conquered the private trader.' But this is only the superficial aspect. . . . We are in the position where we have insufficient resources for the extension of turnover capital, and we cannot yet reject the employment of capital in private trade, if that is of advantage to industry." Cf. also Smilga in *Plan. Khos.*, 1925, No. 1, 52–3.

private capital should have sufficient inducement to perform an essential function in its appointed sphere.[1] By a resolution of STO of March 31, 1925, this revised policy was given definite formulation. To strengthen the co-operatives and extend their rôle, 10 million roubles was to be assigned from the Budget as an addition to the basic capital of the co-operatives, while directions were given to improve and extend the crediting of the co-operatives by the banks. For the rest, the co-operatives were advised to rely on the attraction of resources from their own members by shares and deposits, and on the capitalisation of profits, which could be augmented by quickened turnover and economies of administration. With regard to private capital various modifications were made in the "harsh conditions which obtain at present." The practice by which State industry had made cash payment and the acceptance of a compulsory assortment of goods obligatory for private traders was revoked, while at the same time still leaving the terms of credit and supply rather less favourable in the case of the private trader than of the co-operatives; and the system of differential taxation of private trade was directed to be revised.[2]

In this decree of March 31st, 1925, we have, not a departure from NEP nor the introduction of a new principle, but rather the essence of NEP, which is itself identical with the policy of "encircling capital" that Lenin had tried to follow in 1918. In 1918 it was a question of leaving the capitalist in charge of numerous spheres of industry because he could perform functions for which the State had not at present the apparatus, the personnel or the experience: using him while at the same time controlling and "encircling" him through political measures, through the influence of the Centres and of workers' control. In 1925 it was a question of assigning to the private trader a definite place in retail and to a smaller extent in wholesale trade: using him because as yet the State had not the money nor the apparatus nor

[1] Cf. Rykov, *loc. cit.*
[2] Rosenfeld, *op. cit.*, 484–5.

as yet had learned the art of trade, while at the same time the State kept in the background the controlling instrument of credit and taxation. So long as private capital was bitted and harnessed, the Soviet State was willing to feed and stable it tolerably well. Where private enterprise could perform a service better and cheaper than collective enterprise, administrative and legal barriers were not to be placed in its way. In the competition between private and State or co-operative enterprise, of course, the State did not adopt a policy of *laissez-faire*. Indeed, *laissez-faire* in the development neither of children nor of society can ever mean a freedom from all influences for some *dea ex machina* labelled " Dame Nature " to work her will: it can merely give freedom to influences inherent in the existing environment to have full play. Influence by legal prohibition and overt pressure may be abandoned in favour of the more potent institutional influence which can be exerted by moulding the environment; but whichever method he choose, the teacher must teach and the maker of history must mould. To the extent that in 1925 the Soviet State relaxed its legal and administrative pressure in the economic sphere, the change represented a step towards *laissez-faire*. But competition between State and private enterprise still operated in an environment which favoured the former against the latter, just as in the capitalist world the dice are loaded in favour of the superior competitive strength of the giant business and the trust. The State continued to use the economic measures at its command to give preference to collective enterprise, both in the belief that collective enterprise when passed from infancy to puberty would prove the superior, and also on broader social grounds: as an imperialist employs fiscal preference to cement the Empire, so the communist establishes a preference system to strengthen the trend to a classless society and to discourage opposing tendencies towards the rebirth of a moneyed class. But the preference given was to be moderate rather than excessive, otherwise the harm it did to production might outweigh its social gain, and it might actually defeat its own object by tempting State organs to rest upon their oars. The stronger the position of the State and the less danger there was of the horse " bolting " if given its head, the more easy to discard the whip and spurs for the subtler guidance of the reins— the more moderate and indirect and less obtrusive the methods of preference could be.

Two years after the 13th Party Congress fresh complaints were heard about the private trader prospering on the widened margin between wholesale and retail prices. But this time resort to the old methods of administrative repression, though some probably hankered after them, were not seriously proposed. In reply to these fears Rykov could point to the fact that the participation of private trade since 1923 had steadily decreased, in retail trade from 57 to 39 per cent in 1925–6 and in wholesale trade from 22 to 9. Even if private enterprises were being enriched from the gains of trade, so also must the co-operatives be profiting to an even greater extent, and an absolute improvement in the position of the private trader was not inconsistent with his relative decline.[1] Further economies in the co-operative organisation, which was still too cumbersome and bureaucratic, together with a steady reduction of the retail prices of co-operatives and State retail bodies were pronounced as the surest methods both of overcoming the " goods famine " and of winning the favour of the consumer for co-operative as against private trade. A mere reduction of retail prices, it was true, would do little unless it were accompanied by an increased supply of goods: low prices were of small use to the customer if the co-operative counters were bare; and a lower price in State sales, while the demand remained the same, might merely set free increased purchasing power to be spent at the private shop next door. But the lowered prices, it was hoped, would of itself stimulate increased turnover by which working capital could be economised, and force the co-opera-

[1] Rykov, Report to 15th Party Conference; also Bronsky in *Sozt. Khos.*, 1926, No. 5, 31.

tives to introduce administrative improvements which would lower costs and set free resources for State accumulation. If for no other reason the " cheapening " of goods was valued as the most comprehensive slogan for rallying effort to the task of productive and trading economy. But even if the reduction of prices were to proceed faster than any possible economy of cost and increase of supply, it would not altogather fail to have remedial influence on the situation. It is true that the price-level can never be treated as an entirely independent factor, to be altered at will without reference to the conditions of supply and money-demand on which it depends; but so also in the conditions ruling in Russia it is not entirely a dependent factor. In so far as wages are influenced by considerations of the cost of living, and the demand for credit-advances by the trusts is in turn influenced by their wages-bill; in so far as the price policy of State grain-purchasing organs, and hence grain-crediting, is partly determined by a desire to give to the peasant a fair equivalent in the price he receives for the price he has to pay for industrial goods; in so far, again, as the attitude towards money-hoarding or saving, particularly on the part of the peasants, is largely influenced by anticipations of future movements of the price-level, a raising or lowering of retail prices may itself affect the flow of purchasing power or money-demand on to the retail market.

Trade and trading policy constituted for Russia a problem of special delicacy, because it constituted the link between village and town. The development and improvement of the trading activities of the co-operatives was given particular prominence, because co-operation was depicted as the bridge between peasant and worker, and the drawing of peasant agriculture ever closer into a system of co-operative supply, purchase and credit was regarded as the essential road of transition to socialism in the countryside. For Lenin progress under the conditions of N E P consisted in a series of interactions between industry and agriculture: the growth of the former stimulating the latter, and the growth of agriculture, with its cheaper food and raw materials and widened market, stimulating industry in return. The quickening of this process of sympathetic reactions depended partly on the rate at which capital could be accumulated and applied to extending the base and lowering the costs of both; and it depended also, and in a certain sense primarily, on the perfection of the trading links between the two. But if this progress was to be, not only in quantity but also in quality, of the kind desired, it must proceed along certain lines and within certain limits. The progress must be on the basis of raising all sections of society together, not by raising certain sections, whether *kulak*, State official or Nepman trader, to a position of differential advantage above the rest. Hence a given quantitative growth of trade turnover was weighted more heavily in the final reckoning if it were achieved through co-operative channels than if it had passed through private hands. For some time yet it was both necessary and desirable that from the fruits of exchange between town and country the industrial worker of the towns should enjoy a somewhat higher standard than the peasant: he, indeed, was the senior partner and the pioneer. But the difference must progressively narrow rather than widen; and the economic links with the village must be of such a character as to draw the individualist peasant in his economic relations into closer contact in collective activity with the urban workers and the Workers' State. Only this could provide a channel by which the new technique and the new ideology could invade the darkness of the old semi-feudal village. For the rest, the slow realisation of Lenin's dream of electrification, spreading a new industrial revolution from the urban centres to the countryside, must be relied on to transform the environment of the *moujik*, his habits and way of life and his psychology, and to plough the stiff soil of the old rural economy to receive the new proletarian culture of the towns. This was the reason for the emphasis on co-operation and the preference which it enjoyed. This was the basis both of trading and peasant policy, and the *motif* of the campaign for lowering industrial prices and increasing the real return which the peasant could secure by trade; and it is in the light of this aim that the progress of events in Russia must be judged if it is to be understood.

CHAPTER TWELVE

ECONOMIC PROSPECTS

IF his view of Leningrad and Moscow is confined to the windows of an automobile or even to the stately discomfort of a *droshky*, the foreign visitor probably misses an essential quality of the new Russian life. This quality he will hardly meet on the polished floors of the Europe or the Savoy or the Bolshaia Moscovskaia. When he visits the conservatoire, the opera, or the Art Theatre, or when he shops on Kusnetsky Most or the Nevsky, he may notice little different from the old world. Few starched shirt-fronts or smart ladies will be evident. The *ensemble* may seem a little drab and toneless and less sparkling, like most cities east of the Rhine in the immediate post-war years. Beyond that there will be little to arouse surprise or to be seriously praised or deplored. But should he leave the automobile or the *droshky* for the rough and tumble of a tramcar, and jostle the crowd which throngs the entrance to a suburban cinema; should he chew dried salt herring and sip beer while he listens to the fiddler playing wild gypsy songs of the steppes in a small *peevnaya*; still more if he peep into a factory or workers' club, he can hardly fail to sense that here there is something important and new. At first this novel quality may be hard to define; and when defined it may arouse either a romantic affection or dislike and a secret fear. In a sense intangible and unmeasurable, its effect on the *stimmung* of social life seems as powerful as a new chemical element applied to a chemical composition. The foreigner will notice the absence of cap-touching among workers to "superiors." He will remark a certain confident bearing among the working men and women who walk the Nevsky or the Moscow boulevards after sunset, and how intercourse between managers and men in a factory, or officers and men in a ship or a barrack room has a distinctly novel freedom and lack of restraint. It will seem surprising to find that State officials and persons in authority take pains to be ordinary rather than distinctive in their dress, and a little shocking that a bourgeois bearing and appearance, which in other countries assure a deference so customary as to pass unnoticed, here command no deference, but rather a measure of contempt.

This new social equality which undoubtedly exists in Russia is something more fundamental than the measure of social equality which, in contrast to Europe, is said to exist in the New World. In Russia it is not mixed with an individualist desire to prosper and to climb a social ladder of which the rungs are income-grades. It is divorced from a worship and evaluation of success in money terms and from deference to the man who has won a financial position above his fellows and shows it in his habits and dress and bearing. Rather does the man who makes more money or works more easily than the average strive to maintain an appearance to the contrary, while pride of parentage exists only when parents were toiling and poor. The social equality which is sensed in outward detail strikes deeper to an economic equality. Differences of income certainly exist: the town as a whole enjoys a higher income than the village; a skilled worker may get a wage three or four times that in the lowest wage grade; "specialists" may get special salaries twice or even three times as high as this, and popular journalists and writers may earn by their free-lance efforts a goodly sum. But the differences are small when compared with those in the capitalist world. The difference in wages may lie between 50 roubles a month and 200; "specialist" salaries may range up to 500 or 600 roubles, but very rarely more; and the income-tax is sufficiently "progressive" to make annual incomes above the equivalent of £600, apart from wholesale tax evasion, hardly worth while. Improvement of financial position for the individual, save within fairly narrow limits, is only possible through measures which raise the standard of the whole mass; and an increasing part of the enjoyments which contribute to that standard, in the shape of club rooms and communal services, is assuming a collective rather than an individual form.

A standing threat to break up this approximate equality and to restore the old social ladder and its individualist standards and ideals exists in the shape of the Nepman and the *kulak*, and to a smaller extent in the bourgeois-specialist with the high salary, who are extended a measure of toleration and even of limited encouragement. Less obviously and directly this equality might become endangered from the growth of a new official caste, adopting superior airs along with white collars, and gathering to itself a series of differential privileges. But at present few signs of such tendencies can be seen. The village *kulak* is usually less wealthy than a small English farmer or village grocer. The private trader probably manages to accumulate less capital than the average London coster. The State official and business director more often wears a cap and a Russian tunic than he wears a tailored suit and a collar and tie.

Against the growth of such tendencies in the future several factors are at work. First, there is the instrument of taxation and of credit, differentiating against the higher income and the income gained from private commercial operations, and giving the preference in business competition to State enterprise and co-operation. In addition, every growth of State production and trading narrows the sphere and the possibility for incomes from private business to be made. In the village the *kulak* is less able than formerly to lean on his poorer neighbour, now that co-operation lends aid to the latter and renders him more independent; and in the towns the existence of strongly privileged trade unions with extensive legal powers and State support deprives the private *entrepreneur* of any considerable supplies of cheap labour. With regard to social ideology, the Press, the wireless, the cinema, and the educational system are implanting the new social standards and awakening the new collective loyalties with probably as much success as in other countries these institutions evoke the different ideals and loyalties which prevail in the capitalist West. The higher educational bodies, now peopled to about 80 per cent with students hailing from workers' and peasants' families, have an entirely new atmosphere, nourishing different social ideals and producing a new graduate type. To put an end to the old cloistered intelligentsia and its psychological legacy, and to ensure that the new proletarian intelligentsia should be closely welded to reality and to the mass, a distinctly harsh differentiation was practised until quite recently against students who came from bourgeois homes; and if one were to imagine the difference which would be made if in England Oxford and Cambridge and London Universities were peopled predominantly by trade unionists, who on vacation returned to their union branch, perhaps to teach and to organise, perhaps to work or study in mill or engineering shop or mine, while at the same time the governing bodies of those universities and even some of their teaching staff and their curricula were radically changed, an idea would be gained of the changed psychology that exists to-day in Russia among the new generation who go forth from the universities and technical schools to be engineers and business managers, teachers and doctors and State officials, and receive an income in those occupations little if any higher than the patternmaker or compositor or skilled mechanic. Moreover, a ceaseless vigilance in linking the State machine with the masses in town and country is exercised as the first principle of its policy by the Party, which has its members in controlling positions in every State department, while at the same time its membership consists to over 60 per cent of workers at the bench, and even its central committee of workers to 56 per cent, and which will transfer a member whom administrative work or official responsibility seems to have made too remote from the mass to some humbler work in a locality which will bring him again in contact with the psychology of the rank and file. The leaders of the Party and the Government almost invariably work hard and live simply:

if they have their special automobiles and their *wagon-lits* on the railway, it is to speed them on official business and not on pleasure; and disciplinary measures including expulsion are enforced against those who "live a life unworthy of the Party." Through the Party and through the trade unions, which pursue the rôle of advancing candidates from their ranks for economic posts, a continual upward stream from the mass into the administrative class is maintained, which, so long as it continues, precludes the latter from becoming an exclusive caste, and at present seems to be breaking down the exclusiveness of former times.

Such influences as these, however, would be considerably weakened if State industry, by reason of high costs and inability to provide capital for expansion, were to reach the point where it was unable to advance. Then, not only would private capital find an important field left open to it, but the State itself would be forced to give a freer rein and extended encouragement to the private trader and producer, in order to secure the expansion of production that was necessary to afford to the masses an improved standard of life. The Nepman would then have greater opportunity of growing wealthy; and if population were growing faster than production, nothing could prevent the village *kulak* from finding in the surplus population a profitable field to exploit. The prospects of industrial expansion, and especially the expansion of State industry, accordingly, becomes a matter of prime importance for Russia's future and the future of her communist régime. In the condition in which war and revolution left her capital equipment and in the existing shrunken character of her foreign trade, one might well have prophesied for Russia a serious crisis in her development some time before now, as many in 1925 prophesied both inside the country and outside. It is, therefore, essentially a surprise to find that, while short-lived crises have occurred for special reasons, no such *impasse* in which expansion slowed up to a standstill has appeared; while on the basis of a capital equipment which is probably still seriously depreciated compared with fourteen years ago a level of production has already been attained which, even on conservative estimates, reaches the pre-war. In all such estimates there is, of course, a margin of error, just as there is in Mr. Rowe's estimate of British production as being at present between 90 and 95 per cent of 1913:[1] probably in the Russian figure the margin is greater than in the British. It may be that there is a certain difference in the quality of Russian products which invalidates a little a direct comparison with fourteen years ago. But even when allowance has been made for these considerations, the result still remains surprising; while, whatever the absolute level of recovery may be, the fact that this recovery continues at quite a surprising speed still remains. Had a limit to further expansion been reached in 1924 or 1925, as was expected by many, the position might have been critical for the future of the Soviet State, since at the time she had only a narrow surplus out of which to accumulate new capital; whereas by 1927 she has been able to raise her national "savings" and capital allocations to a figure which approaches the pre-war percentage of her total national income,[2] and out of this accumulation 75–85 per cent represents capital in State hands.

On the basis of this one could have reason to expect a continued rate of economic development that did not fall far behind the annual progress in the two decades before the war. Actually the preliminary estimates of Gosplan, which since the events of 1925 are framed on fairly cautious lines, provide for a considerably more rapid rate of industrial growth over the next few years. These estimates, which were made at the beginning of 1926, provided for an aggregate capital allocation to State industry over the five years, 1925–1930, of some 5 milliard roubles, which, allowing for repair of current depreciation, involved a net addition of some 3300 million roubles to the capital of State industry, raising it from its valuation of some 5 milliard roubles in

[1] Cf. *Economic Journal,* June 1927.
[2] Cf. above, p. 312.

1925 to over 8 milliard roubles in 1930. If we take a more conservative estimate of annual depreciation than does Gosplan, and assume that it is 8 per cent on original value rather than 5 per cent, we arrive at a figure of about 2200–2400 million roubles, as the net addition to Stae industrial capital over the five years. On this basis a percentage growth of production of 34 per cent in 1925–6, of 15 per cent in 1926–7 and of 10–11 per cent in the following three years was anticipated, to be achieved by an annual average cheapening of costs by 6 per cent. This would double production over the five years, so as to bring the level of output by 1930 to between 33 and 50 per cent above the pre-war standard.[1]

Since any such estimates must depend on a number of unknown and incalculable factors, they must necessarily be accepted with a measure of caution; and at first sight one is inclined to greet the conclusions of Gosplan with some scepticism. Other more conservative estimates have been made which place the probable rate of advance rather lower than does Gosplan. Professor Weinstein, for instance, taking the more conservative estimate of net capital accumulation which has been adopted in a previous chapter, prophesied a 12 per cent rather than a 15 per cent rise of production in 1926–7 and for subsequent years no more than 6–7 in place of 10–11 per cent.[2] And on this lower estimate pro-

[1] Strumilin in *Plan. Khos.*, 1926, No. 4, 33–4. Certain minor corrections which seemed necessary in Mr. Strumilin's arithmetic (or his proof-reading) have been made in the text. Adding to the above figure of capital investments other forms of State investments, such as electrification, transport, State agriculture, housing and municipal services, he attains a *total* figure of 13·5 milliard roubles as State investments over the five years. If we make a similar allowance for current depreciation to that made above for industry, we arrive at a *net* figure of about 7 to 8 milliard roubles for all State investments between 1925 and 1930. To reach the aggregate national savings over the period, an amount ranging between 1 and 2 milliard would have to be added to represent private investments in peasant agriculture and private trade and production.

[2] In *Sozt. Khos.*, 1926, No. 4, 23–7. Between 1900–13 (allowing for the change in price-level) the national income showed an annual increase of 2·6 per cent (according to Professor Prokopovitch's estimate) and industry 3·8 per cent. In boom years the increase rose to 6 or 8 per cent.

duction by 1930 would have attained to between 20 and 30 per cent above pre-war. Actually, however, there seems to be little reason for charging the Gosplan estimates with undue optimism. A bad harvest would probably make them too high; but a good harvest might equally make them too low. The plans of the economic organs for 1926–7 are substantially higher than Gosplan's forecast, and the actual progress of production in 1925–6 and in the first three-quarters of 1926–7 do not seem to convict the Gosplan prophecy for these years of over-confidence, rather the reverse;[1] and they suggest that Professor Weinstein's estimate erred considerably on the cautious side. Perhaps this result is attributable to the moderately good harvest of 1926 which may not be sustained in subsequent years; and one who wishes for a thoroughly safe calculation will probably choose a figure of about 8–9 per cent as the annual rate of industrial advance over the next few years.

To find that Russian industry, when it has completed its stage of reconstruction, has prospects of continuing a rate of growth which in pre-war times, with the aid of foreign capital, was hardly attained even in the strongest boom years, comes as a distinct surprise. Equally unexpected is it to find this progress beyond the pre-war level, when industry has not yet repaired the depreciation of capital equipment suffered in the war and civil war years, and may not have completely done so until 1929 or 1930.[2] The fact would seem to indicate that the planning of production by a central body can assure a more even and proportionate expansion of industry in its various branches than can a system of *laissez-faire*, and hence can largely avoid the crises of over produc-

[1] The growth of output in State industry for 1925–6 was 40 per cent. as compared with an estimate of 34 per cent. In the first eight months of 1926–7 the growth over the same period of the previous year has been 21 per cent as against an estimated growth of 15 per cent.

[2] This is written in the autumn of 1927. If we take the minimum figure of 25 per cent depreciation in 1925 as against 1913, mentioned above, p. 295, it follows that this will probably have been repaired by the beginning of 1928. If we take a higher figure which is more probable, the pre-war level of capital equipment will only be attained in subsequent years.

tion which recur so persistently in capitalist countries, thereby securing a more continuous and intensive utilisation of capital equipment.[1] Russia has not, of course, been entirely free from crises in recent years: these occurred for differing reasons in 1922, 1923 and 1925. But in each case the crisis was short-lived, a matter of no more than a few weeks, and in no case did it lead to a general depression, to any general arrest of production and stoppage of work. In the spring of 1922 there was a closing of factories in certain of the finishing trades, but only in order to concentrate resources on greater activity in fuel and the repair of transport; and the closing did not last beyond the summer. In 1923 there was a closing of some concerns in the process of "concentration" of production; but this did not signify any shrinkage of activity as a whole, and in the face of the autumn crisis production and employment continued to expand quite rapidly. Yet, in both of these cases, as also in the winter of 1925, one could reasonably have expected—nay, could hardly have avoided—under conditions which ordinarily prevail in industrial countries, a general hesitancy spreading over the whole market, a speculative drop in demand-prices, and a sharp arrest and even a decline in industrial activity in a general depression developing cumulatively over at least several months. Facts and *a priori* reasoning together seem strongly to suggest as the reason for the absence of such phenomena in Russia the policy of continual price-reduction, correlative with expanded output, which the official policy in 1923–4 proclaimed. Without an adequate planning of production—not *a priori*, but in line with the market—to secure an adequately proportional development of its various parts, a policy of price-reduction alone would not necessarily have sufficed. Similarly a proportional development might not have avoided arrest in a general crisis, if the level of prices and profits in industry in general had remained out of adjustment with the new scale of production. It is true that

[1] To this the factor mentioned in the Excursus to Chapter Five, p. 179, may also have contributed.

under *laissez-faire* conditions an ultimate adjustment of the level of prices and profits to the level of production will tend to take place; but it would seem that in practice the pains of a trade depression are needed to bring this ultimate adjustment into effect; while under monopoly the lowering of prices and profits may meet such keen resistance that adjustment may come rather by contraction of output than by a cheapening of price. The Russian régime of centrally planned production combined with the policy of steady cheapening of price has apparently achieved an important advantage both over private monopoly and over *laissez-faire*.

As additional reasons for the rate of progress in Russian industry some minor influences may also have played a significant rôle. The comparative absence of stoppages through industrial disputes[1] must have had considerable effect, and still more the fact that trade unions, factory committees and most of the politically active workers have turned their efforts to the task of increasing output and improving production instead of to placing a spoke in the capitalists' wheel. Workers' control from being negative and obstructive has become positive; the herd feelings of the workers and the sentiments of class-consciousness have been harnessed to the task of efficient management, not ranged against it. The reason for this important change is that it has always been a cardinal tenet of communist policy to inspire a new spirit of collective unity, based on the sentiment that the control and discipline to which the masses submit is a control of the workers by workers in the interests of the workers, and not by and for a superior class—a sentiment which is certainly present and has considerable power. It is true that in the earlier days the trade unions were often

[1] In 1925 there were 99 strikes covering 34,000 workers in State enterprises and 97 strikes covering 3600 workers in private enterprises. The number of strikers, accordingly, represented only ·5 per cent. of employed trade union members (cf. Ivy Lee, *U.S.S.R., a World Enigma*, 107). The average number of disputes each year in Great Britain between 1893 and 1924 was 732, covering 581,000 workers, or about 3 per cent of all workers. Moreover, the duration of Russian disputes was seldom more than a few days.

ranged in opposition to the introduction of scientific management, bonuses and payment by results. But the communist lead in the trade unions and communist propaganda ultimately secured the waiving of these objections; and often to-day it is trade unions and factory committees which adopt the initiative in criticising administrative inefficiency and introducing improvements in methods of work. The successful continuance of this state of affairs depends largely on the success of the trade unions in democratising their apparatus, making it flexible and giving free play to the complaints, the aspirations and the interests of the rank and file. And it was because of the importance of this that Lenin in 1921 laid such stress on the rôle of the trade unions which he outlined: as co-operation was to be the link between town and village, so the trade unions were to be the organs of contact between the State and the working rank and file.

A further factor which favours productivity is the elimination of a major part of the former luxury production and services, and the reduction of what Adam Smith termed "unproductive" occupations and persons, setting free energies and resources for capital construction or for improving the standard of life and efficiency of the producers. Societies in the past have generally shown the greatest initiative and talent in their leading positions—in English industry, for instance, at the industrial revolution—at times when promotion has been most open to those of humble birth; and the breaking down of class barriers in Russia to-day and the opening of new opportunities of educational advancement to workers and peasants will tend to nourish among future generations genius in more plenty than in the past. Moreover, with an approach to economic equality, and a closer approximation of money-demand on the market to need, a given level of production to-day tends to contribute more to welfare than the same level of production in 1914.

But against these factors which favour economic expansion there exists an important group of influences with a strongly opposite effect. The administration of industry and the efficiency of the managerial personnel is still very low; the shortage of competent managers and technicians, for which pre-war Russia relied extensively on foreigners, is remarked upon with increasing frequency by the heads of industry; while the managers and technicians carried over from the capitalist régime are often handicapped in their work, if no longer by their own hostility to their new masters, at any rate by a certain measure of suspicion under which they work and an extensive system of checks and controls. The administrative system, in spite of improvements, still remains too cumbersome and inflexible. In the administration of industry flexibility is particularly required, since here the conduct of affairs is concerned with continually changing situations, due to changes in technique and in the market, and quick decisions have continually to be made which involve a considerable degree of risk and uncertainty. The trust system in Russia offers a very interesting and very promising combination of centralised direction of general economic policy with a wide decentralisation of operative business decisions to bodies possessing funds of their own and having competence to incur financial liabilities and financial risks.[1] But this system, though it is decentralised in form, is still too centralised in actual practice. The principle of conceding competence to subordinate organs on all " unnamed " cases, which is the essence of a flexible system,[2] is insufficiently established. There is still too much reference of detail to the centre; and general directive orders, deciding issues of policy, are still too often given only after a series of references and appeals from minor bodies, which cause delay and confusion, instead of being planned and laid down in advance. Precisely because a socialist system controls consciously

[1] In a socialist state, however, a considerable part of the risk and uncertainty of an individualist society tend to disappear, namely, uncertainty due to competition and to commercial secrecy, and uncertainty due to the diffusion of economic responsibility among a large number of small units. There remains the uncertainty due to variations of nature (e.g. harvests) and the uncertainty attaching to all economic change and innovation (cf. the writer's *Capitalist Enterprise*, 33–8).

[2] Cf. above, p. 119.

things which are left under individualism to the free play of the market to adjust, the administrative problem becomes greatly magnified and calls for a much higher grade of administrative efficiency and technique. To provide this, a considerable amount of administrative invention, of learning by experience, of education of personnel, is required; all of which requires time and a period of infant clumsiness. An administrative system, like a college or a regiment, requires a tradition, in order to be complete. To find in Russia sufficient persons whose judgment is sound enough for competence to be deputed to them, or to whom regulations can be given in the confidence that they will know how far to observe the letter of them and how far to adapt them and make exceptions, is not easy. For instance, Stalin in 1925 emphasised that " the old type of ' know-all ' worker must make way for a new type of worker who endeavours to be a specialist in some special branch of work. In order to be able to direct in a proper manner, one must know the business and study it conscientiously, patiently and persistently. The old habits of hasty administration which unfortunately replace knowledge are still alive in the Party organisation. This is what explains the fact that the so-called Party leadership sometimes degenerates into a comical accumulation of useless orders and empty and verbal ' direction ' which does not move anyone or anything."[1] About the same time Kamenev declared that " the lack of specialists is now felt seriously for the first time in Soviet Russia. We need specialists now, and we cannot develop our industry at a quick tempo without them; and we must pay them, not only with a higher salary which runs counter to the sentiments of equality among the workers, but we must pay them with different conditions of work, with different hopes for the education of their children, and so forth. This necessity is the result of the gap between our needs and the fact that our educated younger generation has not yet matured."[2]

[1] *Op. cit.*, 23.

[2] Report to the September, 1925, Plenum of the Moscow Committee of the Party.

On administrative inefficiency in general and in detail the searchlight of publicity and of official denunciation has been turned particularly in the last eighteen months. "One of the main thoughts in Djerjinsky's last speech, which was delivered a few hours before his death, was a declaration of determined war against the immobility, the unwieldiness and the bureaucratism of the State apparatus, against conditions which oblige an urgent matter to pass through the hands of ten to twenty authorities before it can be decided upon and executed."[1] A correspondent to *Rabochaia Gazeta* recently cited 15 stages through which the Azerbaidjan budget had to pass before it even reached Moscow. The Azerbaidjan co-operatives had to make reports to six separate bodies. Nine separate organs exercised powers of audit and control. "When there exists an endless chain of organisations through which pass, say, the State budgets or the economic plans, where can one find an institution actually responsible for the budget or the plan? . . . No one is finally answerable for anything; the matter moves on further, deeper, in the *débris* of dozens of institutions and commissions, where it is subjected again and again to reconsideration and deliberation. . . . The Azerbaidjan comrades have now raised their hands: they want to make an attempt on the 'entirety' of their State apparatus."[2] At the 15th Party Conference in November 1926, Rykov, the chairman of Sovnarcom, placed stress on "the backwardness of our technique, the inadequate training of our technical personnel, the gaps in our technical knowledge, the absence of technical experience and technical skill—all these defects act as a hindrance to our whole economics from top to bottom. It is impossible to raise the technical level of the country without improving the training and increasing the number of specialists, without improving the skill and increasing the active participation of the workers in the introduction of the new achievements of

[1] Bukharin in Report to Meeting of Leningrad Party officials, July 28, 1926.
[2] Barkhashov in *Rabochaia Gazeta*, 27.2.27.

technical progress, without bettering the whole training in technical schools and colleges." Turning to the question of the administrative system and "the fight against bureaucratism," he proceeded to read a very illuminating letter from the manager of an important enterprise whom Rykov himself had known personally for many years. The manager complained that for all his enthusiasm in the work and his toil and sacrifices, he had begun to despair of strength to carry through his achievement to the end. In the course of 1926 his time had been occupied and the business of his enterprise upset by the presence of nine separate control commissions and inspections at the works. "My time is wasted," he wrote, "in a most unproductive manner on reports, conferences, negotiations, etc. The central government demands reports, the local government demands reports. The trade union organisations formed three factory councils, three organisations for discussing production and three commissions for setting up standards and settling disputes. I must have time for everything as my presence is demanded everywhere and my absence gives offence. When am I to find time for work?" As a final cup of gall a summons had arrived for the manager to appear before the provincial department of the G.P.U. (political police)—a summons which, in Rykov's words, "had no serious justification, but was only a childish whim on the part of the representative of the G.P.U. who wished to show that he was a person in authority." If this kind of thing was experienced by "a man whom Lenin knew, whom I know, whom Krshishanovsky and Bukharin know, how will other undertakings be treated? Can we with such a system confidently take for granted that the 1050 million roubles allocated for increasing original capital is being used to good purpose?" "This whole system of revision and control," Rykov proceeded, "which is at the same time combined with a lack of personal responsibility, is hardly calculated to ensure successful work in the course of the whole coming period. . . . Our system of economic administration even to-day is still centralised to a degree based on mistrust of every minor link of the chain." Adapted to the simpler tasks of the earlier period of its creation, the "whole machinery of State and economics" now required revision, in order to "adapt it to the new tasks of industrialisation."

How far this administrative inefficiency and red-tape is to-day greater or less than in pre-war times is almost impossible to estimate. Most of those who knew the pre-war Russia can probably recount choice anecdotes of officials, including business officials, in Tsarist times. In some branches of work on which attention has been particularly concentrated it is now probably better; in other branches it is probably much the same. Where to-day the inefficiency becomes more noticeable and significant lies in the much greater tasks which the system has to shoulder. The healthy symptom in the whole matter is that the evils which exist are recognised and are even proclaimed from the housetops, as the public declarations which have been quoted abundantly show. About washing dirty linen in public the Bolsheviks have never had delicate feelings; and while this has meant that the compiler of criticisms of Soviet Russia has not had to search outside official statements for his material, the fact has probably resulted in a larger amount of linen eventually being made white. At the moment the whole forces of the Party are being mobilised to deal with this problem; and newspapers from trade union journals and popular weeklies to *Pravda* and *Isvestia* abound in cartoons of bureaucratic methods and suggestions for improvement.[1] The fact is fully realised that the progress of industry and the growth of capital accumulation largely depends on the achievement of lowered administrative costs; and for this reason a campaign of "economy" and of "socialist rationalisation" was proclaimed in 1926 as the urgent first task in industrialisation. Certainly there is much leeway here to be repaired:

[1] For instance, a cartoon competition on bureaucracy organised by *Krestianskaia Gazeta* (Peasants' Newspaper), of which examples were reproduced in the *Manch. Guardian Weekly*, 11.3.27.

there is a large reservoir for future savings, a large margin for costs to be reduced and productivity to be raised. An official statement recently declared: "Our economic and administrative apparatus swallows up about 2 milliard roubles yearly. There is no reason to doubt that this expenditure could be reduced to 300 or 400 million roubles and additional means for our industry thus won. This is not only possible, but absolutely necessary, if the spirit of bureaucracy and petrification is to be banned from our apparatus and its cheapening and simplification achieved."[1]

It is too early as yet to measure the results of this campaign and to estimate their significance. But already a certain degree of success is to be recorded. The campaign has at any rate to its credit the stimulation of a legion of suggestions for improvement both in the Press and in the "conferences on production" called by the trade unions in each enterprise; and it may prove to have an important indirect value in the long run merely by directing people's thoughts along the right lines. For the first half of 1926 it was reported that the campaign had already resulted in the marking down for reduction of some 55 million roubles of waste expenditure in trusts and syndicates and local industry. Such pruning of superfluous items of expenditure is the more obvious and easier part of the task; but the real cure, of course, requires to cut deeper; and in addition to "economy" in the simpler sense, attention is now being turned to the more difficult problem of revising the administrative system itself. In this connection attention has been directed in two principal directions: first, to a lessening of the number of reports and inspections to which a trust is subject and a simplification of its relations with Vesenha; second, towards a greater freedom of a factory inside the trust.

In a very frank and exhaustive article in an economic

[1] Statement on "The Successes and Defects of the Economy Campaign," Aug. 16, 1926, signed by Rykov, Stalin, and Kuibyshev. The statement stressed that the economy must not be practised at the expense of the workers' standard of life.

monthly at the beginning of 1927 important detailed proposals were made along these lines. At present, the writer declared, a trust was often subject to four different control commissions, while its report on the past year and its plans and estimates for the next customarily passed, not only through about three departments at Vesenha, but also through Narcomfin and Gosplan and S T O as well. This necessitated an interminable series of joint meetings, with a final appeal to S T O to settle disputed points, to each of which the trust representative had to cart round " poods of documents and reports." There was delay in getting the plans for the coming year sanctioned, there was a tendency for the trust to prepare its plans under the knowledge that they would be changed, and the trust was quite unable to arrange its work ahead with any certainty. In the higher economic organs there was a congestion of business and a preoccupation with detail, so that S T O, for instance, had only recently decided a question about the amortisation charges for different trusts in the oil industry which had originated some years before. In place of this confusion and chaos the writer suggested the following simplified system, under which the competence of various departments should be more closely defined, their functions more narrowly specialised, and jurisdiction be allowed to subordinate bodies in all " unnamed " cases. S T O should announce to Vesenha the dimensions of allocations to industry from the Budget for the coming year, and Vesenha should have sole charge of dividing this total between the various industrial sub-departments, and they in turn between the various trusts. Within the financial limits defined by S T O Vesenha would then have complete competence to fix the plans for the coming year. The need for joint conferences with other Commissariats or for appeals to S T O would no longer be necessary, while S T O would be " freed from details " to devote itself to more general work. In other words, a system by which the father parcels out the heritage between the sons once and for all, replaces the system where the allotment is settled by the wrangling of the sons and their ultimate appeal to the father's authority. All the relations between Vesenha and a trust should be through the appropriate sub-department of Vesenha, and not through a succession of departments. To this sub-department the trust would submit its plans for sanction; to this alone would it report and by it alone would its operations be inspected and its books be audited: this sub-department would constitute the trust's direct "boss." In the relations between the trust and the factory the former in concluding commercial agreements, for instance, with a syndicate, should establish only the general terms, leaving details such as quality and delivery for direct arrangement between the syndicate and the factory; and the factory if it had large stocks on hand should be allowed to take the initiative, after informing the trust, in arranging their disposal with the selling organs.[1] Such a suggestion was typical of what was being discussed in every sphere. In details, as in broader questions, similar suggestions were being made: the conceding of greater initiative to technicians, the right of the heads of factory departments to reward as well as to fine, the need for revising and adjusting the scale of wages and salaries to narrow the difference between adjoining categories, to improve the training of engineers, to send them abroad for practical study, and to make the young engineer work his way into the industry through the workshops and not enter it through the trust office direct.[2] If discussion and concrete proposals are at all significant, there should emerge from this campaign of economy, and from the conferences, the speeches and the newspaper articles something much larger than a mouse.

There remain two final questions which are of first importance for any estimate of Russia's economic future. The first of these is the question of credit and currency. On the

[1] Cossior in *Econ. Oboz.*, Feb. 1927. Cf. also Kuibyshev in *Econ. Jizn.*, 1.1.27: "Factories should be given more freedom than before, and trusts have more rights at the cost of the centre."

[2] Engineer Brushkov on "Internal Factory Administration" in *Econ. Jizn.*, 4.1.27. Several of these changes have since been introduced, e.g. revision of wage-scales.

stability of the chervonetz depends, not merely the unhindered movement of foreign trade and the stability of business accounting, but also in large part the smooth growth of private savings in savings banks and co-operatives and State loans, particularly among the peasantry, on which considerable reliance for capital accumulation is at present being placed. Any depreciation of the currency penalises persons who hold their wealth in money form, and it is only at the expense of their impoverishment that inflation is able to yield additional resources to the State or to industry. A renewal of currency depreciation in Russia would, accordingly, discourage accumulation in money-forms and encourage instead an increased buying and accumulation of goods; and the tendency for the peasants to discard their old Asiatic habits of hoarding in goods or in valuable objects in favour of the savings bank and the State loan, which is now being encouraged so vigorously, would be reversed. It was this fact which made the phenomena of the winter of 1925–6 so dangerous, and was the reason for the quick deflation which the Government undertook at that time. After this sharp lesson a further rise in the internal price-level seems improbable, short of a catastrophe. The economic authorities are pursuing a policy of restricting the expansion of credit to the actual expansion of the goods turnover, and are even trying to effect a slow fall in the price-level, at any rate of industrial goods, as production expands. Although wholesale prices may be lowered by administrative pressure on State industry, a fall in retail prices (which is the truer measure of the value of the rouble) will not be maintained, for all the efforts of administrative pressure and trading economies, unless credit expansion proceeds more slowly than the output of goods, involving a strict parsimony in the financing of industry by the banks.[1] But such a parsimony of credit and a year or two of stable currency, linked with

[1] For the first half of 1926–7 a reduction of retail prices by 10 per cent was planned. The actual reduction achieved has been between 6 and 7 per cent (cf. *Econ. Review*, 15.8.27).

peasant prosperity, might manage to transform the hoarding habits of the *moujik* and reveal a powerful new source in peasant savings for capital accumulation in the hands of the co-operative system or of the State.

To understand Russia's currency situation completely, it is essential to realise that she possesses not only a " managed currency " but also at the same time a " managed exchange." The former is achieved through the control which the State Bank exercises over the credit situation, directly as the most important organ of credit to industrial and trading institutions, and indirectly through its rediscounting of bills for other banks. The latter is achieved by virtue of the State monopoly of foreign trade, which, by attempting to plan foreign trading operations so as to maintain a balance of foreign payments, and by appropriate purchases and sales of foreign valuta on the exchange market, keeps the chervonetz at parity with the dollar and the pound sterling. As a result, however, of the depreciation of the chervonetz on the internal market in 1923, and again to a smaller extent in 1925, the internal purchasing power of the rouble is lower than its external, or foreign exchange, value by some 20 per cent according to wholesale prices and by some 40 per cent according to retail prices. If the State foreign trade monopoly did not exist, this divergence between the internal price-level and the world price-level would tend to produce an import surplus, with a purchase of foreign valuta to pay for it, until the foreign exchange-rate of the rouble had fallen sufficiently (or internal deflation been imposed) to wipe out the difference between the two price-levels. At present there is no likelihood that this levelling will occur. And there exists no particular necessity for such a levelling, seeing that the existence of the difference need not impose any real loss upon Russia. The higher internal price-level, having the effect of an export duty, will tend to make export unprofitable; but so also will it act as an import bounty and make imports purchased at the lower world prices equivalently profitable. If, of course, foreign trade transactions are extended only so far as exports, purchased at the internal price-level and sold at the world price-level, are profitable, and no further, these transactions will be unduly narrowed, to the country's loss. This actually seems to be the case at present, with the result that both imports and exports are smaller than they would ordinarily tend to be; and foreign trade is only rendered possible in so far as the Russian prices of agricultural goods subject to export are substantially lower than the price of industrial goods on the home market—a factor aggravating the "scissors" problem and presenting an interesting parallel to Britain's dilemma of "sheltered" and "unsheltered" trades. But there seems no good reason why foreign trade should be limited in this way. There seems no good reason why foreign trade transactions should not be pushed beyond the point where export ceases to be profitable, by subsidising grain export out of the profits obtained from importing at the lower world price. So long as there was profit to be made out of the world market by the extra import sufficient to cover the specific loss on the extra export, no net loss to Russia as a whole would result from this extension of foreign trade; while until this point was reached the *optimum* results from foreign trade would not have been achieved.[1]

[1] The gain to the country would consist in the additional machinery and raw materials which could be procured at a smaller real cost (involved in producing for export) than would be required to produce them at home. The gain from extension of trade would continue until the profit on the marginal increment of imports sufficed to pay the subsidy required to finance the marginal unit of exports. The fact that *money* costs in Russia are higher than outside does not necessarily mean that *real* costs are equivalently higher, or have increased as compared with pre-war; and here Russian statements of the position often do themselves an injustice. Real costs of manufacture were always higher than in other countries, sometimes twice as high, and it is possible that industrial costs are at present rather higher than pre-war owing to depreciated capital equipment and the attempt to supply finished goods from Russian industry which were formerly imported more cheaply from abroad. But because *money* costs (which were somewhat higher than the world price-level before the war because of the tariff) have increased considerably as a result of the rise in the internal price-level, this is not a reason for assuming that *real* costs have risen equivalently, as the representative of Vesenha in a report to STO at the beginning of 1927 seemed to imply (*Econ. Jizn.*, 5.1.27). The change is purely a monetary phenomenon.

The continuance and the success of the new régime in Russia depends, not only upon a progress of production, but also upon the achievement of a steadily rising standard of life; and it is here that the problem of population takes a prominent place. A given expansion of production will clearly involve a smaller expansion of income *per head*, if the population is increasing; and the increase of income per head will be smaller, *ceteris paribus*, the faster the rate at which the population grows. The standard of life will vary, not with the total national income, but with the national income divided by the population. As a result of improved health facilities the death rate in Russia has considerably fallen since 1920,[1] so that despite the results of war and famine the population is now larger by over 6 per cent than in the equivalent area in 1913.[2] The income per head, therefore, has not recovered so far as has total production, the standard of the peasant being slightly lower, that of the industrial worker considerably higher and the income of those who previously formed the middle class being very much lower than in pre-war days. It does not follow from this, as the ardent Malthusian will rush to conclude, that a persistence of this rate of increase of population will spell economic disaster for Russia and a bankruptcy of her hopes. It does not even necessarily follow that in ten years' time the standard of life would be higher if no growth of population in the interim were to occur. Here we have to distinguish two questions: first, whether improvements in productive technique and the opening up of new land as fertile as the old are likely to occur more rapidly than an increase of population; second, whether such improve-

[1] The death-rate for European Russia has fallen since pre-war from about 27 to 21 per thousand, and infant mortality from 25 to 19 per cent. The birth-rate has meanwhile remained almost constant, so that the rate of increase of population has increased. See above, p. 71, footnote.

[2] *Economic Review*, 15.4.27. At present the annual rate of increase is 2·8 per cent as against 1·8 per cent between 1897 and 1914: 82 per cent of the population is at present agricultural. Cf. also Reviakin in *Sozt. Khos.*, 1926, No. 6, 117, where a lower figure of increase is given.

ments, yielding " increasing returns " to labour, are independent, or are in any sense dependent upon a growth of numbers. If the first question has an affirmative answer, while at the same time these improvements would occur whether population were to increase or to remain constant, then the problem of population would not be a pressing one and the standard of life would continue to rise in face of increasing numbers; although at the same time the standard of life would rise more rapidly if the population remained constant than if it increased. If, however, these improvements which brought " increasing returns " to labour were in any considerable measure dependent on an increase of numbers, then it would follow that the *optimum* density of population[1]—if that be a measurable conception—had not yet been reached.

Whether or not in this sense the *optimum* population has yet been reached in Russia it is almost impossible to say. Indeed, this aspect of the population question—the causal relation between numbers and improvements—has nowhere as yet received adequate attention. In some of the more crowded and less fertile areas in Russia, such as the centre

[1] Cf. Lionel Robbins in *London Essays in Economics*, 119–33. The problem of population and of " diminishing returns " is really a question of the combination of the factors of production and of their *optimum* combination from the point of view of labour. The problem arises to the extent that the supply of fertile land is limited, and as the supply of labour increases, resort has to be had to inferior land or to the more intensive cultivation of existing land. Hence the question of the *optimum* " loading " of land, as of machinery. Where new supplies of fertile land can be made easily available with a small expenditure of capital, or economies are available which raise the productivity of labour, the problem does not arise. But if capital, as well as land, is limited, then over-population relative to existing capital facilities soon sets in. The more elastic the supply of capital—the more easy it is to accumulate—the less urgent the problem becomes. In general, however, it will be true that the smaller the supply of labour relatively to capital the greater the productivity of labour per unit. The exception to this will be where improvements in productive methods depend upon an expansion in the labour supply; and improvements require to be classified into (i) those independent of the scale of production; (ii) those dependent on a certain scale of production, as a whole, based on a given combination of capital, labour and land; (iii) those dependent on a certain increase in the supply of capital; (iv) those dependent on a certain increase in the supply of labour.

and north-west, this point has probably been passed. In other thinly populated and fertile areas a larger population might probably lead to a more successful combination and division of labour,[1] and might make profitable the introduction of large units of capital in the form of machinery and transport facilities, which formerly, in combination with a smaller labour supply, were not sufficiently worth while. Industry as a whole has possibilities of considerable economies, both internal and external, from an expansion of scale which would require a larger supply of industrial workers. Such improvements are certainly dependent on an increased supply of labour in particular areas or particular spheres, but whether on an increase of population for the whole country, as distinct from an improved distribution of the existing population, it is difficult to say. But whatever the answer to this question may be, there are a number of considerations which suggest that the problem of absolute over-population is some distance from approaching an urgent stage. The possibility of a technical revolution in the methods of agriculture, which may have more sweeping results than the agricultural changes in England at the end of the 18th century; the possibility of opening up new fertile areas beyond the Urals, such as that to be tapped by the new Semipalatinsk railway, which may do for Russia something of what the opening of the Middle West did for America in the 19th century; the possibility of a new, or at least a completed, industrial revolution, based on the progress of electrification—possibilities such as these suggest that the tendency to "diminishing returns," in so far as it has begun to operate, is likely to be offset fairly strongly in the future by improvements which increase the productivity of labour and raise the standard of life. The expenditure of a comparatively small amount of capital—for instance, in

[1] Prof. Prokopovitch, for instance, on the basis of correlation of farm statistics, points out that in new farm colonies the number of workers is more important to success than the amount of capital, while in older, more populated villages the reverse is the case (*Russian Economist*, Vol. III, No. 9, 3108).

building railways, in spreading agricultural knowledge, in transferring population from crowded villages to more thinly-peopled districts—may open up very considerable prospects of "increasing returns."

Nevertheless the realisation of such improvements requires at least some initial capital outlay; and for an increase of population to be accompanied by an equivalent increase of product, it will be necessary for population to advance more slowly than the expansion of capital equipment. The productivity of labour will not increase, but decrease, if the population of the village increases faster than the supply of agricultural implements. The workers' standard of life will fall, and not rise, if their numbers increase more rapidly than housing facilities. The phenomenon of increasing unemployment in face of expanding industrial employment is witness to the fact that expansion of industrial equipment at present proceeds more slowly than the migration of the surplus population of the village into the towns.[1] If in the next ten years when capital is scarce and the tasks of the new society are still in the pioneer stage, population should expand rapidly, it might well cause serious over-population in certain areas of the countryside and an influx into the towns at a faster rate than industrial expansion and employment could proceed. Not only would such an increase swallow up the principal gains of increased production: it might offer precisely the field of cheap labour which the *kulak* and private *entrepreneur* require, and breed in the towns and villages an army of unemployed discontent. If at any one time there be an *optimum* density of population, there should also presumably be an *optimum* rate of growth —an *optimum* which is probably exceeded if the increase of persons is more rapid than that of capital equipment to enable them to work. Although no dogmatic answer is at

[1] The urban population, for instance, increased between 1925 and 1926 from 20 to 25 million, of which 1·5 million represented natural increase and 3·5 million the influx of rural population (*Econ. Review*, 15.4.27) The population of Moscow is now 2 million as against 1 million in 1920, and that of Leningrad is 1·6 million as against ·7 million in 1920.

present possible to Russia's population question, it remains a matter of importance which requires study, and may soon demand a greater degree of attention than it has hitherto received. The increase of population may well prove to require some kind of regulation as much as the other economic factors which Gosplan seeks to co-ordinate and to plan; and contraceptives may to-morrow prove as important a slogan in the campaign for a higher standard of life in Russia as are rationalisation and economy to-day.

In Moscow one meets the breath of Asia in the Kremlin Towers, the minarets, and the Tartar faces; and whatever her future destiny may be, in Russia the East still marches with the West. Whatever emerges from the present must be a blending of the two. It is not impossible that the next decades may hold for Russia an industrial revolution as rapid as in Japan or Germany half a century ago. Some declare that Moscow already wears the signs of an American city, with a drive and activity which she did not have before. In her streets there is certainly a new rhythm of life to be felt and heard. A new spirit of creation is abroad, elemental and crude and strong. On the lump of the old Russian temperament the Communists are ruthlessly working as a new leaven—an energising, a levelling, a Westernising force. Perhaps in this " laboratory of life," as one observer calls it, the scientist is evolving some new historical element of great moment to the world. Those who prefer Tolstoy to Marx, and the slow rhythm of the plough to the more complex rhythm of the machine, may dread the outcome of the experiment and loathe to look upon its face.

The engine is not dead
It lives ! It lives ! It reaches out a claw
To clutch the hearts of men
And men are governed by a cruel clock
That beats a doleful time—tick-tack, tick-tack
For morning, noon and night—tick-tack, tick-tack.
One shall be arm, another leg, a third
Brain—but the soul, the soul is dead.

But the world to-day needs engineers in leather-jackets more than it needs dreamers and mystics to charm it to reverie and to sleep. For the social engineer the experiment must hold an absorbing interest. For the exploited proletarian it will hold an important hope. It may hold a key for the tired searchers who grope, not after the spinning-wheel and home-spun, but towards some new synthesis where

> The Demon Steam is overthrown
> By right of numbers, and the power
> Pluck'd from the tyrant's throne is made
> Obedient to his former subjects !
> Once you were slaves to elements
> But now their masters, royal masters !
> And in Creation's last high hour
> The bow of freedom spans the sky,
> Your arch of promise. Man becomes
> The captain of his earth !

A GLOSSARY OF TERMS

Centrosoyus. Central Union of Consumers' Co-operative Societies.

Dessiatine = 2·7 acres = 1·09 hectares.

Ekoso. Economic conference: conferences called together from time to time of representatives of industry, etc. in any district, e.g. Gubekoso.

Esenha. Economic Council, whether of the Union, republic, or local body unspecified.

Glavki. Committees or Boards set up by the Centres, or directly by Vesenha for a whole industry or a branch of an industry. (See page 99 *seq.*)

Gosbank. The State Bank.

Gosplan. State Economic Planning Commission: a permanent advisory body attached to STO, composed of experts, and itself divided into specialised sub-departments and *ad hoc* sub-committees.

Gostorg. A wholesale trading company set up with State capital to operate on the internal and on foreign markets.

Gubernia. An administrative unit or province, e.g. Tambov, Vladimir, Moscow, Vologda, Perm.

Gubsovnarhoz. The industrial department of the gubernia Soviet.

Gubtorg. Trading company set up by a gubernia Soviet.

Kulak (literally, "fist"). A rich peasant employing labour, making a living by trade and/or acting as village usurer.

Narcomfin. People's Commissariat of Finance.

Narcomprod. People's Commissariat of Supplies (merged in Narcomvnutorg at the beginning of 1924).

Narcomput. People's Commissariat of Ways and Communications.

Narcomzem. People's Commissariat of Agriculture.

Narcomtorg. People's Commissariat for Trade (formed in 1926).

Narcomtrud. People's Commissariat of Labour.

Narcomvneshtorg. People's Commissariat for Foreign trade (merged in Narcomtorg in 1926).

Narcomvnutorg. People's Commissariat for Internal Trade (created in 1924 from the previous Commission attached to STO, and merged in Narcomtorg in 1926).

NEP. The New Economic Policy.

Nepman. Private Trader.

Pood = 36·11 lb. (English) = 16·38 kilograms.

Prombank. Industrial Bank.

R.S.F.S.R. Russian Socialist Federal Soviet Republic.

Samagonka. Peasant home-distilled spirit from rye or potatoes.

Sovnarcom. Council of People's Commissaries, elected by the Central Executive Committee of the Soviet Congress, and equivalent to the Cabinet or Council of Ministers in other countries.

STO. Council of Labour and Defence: the highest authority in the economic sphere; appointed by Sovnarcom. (See pages 140 and 241.)

U.S.S.R. Union of Socialist Soviet Republics.

Uyezd. An administrative unit equivalent to a county.

Verst. = ·66 mile = 1·06 kilometres.

Vesenha. All-Union Supreme Economic Council. (See page 98.)

A LIST OF SOURCES

Abregée des Données Statistiques de l'U.R.S.S. (1925, Cent. Statistical Dept., Moscow.)

All-Union Textile Syndicate (Vesenha, Moscow).

ASKNASIE, S. *Narodnoe Khosiaistvo Sovetskikh Rep.* (National Economy of the Soviet Republics): an explanatory bibliography.

BAERLEIN. *The March of the Seventy Thousand.*

BALABANOV. *Ochorki po Istorie Rabochevo Klassa v Rossii.* (Outline History of the Working Class in Russia), Vols. 1–3.

BRAILSFORD, H. N. *The Russian Workers' Republic.*

BRITISH LABOUR PARTY. *Report on Russia*, 1920.

BUCHANAN, SIR GEORGE. *My Mission in Russia*, 2 vols.

BUKHARIN, N. *Economika Perekhodnovo Perioda* (Economics of the Transition Period).

BUKHARIN, N., and PREOBRAJENSKY. *The A.B.C. of Communism.*

BUKHARIN, N. *Building-up Socialism.*

BUXTON, C. R. *In a Russian Village.*

DENIKIN. *The Russian Turmoil.*

DILLON. *Russia in Eclipse.*

DJERJINSKY. *Perspectivi Promishlenosti 1925–6* (The Industrial Outlook, 1925–6).

DJERJINSKY. *Promishlenost S.S.S.R.* (Russian Industry).

DUKES, SIR PAUL. *Red Dusk and the Morrow.*

EPSTEIN, E. *Les Banques de Commerce Russes.*

Export, Import i Consessii Soyuza S.S.R. (Export, Import and Concessions in U.S.S.R.): in Russian and English.

FARBMAN, M. *Bolshevism in Retreat.*

FARBMAN, M. *After Lenin.*

GESSEN. *Istoria Gornorabochikh S.S.S.R.* (History of the Miners in Russia), Vol. 1—.

GOLDMAN, EMMA. *My Disillusionment in Russia.*

GORDON, PROF. M. *Ochork Economicheskoi Borbi Rabochikh v Rossii* (A Sketch of the Economic Struggle of the Workers in Russia).

GOSPLAN. *Kontrolnie Tsifri, 1927–8.*

GUEST, L. HADEN. *The New Russia.*

HELLER, A. *The Industrial Revival in Soviet Russia.*

HINDUS, M. *Broken Earth.*

I.L.O. *Report on Economic Conditions in Russia.*

I.L.O. *Labour Conditions in Soviet Russia* (1920).

I.L.O. *Industrial Life in Soviet Russia*, 1917–23.

I.L.O. *Organisation of Industry and Labour Conditions in Soviet Russia.*

I.L.O. *The Co-operative Movement in Soviet Russia* (1926).

I.L.O. *The Trade Union Movement in Soviet Russia* (1927).

Institute of Economic Research (Moscow), *La Situation Economique de l'Union Sovietique.* Published in Paris.

Institute of Commercial Research (London), *Russia : General Review and Commercial Report*, 1926.

KARLGREN, PROF. A. *Bolshevist Russia.*

Katalog Knig po Obschestvennim Voprosam (Catalogue of Books on Social Questions).

KATZENELLENBAUM, PROF. S. *Russian Currency and Banking*, 1914–24.

KEYNES, J. M. *A Short View of Russia.*

Khosiaistvennie Itogy, 1922–3 (The Economic Year, 1922–3).

KOLLONTAI, A. *The Workers' Opposition in Russia.*

KRITSMANN, L. *Geroicheski Period Velikoi Russkoi Revolutsii* (The Heroic Period of the Great Russian Revolution).

KRSHISHANOVSKY, G. *Khosiaistvennie Problemi R.S.F.S.R.* (Economic Problems of R.S.F.S.R.).

KRUMIN, G. *V Borbye Za Sozialism* (In the Struggle for Socialism).

KRUMIN, G. *Puti Khosiaistvennoi Politiki* (Paths of Economic Policy).

LABRY, R. *Une Legislation Communiste.*

LARIN AND KRITSMANN. *Ochork Khosiaistvennoi Jizni i Organisatsii Narodnovo Khosiaistva Sovietskoi Rossii* (A Sketch of the Economic Life and Organisation of the National Economy in Sov. Russia).

LEE, IVY, *U.S.S.R. : a World Enigma.*

LEITES, K. *Recent Economic Developments in Russia.*

LENIN, N. *Collected Works* (in Russian).

LENIN, N. *State and Revolution.*

LENIN, N. *Will the Bolsheviks Maintain Power ?*

LENIN, N. *Left-wing Communism : an Infantile Sickness.*

LENIN, N. *On the Road to Insurrection.*

LONDON AND CAMBRIDGE ECON. SERVICE. *Memorandum No. 25*, prepared by the Conjuncture Institute, Moscow.

LUKHOMSKY. *Memoirs of the Russian Revolution.*

MAKEEV AND O'HARA. *Russia.*

Materiali dla Dokladov, Mosc. Komitet R.K.P. (Materials for Reports, Moscow Committee of the Russian Comm. Party).

MAVOR, PROF. J. *Economic History of Russia*, 2 vols.

MAVOR, PROF. J. *The Russian Revolution.*

MILIUKOV, P. *Russia To-day and To-morrow.*

MILLER, MARGARET. *Economic Development of Russia, 1905–14.*

MILIUTIN. *Novy Period Mirovoi Economiki* (The New Period of World Economics).

Na Novikh Putyakh (On New Paths), vols. 1–3.

NORDMAN, N. *Peace Problems : Russia's Economics.*

PALÉOLOGUE, M. *An Ambassador's Memoirs*, vol. 3.

PARES, SIR BERNARD. *A History of Russia.*

PASVOLSKY, L. *Economics of Communism.*

PASVOLSKY, L., and MOULTON, H. G. *Russian Debts and Russian Reconstruction.*

POLLOCK, JOHN. *War and Revolution in Russia.*

POKROVSKY, PROF. M. *Russkaia Istoria s. Drevnieyshikh Vremen* (Russian History from the Earliest Times), vols. 3, 4.

PREOBRAJENSKY, E. *Economicheskie Crizisi pri N E P* (Economic Crises under N E P).

PREOBRAJENSKY, E. *Novaia Economika* (The New Economics).

PRICE, M. PHILIPS. *Reminiscences of the Russian Revolution.*

PROKOPOVITCH, PROF. S. N. *Economic Conditions in Soviet Russia.*

RAFFALOVITCH, A. *Russia : its Trade and Commerce.*

RANSOME, A. *The Crisis in Russia.*

REED, JOHN. *Ten Days that Shook the World.*

Restoration of Agriculture in the Famine Area of Russia, issued by the Information Dept. of the Russian Trade Delegation in London.

ROSENFELD, J. S. *Promishlennaia Politika S.S.S.R.* (Industrial Policy of U.S.S.R.).

ROSS, E. A. *The Russian Soviet Republic.*

ROTHSTEIN, A. *The Soviet Constitution.*

RUSSELL, BERTRAND. *The Practice and Theory of Bolshevism.*

Russkaia Promishlenost, 1922 (Russian Industry, 1922).

RYKOV. *Osnovnie Voprosi Khos. Politiki S.S.S.R.* (Basic Problems of Economic Policy in U.S.S.R.).

SMUSHKOV. *Economicheskaia Politika S.S.S.R.* (The Political Economy of U.S.S.R.).

SOROKIN, P. *Leaves from a Russian Diary.*

STALIN, I. *Bolshevism : some questions answered.*

STALIN, I. *Leninism.*

State Bank of the U.S.S.R., 1921–6.

STRUMILIN, S. *Na Khosiaistvennom Fronte* (On the Economic Front).

Systematicheski Ukazatel Sozialno-Economicheskoi Literaturi Izdannoi Gosizdatom, 1919–24 (Systematic Index to Social and Economic Literature). Published by the State Publishing House, 1919–24.

Trade Union Congress. *Russia : Official Report of T.U. Delegation*, 1924.

TROTSKY, L. *Novy Kurs* (The New Course) : in French as *Cours Nouveau.*
TROTSKY, L. *Lenin* (in English).
TROTSKY, L. *Defence of Terrorism.*
TROTSKY, L. *Problems of Life.*
TROTSKY, L. *Towards Socialism or Capitalism?*
Tyajolaia Industria S.S.S.R. : Ugol, Nieft, Jelezo (Heavy Industry in U.S.S.R.: Coal, Oil, Iron): Ed. by Prof. Den.
USTINOV, PROF. V. M. *Evolutsia Vnutrennoi Torgovli v Rossii, 1913–24* (Evolution of Internal Trade in Russia, 1913–24).
VARGA, PROF. E. *La Dictature du Prolétariat : Problèmes Economiques.*
Voprosi Khosiaistvennovo Stroitelstva (Questions of Economic Construction).
WELLS, H. G. *Russia in the Shadows.*
YAKOVLEV, Y. *Dierevnia, kak ona yest* (The Village as it is).
YAKOVLEV, Y. *Nasha Dierevnia* (Our Village).
Yejegodnik Cominterna, 1923 (Comintern Year-book, 1923).
YUROVSKY, PROV. L. N. *Currency Problems of the Soviet Union.*
WIEDENFELD, PROF. KURT. *The Remaking of Russia.*
ZAGORSKY, S. *La République des Soviets.*

PERIODICALS

IN ENGLISH

Communist International (monthly, later bi-monthly; Moscow and London).
Economic Review (weekly).
Economist (weekly).
Economic Journal (quarterly).
International Labour Review (monthly ; I.L.O., Geneva).
Industrial and Labour Information (weekly ; I.L.O., Geneva).
International Press Correspondence (Vienna).
London and Cambridge Economic Service, 1926.
Manchester Guardian Commercial, special Reconstruction supplements, 1922–4.

Monthly Survey of the State Bank of U.S.S.R.

Russian Economist (bi-monthly, issued by Russian Econ. Association in London, 1920–3).

Russian Information and Review (monthly, issued by Information Department of Russian Trade Delegation, London, 1921–5).

Soviet Union Monthly (monthly, issued by Information Department of Russian Trade Delegation, London, 1925–7).

Soviet Union Year-book, Ed. by Segal and Santalov (for 1925 1926, 1927, 1928).

IN RUSSIAN

Economicheskaia Jizn (Economic Life), daily organ of S T O, Ekoso, etc.

Economicheskoe Obozrenie (Economic Review), monthly review, issued by S T O.

Economichesky Bulletin Konyunkturnovo Instituta (Economic Bulletin of the Conjuncture Institute), a monthly survey of economic conditions.

Isvestia (News), daily organ of the Soviet Government.

Isvestia R.K.P., monthly report of the proceedings of the Central Committee of the Russian Comm. Party.

Narodnoe Khosiaistvo (National Economy), annual economic survey of the year, issued by Gosplan.

Planovoe Khosiaistvo (Planned Economy), monthly review issued by Gosplan.

Pravda (Truth), daily organ of the Central Committee of the Comm. Party.

Rabochaia Gazeta, workers' daily.

Sozialisticheskoe Khosiaistvo (Socialist Economy), bi-monthly theoretical review.

Statistichesky Bulletin, monthly abstract of industrial statistics published by Vesenha.

Vestnik Communisticheskoi Akademii. The proceedings of the Communist Academy.

Vestnik Truda (Labour Record), monthly organ of Narcomtrud.

APPENDIX TO THE SECOND EDITION

ON AGRICULTURE AND INDUSTRY IN 1927–28

UNLESS it be already very wealthy, a country is unlikely by voluntary individual saving to obtain a sum of capital sufficient to transform an agrarian into an industrial nation within a narrow stretch of time. And in no country does the process of industrialisation seem to have been separable from some extraordinary measures which offend—and often designedly so—against the precepts of *laissez-faire*. One form of these measures, historically of great significance, has been the exploitation of agricultural areas for the benefit of nascent industry, either areas which lay within the national boundaries or were satellite colonies outside. Such exploitation, whether formulated as a conscious policy or not, had its *leitmotif* in the cheapening of agricultural goods relative to industrial, so that the reduced consumption of agricultural producers (relative, at least, if not absolute) could place surplus resources in the hands of industry from which capital could be accumulated and industrial construction could be financed. To this system of forced accumulation Protectionist measures in favour of industry were generally essential. In Britain it appeared in the guise of the Mercantile System, regulating trade between the capitalists of the home country and the colonial areas across the seas to the former's aggrandisement. In the industrial countries which developed later and had few colonies the pursuit of a tariff policy for the benefit of industry had the effect of raising the industrial price-level inside the tariff wall, and, by raising it above the agricultural level, of drawing in resources for the benefit of industry at the expense of the population of the countryside. Where industrial development came later in the day and could be financed by capital borrowing from abroad, this special function of a Protective policy was less required. But even here Protection probably fulfilled in this way a quite important rôle. With this form was combined in all capitalist countries the process of class differentiation, creating a proletariat both in the village and in the town. Here it was the special cheapening, not of agricultural products, but of labour-power that was significant; and in general the lowered consumption of the urban and rural proletariat probably played a larger part even than the exploitation of peasant producers in enabling a surplus to accrue to industrial capitalists, out of which alone industrial development could be financed.

By the decision of the 14th Party Congress[1] Russia had definitely set her face on the road to industrialisation as the *sine qua non* of Socialism in a backward agrarian land. And, in Russia, as elsewhere, the problem of the means to finance industrial construction became the dominant theme. If factories were to be built, irrigation schemes and power-stations and railway extension undertaken, which would yield their fruit only after a period of years, somebody in the present would have to lack the cloth trousers or linen tunics, the leather boots or sandals, the food products or metal wares which might have been available, had not labour and materials been diverted to constructional work. To finance the import of constructional material by foreign capital was for Russia in existing circumstances virtually impossible on any considerable scale. Preobrajensky had been right in pointing out that something would have to be obtained at the expense of the village—by giving to the village less textile goods in proportion to the food and raw materials that it furnished in return. Where a quarrel could be made with his policy of "squeezing" the peasant lay in the

[1] Cf. above, pp. 318–20.

effect of such exploitation on the expansion of agriculture.[1] While in a short period—say, 5 or 10 years—a " squeezing " policy might yield more to industry, and yield it more quickly and immediately, a moderate policy towards the village might eventually yield more in the aggregate over a long period—say, 20 or 30 years—even if the *immediate* yield were less. At the present time something still continues to be obtained at the expense of agriculture to the extent that the " scissors " continues—a situation impossible of continuance without the degree of " protection " to industry which the foreign trade monopoly and its control of imports affords.[2] In some measure this acts as a brake on agricultural development, and by lessening the grain and raw materials available for the towns and for export ultimately lessens the amount which industry can obtain and the rate at which it can advance in the future. On the other hand, to forego this advantage would necessitate either a lower rate of capital accumulation and industrial construction in the *immediate* future or else a reduced consumption of the urban worker—either his consumption of grain or of industrial products. And it is against the background of this crucial issue—the choice between industrial construction, the consumption of the town worker, and the consumption of the peasant—that the discussions and events of the past year in Russia must be set.

The Central Committee of the Party in the autumn of 1927 had issued a preliminary Five Year Plan, embodying

[1] Exploitation would tend to check agricultural production unless peasant demand for money-income was inelastic (See above, p. 283.) In the case of a proletariat this condition for the maximum success of exploitation is probably fulfilled.

[2] To the extent that agricultural export is to be possible, agricultural prices (in terms of gold) have to remain at the world level. To the extent that the " scissors " still prevails, industrial prices remain above the world level, and the internal value of the rouble is less than its external (cf. above, pp. 393–4). Unless import was restricted, foreign manufactured goods would flow in and lower the industrial price-level. This would mean a lowering of industrial profits in the present, and would mean that finished goods rather than constructional materials would be imported in exchange for agricultural exports—in other words, a slackened present rate of industrial accumulation.

reports of Gosplan which from estimates of possibilities proceeded to the formulation of the policy by which economic activities should be guided in the ensuing years. At this draft plan, the opposition, which from its Trotskyist nucleus in 1923–4 had been reinforced in 1925–6 by Kamenev and Zinoviev and Smilga, levelled strenuous criticism, outlined prior to the 15th Party Congress in two trenchantly worded "Counter-theses." The onus of their complaint was that by the official policy towards the peasants, and particularly by the "concessions" made to encourage agriculture in 1925, the village *kulak* had been enriched, his influence in the village and his exploiting tendencies increased, so that the old pre-war tendency to class differentiation in the village had reappeared. Bukharin in a rash moment two years before had let loose the phrase towards the peasantry, "enrich yourselves"; and this was fastened upon by the opposition as the obtruding horns of the official policy. The charge was supported by abundant figures. Rich peasant husbandries constituted 15 to 25 per cent of the total number, covered 25 to 45 per cent of the cultivated area, and possessed 40 to 60 per cent of the machinery. The easier policy with regard to land-leases and the employment of wage-labour had benefited predominantly this *kulak* class: three-quarters of the land leased was concentrated in the hands of 16 per cent of the richer farms; and in the last two years the area cultivated by the rich peasant had increased by 100 to 200 per cent. At the same time there had been an appreciable increase in the number of landless persons in the village, forced to rely on wage-labour for subsistence. Even the co-operatives were becoming perverted by *kulak* influence and were ceasing to perform their Leninist function as aids to the poorer peasants and instruments for introducing collective methods in the countryside.

Nor was this all. The fact that the *kulak* had been enriched enabled him to hoard large stocks of grain and to hold them back from the market: being rich he was strong enough to resist the pressure of the "scissors" upon himself. Grain reserves the Counter-thesis estimated to amount to some 800 to 900 million poods—considerably greater than before the war—of which some 58 per cent was in the hands of one-sixth of the richer farms. This holding back of grain from the market threatened a crisis in the exchange between village and town, lessened the available grain export, and hence the possibility of importing machinery for industrial construction in return, and lowered the urban worker's real wage by raising the price of food. It was this that was responsible for the slow rise in the workers' standard of life of which the opposition particularly complained—his real wages, his receipts from social insurance, his housing conditions—and for the rate of industrial construction provided in the Five Year Plan being, in the opposition's opinion, much too small. This in turn by retarding the growth of industrial production accentuated the "goods famine" and the shortage of goods supplied to the village, and so led to an aggravation of the crisis in the turnover between town and village in a vicious circle. And if the only method of handling the situation was to impose "administrative" pressure to reduce industrial prices, this, so far from curing the root of the evil, would merely enrich private speculators who fattened on the difference between factory prices and the retail prices which consumers were willing to pay. The lowering of industrial prices which the official policy endeavoured to pursue could only be properly achieved as a result of increased accumulation and the re-equipment of industry: at present the policy merely reduced accumulation by lowering industrial profits.

To strike at the root of the situation they proposed a sharp change in the policy towards the *kulak*: an offensive against the rich peasant, of which the first instalment should be a compulsory grain loan of 200 million poods levied on the richest 10 per cent of peasant farms.[1] With

[1] This would amount to between a third and two-fifths of the annual pre-war grain export, and to more than the average annual grain export for 1925–6 and 1926–7.

the proceeds of this loan the means could be found for increasing grain exports, for importing industrial equipment in return—possibly of doubling that import—and so of increasing the rate of industrial construction, so necessary if manufacturing costs were to be cheapened and the margin of urban unemployed absorbed. "Those who reject this way," it was declared, "are left with the sole alternative of abandoning the foreign trade monopoly, of resorting to foreign capital for export and import, and of importing foreign goods for the village in exchange for the export of the accumulated reserves of grain."[1]

Some of this cogent criticism was certainly valid, and in a less polemical atmosphere would probably have been frankly admitted by the leaders of the Government. But when the defenders of the Five Year Plan replied with equal warmth that the charges were a demagogic caricature, they seem to have had considerable reason on their side. It was true that unemployment in the towns assumed serious proportions. Nevertheless this coexisted with an increase in the total number of employed wage-earners by 25 per cent and of workers employed in State industry by 30 per cent over the previous two years; and this unemployed margin was mainly due, not to the stagnation of industry, but to the continual immigration of villagers into the large towns. It was true that the workers' standard of life was distinctly low as compared with that in western countries. At the same time it seems generally agreed that the real wage of the industrial worker was in 1926–7 on the average some 10 per cent higher than the pre-war

[1] Counter-Theses of the Opposition on the Five Year Plan and on the Work in the Village, published in Discussion Supplements Nos. 3 and 5 of *Pravda*, 5.11.27 and 17.11.27. The signatories to the latter thesis were Trotsky, Zinoviev, Kamenev, Smilga, Rakovsky, Bakaiev, Yevdokimov, Peterson, Muralov. The expulsion of certain of the opposition in November was occasioned, not by their criticism, but by offences against Party discipline in organising secret agitational work outside the boundaries of Party discussion against the official policy, and so of virtually setting up a second Party. Several of the expelled members, including Kamenev, Zinoviev and Piatakov, have since been readmitted.

level; while including various social insurance benefits his standard of life was some 30–34 per cent higher than in 1913. At the same time his hours of work were shorter by about a quarter, and his daily output only some 96 per cent of the pre-war amount.[1] While the rate of accumulation might well be painfully slow for those impatient for industrial progress, it remained true that the volume of net capital investment had by 1926–7 attained and even exceeded the pre-war proportion of the national income, and continued on an upward curve.[2] True, there were serious deficiencies in the grain surplus and the grain export; but the causes of this seem to be considerably less simple and less easily exorcised by a magical formula than the opposition imagined.

The opposition was charged, moreover, with presenting figures that were misleading and even false. The gloomy picture of a growing *kulak* domination in the village was only obtained by the quite unjustifiable device of including all peasants with holdings of over 6 dessiatines in the *kulak* category, whereas farms up to 8 dessiatines, and even up to 10 dessiatines, usually employed wage-labour only as auxiliary labour at certain seasons of the year such as the harvest, and were hardly to be classed as regular employers of labour. What could truly be classed as *kulak* farms still remained quite small, covering little more than 10 per cent of the arable area and supplying no more than 15 per cent of the grain surplus. True, their number was growing; but, in Yakovlev's words, only by the illegitimate use of "the large percentage leaps taken by small numbers" could this growth be construed as serious or as at all comparable in scale to the growth of "middle peasant" farms.

[1] Prof. Weinstein, in *Econ. Bulletin Konyunkturnovo Instituta*, Nos. 11–12, 1927, *cit. Volya Rossii* (Prague), July 1928; Strumilin in *Pravda*, 30.11.27. The Narcomtrud Index Number of Real Wages for March 1928 gave an average figure of 120 for the whole Soviet Union (1913=100). In 1928 a start was made in the introduction of the Seven-Hour Day. This has been introduced in several textile factories, in combination with a transfer to a three-shift system.

[2] Weinstein, *loc. cit.*: *Kontrolnie Tsifri Nar. Khos, S.S.S.R., 1927–8*, pp. 19–31.

Similarly with regard to the opposition charge that the lower ranks of the village were in process of a steady proletarianisation: true, a considerable proportion of poor peasant farms, ranging from 9 per cent in White Russia to 21 per cent in Siberia, had been liquidated in recent years and their owners become landless; but at the same time a much larger proportion of formerly landless peasants, ranging from 20 to 40 per cent, had been provided with land, while the proportion of peasant farms which lacked horses or working cattle was showing a slow but steady decline.[1]

Equally mistaken, it was alleged, were the statements in the Counter-theses concerning the hoarding of grain. The estimate of the Central Statistical Office placed the figure of peasant grain reserves at 700 million in place of the opposition's figure of 800–900 million poods—a difference equal to the amount of the proposed compulsory loan. Moreover these reserves, which were certainly large and had been on the increase, were not predominantly in the hands of the *kulak*. The geographical distribution of the reserves suggested that they were "for the most part safety reserves, predominantly stored up in districts subject to drought," and no correlation existed over the various districts between the size of grain reserves per head and the preponderance of the rich farmer.[2]

With the smoke of the Counter-theses went the fire of the grain collection difficulties of the winter of 1927–8; and while the prescription which the opposition served might be questioned, little doubt remained by the time of the 15th Party Congress in December that there was something to be diagnosed. The harvest of the summer of 1927 had been above the average, being the third good harvest

[1] Yakovlev in *Pravda*, 5.11.27; Molotov's report to 15th Party Congress, *Econ. Jizn*, 22.12.27, and *Rabochaia Gazeta*, 23.12.27. The Counter-Theses had made considerable use of an investigation undertaken by Gaister for the Communist Academy into a sample of 1200 peasant farms. Gaister subsequently wrote disclaiming the interpretation placed upon his figures by the opposition (*Econ. Jizn*, 5.12.27, 6.12.27).

[2] Goldenburg in *Pravda*, 17.11.27.

in succession, and the arable area had recovered to within a small percentage of pre-war. But despite such a fair appearance, the volume of grain which the collecting organs were able to purchase in the autumn fell considerably short of the anticipated amount, and in November and December showed a sharp drop to a level of less than half the amount collected in the same months of the previous year. The situation seriously threatened both the food supply of the towns and the grain export surplus, this latter endangering the import plan and the program of capital construction for the year, if the stability of the chervonetz exchange was not to be sacrificed. In the first two months of the new financial year grain exports were less than half the monthly average of 1926–7; and in the remaining months of 1927–8 the figure of monthly grain export fell to a few thousand tons. July 1928, on the eve of the new harvest, actually witnessed a large buying of grain abroad, to the amount of some 12 million poods, or about two-thirds of the total amount exported since the previous October. Nor did this shortage of agricultural products on the market stand alone. The winter months also saw a sharpening of the industrial "goods famine" and the appearance in a less acute form of many of the features of the inflation crisis of two years before.

The immediate causes of this situation were not dissimilar to those which were operative in 1925. In the summer of 1927 there had occurred both the usual seasonal fall in industrial production, following the holiday season and the migration of workers in some districts to aid their families in the harvest, and at the same time a reduction in factory prices in conformity with the directions of the higher economic organs. The autumn commenced, accordingly, with a somewhat shrunken total of industrial supplies as valued at the ruling prices. Meanwhile a mild boom of constructional activity had taken place, financed in part by trusts drawing upon accumulated reserves,[1] in part

[1] In other words, by a lessening of bank deposits.

by an expansion of long and short-term credits by the banks. This constructional boom was to some extent due to the inauguration of schemes which had been postponed from the first half of the year for lack of funds; but even over the year as a whole, while the production of finished goods fell short of what was envisaged in the annual plan, that of constructional goods exceeded the planned quota.[1] The purchasing-power, both urban and rural, which was increased through the additional employment afforded by this constructional work, was still further swollen in the towns by a rise in wage-rates and in the villages by a record increase in peasant receipts from the sale of certain raw materials at a relatively favourable price. This provided the basis for a " break in the equilibrium between supply and demand," which Mikoyan, the Commissar for Trade, estimated to amount at the prevailing prices to a deficit in supply of 300 million roubles; while *Economicheskaia Jizn* estimated that between July and December the purchasing-power of the country had grown by 11·6 per cent and the supply of finished industrial goods by only 3·2 per cent. On a free competitive market such a situation would have shown itself in a rise of prices—in a word, in the usual phenomena of credit inflation. This actually occurred at the end of the autumn on the private market, both in the case of industrial and of agricultural goods. But State policy exerted its influence to prevent the prices charged by State institutions from rising; while in the grain market the monopolist position of the State buying organs was sufficiently strong to control the price of grain. The shortage accordingly expressed itself simply in a margin of unsatisfied demand; and since urban demand, being nearer to the source and more insistent, was able to intercept an undue share of the current supply, the chief burden of the shortage fell upon the village. When in the local store

[1] The growth of constructional industry over the year amounted to some 22 per cent, and of the production of finished goods by 14 per cent (Pervushin, *Econ. Oboz.*, Nov., 1927, 16).

the goods he required were either inadequate or absent, while he himself for the moment was relatively well supplied with funds, the peasant, and particularly the well-to-do peasant, was naturally in no hurry at existing prices in the grain market to part with the produce in his barns. To this diffidence a further factor contributed. In the previous year the relation between the prices of grain and of other agricultural production, such as raw materials and live-stock, had been unfavourable to the latter, so that collections of these had seriously fallen. This year, in the attempt to ensure the raw material supply for industry, the see-saw had been allowed to swing too far the other way, so that it was now the turn of grain to be undervalued. The collection difficulties did not apply, therefore, to all agricultural products. During the autumn and winter months purchases of certain products, notably oil seeds, flax, hemp, mahorka and butter, were maintained and even increased; and the crisis remained principally a grain crisis, since it was upon the grain supply that the onus of the situation was heaped.[1]

But one blade of a shears cannot achieve its task alone; and without the aid of some more fundamental factor these transitory errors of economic forecast would probably have had quite an unimportant effect. The autumn difficulties suggested that capital construction work and the urban standard of life were increasing faster, at least at the moment, than the actual economic situation would allow, with a resulting inadequacy of finished industrial goods on village markets to evoke in exchange the requisite quantity of peasant produce. But why should this be so? With agricultural yield restored to the pre-war level, and industrial production above that level, why should it be impossible, now that the luxury consumption of the former propertied class was no more, to maintain as large a capital

[1] Zalkind in *Econ. Oboz.*, May 1928, 143 *seq.*; Prof. Pervushin, *ibid.*, 115 *seq.*; *Econ. Jizn.*, 2.2.28; Pervushin, *ibid.*, 1.10.27; Mikoyan's report, *ibid.*, 20.12.27; Zalkind's report, *ibid.*, 23.12.27; Editorial in *Econ. Jizn*, 13.12.27 and 5.1.28.

accumulation as before the war and a working-class standard of life that was somewhat higher? If the expansion of credit facilities to finance constructional work, which in the actual circumstances of the summer and autumn proved excessive, had met the increase of agricultural goods on the market that had been anticipated, no inflationary tendency would necessarily have been manifested. The fact that inflationary symptoms reacted so catastrophically on the agricultural surplus, if only temporarily, suggested the existence of some fundamental maladjustment between industry and agriculture.

An answer to this riddle is indicated if we examine the relation between the marketed surplus and the total harvest in the previous year, 1926–7, when conditions particularly favoured the flow of peasant grain on to the market, and the peak of post-war grain collections and grain export was attained. The fact which at once strikes the attention is the very small proportion of the total harvest which was marketed even in this particularly favourable year. In pre-war years the percentage of grain placed on the market outside the village was only some 26 per cent of the total harvest: in 1926–7 the percentage was actually no greater than 13 to 14 per cent. As a result, while the area under grain stood at some 80 per cent and the total harvest at over 90 per cent of the average pre-war level, the marketed surplus available for the towns and for export stood at no more than a half of the pre-war amount. If we take account of other agricultural products, some of which have increased considerably both in area and yield over pre-war levels, the picture is less dark. But even when these other products have been included, the surprising fact remains that, while the total agricultural area stood in 1925–6 at 95 per cent of the normal, no more than 17 per cent of the total yield was marketed, so that agricultural supplies available for purchase were only 70 per cent of pre-war.[1] The opposition had maintained that " the slow develop-

[1] *Kontrolnie Tsifri 1927–8*; Weinstein, *loc. cit.*

ment of industry retards the development of agriculture." The actual situation seemed to be that the decline in the marketable surplus of agriculture was the fundamental barrier to the further advance of grain export and of the urban standard of life.

Clearly the phenomenon could not be wholly or even mainly attributed to the evil genius of the *kulak*, seeing that as much as 85 per cent of the total grain production now fell to " middle " and " poor " peasants as against some 50 per cent before the war. At first sight an opposite view is tempting: to lay the blame upon the " scissors." But the relative undervaluation of agricultural products, while doubtless it exercises some influence, can hardly be debited with the whole magnitude of the result; and if it were indeed the factor of prime importance, its influence would be shown by now as much on the sown area as on the marketed surplus. The slow recovery of the former is certainly important; but it is the exceptional fall of the latter which is the dominating phenomenon to be explained. Had there been no other reason, the " scissors " would hardly have achieved so serious a result.

The missing reason is not far to seek. It lies in the very character of the agrarian revolution of 1917. The large farm, particularly when worked by proletarian wage-labour, yields a proportionately larger surplus of produce over internal consumption than does the small family holding. Before the war the estates of the large land-owners placed nearly a half and the rich peasant farms about a third of their total produce on the market; and these two categories, while producing no more than a half of the total harvest, were responsible for nearly three-quarters of the marketed grain. After the revolution the whole centre of gravity was changed. The landowners' estates disappeared, being replaced by State and collective farms which covered no more than 3 to 4 per cent of the cultivated area. Rich peasant farms declined to about a quarter or a third of their previous number, while those which remained were generally of smaller average size and their marketed surplus constituted a fifth instead of a third of their produce. Eighty-five per cent of the harvest now fell to farms which were classed as "poor and middle peasant," which produced on the average no more than a small surplus above their own requirements. Greater equalisation in the village had placed the majority of the peasants in a stronger position and enabled each family to increase its consumption of its own produce. Formerly peasant consumption had been reduced, and a surplus created, by the impoverishment and even proletarianisation of large sections of the peasantry. Now that this cheapening factor had been removed, the "cost," as it were, of raising produce for market was increased;[1] and to coax from the village the same marketable surplus as before required the offer of terms, not only equally, but considerably more favourable to agriculture than had formerly reigned. To this result had further contributed the decreased burden on the village as a whole of rent- and tax-obligations.[2] The central fact of the situation, as Stalin declared in the spring, is that "the basis of agriculture is the small peasant farm putting the minimum of grain on the market."[3]

The obvious remedy if one assigned main responsibility to the "scissors" was to remove the relative undervaluation of agricultural goods, at the expense of the urban standard of life and of the plans of capital investment. This would need to be done by a deflationary lowering of industrial prices, since to do so by raising grain prices would hamper grain export still further. To this end finished

[1] In terms of our analysis above, p. 280 *seq.*, the village demand for industrial goods in terms of effort had decreased, and the "curve" of village demand had consequently moved to the left, owing to the removal of factors which formerly cheapened the peasants' valuation of effort in terms of income.

[2] Cf. above, p. 349 footnote.

[3] Speech of Stalin to a joint meeting of students of the Comm. Academy, Sverdlov Univ., and the Institute of Red Professors, reprinted in *Int. Press Corr.*, 14.1.28; Molotov's report, *Econ. Jizn*, 22.12.27 and *Rabochaia Gazeta*, 23.12.27; Prof. Litochenko in *La Situation Econom-*

industrial goods might be imported, instead of constructional materials, and thrown upon the internal market—the so-called "goods intervention" of 1923; or, more drastically, control of imports could be relaxed to allow manufactured goods to flow in more freely, at the expense of an import surplus and a fall in the chervonetz exchange. In the winter and spring policies of this nature were being canvassed among economists in State institutions and even in certain circles of the Party; and it was to the extremer form of such proposals that the Counter-theses referred as "the abandonment or 'modification' of the State monopoly of foreign trade." But it was now becoming clear that a deflation of industrial prices, pursued on the modest scale of the last two years, was inadequate in the long run to stimulate agriculture to the required extent; while, if such price-concessions to agriculture were to be adequately generous, they would virtually sacrifice all considerable present hopes of capital accumulation in industry, requiring as they would a large import from abroad and the concentration of all available resources on increasing the immediate supply of finished goods. Such policies, to be successful, would assuredly need to be

ique de l'Union Sovietique (Inst. of Econ. Research, Moscow). Stalin quoted the following estimates made by the Central Statistical Department:

BEFORE THE WAR	Total Grain Prodn. (million poods)	Per cent of Total	Grain placed on market outside the village (million poods)	Per cent of Total	Percentage of Total harvest which is marketed
Landowners	600	12	281·6	21·6	47
Kulaks	1,900	38	650	50	34
Poor and Middle Peasants	2,500	50	369	28·4	14·7
Total	5,000	100	1,300·6	100	26
1926–7					
State and Collective Farms	80	1·7	37·8	6	47·2
Kulaks	617	13	126	20	20
Poor and Middle Peasants	4,052	85·3	466·2	74	11·2
Total	4,749	100	630	100	13·3

combined with some definite encouragement to the growth of the rich peasant farm which had a surplus to sell. If greater equalisation in the village was the chief reason for the shrunken surplus, concessions to the peasantry were of minor use unless in some way they handled this fundamental cause; and between the horns of this dilemma, it is scarcely surprising that the leaders of the Party rejected this line of policy as being either inadequate for a permanent solution or else the wedge of a reversal of the agrarian revolution and the revival of class differentiation in the countryside. To have pursued the policy further, at least, would have been to play into the opposition's hand.[1]

The direct alternative to remedies of this nature lay in the proposals of the Counter-theses to exert pressure upon peasant agriculture, forcing it to yield a larger surplus, either by taxation or by overt measures which savoured of "war communism." And for the moment it seemed at the turn of the year as though this was the policy which had won. There was much gossip at this time in Moscow clubs and restaurants about a "return to 'war communism.'" It was a common aphorism both in Soviet and in *emigré* circles that Stalin, having banished the opposition, had stolen its policy. Newspaper correspondents, such as Paul Scheffer of the *Berliner Tageblatt*, proclaimed to the world that the Kremlin had taken a sharp "turn to the left." In this journalists' chatter there lay an element of truth. The Agricultural Tax, which in its absolute incidence had been lightened two years before, had been reorganised and was now imposed in a much more progressive form, steeply graduated against the rich peasant, with 35 per cent of the poorer peasantry entirely exempt. A number of local agricultural co-operative societies, alleged to have come under the influence of *kulaks* and to be serving their in-

[1] The attempt was still continued, of course, to lower industrial prices in so far as costs could be reduced by rationalisation; and in the summer of 1928 grain prices were actually raised. But no new departure in this direction was taken; and to meet the special problem of the agricultural surplus another policy was adopted as the long-period cure.

terests, were dissolved and reorganised with a membership of " poor " and " middle " peasants. Administrative directions were issued to local authorities that the law against profiteering was to be enforced where grain hoarding was being undertaken on a considerable scale for speculative ends. In many districts this order was interpreted in excess of the intention of its authors, and in execution was sometimes used in wholesale fashion to effect forced sales by the peasantry at existing prices to the collecting organs; while in a number of cases pressure was actually exerted by rural authorities in procuring subscriptions to the newly-issued Industrialisation Loan.[1]

But any intention to retreat from NEP in favour of pressure on peasant sales of grain was quickly disclaimed by the central authorities.[2] A tightening of administrative measures against what were considered to be clear cases of grain speculation was admitted as a temporary measure. But efforts were quickly made to curb the " excesses " and " abuses " in interpretation which had occurred; while measures were taken to accumulate a fund of industrial goods, even at the expense of creating a shortage in the towns, and to place them upon the rural market. More emphatically still a pronouncement of the Plenum of the Central Committee of the Party in June disavowed all forms of administrative pressure which curtailed the freedom to trade in grain, and further proposed to make certain concessions to the village in the shape of a raising of grain prices and the arrangement of forward contracts in purchase of the forthcoming harvest, paying down cash to the peasant in return for a guaranteed future delivery of a certain quantity of grain. Such measures, however, whether temporary assaults on speculative hoarding or price-concessions to the village, afforded passing stimuli rather than an enduring tonic to the situation. Of much more funda-

[1] Cf. Speech by Stalin to meeting of Moscow officials of the Party, April 13th, 1928; Rykov at Plenum of Moscow Soviet, March 9th, 1928.

[2] Cf. Krumin in *Econ. Jizn*, 3.3.28, and in *Econ. Oboz.*, Feb. 1928, 10.

mental importance was the policy outlined in the resolution of the 15th Party Congress in December and given more explicit formulation in the spring. In the circumstances it remained the sole alternative, if industrial development was to continue, to the methods of "war communism" or to the revival of the large capitalist farm. The State and collective farms, like the pre-war landlords' estates, placed nearly a half of their total produce on the market; and if the marketable surplus of grain was to be increased, the shortest way, consistent with a communist policy, was evidently to hasten the development of these large-scale farms. It was a question, at least, of developing either these or the *kulak* farms. Two years previously the investment of capital in new State farms had been rejected as the primary object of rural policy, both because capital at that time was more scarce and because certain important disabilities remained to be removed which hampered the growth of the "middle peasant." Two years had now shown that the limit of further expansion of industry, in the present condition of agriculture, was being reached; and the collectivisation of agriculture was proclaimed as the principal task of the next few years. Plans were set on foot for increased capital investment in agriculture in the institution of large State farms; and schemes were actually prepared for gargantuan farms in Siberia of 100,000 acres, large even by American standards. Stalin announced the hope that these could be made annually to yield some 150 million poods of grain for the market at the end of 5 to 6 years (or about 50–60 per cent of that furnished by the landlords' estates before the war), and that improvements in peasant agriculture could be made to yield another 100 million in the same period. It is inevitable that the sinking of capital in such enterprises must in some degree retard the possibilities of industrial development in the immediate future, or else delay the advance of the urban standard of life. But its result at a later date on the possibilities of grain export may be considerable; and on the success of the new policy of agricultural collectivism the future industrialisation of Soviet Russia appears to depend.

Equipped by previous experience to handle such a situation, the authorities were able to curb the crisis of the autumn months even more quickly than in 1925 and to prevent its symptoms from assuming such a pronounced form. The expansion of credit and currency of the autumn was successfully curtailed, being succeeded in the New Year by a certain measure of deflation. Between July 1927 and the end of the year the currency in circulation had swollen by some 13 per cent; but in the New Year a contraction set in, and by April 1st some 150 million roubles had been withdrawn from circulation, as against an average of about 65 to 66 million in the same quarter of the two previous years. At the same time the loan and discount operations of the five principal banks, which had risen by 300 million between October and January, were reduced by some 80 million in the first quarter of the New Year, while deposits increased by some 200 million. To deal with the breach between supply and demand in the village, stocks of industrial goods were drawn upon, and their distribution altered in favour of the countryside; while at the same time the speeding-up of tax collections and the vigorous canvassing of the Industrialisation Loan decreased the idle funds of purchasing-power in the village, and, combined with the administrative measures adopted as a temporary expedient against speculation, increased the willingness of the peasantry to market their grain. As a result the month of January showed an abrupt recovery of grain collections, which continued in the ensuing months to remain at a figure some 50 to 60 per cent higher than in the corresponding period of the previous year. So successfully, indeed, did these months repair the deficiencies of the previous quarter, that by the beginning of the summer the total grain purchases for the whole harvest year, while they failed to show the anticipated increase, nearly attained the figure of 1926–7, and exceeded that of the previous critical year of 1925–6 by some 20 per cent. But since in the last twelve months urban consumption had grown by some hundred million poods, the surplus available for export still remained insignificant and grain reserves unduly low.[1]

Some fear was expressed in the spring that the new taxation policy and the administrative "excesses" of the early months of the year might have a detrimental effect on the area sown for the ensuing harvest; and when in July certain large grain shipments to Russia occurred, this was assumed in the West to be evidence that a new catastrophe was due to appear. So far, however, no serious effect on the area of the new harvest is discernible. It may even be that the marketed surplus will increase in the next two years, since there is presumably a limit to the amount of grain that can be reasonably hoarded, and in recent years grain has been used to replenish reserves after a period of extreme depletion. For climatic reasons the winter-sown rye in certain areas has been a partial failure, as also the less important crops of winter-sown wheat; and since these are the first to be harvested, a temporary shortage of grain faced the towns towards the end of July. The grain imports which at this time caused such excitement in the English Press amounted to about one month's export in 1925–7 and to perhaps a fortnight's consumption in the larger towns, and were evidently prompted both by the lateness of the bulk of the harvest and by the desire to place some reserve in the hands of the State to aid the manipulation of grain prices in the critical early months of the collection campaign. But while the winter-sown crops were below those of the previous year by some 10–12 per cent, the spring-sown cereals, according to available reports, appear to be sufficiently above the average to compensate fully for the deficiency of the former, and even possibly to make the total harvest a little larger than in 1927.[2]

[1] Krumin in *Econ Oboz.*, Feb. 1928, 5 *seq.*; Zalkind, *ibid.*, May 1928, 144 *seq.*; and Pervushin, *ibid.*, 115 *seq.* The ratio of grain collections in the four years, 1924–5 to 1927–8 were as follows (1923=100): 70, 129, 160, 156 (*Econ. Jizn*, 20.7.28).

[2] Report of Mikoyan to All-Union Grain Conference, *Econ. Jizn*, 18.8.28.

While the prospects of industrial advance in the future will be conditioned both by the chance of harvests and by the success of the new agricultural policy, nothing has so far occurred to invalidate the tentative estimates which were made by the writer a year ago. Such errors as events may have revealed are probably of caution rather than of rashness. In the course of 1926–7, according to the official figures, the production of large-scale State industry increased by some 18 per cent over the previous year, and that of all factory industry by 15 per cent. The agricultural area grew in the twelve months by 6 per cent and agricultural output by some 4 per cent; while the rise of the total national income was estimated at 10 per cent. According to preliminary plans, a similar level of progress is to be maintained in the present year. The production of factory industry is estimated to increase by a further 14 per cent, agricultural production by 3 per cent, the gross production of agriculture and industry combined by 7 per cent and the national income by about 10 per cent. In this expansion it is intended that constructional industry shall share to the greatest extent and the production of finished goods on a more modest scale. According to a conservative estimate by Prof. Weinstein, the *net* capital accumulation for the whole economic system amounted in 1926–7 to some 2·6 to 2·7 milliard roubles.[1] For 1927–8 it is planned to increase State allocations for capital purposes by 20 per cent to a gross figure of some 3.5 milliard roubles.[2] These plans were originally constructed under the influence of unfavourable harvest forecasts, and hence seem unlikely to be guilty of a rash optimism. So far, indeed, events have confirmed them fairly well, industrial production in the first half of the financial year, despite the grain crisis, showing a 15·2 per cent increase, according to the available

[1] For a comparison with the writer's own earlier estimate, cf. above, pp. 310–13, 331, 379.

[2] *Kontrolnie Tsifri, 1927–8,* 9–30; Prof. Weinstein, *loc. cit.*; Prof. Pervushin in *Econ Oboz.*, Nov. 1927, 16 *seq.*

figures, over the similar period of the previous year.[1] Unless one is willing to regard all Russian figures as gigantic falsehoods, devised with surprising cunning to deceive, the continued rate of industrial growth in Russia must be admitted as one of the most interesting phenomena of our age.

[1] Prof. Pervushin in *Econ. Oboz.*, May 1928, pp. 115, 119.

INDEX

ABSENTEEISM, 95
Accounting, 166 *seq.*, 336
Accumulation, Chapter 10; — socialist, 259–267, 269, 272, 300–13, 353, 378–9, 392, 415, 429; — private, 258, 320, 351, 352–3; — primitive, 260–2, 409–10
Administration, — personnel, 71, 123–5, 165, 189, 197, 385; — industrial, 98 *et seq.*, 249, 331–2, 384–91; — problems of, 112–27, 133 *seq.*, 159, 188, 197 *et seq.*, 384 *seq.*
Agriculture, 341–51, 353–9; — land distribution, 20–1; — size of farms, 20–1, 341–4, 411–6, 421–3; — and industry, 212 *seq.*, 221 *seq.*, Chapters 8 and 9 and EXCURSUS, 320–6, 419 *seq.*; — production, 223–4, 323–4; — methods, 341–2, 348–50, 356–9. See also GRAIN, PEASANTRY
Agricultural Tax, 164–5, 188, 283–4, 315, 320, 343, 349, 354, 424
American methods, 3, 56, 332. See also RATIONALISATION
Amortisation, 180, 293 *seq.* See also CAPITAL
Anarchists, 33, 48, 53–4
Angell, Norman, 2, 3
Azerbaijan, 386

BAERLEIN, 77
"Bagmen," 82, 132
Baku, 88, 129; — Letter to B., 298, 336
Banking, — nationalisation, 31–2; — policy, 243–5; — deposits, 303, 307, 331–2, 356. See also STATE BANK, PROMBANK, CREDIT
Barter, 172; — State B., 57, 64, 205–6, 211
Bauer, Dr. Otto, 3, 17
Biedny, Demian, 141
Bierbrauer, 230
Blanquism, 12, 13
Bogdanov, A., 334
Bourgeoisie, 67–70; — new B., 333, 335, 340, 375
Brest-Litovsk, 47–8, 52, 53
Bribery, 125, 344, 348
Bronsky, 212, 327
Budget, — deficit, 77, 253; — stabilisation, 131, 225, 242, 253; — financing industry, 307–8
Bukharin, 53, 86–7, 153, 158, 163, 266–8, 320, 350–1, 352, 386, 412
Bureaucracy, 30, 116, 119 *seq.*, 137 *seq.*, 331–2, 362–3, 369–70, 386 *seq.*

CAPITAL,—foreign, 70–1, 186–7, 336; — depreciation, 74–6, 84, 97, 180, 293 *seq.*, 313, 379; — as a cost, 174 *seq.*; — private, 255, 288, 312, 320, 342, 352–3, 364–6, 368–9, 377; — investment, 174–5, 176–181, 312–14, 330–1, 378–9, 392, 398, 415, 429; — circulating, 182 *seq.*, 198, 206, 207 *seq.*, 250, 294–5, 309, 313; — basic, 198, Chapter 10. See also ACCUMULATION, SAVING
Capitalisation, 198; — over-c., 178–9
Capitalism, 7–11, 27, 29, 56, 78, 167, 178, 262, 267, 300, 381–2; — "encircled C.," 38, 43, 50–2, 99–100, 162, 367–9; — State C., 50, 54, 57, 161–2, 260, 262, 269, 334–5, 337–9, 371
Cattle, 148, 340, 349, 353–4
Centralisation, 27, 58–9, 62–4, 87, 104 *et seq.*, 112–28, 137–44, 155–6, 159, 164, 200 *seq.*, 384
Centres, 51, 100 *et seq.*, 114–15 199

Centrosoyus, 108–12, 205–7, 210, 211, 235, 237, 331, 362–6
Centro-textile, 51, 100, 105
Chemugol, 203, 235
Chernov, 22–3
Chervonetz, 132, 225–6, 228–35, 252, 392–4, 423, 427
Class, 7–8, 78, 83–4, 113, 116, 123, 300–3, 383 ; — classless society, 8, 10, 30–1, 61, 113, 117, 338–9, 368, 374–6, 383 ; — C. monopoly, 7–9, 26, 123, 337–8 ; — C. and State, 29 ; — C. differentiation, 340 *seq.*, 352 *seq.*, 375–7
Class Struggle, 9–10, 78, 83–4 ; — in the village, 149, 154, 163–4, 350–1
Collectivism, agricultural, 425 *seq.*
Colonies, 261–7, 275, 278–9
Communism, 61 *seq.*, 160 *seq.* ; — English ideas of, 2–3, 6–7. See also LENIN, CLASSLESS SOCIETY
Competition, 172, 215, 216, 219, 221, 236–8, 363 *seq.*
"Concentration," 191–2, 250–2, 292
"Concessions," 51–2, 186
"Consuming Areas," 147–8
Contact, 116–18, 122, 144 *seq.*, 150
Control, — State c., 27, 98 *seq.*, 126–7, 162, 367–9. See also STATE, WORKERS' CONTROL, DICTATORSHIP, DEMOCRACY, PARTY, CREDIT, etc.
Co-operatives, 108–12, 162, 164, 199, 205–7, 256, 269, 346, 347, 354–6, 360–71, 424–5 ; — "Co-op. Collectivism," 346
Cost, 133 *seq.*, 174 *seq.*, 362, 369–70 ; — industrial, 209, 230–1, 241–2, 247 *seq.*, 291 *seq* ; "real c.," 174–5, 275, 282. See also OVERHEAD
Counter-Theses, 412 *seq.*
Credit, 181, 207–8, 229, 242, 243, 247, 253, 304 f., 309, 328–9, 354, 391–2, 418, 427 ; — foreign, 186–7, 297 ; — agric., 354–6 ; — "goods c.," 362. See also DEFLATION, STATE BANK, PROMBANK
Crises, Economic, 168, 212–15, 221, 235 *et seq.*, 256–7, 268–9, 284 *seq.*, 314–16, 323, 326–9, 377–8, 380–2, 416 *seq.*

DECENTRALISATION, 192, 200 *seq.*, 363–5, 384, 390–1
Deflation, 242–4, 246–7, 253–5, 329–30, 392, 411, 413, 422–3
Demand, — peasant, 79–80, 264–6, 268–9, EXCURSUS to Chapters 8 and 9. See also NEEDS, MARKET, MARKETING
Democracy, 112 *seq.*, 158–9 ; — in industry, 39, 53, 99–100, 152, 156 *seq.* ; — Soviet d., 344–5, 347–8 ; — workers' d., 383. See also TRADE UNIONS, SOVIET, WORKERS' CONTROL
Denationalisation, 188–9
Denisov, 343, 346, 355
Depreciation, —. See AMORTISATION, CAPITAL
Diarchy, — industrial, 42–4, 54–5
Dictatorship, — workers', 19, 21–2, 29–30, 84, 337–8 ; — of industry, 257, 259 *seq.*, 322
Djerjinsky, 235, 305–6, 322, 386
Dolgov, Prof., 231
Domestic Industry, 66 *seq.*, 281, 349
Donetz, 44, 51, 59, 68, 70, 83, 88, 129, 185, 191–2, 202, 211
Donugol, 191, 202, 218

ECONOMICHESKAIA JIZN, 159, 214, 226–7, 418
Economists, — classical, 126 ; — orthodox, 8–9
Economy, 182, 189–90, 225, 253, 331–2, 389
Education, 348, 359, 375–6, 386–7, 391
Effort, 174 *seq.*, 275, 282
Electrification, 162, 312, 371, 397
Exploitation, 8, 276–9, 282–3, 288 ; — of peasants, 146–7, 221–4, 233–4, 238–9, 260–7, 282, 288, 289, 300–1, 304, 409

FACTORIES, 66–8, 391
Falkner, Prof., 227–8, 230
Famine, 77–9, 94–5, 186–7, 192–3, 212, 221. See also HUNGER, "GOODS F."
Farms, — State, 20, 345–6, 350–1, 426 ; — large and small, 20–1, 341–4, 357, 412–6 ; — new methods, 356–8. See also AGRICULTURE, GRAIN, PEASANTRY

Feudalism, 67–8, 78
Fisher, Prof. Irving, 208, 231
Fuel, — crisis, 83, 88, 182 *seq.*, 187–92

GENOA, 187, 297
Glavki, 100–6, 110, 114–15, 127, 137 *seq.*, 142–4, 196–8, 216
Glavmetal, 99
Glavneft, 102
Glavtop, 102, 191
Glavugol, 99, 102
Gold, — prices, 132 ; — standard, 242–3, 256, 258, 393
" Goods famine," 316, 320, 321, 323, 326, 330, 351, 369, 413 *seq.*
" Goods Intervention," 247, 256, 422–3
Gorki, Maxim, 15, 56
Gosplan, 180, 214, 219, 230, 241, 244–5, 257, 330, 352, 379, 390, 399
Gostorg, 237, 359
Grain, — monopoly of g. trade, 82, 109 *seq.*, 132 ; — nationalisation of g. trade, 32 ; — supply of, 77, 78–80, 93–4, 129, 132, 146–8, 188 *seq.*, 192–3, 223–4, 265–6, 289, 314 *seq.*, 357–8, 428 ; — requisitions, 96–7, 109 *seq.*, 127, 144–50, 164, 184 ; — area of, 148–9, 223 ; — marketable surplus, 224, 283–4, 321, 412–3, 417 *seq.* ; — export of, 246, 414, 417 ; — purchase, 288–9, 314 *seq.*, 328 ; — loan, 413 *seq.*
Gubsovnarhoz, 102 *et seq.*, 114–15, 138, 141–3, 204, 211
Gubtorg, 231, 359

HARVEST, 148, 220, 221–2, 227, 286, 288–9, 290, 296, 314–16, 324, 328, 331. See also FAMINE, GRAIN
Hawtrey, R. G., 8–9, 122, 176–7
Hensel, Prof., 297
Hobson, J. A., 8

IMPERIALISM, 278–9
" Incentive limit," 73 *seq.*, 79–80
Index Numbers, 131–2, 213, 222, 225, 226, 228, 232, 316, 324, 393
Industrialisation, 66–71, 318–20, 378–80, 388, 397, 399, 409 *seq.*
Industrialists, 241 *seq.*, 354 *seq.*
Inflation, 63–4, 77, 81, 85, 89–95, 131–2, 183–4, 220, 225–6, 242, 253, 286, 307, 316, 326 *seq.*, 392, 411 f.
Intelligentsia, 29, 69, 376, 385–6
Interest, 174 *seq.*, 208

KAKTYN, 248–9
Kalinikov, Prof., 230, 241
Kalmanovsky, 295
Kamenev, 15, 153, 315, 317, 318, 350–1, 361, 385, 412, 414
Karlgren, Prof., 261, 294, 344, 349
Kerensky, 13–15, 35–7, 83
Keynes, J. M., 10, 337
Kollontai, 156–7, 159, 334
Kondratiev, Prof., 220, 231–4, 240, 241
Krassin, 46, 257–8, 297
Krestinsky, 53
Kritsmann, 124–5, 137, 146–7, 350
Kronstadt, 86, 151–2
Krshishanovsky, 141
Kuibyshev, 332, 391
Kulak, 147–8, 320, 322, 335, 339, 340 *seq.*, 350–5, 375, 412 *seq.*
Kust, 103, 199, 202
Kustar. See DOMESTIC INDUSTRY
Kutler, N., 231, 352

LABOUR, — compulsory, 96, 150–1, 155–6 ; — l.-value, 174 *seq.*, 274–5, 282 ; — quality of, 185–6 ; — productivity, 293, 305–7, 395–8
Laissez-faire, 5–6, 10, 27, 367–9, 382, 409
Land Decree, 20–1
Land tenure, 341–2, 348–50, 412–4
Larin, 46, 51, 146, 242, 350–1, 360–3, 365–6
" Left " Communists, 52 *seq.*, 61, 154
Left Social Revolutionaries, 21–3, 33, 48, 53, 60
Lenin, 11, 13 *seq.*, 27–9, 41, 48–54, 58–9, 60–1, 63, 87, 152, 153, 160 *seq.*, 260, 266, 346, 370–1, 383
Leningrad, 15–16, 22, 36, 45, 78, 103, 139, 189, 193, 373–47
Libedinsky, 150

Lloyd, E. M. H., 119
" Loading," 250–1, 291–3
Loans, 186–7, 198, 297, 298, 303, 308, 332, 392, 413–5, 427
Localism, 33–4, 142–3, 165, 201

MAKEEV, 2
Managers, 56, 101, 106, 162, 384, 387
Market, 125–7, 130, 167, 170–4, 205–6, 210 *seq.*, 257, 268, 336; — " free " m., 96, 132–4
Marketing, 210 *seq.*, 237 *seq.*, 359 *seq.* See also TRADE
Marx, 5, 7 *seq.*, 17, 160, 260–1, 263, 266, 284–6
Medvediev, 298, 336
Mensheviks, 37. See also KERENSKY
Meschersky, 51–3
Metal industry, 43–5, 67, 68, 88, 95, 99, 103, 136, 139, 184, 193, 195, 201, 217–18, 223, 251–2, 271
Miasnikov, 334
Mikoyan, 418
Mining, 70, 88, 99, 185, 191–3, 202–3, 218, 271
Mirbach, Count, 47, 60
" Mixed Companies," 51–2, 199, 237 f.
Money, — moneyless system, 62 *seq.*, 130 *seq.*, 166 *seq.*, 336; — theory of, 91–3, 227 *et seq.*, 370; — and accounting, 166 *seq.*; — stabilisation, 242–3, 252–5, 270 392–3. See also INFLATION, DEFLATION, ROUBLE, CHERVONETZ, CREDIT
Monopoly, — State, 82, 109 *seq.*, 115, 126–7, 132–3, 164, 172; — industrial, 216, 236–40, 246, 249, 254, 261–2, 264–9; — theory of, 277 *seq.*; — trading, 205–6, 363
Moscow, 15–16, 36, 60, 189, 192, 202, 211, 228, 240, 365–6, 373–4

NARCOMFIN, 132, 240, 243–5, 246, 253, 254, 390
Narcomprod, 108 *et seq.*, 114–16, 127, 139, 149, 206, 237
Narcomput, 104, 152, 192
Narcomvneshtorg, 237
Narcomvnutorg, 247, 361–2
National Income, 71, 95, 311–12, 378–80, 429; — distribution of, 374
Nationalisation, 25 *seq.*, 31–5, 46–7, 49–50, 54, 57–60, 99 *seq.*, 138
Naturalwirtschaft. See MONEY
Needs, 133–4, 168–70
NEP, 4, 131–2, 144, 163–5, 173–4, 180, 196 *seq.*, 213, 245, 256, 267, 272, 320, 334 *seq.*, 346, 352–3, 367–8
Nepman. See TRADER
Nogin, 241–2, 363
Novaia Jizn, 15, 56

OBROK, 68
Oil industry, 70, 88, 140, 185, 202, 216, 390; — nationalisation of, 32
Opposition, The, 156–8, 254 *seq.*, 286, 316 *seq.*, 334 *seq.*, 412 *seq.* See also WORKERS' OPPOSITION
Organisation, 74–5, 133 *seq.*, 197 *seq.* See also ADMINISTRATION
Ossinsky, 53, 149, 158, 162–3, 254–6
Ossovsky, 335
Overhead charges, 177 *seq.*, 241–2, 248–52, 291, 362, 389
Overproduction, 235, 240, 268–70, 284–7, 380–2

PALÉOLOGUE, 77–8, 83, 85
Party (Communist), 12–13, 30–1, 47–9, 52–6, 107, 117–18, 121, 150, 161–2, 190, 348, 376–7; — 9th Congress, 142–4; — 10th Congress, 152 *seq.*; 12th Congress, 250, 268, 297; — 13th Congress, 245, 254 *seq.*, 268–70, 361–2, 364; — 14th Congress, 317–22, 345, 350–2; — 15th Conference, 318, 353, 369, 386 *seq.*; — 15th Congress, 416, 426
Pavlovka, 357
Peasantry, — and food supplies, 78–80, 85, 93–6, 144 *seq.*; — p. revolts, 82, 150; — and workers, 19–23, 69–70, 118, 144 *seq.*, 155, 163–4, 221 *seq.*, 260 *seq.*, 304, 333, 370–1; — " middle " p., 148, 266, 349, 355; —

psychology, 358; — and market, 224, 233–4, 238–9, 246, 264–6, 357–8; — accumulation, 310; — class differentiation, 341–5, 350 *seq.*, 353–5, 412–5. See also AGRICULTURE, AGRICULTURAL TAX, GRAIN
"Permanent Revolution," 155, 163, 267, 346, 350–1
"Perversion" of State, 156–7, 159, 322, 334–5, 340
Peter the Great, 67, 83, 85
Petrograd. See LENINGRAD
Piatakov, 31, 44, 46, 53, 256, 270, 352
Plan, Five Year, 411 *seq.*
Planning, — economic, 27, 133 *seq.*, 168 *seq.*; 173, 245, 254–5, 257, 258, 268–9, 286–7, 336, 380–2, 390, 411 *seq.*
Pravda, 152, 388
Preference, 199, 363, 367–9, 371
Preobrajensky, 53, 258–9, 259–67, 287, 297, 321, 410
Population, 71, 76, 395–9
Prices, 167, 170–1; — discrimination, 177–9; — regulated, 205–6, 247, 315, 360, 392, 418–9; — agric. and industrial, 212–13, 220, 221–3 *et seq.*, 246 *seq.*, 261, 271, 323–7, 394, 409–11; — lowering, 268, 271, 329–31, 369–70, 381–2, 392; — wholesale and retail, 323, 325–7, 369–70, 392. See also INFLATION, DEFLATION, INDEX-NUMBERS
"Producing Areas," 147–8
Production, — decline of, 83, 88–9, 95; — recovery of, Chapter 6; — industrial, 223, 290, 323–4, 331, 377–80, 429
Prokopovitch, Prof., 84, 95, 224, 311
Profit, 9, 180, 200, 240, 247, 255, 261 *et seq.*, 271, 285–6, 307–13, 352; — "super-p.," 260–3, 276–80, 305
Prombank, 243–5, 309
Proportionality, 168–9, 178, 284–8, 316, 380–2
Protectionism, 261, 279, 319–20, 363–4, 367–9, 409–10
Provisional Government, 13–15, 82 *et seq.*
Pugachev, 67

RABOCHAIA GAZETA, 386
Radek, 53
Railways, 57, 69, 76–8, 82–3, 88–9, 104, 131, 136, 139, 152, 187, 189, 192–3, 397
Rasbazarivania, 210–15, 219–20, 238
Rationalisation, 306–7, 331–2, 388–91
Rationing, 167, 169, 176; — credit, 247, 331
Rentier, 175–6, 337
Requisitioning. See GRAIN
Reserves, — goods, 97, 139, 184–8, 289, 310, 316, 324, 413–6; — money, 208–9, 210–12. See also AMORTISATION, CAPITAL
Riazanov, 56
Rosenfeld, 202
Rotation of Crops, 341–2, 357–8
Rouble, 77, 81, 94, 131–2, 225, 252, 270. See also MONEY, INFLATION, CHERVONETZ
Rousseau, 29
Rudzutak, 153
Rykov, 46, 174 f., 268–70, 312, 329, 331–2, 353, 362, 366, 369, 386–8

SABOTAGE, 31, 34–6, 39, 85, 125
"Saving," 174 *seq.*, 182–4, 300–3, 307, 311–12, 327, 332, 352–3, 356, 367, 388–9, 392–3, 429
Scheffer, Paul, 424
"Scissors," 212–14, Chapters 8 and 9 and EXCURSUS, 323–7, 394, 411, 421–3
Serebrovsky, 332
Serfs, 67–8
"Shock" system, 136–8
Shliapnikov, 298
Skobolev, 37
Skorotchkin, 343, 355
Siberia, 76, 129
Smilga, 191, 321–2, 323, 325–6, 412, 414
Smith, Adam, 40
Smytchka, 23, 118, 144, 147–8, 161–2, 163–4, 266–7, 272, 346–7, 359
Sobolev, Prof., 311–12
Socialism, — English, 5, 8, 10, 277; — Guild, 10, 17; — in industry, 26–8; — in Russia alone, 299, 317–20; — theory

of, 263 ; — tendencies to, 335, 338–9, 354–8. See also NATIONALISATION
Sokolnikov, 240, 242, 252, 258
Soviets, 13–15, 18, 23, 35–8, 42, 157, 158 ; — village, 344 *seq.* ; — elections, 347–8, 351 ; — 8th Congress, 142–3, 149–50 ; — 10th Congress, 239, 242, 243
Sovnarcom, 60, 132, 198, 331
Specialists, 40, 45, 53, 58, 100, 106, 124–5, 156, 162, 333, 374 384, 385–7, 391
Speculation, 132, 425
Spiridinova, Marie, 22–3
Stakhaev, 49–50
Stalin, 153, 318–19, 345, 350, 385, 424, 426
State, 11, 18, 28–30, 50, 150, 157, 165, 371 ; — degeneration, 322, 334–5, 340 ; — personnel, 189–90, 340. See also ADMINISTRATION
State Bank, 31, 132, 207–8, 243–5, 247, 254–5, 309, 329–30, 393
S T O, 140, 241, 331, 390
Stocks. See RESERVES
Strikes, 31, 39, 151, 382
Strumilin, 224, 241, 247–8
Subsidies, 294, 304, 307–12, 394
Super-Profit. See PROFIT
Supply, 133 *seq.*, 167, 182–4 ; — State S., 189–90, 200–1 ; — raw materials, 193–5, 212 *seq.* ; — agric. and industrial, 212 *seq.* See also GRAIN, NARCOMPROD, PRODUCTION
Surplus-value, 8–9, 261, 276–9, 301, 302. See also EXPLOITATION, PROFIT
Syndicalism, 33 *seq.*, 44–7, 59, 156–7, 163, 219
Syndicates, 215–19, 238, 241, 271, 359, 362–5, 391

TAXATION, 57, 85, 200, 225, 242, 247–8, 349, 354, 367 ; — for war purposes, 72 *seq.* See also AGRICULTURAL TAX, INFLATION
Taylorism, 56, 332
Textile industry, 36, 70, 94–5, 100, 129, 139, 185, 189, 194, 203, 209, 216–17, 223, 251–2, 271
Thermidor, 322
Trade Cycle. See CRISES
Trade, foreign, 237, 319, 393–4, 411 ; — nationalisation of, 32 ; — trade balance, 186–7, 253, 256
Trade, internal, 109–12, 164, 199, 205–7, 210–19, 236–9, 255–6, 359–70
Trade Unions, 33, 47, 55, 100, 105, 107–8, 115, 150, 279, 375, 377, 382–3, 389 ; — Party discussion on, 152 *seq.*
Trader, private, 212, 255, 258, 269–70, 316, 333, 339, 340, 351–2, 355, 359–61, 364–70, 377
Transition Period, 49–50, 58–9, 160–2, 260–8, 337–41, 345–6, 350–2, 370–1 ; — State in, 29
Trotsky, 3, 16, 27, 47, 62, 148 f., 150–1, 152 *seq.*, 155–6, 159, 163, 192, 256–7, 267, 268, 286, 298, 321, 339, 412 *seq.*
Trusts, 144, 196 *seq.*, 236, 241, 250–2, 255, 293–4, 384, 387, 390–1
Turkestan, 94, 129, 185, 194

UKRAINE, 47, 55, 59, 235, 240
Unemployment, 189–90, 398, 414–5
Ustinov, Prof., 363
Utopianism, 61, 335–6

VARGA Prof. E., 27–8
Vertical combination, 203
Vesenha, 32–4, 46–7, 57, 62, 98 *et seq.*, 114–15, 139–40, 159, 191, 197, 198, 200, 204, 214, 219, 231, 237, 241, 243, 255, 331–2, 390–1
Vieselova, 343, 346, 355
Village, 228 ; — and towns, 145 *seq.*, 159–60, 212–15, 221 *seq.*, 260–8, EXCURSUS to Chapters 8 and 9, Chapter 11 ; — class differentiation, 340 *seq.*, 350 *seq.*, 353–5, 412–5 ; — commune, 341–2, 357. See PEASANTRY, GRAIN, AGRICULTURE
Vladimirov, 240
Voronsov, 355

WAGES, 81, 95, 190, 194, 305–6, 316, 322, 374, 414–5 ; — piece-rates, 56
" Waiting." See " SAVING "

War, — real burden of, 72 *seq.*; — civil war, 87 *seq.*, 115 *seq.*, 129; — destruction of, 89
"War Communism," 4, 57–65, 95–7, 112 *seq.*, 129 *seq.*, 173, 196, 267, 320, 333 *seq.*, 344 *seq.*, 424 *seq.*
"War Socialism," 33
Webb, Sidney, 3, 8, 27
Weinstein, Prof., 240, 310–12, 379–80, 429
Witte, Count, 69
Workers' Control, — in factories, 35–46, 106–7; — in industry, 99 *et seq.*, 156–8, 382–3. See also TRADE UNIONS, DEMOCRACY, SYNDICALISM
Workers, — standard of life, 185–6, 190, 194, 374, 379–80, 395–9, 414–5; — number, 66, 223, 292, 398; — and peasants, 69–70, 263 *seq.*, Chapter 11
"Workers' Opposition," 156 *seq.*, 334
"Workers' Truth," 334–5
Wrangel, 130

YAKOVLEV, 343, 346, 355, 357, 415
Yefimov, 343, 355

ZINOVIEV, 15, 22, 153, 317, 318, 320, 350–1, 412, 414
Znamenka, 343, 355